IDEOLOGIES AND INSTITUTIONS IN URBAN FRANCE

Ideologies
and institutions
in urban France

The representation of immigrants

R. D. GRILLO

University of Sussex

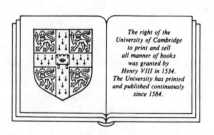

The right of the
University of Cambridge
to print and sell
all manner of books
was granted by
Henry VIII in 1534.
The University has printed
and published continuously
since 1584.

CAMBRIDGE UNIVERSITY PRESS

Cambridge
London   New York   New Rochelle
Melbourne   Sydney

Published by the Press Syndicate of the University of Cambridge
The Pitt Building, Trumpington Street, Cambridge CB2 1RP
32 East 57th Street, New York, NY 10022, USA
10 Stamford Road, Oakleigh, Melbourne 3166, Australia

First published 1985

Printed in the United States of America

Library of Congress Cataloging in Publication Data
Grillo, R. D.
Ideologies and institutions in urban France.
Bibliography: p.
Includes index.
1. Lyon (France) – Foreign population – Case studies.
2. Lyon (France) – Ethnic relations – Case studies.
3. North Africans – France – Lyon – Case studies.
4. France – Foreign population – Case studies.
5. France – Ethnic relations – Case studies. I. Title.
DC801.L968G75   1985   305.8'00944'5823   84–23820
ISBN 0 521 30179 3

FOR BRON, CLAUDIA, PIPPA, AND IOAN

Contents

Tables, figures, and maps

Acknowledgments

All anthropological research is dependent on the anthropologist's informants. Many hundreds of people in Lyon gave freely of their time and allowed me to discuss with them the issues that formed the basis of this book. They are too many to thank individually, and it would be invidious to single anyone out for mention. In some circumstances it might also be against their best interests. I would, however, like to record my thanks to the Groupe Tiers Monde of Caluire for allowing me to consult material they collected in connection with a report on their commune.

Findings from my research have been presented to seminars at the universities of Amsterdam, Belfast, Cambridge, Durham, Kent, Oxford, Sussex, at the School of Oriental and African Studies and University College, London, to members of the Ethnic Relations Research Unit, Wandsworth, and in a variety of forms to meetings of the Social Science Research Council's "European" seminar. I would like to thank all who offered comments at those seminars, as well as the many others with whom I discussed my material, in particular two postgraduate students, Andrea Caspari, an anthropologist from Sussex, and Peter Jones, a geographer from Sheffield, who in the late 1970s undertook research in Grenoble and Lyon, respectively, in fields very close to my own. Richard Burton, a Sussex colleague, gave me guidance on numerous aspects of French social and racial thought, and A. L. Epstein offered me encouragement and the benefit of his considerable experience of urban anthropological research from beginning to end of this project.

The project would not have been possible without an initial grant from the University of Sussex to visit Lyon in 1974, and a generous award from the Social Science Research Council for fieldwork in 1975–6. I should like to express my gratitude to Irene Sheard and the staff of the School of African and Asian

Studies, University of Sussex, for their immense help with the preparation of this book.

Finally, to my family, who participated and endured, this work is respectfully dedicated.

R. D. Grillo

Glossary of abbreviations and acronymns

ACFAL: Association de Coopération Franco-
                Algérienne du Lyonnais
ADCFA: Association Dauphinoise de Coopération
                Franco-Algérienne
ADIF: Association pour la Diffusion de
                l'Enseignement Linguistique
AEE: Amicale pour l'Enseignement des Etrangers
AEFTI: Association pour l'Alphabétisation et
                l'Enseignement du Français aux
                Travailleurs Immigrés
ALHTRAM: Association Lyonnaise pour l'Hébergement
                de Travailleurs Migrants
APACS: Association pour l'Animation Culturelle et
                Sociale
ASEV: Association des Educateurs de Villeurbanne
BEP: Brevet d'Etudes Professionnelles
BTP: Bâtiment et Travaux Publiques
CAIO: Centre d'Accueil, d'Information et
                d'Orientation des Travailleurs Etrangers
CAP: Certificat d'Aptitude Professionnelle
CEFISEM: Centre d'Information et de Formation des
                Personnels Concernés par la Scholarisation
                des Enfants de Travailleurs Migrants
CES: Collège d'Enseignement Secondaire
CET: Collège d'Enseignement Technique
CFDT: Confédération Français Démocratique du
                Travail
CFI: Comité(s) Français-Immigrés
CGT: Confédération Générale du Travail
CIMADE: Comité Inter-Mouvements auprès des
                Evacués

CLAP:	Comité de Liaison pour l'Alphabétisation et de la Promotion
CLORATE:	Comité de Liaison des Organisations du Rhône d'Aide aux Travailleurs Etrangers
COURLY:	Communauté Urbaine de la Région Lyonnaise
CPA:	Classes Préparatoires à l'Apprentissage
CPPN:	Classes Préprofessionnelles de Niveau
CREDIF:	Centre de Recherche et d'Etude pour la Diffusion du Français
CRS:	Compagnie Républicaine de Sécurité
DDASS:	Direction Départmentale de l'Action Sanitaire et Sociale
EEC:	European Economic Community
ETDA:	Employés, Techniciens, Dessinateurs, Agents de Maîtrise
FEN:	Fédération de l'Education Nationale
FLN:	Front de Libération Nationale
FO (or FO-CGT):	Force Ouvrière (CGT)
GAEC:	Groupement Agricole d'Exploitation en Commun
GISTI:	Groupe d'Information et de Soutien des Travailleurs Immigrés
GSHH:	Groupement Social de l'Hygiène et de l'Habitat
GSU:	Groupe de Sociologie Urbaine
HLM:	Habitation à Loyer Modéré
INED:	Institut National d'Etudes Démographiques
INFAC:	Institut National de Formation des Animateurs des Collectivités
INSEE:	Institut National de la Statistique et des Etudes Economiques
IREP:	Institut de Récherche Economique et de Planification
LOGIREL:	Société d'HLM de Logement, Région Lyonnaise
MRAP:	Mouvement contre le Racisme et pour la Paix
MTE:	La Maison du Travailleur Etranger
NDSA:	Notre-Dame des Sans-Abri

ODTI:	Office Dauphinoise des Travailleurs Immigrés
ONAMO:	Office National Algérien de la Main d'Oeuvre
ONI:	Office National d'Immigration
PACT:	Centre de Propagande de l'Action Contre le Taudis
PCF:	Parti Communiste Français
PCR – ML:	Parti Communiste Revolutionnaire – Marxiste Léniniste
PS:	Parti Socialiste
PSU:	Parti Socialiste Unifié
SCET:	Société Centrale pour l'Equipement du Territoire
SERL:	Société d'Equipement pour la Région Lyonnaise
SES:	Section d'Éducation Spécialisée
SGEN:	Syndicat Général de l'Education National
SLEA:	Sociéte Lyonnaise pour l'Enfance et Adolescence
SLPM:	Service de Liaison et Promotion des Migrants
SMIC:	Salaire Minimum Interprofessionnelle de Croissance
SNAV:	Société Nouvelle des Ateliers de Vénissieux
SNI:	Syndicat National des Instituteurs
SONACOTRA:	Société Nationale de Construction de Logements pour les Travailleurs
SSAE:	Service Social d'Aide aux Emigrants
SSFNA:	Service Social Familial Nord-Africain
SSRC:	Social Science Research Council
UDCGT:	Union Départementale de la CGT
UIB:	Union Interprofessionnelle de Base
ZUP:	Zone à Urbaniser en Priorité

1

Introduction

The ethnography on which this monograph is based derives from an anthropological study, undertaken in 1974–6, of immigrants, mainly of North African origin, living in a French provincial city. This book is, however, only partly concerned with such immigrants, and it has not been conceived in any straightforward way as a contribution to migration studies.

The discussion moves on three levels, or to put it less pretentiously, approaches the data from three directions, each leading toward a somewhat different, if ultimately related, range of analytical problems. The implications of "level," which suggests differences of depth, subtlety, and perhaps sophistication, are not, however, wholly misleading, in that each raises problems of greater generality within the social sciences and greater complexity, at least for this analyst. They also represent phases in the analyst's perception of his ethnography. We are rarely told so, but it is usual in anthropology, as in other disciplines, for the researcher to move through many stages in understanding a society in which intensive fieldwork has been undertaken. This occurs in the field itself and, in the aftermath, in the writing. In a sense, the process never stops, even after, perhaps especially after, results have been published. The anthropologist's material is not something in which one can find a final, conclusive answer, any more than one can with a painting or a piece of music. If we are honest, any anthropological publication is a report on analysis in progress; and this is no exception.

The three levels formed, then, successive stages in the perception of ethnography obtained during fieldwork in the city of Lyon, France. Briefly, they are as follows.

The first is concerned with *immigrants,* and in the course of the book I deal at some length with the situation of migrant workers and their families who are recent arrivals, for the most part, in an urban and industrial milieu. In doing so, a number of issues are raised that are comparable to those encountered elsewhere in the literature of anthropology and other disciplines that focus on labor migration, ethnicity, race relations, and so on, in both Europe and the Third World.

Such issues were, in fact, my starting point; but as I will explain, experience in the field forced a switch in focus from immigrants to the *society of immigration*. Thus the second level of analysis, which is the most fully developed in this book, is concerned with the general milieu in which the immigrants are located: a major urban center in a highly advanced industrial society. Its focus is the attributes of such a milieu. It happens, therefore, that this book is as much about France and the French as it is about migrants.

The link between these two levels is that the analysis of French society concentrates on how the institutions of that society and their (mainly) French personnel perceive and manage what they call the "problem" of a defined section of the population: immigrants. There are two aspects of this.

First, any reader who goes through the speeches recorded in the "Events" described at intervals in the text will be struck by the frequency with which the word "problem" occurs, almost regardless of the ethnic identity or ideological persuasion of the speaker. No researcher in France could fail to note how orally and in writing (in reports, articles, books of every description) the words "immigrant" and "immigration," or less euphemistically, "Arab" or "North African," produce the word "problem." So much so that early in his fieldwork it occurred to this investigator that this fact itself was worthy of investigation: How and why is the situation of immigrants in France viewed as "problematic," and what is the role of French institutions in the "representation of problems"?

"Representation" here refers to perception and conception, an ideological dimension. But if there is "representation" of problems, there is also a problem of "representation." The point is this: If the situation of immigrants is "represented" as problematic – perceived, conceived, analyzed, and finally handled in terms of the "problems" that immigrants pose or are believed to experience – and these "representations" are taken into the institutional system through which policies are formulated and implemented, then we must examine who presents the "representations," that is, whose view is "represented" in a political sense, by what means, and how evaluated.

The general approach taken here was outlined first in my report to the Social Science Research Council on the Lyon project (Grillo 1978). It is one that has received relatively little attention in the literature, although in France the work of Catani (1973) and Pinot (1973) has a generally similar focus, as does the compilation by Tewfik Allal and others (1977). In Britain, if such matters are discussed at all, it is in the context of policy studies or in accounts of the politics of race. (But see Rex and Tomlinson 1979:198, 244.) Gary Freeman's (1979) stimulating comparison of British and French policies toward immigrants since World War II adopts a perspective close to my own, although his concern is with the perception of problems at the center, rather than with their handling at the local level and in practice.

The analysis of the perception and management of "problems," with what I term their "representation," deals with ideas and beliefs. This leads to my third level: the nature and structure of ideological systems in advanced industrial societies. Here I touch on a number of themes tackled by scholars in the fields of "discourse analysis" and the sociology of knowledge. The link between this level and the others is provided by a question that runs through this book and presents a central organizing theme: What can be said about the construction and contextualization of ideologies in our type of advanced industrial society, having regard to their application via an institutional framework to a defined segment of the population (immigrants)?

URBAN SYSTEMS IN ADVANCED INDUSTRIAL SOCIETIES: THE INSTITUTIONAL FRAMEWORK

I have said that this study is concerned as much with the milieu in which immigrants are located, and in particular with the "institutional complexes" that operate therein, as with immigrants themselves. Let me elaborate this, describing first in broad outline the characteristics of that milieu, which may be described briefly as advanced industrial and urban.

An anthropologist undertaking an urban study in France receives little guidance from the writings of colleagues who have hitherto worked in Europe. By and large, their research, so ably summarized in Davis's *People of the Mediterranean,* is irrelevant. So, too, is the bulk of urban anthropological research concerned with Third World cities. Not surprisingly, when analyzing my own data, I initially found the greatest stimulus in the ideas of a number of contemporary French urban and industrial sociologists – Touraine, Castells, and Lojkine, the last of whom happens to have written a monograph (1974) on Lyon.

One concept, found useful as a starting point, was that of the "post-industrial" or "programmed" society, as Touraine variously calls it:

> A new type of society is now being formed. These new societies can be labeled post-industrial to stress how different they are from the industrial societies which preceded them, although – in both capitalist and socialist nations – they retain some characteristics of these earlier societies. They may also be called technocratic because of the power that dominates them. Or one can call them programmed societies to define them according to the nature of their production methods and economic organisation.   [Touraine 1974:3]

Touraine makes it clear that this type of society occurs in both capitalist and socialist versions. Castells, whose vision of contemporary society in France is similar, equivocates (1976b:66). Lojkine, who like Castells is a more obviously Marxist writer than Touraine, confines himself to "the current phase of monopoly capitalism, State monopoly capitalism marked by the systematic and generalized intervention of the State to facilitate monopolistic accumulation" (Lojkine 1976:136). His book on Lyon may be read as an extended case study of such a system in operation.

An outstanding feature of writers such as Castells, Lojkine, and Touraine is that they firmly incorporate the study of an urban and industrial milieu within the framework of the broader social system. Thus, for Castells, the classic Wirthian definition of urbanism is no more, but no less, than "the cultural expression of capitalist industrialization, the emergence of the market economy and the process of rationalization of modern society" (Castells 1976a:38). Although not denying the existence of differences between town and country, he claims that the "fundamental features of . . . urban culture are the direct consequence of industrialization, and, in certain cases, capitalist industrialization" (p. 54).

The logic of this is that an anthropological study set in a city such as Lyon is, at one level, about the wider social and economic system of which the city is a manifestation. But how are we to approach the study of such a system? Castells, having with one hand abolished urban sociology as an autonomous discipline

(1976a:59), with the other resurrects it by offering two fields for urban research: the study of relationships in space and of what he terms the "process of collective consumption" (1976b:74).

On this point there is a convergence in the views of Castells and Touraine. Both, while acknowledging the overriding importance of the system of production, insist on the significance of consumption, both public and private, and of what might be termed "relations of consumption," in contemporary society. And both are concerned with "social movements" that arise from contradictions in the consumption system. As Touraine puts it, "It is both true and false that today's conflicts are located more on the level of *consumption* than of production" (1974:84, his emphasis).

The analysis of consumption, individual and collective, public and private, forces attention on the organization of consumption, and thence on "consumer relationships." Here I must stress that the term "consumer" is used very broadly and implies some similarity among people who buy a product in a shop, rent a house, go to school, and are patients in a hospital. Ahmed, a *cuisinier* in an Algerian-owned café in central Lyon, had been trying to find an apartment for himself and his family. Eventually he succeeded, and I asked him how it was. "Oh, it's fine. The apartment's very well placed. The school's nearby, there's the supermarket, the medical center, the social worker . . ." The relationships implied by the apparently heterogeneous collection of what I shall term "institutional complexes" in which they are embedded (landlord/tenant, teacher/parent or pupil, doctor/patient, salesperson/customer, social worker/client), of course, differ significantly in content and structure; but there is sufficient similarity to enable us to treat them collectively in the first instance.

One feature they share is a characteristic of the type of society we are discussing, which in fact cuts across other divisions such as that between private and public and, indeed, that between production and consumption. For many of the social relationships in which people engage are increasingly conducted within, or with the personnel of, an institutional complex: a network of formal organizations bureaucratically ordered in Max Weber's sense. "Institutional complex," rather than simply "institution," as in most cases there are several linked organizations, or parts of organizations, operating in a specifiable domain. Of special interest and importance are those concerned with the domains of housing, education, health, welfare, and work.

These institutional complexes significantly affect the day-to-day life of society's members. Indeed, it is impossible to exist in France without being continually touched, directly and indirectly, by their activities. Let me make five further points about them and their analysis in this book.

First, many of the institutional complexes with which we will deal are concerned with relations of *consumption* (e.g., in Chapters 4 and 5 on housing, 6 on the social services, 7 on education). This is not to say that relations of *production* will be ignored. (See Chapters 8, 9, and 10.) Nor does it mean that the former are thought to have greater theoretical importance than the latter. The two great fields of relations are linked, and ultimately one must suggest what the nature of the linkage is.

Second, behind much of the material to be presented lies the state (or the State, as most French writers would have it). Many of the institutions that make up a complex are, directly or indirectly, formally or informally, linked to the state system. A major problem we will have to tackle is the nature of the state's role in a society such as France.

Third, central to the analysis is the relationship between the personnel of institutions and their "clients," using that term in a broad sense. While, on the one hand, emphasizing an essential similarity among all such relationships, I recognize that there are differences between the personnel of different institutions and the clients they encounter. It is in respect of these differences that the value (and the limitations) of a study concentrating on one type of client – immigrant workers and their families – will become apparent.

Fourth, somewhat apart, at least in analytical terms, from the institutional complexes that organize production and consumption, are a variety of bodies that often share important organizational features with the institutions (e.g., a bureaucratic order) and, indeed, may be part of them (as is true of some social workers) but that *act on* relations in production and consumption. By that I mean in the way a trade union "acts on" the relationship between employer and employee. In some cases, such bodies may form or represent a relatively organized opposition to the activities of the institutional complexes.

Fifth, the study of the institutional complexes and their personnel, and the relationships with clients, has much to commend it from an anthropological point of view. The relationships they

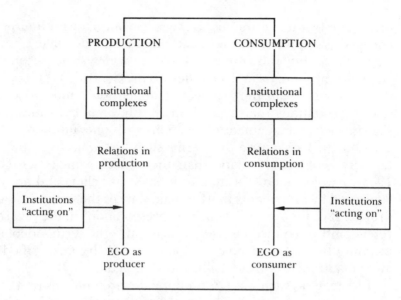

Figure 1.1. Relations of production and consumption.

entail are "pivotal," or "nodal" (Grillo 1980a), linking a multiplicity of social fields at different levels of social organization. They thus provide a means of tackling the problem of relating macro- and microanalyses. They also provide a way into the difficult question of the relationship between institutional organization and ideological structure, both in terms of particular institutions and their personnel and in terms of the system as a whole.

The elements of this "system" are presented in a deliberately abstract form in Figure 1.1. Much of what happens in a city such as Lyon cannot, of course, be fitted into the framework suggested by that diagram. To attempt to make such a fit would be reductionism of the worst kind. The diagram simply indicates certain key relationships, and the linkages between them, that engage people in the kind of society Lyon is. Given the time devoted by my informants, French and immigrant, to discussing them, they clearly were crucial to those involved.

THE IDEOLOGICAL FRAMEWORK

When the Lyon project was proposed and I tried to define the contribution a British social anthropologist might make to a study of immigrants in an urban and industrial milieu, I argued that a distinctive feature of the discipline is its concern with interaction and process studied through the medium of detailed cases interpreted within the framework of the wider social, economic, and cultural contexts in which they occur. Central to this is what I then wished to call the "subjective dimension": models, definitions, orientations that actors consciously or unconsciously employ in their management of relations with one another.

Although I recognize that terms such as "subjective" and "actor" are more problematic than they once seemed (see Grillo 1983), I would maintain that an interest in beliefs and attitudes expressed by informants must remain part of the anthropological project. It is this aspect to which "representation" in the first sense refers, and in connection with which I use the term "ideology," meaning by that a relatively organized and organizing body of ideas manifested both verbally and in practice.

"Ideology" as such was not traditionally presented as part of the subject matter of British social anthropology, although there has, of course, been a long-standing interest in ideational systems, their "function" in the social order, and the meanings they convey. This absence of "ideology" from anthropological vocabulary was, one suspects, due partly to a belief in a fundamental difference between the systems of thought of traditional societies and those of the modern world. (See Gellner 1978:81.) It also probably owed much to the political connotations of the word. In the early 1970s, however, ideology (so termed) began to appear on the anthropological agenda in the writings of, for example, Asad (1979) and Bloch (1974 and 1975a:Introduction, 1977). Their work and that of others (e.g., in Bloch 1975b) drew extensively on a Marxist interpretation of ideology, in particular that recension of it associated with Louis Althusser.

Let me say at once that for reasons discussed in Chapter 12, my approach to ideology does not derive from an Althusserian perspective, which I believe preempts both questions and answers in the study of ideational systems. A much more fruitful approach to ideology in the sense used here may be found in the writings of Michel Foucault (1970, 1971, 1972, 1980), whose work has been curiously ignored by British anthropologists, although that of several of his compatriots – including, recently, Jacques Derrida – has made a considerable impact.

A key concept in Foucault's writing is that of "discourse," a term that designates a "group of statements in so far as they belong to the same discursive formation" (1972:117). Statements are "groups of verbal performances . . . linked at the statement level" (p. 115), identified by the way a statement has a "referential" (p. 91), which consists of "laws of possibility, rules of existence for the objects that are affirmed or denied in it" (ibid.). In this sense, discourse bears a family resemblance to Kuhn's modified concept of "paradigm" (Kuhn 1970:182), although in Foucault, as in Pêcheux (1969, 1978, 1982), there is a much greater concern with the language in which discourse is embodied and – much more problematically – in which it is embedded.

This perspective may be allied to that of the French anthropologist Louis Dumont, whose ideas are perhaps in certain respects closer to those of Foucault than the former might care to admit (compare Foucault 1972:184–6 with Dumont 1977:17–22 on the status of scientific discourse). Dumont is concerned with what he calls "modern ideology": "a set of ideas common to many societies, countries or nations" (1977:7). This ideology consists of "configurations" (p. 14), particular ways in which ideas drawn from the set are constructed by, for example, different national or cultural groups. Thus, to rephrase what I said earlier, the discussion of the "representation" of problems in this book examines the structure and content of a variety of discourses and seeks to identify the ideological configurations embodied therein.

In a society such as France, however, there are always a multiplicity of discourses and ideological configurations, which interact and interrelate in subtle ways. This has been ably demonstrated by Gill Seidel in a fascinating series of papers concerned with right and left in both Britain and France (Seidel 1975, 1979a, 1979b, 1983; Seidel and Billig 1979). Besides revealing the complex semantic structure of political discourse and the morphology of its language, she also shows how discourses "play" on one another. There are, in addition, complex levels of similarity and dissimilarity among discourses in respect of the configurations they project.

Beyond that, of course, not all discourses are of equal status, power, and authority. Much of Seidel's work tries to identify what she terms the "dominant discourse," which she defines as a dominant "mode of argument and selection of meanings enmeshed in institutional norms and practices" (1979a). In this she follows Foucault, who like Althusser and Pêcheux, is much exercised by the relationship between discourse and power (cf. Foucault 1971,

1980), whether that concerns the power of discourse vis-à-vis the "subject" or, more simply and with greater relevance to this book, the discourse that is powerful: the discourse that prevails.

In discussing the "representation" of problems, therefore, we are dealing not with passive systems of philosophical reflection but with views that are in more or less constant conflict. Discourse, as Seidel and others frequently state, is a "site of struggle." The point is that the study of discourse is not primarily the study of ideas alone, of disembodied ideology; and this study is as much concerned with society as with ideology and, of course, the relationship between the two.

Here the link is made in two ways via the institutional framework described earlier. First, what are construed as "problems" are often, though not always, associated with the relationship between the migrant and the institutional complexes of French society. It is their roles as producers and consumers that frequently form the subject matter of discourse. Second, it is within and through the institutions themselves, at least some of them, that the "representations" of problems are "represented" in a political sense. The institutions themselves are one site of ideological struggle.

Throughout the text, discussion of "representation" in both senses alludes to what might seem a straightforward opposition in French thought and practice between ideologies and institutions of the right and left. (See Figure 1.2.) Although this opposition provides a constant frame of reference, both for participants and for the observer, it should be stated at the outset that it is by no means as simple as it seems; and, indeed, the validity of the opposition itself will eventually be questioned.

Analysis of these themes begins in Chapter 3. Chapter 2 presents an introductory account of the immigrant population of France and Lyon. The rest of this chapter is also introductory. It explains how my research in Lyon began and developed. It is intended partly to illustrate certain features of an advanced urban system, partly to demonstrate how and why I arrived at an understanding of that system.

Finally, regarding the use of French in the text, readers may note that all citations from written sources are given in the original language. Citations of the spoken word are in English, unless an analytically arresting word or phrase was used.

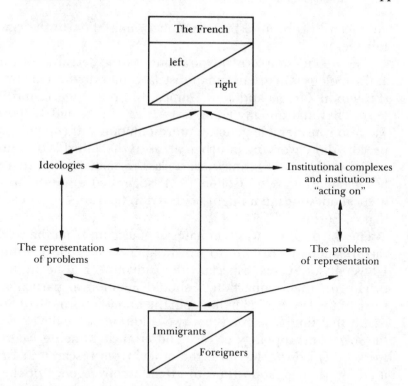

Figure 1.2. Ideologies, institutions, and immigrants.

A PROJECT AND ITS DEVELOPMENT

The research project that generated the material for this volume was initially inspired by work in three fields of research, each represented at the University of Sussex when the proposal was first formulated. Between 1966 and 1971 Professor F. G. Bailey and his students had undertaken a series of studies, financed by the Social Science Research Council (SSRC), of Southern European peasant societies (Bailey 1971, 1973). Although Bailey left Sussex in 1972, research in Europe continued. It had been Bailey's intention to switch the focus of interest from the countryside to the towns, and to the movement of people from one to the other in search of employment. Several of the later projects in the Bailey program had begun to reflect this (e.g., Griffin 1973; Palmer 1981; Pratt 1973). My own research was conceived in terms of this development and was intended originally as a contribution to the study of

Southern European, especially Italian, migration to the cities of Europe.

The second source of inspiration was the research of Sussex anthropologists in urban and industrial centers in the Third World (Epstein in Zambia and New Guinea, Lloyd in Nigeria and Peru, Pocock in India, and myself in East Africa). In the mid-1970s there was also considerable general interest among anthropologists, especially those working in urban areas in the Third World, in the linked problems of ethnicity and class formation. Research then being published (e.g., Cohen 1974) suggested a number of theoretical questions that might be tested in fieldwork in a new area, that is, Europe.

The third source was the material emerging from the study of race relations in Britain, to which again some colleagues at the University of Sussex, especially the Indianists, had begun to contribute. In that connection, I should mention in particular the work of the late Paul Hershman in the London borough of Southall. At that time it seemed that two traditions were developing in the social anthropology of race and ethnicity: one derived from work in Third World cities; the other, from research in Britain itself. It seemed opportune to effect a convergence of the two traditions and also test in another European society some of the hypotheses research on race in Britain had generated. A major publication (Castles and Kosack 1973) by two Sussex political economists offered a broad theoretical and comparative framework within which such material might be located.

From these sources, then, came the main theme of a research proposal that was submitted to the SSRC in 1974–5: the application of anthropological methods of inquiry to the study of ethnic and class identity among immigrant workers in a major European urban center. This theme remained at the heart of the research. A further specific subtheme concerned *variation* in identity: what circumstances, structural conditions, affected the choice of identity and the intensity with which it was expressed.

A number of factors influenced the direction the research was to follow in both the long and the short term. First, an early decision was made to locate the project in France (rather than, say, Germany), partly for personal reasons, partly because it was felt that such research might build on the findings of Griffin's work in Nice (1973). A reading of official publications suggested that one of the industrial centers in the Rhône-Alpes region would prove a suitable field site.

Second, in the initial stages it was thought that the project would concentrate on Italian migrants. Discussions with F. Wilson of the University of Cape Town, who had spent part of 1973 in Lyon, forced me to realize that no study of immigration into France could ignore migrants from North Africa. Reading of French accounts of immigration, and a preliminary field visit in 1974, strongly reinforced this view. In consequence, comparison between Southern European (Italian) and North African (Algerian) migrants was built into the research proposal.

Third, given an interest in the situational variation of identity, further types of comparison had to be undertaken. It was, therefore, proposed to study ethnic, class, and status identities within a variety of fields of social relations, and between different structural contexts within those fields, for example, between factory work and work in the building industry in the field of employment, between inner-city tenements and new suburban-housing estates in the field of residence. It was this comparative framework that provided the strategic and tactical guidelines for the research in its initial stages.

Preparation for the project began in 1972. In the summer of 1974 the University of Sussex funded a short trip to the Rhône-Alpes region. I cannot overstress the value of this early contact with a new field area, and the extent to which it enhanced the subsequent preparation of a research proposal and guided work and reading in the year prior to entering the field. It also provided an early and useful familiarity with the ground, and an incentive to begin the study of North African dialect Arabic that continued throughout fieldwork.

Fieldwork proper began in July 1975 and continued until August 1976. The choice of location had been narrowed to two of the main centers in the region: Lyon and Grenoble. It fell on Lyon, partly for practical reasons – the availability of family accommodations – partly for reasons concerned with the structure and size of the city. The relative complexity of Lyon was itself enticing.

A fuller description of Lyon will be given later. In brief, the Lyon area constitutes the most important urban and industrial complex in France outside of Paris. Its significance is indicated by the cities with which it is twinned: Birmingham, Frankfurt, Milan.

The *agglomération,* the Communauté Urbaine de la Région Lyonnaise, or COURLY* consists of Lyon itself (population over
500,000) and some four dozen communes, making a built-up area
35 kilometers in diameter with a total population of nearly 1.2
million. Traditionally the center of the silk industry, it is now
better known for artificial textiles and chemicals and for its heavy
and light mechanical and electrical engineering, especially the
production of heavy vehicles and their parts. There is also a large
construction industry and a substantial tertiary sector. Some
200,000 first- and second-generation foreign immigrants live in
the area.

Despite (indeed, perhaps, because of) its complexity, Lyon
proved an immensely fruitful location for fieldwork. Grenoble –
one-third its size – would undoubtedly have been simpler and
easier. Lyon has a reputation as socially the "coldest" city in
France, a belief the Lyonnais themselves do little to dispel. It is
also thought to be a "hard" city so far as relations between French
and immigrants are concerned. The social structure and political
complexion of the French population – as compared, say, with
that of Grenoble – might be thought to be partly responsible, and
I will discuss in a moment the implications of the city's social
structure for the type of fieldwork that was possible.

So, then, the project was centered on Lyon, where my family
and I established ourselves for some fourteen months. For the
first year we rented a flat in the VIth Arrondissement (see Map
3),† in a quartier that was losing its immigrant population because
of urban renewal. The area was within walking distance of several
areas of immigrant concentration and was centrally placed for
travel by public transportation to most parts of the metropolis.
The last months of our stay were spent in a suburb southwest of
the city. We thus experienced at first hand the contrasting life-
styles of two distinct types of residential areas. That our children
attended the neighborhood school, which had an immigrant intake of 20 percent, gave us immediate experience of what otherwise would have been a relatively closed world.

I have spent some time outlining the background to this research to suggest the kind of project it might have become. A brief
account of my initial expectations about fieldwork in a large Euro-

*I generally follow French custom by employing acronyms, a glossary of which
has been provided near the beginning of this book.
†Maps follow the Bibliography near the end of this volume.

pean city and of the strategy I attempted to follow in the early stages of research will reinforce this.

My experience of urban research in East Africa, where I had devotedly followed the methods suggested so brilliantly by Whyte (1943), indicated that the best line of approach was to attempt to make direct, informal, personal contact with a limited number of informants with whom one could establish enduring rapport. Such contact should be permanent and continuous. As one became part of their network of relations, part of their lives, and allowed oneself to be guided by them, the rest – the data – would follow. Second, the comparative framework developed in the original research proposal involved a number of issues that could not be tackled simultaneously. The two immigrant groups chosen for comparison (Italians and Algerians) occupied social milieus that at the outset appeared rather different. Consequently, I decided at first to seek contacts with the Algerians, who at least had the advantage of visibility. Third, contacts had to be sought where people gathered. There are no ghettos in Lyon, but certain areas are frequented by North Africans, and it was to these that I directed my attention. In effect, the research was set to become a study of the "community" of immigrants from within. The end result was very different.

ANTHROPOLOGICAL FIELDWORK IN AN ADVANCED URBAN AND INDUSTRIAL SOCIETY

Anthropological analyses do not always make clear that the type of society in which research is located "structures" the anthropological enterprise (Grillo 1980c). If pressed, I might admit to being in some sense an "urban anthropologist," without being able to say precisely what that means. "Everyone knows what a city is except the experts," says Horace Miner (1967). Agreed. At the experiential level, the contrast between town and country is obvious; but so is that between various kinds of towns. Early on in Lyon I concluded that I had never really undertaken *urban* research before. There was something about this city that struck me at the time as quintessentially urban (perhaps in a Wirthian sense) and very different from what most British anthropologists had previously encountered. This at the end of a particularly frustrating day in an area believed to contain a certain concentration of Italian immigrants. The vast thoroughfares and featureless apartment blocks contained no sign whatever of the kind of "urban village" so readily apparent in Kampala. I consoled myself with the Chandlerian dictum "Down these mean streets a man must go."

Traditional anthropological methods require a certain openness, or public accessibility, on the part of the society under observation. When many areas of the society are closed, or private, continuous participant observation becomes very difficult. In an urban and industrial society like Lyon's, one's informants spend a large part of their lives within formal organizations to which an outsider gains access in only a limited way. For example, entry into a factory as an independent anthropologist may be virtually impossible. One can gain access via management; or if jobs are available, one can obtain employment (see Mars and Nicod 1984). In both cases, one's relationships within the institution are structured. If occasions for meeting people are restricted to those outside the work context, there is a practical problem in that there are relatively few times when people are available. It comes down to evenings, weekends, and public holidays.

If availability is reduced to a limited range of times and places, it is important that there should then be accessibility. I was, however, faced with a life-style that is characteristic of much of urban Europe but is highly marked in Lyon: the privatization of behavior and relationships. For example, according to my informants and my own experience, it is in Lyon extremely difficult to establish a relationship and maintain it on an informal basis until it is already of considerable duration. There is a positive hostility toward the casual call at home, among both French and immigrants. Casual visiting may, in fact, be *physically* impossible. It was thought "typically Lyonnais" that in an inner-city apartment block the main door of a building is closed, locked, from about 9:00 P.M. Unless the person one wishes to visit has a telephone (not common), there is little one can do even to bring that person to the door.

"Chacun chez soi!" is a remark often made about life in Lyon, especially perhaps life in the new housing developments, where in a fifteen-story–tower block the limits of a relationship with a neighbor are "Bonjour. Bonsoir" on the staircase or in the elevator, should it be working. A life-style that on weekdays encompasses work-meal-TV-bed, encapsulated within the work place, on the one hand, and the apartment, on the other, implies great frustration for an anthropologist pursuing traditional methods of inquiry. Even when a casual contact is made, or a contact derived from another source is encouraged, even when rapport seems excellent, it is difficult to maintain continuous relationships of the kind I had had with informants in Kampala. These are busy people leading a highly organized existence, with little time to talk to an anthropologist and little interest in, or opportunity for, incorporating him in their lives, other than strictly on the society's terms.

A small example may illustrate some of the frustrations that are encountered even when circumstances might otherwise seem propitious. One of my daughter's classmates in the primary school opposite our flat shared our surname. The father, an Italian immigrant, was an electrician whose wife kept the stationery store around the corner. I arranged to meet him and discovered that our families came originally from the same part of Italy. We speculated that we might be related and promised to see much of each other. Despite this auspicious start, we managed to meet only twice throughout the whole year. There were good reasons (there always were), but the frustration generated may be appreciated.

What I say here applies to the great majority of family heads – immigrant and French, middle class and working class. The rhythm of life of the large numbers of male migrants who are unmarried or who have left their families behind is only marginally different: work-shopping-cleaning-cooking-meal-TV-bed. Many of them also live in accommodations where access by outsiders is formally restricted. Thus, the rules of the hostels run by the Maison du Travailleur Etranger (MTE) state; "Dans l'intérêt de chacun, pour éviter des désordres, l'accès des locaux à toute personne étrangère au foyer est soumise à l'autorisation préalable du Directeur. (Maison du Travailleur Etranger, 'Foyer de Travailleurs: Règlement Intérieur.')"

There are a number of exceptions – occasions, areas – when or where access is easier: public spaces (parks and the like), meetings, ceremonies, gatherings of all kinds, where observations may be made. Even here, however, introductions may be necessary. Then there are the cafés. North African society is in France a café society; and the café would seem, on the surface, an obvious place where there is an open public arena in which contacts might be made and established. On that assumption, I began frequenting the cafés and restaurants of the Place Gabriel Péri, the "Place du

Pont." Throughout the whole of our stay in Lyon, I regularly visited the cafés there and in the nearby Place Guichard, whose Sunday market attracts many North Africans.

In the very long run, this type of research proved fruitful. The cafés are the meeting place not only for those who live in rented rooms adjoining them but also for many others who come into the center of the town from the suburbs or from farther afield on a visit or in their travels. Through the cafés I established a network of contacts of a relatively long-term nature and also made casual acquaintances. For various reasons, however, the value of the café as a locus for fieldwork is restricted.

First, relating to their function for their customers, is the pattern of café activity. Crowded to the bursting point – and noisy with talkers attempting to make themselves heard over the TV, jukebox, or record player – at mealtimes during the week, and on Saturdays and Sunday mornings, they are almost deserted on other occasions.

Second, contacts made in cafés are made with a floating population. There is considerable mobility between lodgings, for example, and between jobs (less, perhaps, than usual during the period of my fieldwork because of the employment situation). Moreover, someone met in a café may live in a distant suburb, and because until real progress has been made such relationships are kept as café relationships, it may be weeks or months before a good contact is seen again.

Third, non-Arab customers of such cafés are extremely rare and by and large not welcome or, rather, treated with great reserve. There is never discrimination of a kind an Arab experiences in many "European" cafés. I was never *refused* service, for example. It is just that relations between French and Arab immigrants are such that *all* Europeans are regarded with suspicion, especially perhaps one whose situation was as difficult to diagnose as my own (student? teacher? unemployed?). Rapport could be established only after many months of assiduous work. Fluent knowledge of Arabic, which I certainly did not have, is of only marginal help. In fact it can increase suspicion, for who, in France, other than a *pied noir*, a former *colon*, knows Arabic? A French worker-priest, committed to the Algerian cause since the early 1950s and a fluent speaker of the Algerian dialect, with many Algerian friends, admitted that he never went to the cafés, because he felt so uncomfortable there. These remarks apply especially to Algerians, who form the majority of North Africans. Relations with Tunisians, for the French and for me, were less tense. There are good historical reasons for this. Algerians maintain a firm ethnic boundary through which it is extremely difficult to break.

Although working the cafés paid off in the very long run, it was not the best way, the way established in the society, of developing a relationship, especially between an Arab and a European. I soon realized that my best contacts came when a third party had made an introduction, when my credentials were above suspicion. Then, and virtually only then, could rapport be established. It was a vicious circle. One could make friends only after one had made friends. It is probable, however, that someone who had previously worked in Algeria for a long period in an area of high emigration and had established contacts "over there" that led to introductions in France would have fared differently.

In the course of the year, I found that there were various channels through which firm contacts could be established. Of these, the most important for my fieldwork were networks arising from the trade-union movement and certain private associations. These were of immense value, provided one recalled that through such networks one was drawn into a specific milieu, with its own perspective. But such contacts – or, rather, the rate and intensity of contact with such informants – are affected by the structure of urban society. Leaving aside the rhythm of life mentioned earlier, the most important single constraint is that a network of individuals based on a private association, say, may consist of people living throughout the urban area. For example, some of my best informants came from the suburbs of Saint-Genis-Laval, Tassin, Caluire, Rillieux, Vaulx-en-Velin, Décines, and Vénissieux, that is, from all corners of the urban periphery. Even from central Lyon, these places are difficult to reach by public transportation at the best of times, in other words, during the day in midweek – much more so in the evenings and on weekends. Moreover, many people, especially Arabs, hesitate to cross the city at night, by either public or private transportation, for fear of casual violence or "controls" by the police.

Aside from these physical constraints, which meant that meetings had to be arranged by appointment, at infrequent intervals, and well in advance, the development of these contacts was affected by life-styles that emphasized the privatization and compartmentalization of social relationships. A trade-union contact, like a café contact, remained essentially that, and for a long time would be bound by highly formal rules of conduct. For example, I was a member of an association concerned with Franco-Algerian relations, the Association de Coopération Franco-Algérienne du Lyonnais (ACFAL), whose members all appeared to be one another's good friends: At meetings everyone gave and received *tu*. One evening I arrived to find that the door of the clubhouse was locked and no one could get in. The key was with the director, André. But where was André? How could we reach him? The fact was that not one person knew where André lived, although we subsequently discovered that his apartment was less than half a mile away, in the center of Lyon.

In the end, the long-term relationships I had been seeking at the outset did materialize, from either the cafés or the institution-based networks of the kind mentioned above. By the time I left the field, I had a reasonable number of "working" relationships among both immigrants and the French and was in a position to begin the kind of research I had originally envisaged. But it had taken a year to reach that stage.

I could probably have reached that position somewhat earlier if developments had not occurred that caused me to alter my original strategy. The difficulty in establishing lasting contacts, and the restricted number of occasions on which contacts could be made (and the fact that I was bored sitting in empty cafés watching *Kung Fu* dubbed into French on TV), left me wishing for a more active research role. After a month of fieldwork, when it was clear that the cafés would pay dividends only after considerable effort, I came by chance on an organization, the Maison du Travailleur Etranger, that runs hostels for foreign workers in Lyon. After a false start I met and talked at some length with the staff of this organization. Originally, I had intended to discover some "facts," such as how many residents there were in the hostels; but as one meeting led to another, one organization to another, a wholly unexpected avenue of inquiry became apparent.

First, it transpired that in Lyon there was a wide range of mainly French organizations – public and private – concerned wholly or partly with immigrants. Second, although these bodies could provide factual information, they were much more significant as a source of attitudes and as examples of the structural response of French society to immigrants. Third, they and their personnel were linked (and divided) in complicated ways that revealed much about the workings of the urban social and political systems. Fourth, they were open to people like myself. Their staff were willing, indeed expected, to talk at great length about immigrants. My role as investigator fitted exactly their role as informants.

Once I had started this line of inquiry, and as fresh points developed almost day by day, it became clear that here was a most interesting area of research, which in the French context, and indeed elsewhere, was hardly ever tackled, although two short articles (Davis 1975; Rew 1975) read while in the field indicated that other scholars were in different ways beginning to attack the same kind of material. To do it justice, however, required a full-scale deployment of time and resources. Thus, what began as a casual attempt to keep busy while the relationships at the core of the original strategy matured became itself the central strategy of the research.

The two lines of research could, in fact, be conducted simultaneously, since the (French) personnel of the institutions were most accessible, initially, during times when my immigrant contacts were otherwise engaged. By maintaining these two strategies, findings from rather different contexts could be counterpointed. None of this, however, should be taken to imply an identification of institutionally derived, formal contacts with French informants, and casually derived, informal contacts with immigrants. A number of my French contacts were established on an informal basis, and certain contacts with immigrants were institutionally based. And, of course, some of those I met in formal settings (especially in the trade unions and in the associations I joined) were also encountered in other, less formal contexts. Life was never completely compartmentalized.

As research gathered pace and I perceived the range of institutions involved, I worked out a rough plan to obtain maximum coverage by dividing them, for convenience, into those concerned with housing, work, education, and the social services. It seemed best to concentrate as far as possible in any period on those concerned with a particular facet of social relationships. This compartmentalization was only partly artificial, in that many of the institutions were specialized in these fields. Others, of course, cut across these categories.

There was, however, another practical advantage to be derived from this specialization, and from this whole line of inquiry. The complex nature of urban and industrial society means that a great deal of technical knowledge is required to understand the background of what might otherwise seem a straightforward matter. If told, for example, that "Ahmed lives in an F3 in an HLM on a ZUP," it might be enough to know that this could be translated as "Ahmed lives in an apartment with three principal rooms in a low-rent housing development on a very large property or estate." But what exactly is an HLM or a ZUP, what is their significance in terms of the urban housing system, and what is the significance of that for Ahmed? This is not just a question of acquiring a limited amount of knowledge to clarify matters that are otherwise on the boundary of one's interest or at the limits of one's näiveté. There is in this a theoretical point of some importance.

I would argue that it is theoretically unsound and practically impossible to treat "immigrants" as if they were an isolated community, or one whose principal relationship with the society of immigration is determined by a difference of color, culture, or "race." Immigrants are sociologically members of the society into which they have migrated – the receiving society – and their position must be understood, in part at least, in terms of the institutions and processes of that society, although this does not preclude the incorporation of other factors, for example, the immigrant's membership in a sending society, into the analysis. This is the logical conclusion to be drawn from Gluckman's (1961) dictum that "an African miner is a miner." Yet the fieldworker who operates on this assumption is driven to pay as much attention to the society that receives the immigrants as to the immigrants themselves.

The elucidation of the statement "Ahmed lives in an F3 in an HLM on a ZUP" required, eventually, systematic analysis of the nature and operation of the urban-housing market and its particular significance for immigrants of various backgrounds, of French housing policy and its application in an urban area such as Lyon, of the structure of municipal government, and of the process of urban development in France over the past twenty years, as well as consideration of changing patterns of migration, and hence the changing structure of the sending society, over a similar period.

In this respect, the organizations and associations I term the "institutions" are crucial for both immigrants and others. They are the principal manifestation of the societal system whose instruments they are and often the principal forums within which alternatives to that system are elaborated. In every respect, they are at the core of the relationship between immigrants and French society, and their structure, organization, and function reflect this.

In previous research on immigration and urban society, I had accepted the Gluckman dictum, at least as a working hypothesis, and the present research was originally influenced by that and by other writings on migration in Europe that adopted a similar line (e.g., Castles and Kosack 1973; Rex and Moore 1967). The research I undertook in Lyon confirmed the value of that hypothesis in the strongest possible way. The logic of that position, together with the exigencies of fieldwork, forced me to see eventually the contradictions in the fieldwork strategy I had tried to implement at the outset. Thus, what might have become, perhaps inadvertently, a study of the internal structure of a "community" of immigrants, working from the inside looking out, became instead what my basic theoretical position had demanded all along, a study of the relationship between that community (if such it be) and the society in which it was located, working from the outside looking in. So the research, and thus this book, is concerned as much with the *French* and French-immigrant relations as with the immigrants themselves.

Let me return for a moment to an earlier point. Given the need to learn about French society, the specialized nature of the institutions had a practical value. For while recognizing the connectedness of different facets of social life (housing, work, school, etc.), the fieldworker could concentrate on one aspect at a time. This specialization of the inquiry is not to be seen as a simple heuristic device, however. The specialization of the institutions is itself a social fact of considerable significance. The categorically distinct fields of social relations that the French often present the observer – *logement, travail, scolarisation, formation* – reflect both the organization of the society and an ideological view of that organization. This provides further illustration of the way in which the fieldworker's experience – in this case, of the way in which data are presented – is structured by the society under investigation. That some informants, operating with a different ideological perspective, did not categorize social relations in this way illuminates other aspects of the society's structure.

The preceding remarks have been intended to offer some general reflections on fieldwork in a "complex" society and on the ways in which the fieldworker can be driven by the society he is studying into a particular style and pattern of research. I hope they also explain how and why the initial aims of the Lyon project were altered in the course of the research. The analytical and theoretical issues that ultimately arose from fieldwork were in certain respects totally unexpected, although I believe they were implicit in the original aims. In many ways, of course, the research remained within its terms of reference. It was "about" immigrants, even if the focus shifted to the French and French-immigrant relations. It was also "about" migration, class, and ethnicity, as subsequent chapters will show. Immigrants as such, however, ceased to be the center of interest.

In this section, various points have been made about the structure of Lyon as a system of social relations partly to illustrate the problems this posed for fieldwork. Many factors may be said to characterize that system: the privatization of social life, the formality of relationships, their compartmentalization, the specialization of roles and institutions, the existence of an "institutional complex" of great social, economic, and political significance, as well as a multitude of other factors, which are discussed elsewhere. The system of relationships found in Lyon, and in France generally, is characteristic of what, along with many others, I describe as "advanced" or "post-" industrial society. This type of society was represented dramatically, and hilariously, in two French films of the 1960s: Jacques Tati's *Playtime* and Jean-Luc Godard's *Alphaville* (just as two films of the 1930s, Chaplin's *Modern Times* and René Clair's *A Nous la Liberté,* portrayed the postindustrial society's "industrial" predecessor). In a sense, Lyon *is* "Alphaville," and this book is about such a city and such a society. Immigration and immigrants provide only a case in point, an instance of how such a society affects the lives of its members, albeit an important and particularly instructive instance. It was *in* and *through* the fieldwork that I was led to see this.

SOME FURTHER NOTES ON METHODS AND SOURCES

Doing research in Lyon, I sought information from a variety of sources, the most important of which was discussion with, and observation of, informants, both those encountered "on the street" and those approached via the institutions. Between September 1975 and July 1976 I met some two hundred French persons and several dozen immigrants (Algerian, Italian, Moroccan, Portuguese, Spanish, Tunisian, etc.) in the latter category. For the most part these people gave freely and fully of their institutional time. I was never directly refused a meeting, and only once was I unable to make the contact I wished. I thus talked with representatives of the great majority of institutions, public and private, concerned directly and indirectly with immigrants in Lyon. There remained, however, a number of gaps I did not have time to close, especially among employers and in police and judicial circles (e.g., the children's "judges").

Interviewing technique varied somewhat according to the context and the type of contact. In informal meetings in cafés or homes, with individuals or groups, I rarely took notes. Events, remarks were committed to memory and recorded later. About half the time, however, meetings were of a more formal nature (often held in offices). Then I took notes, which when written up provided a full, often verbatim record of the information obtained. The awkwardness that note-taking can introduce into a relationship was offset by the richness of the material retained. These more formal interviews were loosely structured in that although I did not use prepared questionnaires, previous conversations and sometimes published reports provided guidelines, or at least a checklist of points to be covered. Other occasions when I was almost always able to take notes overtly included many of the public and private meetings I attended simply as an observer.

Although my informants were scattered across the whole urban area and were involved in many different types of situations, it was both possible and desirable to concentrate attention on a number of locations. There were, for example, two central cafés that I visited as frequently as possible both during the week and on weekends. I belonged to one of the voluntary associations whose meetings I attended regularly. In addition, I tried to organize the institutional interviews so that they focused on particular areas that I knew well and where I had contacts. These included the central zone of the Zone à Urbaniser en Priorité (ZUP) Les Minguettes at Vénissieux, a part of the ZUP at Vaulx-en-Velin, an area of Vaulx-en-Velin Sud, the neighborhood around a *cité de transit* at Caluire and another at Oullins, a hostel on the Croix Rousse in Lyon, the areas around the Place Gabriel Péri and the Place Guichard in Lyon IIIrd, and the rue Olivier de

Serres in Villeurbanne. I also looked intensively at a small number of firms that were particularly important as sources of employment.

A glance at the maps near the end of this book will show the dispersal of these locations. In effect, they are sample areas that reflect the current distribution of immigrants in Lyon and the different types of areas and housing in which they live. Within the limits of the capacity of a single researcher, my aim was to obtain as comprehensive a picture as possible of the total context (and patterns of variation). It may be argued that any *one* of the above locations could have provided the basis for an intensive study. It should be clear, however, that the "urban village" approach that characterizes much anthropological research in urban Africa and elsewhere, if not impossible, is practically extremely difficult to implement in the short time available to most fieldworkers (i.e., twelve to fifteen months). Moreover, no one quartier is representative, in an amoeba-like way, of the totality. The local "community" has to be placed in the perspective of its relationship with the totality and studied comparatively, having regard to the other elements that make up the totality. When these elements and relationships can be defined, the study in depth can be undertaken with greater confidence.

A considerable amount of information is available in a substantial local literature on immigration in Lyon and more generally in the Rhône-Alpes region. There is relatively little of interest prior to about 1960 (cf. Baroin 1935; Chatelain 1934; Laroche 1955), but from the early 1960s onward there was a rush of studies, few of which found their way into print (e.g., Aboubacar 1972, Autenrieth 1971, Crozat 1970, Daille 1974, Mazzoleni 1970, and Sandillon 1969 concerned with Roanne; Vallet 1971 dealing with Givors; and that of Cordeiro and his associates – Cordeiro 1970, Cavard et al. 1973 – located in Grenoble).

Of the earlier studies, two (Mathieu 1961; Institut d'Etudes Politiques de Lyon 1966) may be cited for the intrinsic historical interest of the material they contain. Faidutti-Rudolph's mammoth 1964 description of the Italianate population of southeastern France also contains a brief but detailed section on Lyon. Otherwise, many of these studies are descriptive and repetitive, as are the *Mémoires* and *Rapports de stage* produced by trainee social workers, teachers, and the like, useful collections of which are possessed by a number of organizations in Lyon. Some of these are worth consulting for the attitudes they reveal, although occasionally they also contain other information of value (e.g., Courteuge 1971; Perez 1973).

Some of the most interesting and useful studies are those that have emerged from public and private research on housing (Caillot 1969; Chazalette 1972; Crétaine 1974; Deschamps 1976; Dubreuil 1975; GSU 1974a, 1974b; MATELT-SAEI 1974; SONACOTRA 1975b). A thesis by Michaud (1975), which he kindly allowed me to consult while in the field, helped me considerably to understand the implications of urban-development plans for the housing of immigrants just when I was becoming aware of them in my own research. Of the studies concerned with North Africans, Le Masne's thesis (1974) is outstanding.

Research of a kind is sometimes published by a variety of private groups, perhaps examining the operation of their own institution, perhaps as part of their contribution to some ongoing debate. The private associations also publish annual assessments of their activities, which are a gold mine of fact and opinion. Some also publish monthly journals of articles, letters, and comment, and in one case a monthly review of press reports relating to immigration. Membership in these associations is worthwhile simply for these.

Various public bodies provide information. The staff at the Institut National de la Statistique et des Etudes Economiques (INSEE) *Observatoire* at Lyon is exceptionally helpful, and INSEE's monthly bulletin *Points d'Appui* is invaluable. The prefecture is also, obviously, an important source of information of all kinds, published and unpublished, as are the foreign governments whose nationals migrate to France. Particularly useful were the reports, journals, newsletters, and so forth of the Amicale des Algériens en Europe.

Many publications, handouts, leaflets, posters, memoranda, "analyses," and so forth of a more ephemeral nature were readily available to the assiduous collector. The material issued by trade unions and political parties in connection with strikes, days of protest, and the like was especially interesting. From time to time it was possible to obtain – for reanalysis – the original data, schedules, and so forth, on which reports, surveys, and the like may have been based.

In addition, there is the press – local and national. For the purposes of this study, *Le Monde* was invaluable at the national level. Locally, the *Progrès* group of papers dominates the scene. It was found immensely helpful to maintain a press-clippings file dealing with the main areas of research interest throughout the fieldwork and afterward. Of value, too, were the newspapers, newsletters, magazines, and so forth published in French and other languages by the trade-union movement and the political parties.

2

Immigrants in France and in Lyon

In the previous chapter I stated that in this book the phenomenon of immigration provides the material for an extended case study through which to explore the working of institutional complexes and ideological systems that characterize French society. Nevertheless, the French-immigrant relationship is at the core of the study and immigrants themselves do figure prominently in the narrative. Some information about their situation in France and in Lyon is therefore essential.

It is not proposed to discuss here the general background to immigration: the factors – social, political, and above all economic – that have led to the fluctuating demand for labor in the core countries of Western Europe and in the United States, the principal receiving societies in the modern system of international migration, and the relationship that existed and still exists between such countries and those that have historically exported labor – the sending societies either on the periphery of the European core (southern Italy, Spain, Portugal, Greece, Yugoslavia, Turkey, Ireland) or in the former colonies of Africa, Asia, and the Caribbean. No understanding of modern migration can be complete without an appreciation of the significance of the broad intersocietal context within which it occurs. Nevertheless, I will in general take that broad context as given and for the moment simply refer the reader to the large number of excellent texts where it is discussed (see especially Böhning 1972; Descloîtres 1967; Grandjeat 1966; Kayser 1971, 1972; Kindleberger 1967; Klaasen and Drewe 1973; Marshall 1973; Piore 1979; Power 1979; Rose 1969; Schechtmann 1962).

The best account of migrant labor in Western Europe is still that of Castles and Kosack (1973), whose comparative work enables us to put the French material into a broader perspective from which the similarities and differences between France and the other countries of Western Europe can be assessed. Like those other countries (e.g., Britain, see Freeman 1979, or Holland, Marshall 1973), France has, for the last century, for reasons of economic and demographic necessity (Armengaud 1973), been obliged to import labor from abroad. The countries that have acted as labor reserves for French industry and agriculture include France's neighbors to the south (Italy, Spain, Portugal) and more distant countries of Eastern Europe (Poland, Czechoslovakia, and Yugoslavia). There has also been heavy reliance on the territories along the southern Mediterranean littoral with which France had a colonial relationship: first and foremost Algeria, but also Tunisia and Morocco. Occasionally there have been other sources, too, such as the influx of refugees from Armenia in the 1920s.

It is worth stressing that labor immigration has long been important to French society and is not just a phenomenon of late capitalism, although it has been given a particular shape and function in the post–World War II economy. (See Mandel 1978:181.) The general features of immigration since about 1950 have been amply documented elsewhere (see especially Armengaud 1973; Calame and Calame 1972; CEDETIM 1975; *Esprit* 1966; Freeman 1979; Granotier 1970; Hervo and Charras 1971; Minces 1973; Pétonnet 1968; Pinot 1973; Tapinos 1966, 1969, 1975; Valabrègue 1973; Vieuguet 1975; Wisniewski 1974, among many others). In this chapter, I will discuss briefly, with special reference to the Lyon area, some of the more general aspects of contemporary French immigration, to provide a necessary background to subsequent discussion.

NUMBERS AND DISTRIBUTION

In 1976 there were some 4 million foreigners registered in France (Table 2.1), more than half a million of whom lived in the Rhône-Alpes region, a cluster of eight departments centered on the Rhône. Within the region there are three main concentrations around the cities of Grenoble, Saint-Etienne, and Lyon. The Rhône Department, which includes Lyon, contains some 184,000 foreign nationals, about 12 percent of the 1975 population. The Lyon metropolitan area (COURLY), which accounts for 80 percent of the department's population, is the most important center of foreign immigration outside the Paris region. It is also a major pole of attraction for French national migrants: 20 percent of the

Table 2.1. *Foreigners in France, 1975–6*

Nationality	Census 1975	Min. de l'Int., Jan. 1, '76
Algerian	720,690	884,320
Portuguese	758,925	858,929
Italian	462,940	558,205
Spanish	497,480	531,384
Moroccan	260,025	322,067
Tunisian	139,735	167,463
Polish	93,655	86,408
Yugoslav	70,280	77,810
All others	448,685	709,548
Total	3,442,415	4,196,134

city's 1975 population had resided outside the urban area at the time of the previous (1968) census.

Quantitative accuracy with regard to the foreign population of France is impossible, and I do not wish to enter into any general discussion of the vexed question of whose numbers to believe. Several series are available, not all of them reconcilable. Each researcher has to make his own judgment. When the point is important, I will explain and justify the choice of figures presented in this book. The trends of recent years can, however, be charted in general terms. Tables 2.2, 2.3, and 2.4 give details from two sources. The late 1960s and early 1970s saw a rapid growth in the foreign population of the Rhône Department. North Africans increased by some 80 percent, the influx of Tunisians being especially marked. Although the important groups of Italians and Spaniards declined in absolute terms, the Southern European population as a whole climbed substantially because of a tripling of Portuguese immigrants.

These figures refer to those of foreign *nationality* and do not include children born to foreign parents but registered at birth as French nationals. Nor do they include those who have acquired French nationality, of whom a further 47,000 were counted in the Rhône Department at the 1975 census (Ministère du Travail 1977:72). Among them would be included the Harkis, Algerians who at the time of independence opted for France. Mention should also be made of the presence in the area of a substantial number of the former settlers in North Africa, a million of whom returned to France in the 1960s.

Table 2.2. *Foreigners in the Rhône Department: census data*

Nationality		1962	1968	1975
(a)	Algerian	26,571	37,048	58,300
	Moroccan	463	1,504	4,710
	Tunisian	1,748	4,416	14,430
(b)	Italian	24,657	26,496	22,970
	Portuguese	995	7,376	23,125
	Spanish	14,254	24,856	20,605
	Other	9,549	10,772	14,455
Grand total		78,237	112,468	158,625
Total (a)		29,782	42,968	77,440
Total (b)		39,906	58,728	66,730
Total population of Department		1,181,101	1,325,611	1,432,910
% Foreign		6.6	8.5	11.1

Table 2.3. *The foreign population of the Rhône Department: prefecture data*

Nationality		1968 (Jan.)	1975 (Dec.)
(a)	Algerian	(44,000)[a]	72,300
	Moroccan	2,684	6,454
	Tunisian	6,884	16,044
(b)	Italian	30,649	25,479
	Portuguese	8,755	26,176
	Spanish	23,255	21,169
	Other	11,436	16,519
Grand total		(127,663)	184,141
Total (a)		(53,568)	94,798
Total (b)		62,659	72,824
% Rhône population		(9.6)	12.9

[a]The actual figure cited by prefecture sources for the 1968 Algerian population is 31,143. This was an estimate out of accord with national figures for the same date and with the prefecture figure for the following year (1969) of 50,143 Algerians. The figure presented here is the best estimate available in the light of other data.
Source: Préfecture du Rhône.

In demographic terms, a broad contrast may be drawn between two main clusters of immigrants. Figures for France as a whole (Tapinos 1975; Wisniewski 1974) show that among North Africans adult males constitute some 60–70 percent of the immi-

Table 2.4. *Change in foreign population of the Rhône Department, 1968–75*

Nationality	Census data		Prefecture data	
	Absolute change	% change	Absolute change	% change
(a) Algerian	+21,252	+ 57.4	+28,300	+ 64.3
Moroccan	+ 3,206	+213.2	+ 3,770	+140.5
Tunisian	+10,014	+226.8	+ 9,160	+133.1
(b) Italian	− 3,526	− 13.3	− 5,170	− 16.9
Portuguese	+15,749	+213.5	+17,421	+199.0
Spanish	− 4,251	− 17.1	− 2,086	− 9.0
Other	+ 3,683	+ 34.2	+ 5,083	+ 44.4
Grand total	+46,157	+ 41.0	+56,478	+ 44.2
Total (a)	+34,472	+ 80.2	+41,230	+ 77.0
Total (b)	+ 8,002	+ 13.6	+10,165	+ 16.2

Table 2.5. *Foreign population of the Rhône Department, 1975: demographic structure of principal groups*

Nationality	Men	Women	Children under 16	Total	% men
Algerian	41,090	8,553	22,657	72,300	56.8
Moroccan	4,575	871	1,008	6,454	70.9
Tunisian	11,984	1,842	2,218	16,044	74.7
Italian	12,486	8,536	4,457	25,479	49.0
Portuguese	11,807	7,184	7,185	26,176	45.1
Spanish	8,630	7,034	5,505	21,169	40.8
All others	9,861	4,792	1,866	16,519	59.7
Total	100,433	38,812	44,896	184,141	54.5

Source: Préfecture du Rhône.

grant population. Among Southern Europeans the figure for adult males is about 45 percent. Table 2.5 shows that the situation in the Rhône Department is of much the same order. North African immigration has always been predominantly masculine. The migrants are predominantly bachelors or else married men who have left their families at home. Of the North Africans resident in a group of hostels in Lyon, 77 percent were stated to be married, separated from their families (Maison du Travailleur Etranger 1974, 1975). Southern European migration has become, fairly rapidly in the case of each of the three main groups, a family affair. The growth of the Portuguese population during the early 1970s was in no small part due to the arrival of families. This and the high rate of intermarriage with Frenchwomen on the part of Italian men mean that North Africans and Southern Europeans often have very different domestic and residential circumstances.

Although North African migration is still predominantly male, the number of North African families in France has increased significantly over the last twenty years. In the Rhône Department, for example, there were in the late 1950s no more than a few hundred such families (Mathieu 1961). By the mid-1970s there were almost certainly more than ten thousand, the bulk of whom arrived after 1968 during a period when considerable numbers of Portuguese families were also entering the area.

An important factor in comparing the two main groups of nationalities is relative family size. A survey undertaken on the ZUP at Vaulx-en-Velin, one of Lyon's eastern suburbs, showed that the average number of children per French family was 1.3; per Southern European family, 2.2; and per "African" family, 3.3. Arab families of six or more children are not uncommon. The North African population in the mid-1970s, therefore, contained a small but rapidly growing proportion of what were in French terms abnormally large families.

The rough contrast made here between immigrants from Southern Europe and those from North Africa may be extended in other directions (employment, education, language, religion, colonial experience, and so on) and is perhaps a useful one for the reader to bear in mind. Whether or not it is an analytically important distinction is a matter on which I will reserve judgment. Certainly much, though by no means all, of the migration literature in French is coded in terms of this contrast (see Papyle 1973), and there is considerable published work on each of the principal nationalities. That on Algerians is particularly rich. (See especially Augardes 1970; Belloula 1965; Bendifallah 1974; Chevalier 1947; Cordeiro 1970; FLN 1966; INED 1954, 1955; Le Masne 1974; Leriche 1959; Michel 1955; Mohammed 1973; Montagne 1953, 1954; Muracciole 1950; Rager 1950, 1956; Trébous 1970; Wisniewski 1973; Zehraoui 1971.) There are far fewer studies of other North African groups (but see Ben Sassi 1968 and INED 1977). For Southern Europeans, detailed information may be found on Italians (Faidutti-Rudolph 1964; Griffin 1973), Portuguese (Brettel 1977; Hommes et Migrations Etudes 1967), and Spaniards (Aguilo 1968; Hermet 1967).

Chapters 4 and 5 discuss in some detail the distribution of the foreign population by national group in the Lyon conurbation. Here I summarize briefly the salient points that might be borne in mind. In the city of Lyon itself there are relatively high concentrations in the Ist Arrondissement and on the borders of the IIIrd and VIIth (see Maps 2 and 3). This is the Place du Pont quartier. In the suburbs are large numbers of foreigners in the working-class communes to the east and southeast, especially at Vaulx-en-Velin (28.8 percent foreigners in the population in 1975) and at Décines, Vénissieux, Saint-Priest, Saint-Fons, and Feyzin (all over 18 percent). In the northern and western suburbs (with the exception of Pierre-Bénite: 16.2 percent), the proportion is generally much lower. The factors that produce this distribution include the structure of the housing and job markets. The next section discusses the employment of immigrants.

EMPLOYMENT

We are concerned with labor migrants and their families who come to France to seek work, which they find mainly in the lower echelons of the industrial order. The 1960s and 1970s were boom years for employment in France. Between 1962 and 1975 the active population (wage and salary earners) in the Rhône Department increased by 26 percent (Table 2.6). There was, however, a shift within overall employment from the secondary to the tertiary sector (see Table 2.7).

Table 2.6. *Active population of the Rhône Department, 1962–75*

	1962	1968	1975
All employment	527.3[a]	562.8	615.1
Waged/ salaried	428.6	471.9	539.9
Women in total employment	n.a.[b]	207.0	234.9

[a]Numbers in thousands.
[b]Figures not available.
Sources: INSEE, "Les actifs dans Rhône-Alpes," *Points d'Appui* No. 9. October 1977; census data.

Table 2.7. *Active population of the Rhône Department by main sectors of employment, 1962–75 (percentage distribution)*

	1962	1968	1975
Primary	1.4	1.1	0.7
Secondary	57.7	52.4	47.3
Tertiary	40.9	46.5	51.9
Number (thousands)	428.6	471.9	539.9

Sources: As for Table 2.6.

The general increase in the labor force was made possible part-ly by the entry into the labor market of substantial numbers of French women workers. However, perhaps as many as one in three of the additional people employed have been of foreign origin. These migrant workers sometimes found employment in the growth industries in the tertiary sector, but more usually they were sought as replacements for French workers leaving the sec-ondary, industrial, sector. For example, in the period 1970–4 the Office National d'Immigration (ONI) placed 33 percent of for-eign entrants in the Rhône Department in the construction indus-try and a further 24 percent in mechanical engineering (INSEE, *Points d'Appui,* October 9, 1975). Table 2.8 shows the distribution of French and foreign workers by sector of economic activity and shows clearly the contrasting employment profiles of the two groups. The table also shows the percentage of foreign workers among those employed in each sector. It is in industries such as construction, electrical and mechanical engineering, automobiles, textiles, and chemicals that foreigners have the highest represen-tation (for France, see Ministère du Travail 1975). Because of French law there are hardly any foreign employees in the public sector (e.g., transport), which makes the distribution of foreign workers in France quite different from that found in many British cities.

In addition to considerable variation between the main sectors of economic activity, there is significant variation between firms *within* the sectors that are the principal employers of immigrant labor. There is also variation at the level of the firm, in that some departments or work sections recruit far more foreign workers than others. I will look at this variation in some detail later in this chapter. Suffice it to say that many foreigners find employment

Table 2.8. *French and foreign workers by sector of economic activity, Rhône Department, 1975*

Sector[a]	French		Foreign		% foreign in sector
	No.	%	No.	%	
1	21,330	3.9	655	1.0	3.0
2	11,805	2.2	1,440	2.2	10.9
3	6,555	1.2	145	0.2	2.2
4	47,880	8.7	10,315	15.4	17.7
5	62,380	11.4	13,315	19.9	17.6
6	53,875	9.8	6,980	10.4	11.5
7	35,615	6.5	16,830	25.1	32.1
8	67,250	12.3	4,120	6.2	5.8
9	41,080	7.5	1,890	2.8	4.4
10	96,695	17.6	7,130	10.6	6.9
11–13	16,725	3.1	560	0.8	3.2
14	86,665	15.8	3,770	5.6	4.2
Total	548,035	100.0	66,970	100.0	10.9

[a]*Key to sectors:* 1. Agriculture 2. Agricultural industries 3. Energy 4. *Industries des biens intermédiaires* 5. *Industries des biens d'équipement* 6. *Industries des biens de consommation* 7. Building and construction 8. Commerce 9. Transportation and communications 10. *Services marchands* 11–13. Insurance, finance, etc. 14. *Services non-marchands*
Source: Census table.

where, as the saying goes, the work is "hardest, dirtiest, and poorest paid."

Confirmation of this may be found in a comparison of the distribution of French and foreign workers among what official statistics call *catégorie socio-professionnelle*. Table 2.9 shows the relatively small proportion of foreigners in administrative and white-collar jobs and their concentration among skilled workers – *ouvriers professionnels* (OP) or *ouvriers qualifiés* (OQ) – and even more markedly among the so-called *ouvriers specialisés* (OS), the principal category in which ordinary workers on building sites and on factory production lines are placed.

So far as the main national groups of immigrant workers are concerned, there is relatively little difference between North Africans and Southern Europeans in terms of the sector of economic activity in which they are employed. There is, however, a significant difference in terms of *catégorie socio-professionnelle* in that the great bulk of North Africans are OS while a far higher proportion of Southern Europeans are skilled workers. One further dif-

Table 2.9. Catégories socio-professionnelles, *Rhône-Alpes region,*
1968–75, by nationality

Category[a]	1968			1975		
	French	Foreign	% foreigners in category	French	Foreign	% foreigners in category
Professions libérales + *cadres supérieurs*	81,172	1,572	1.9	123,750	2,685	2.1
Cadres moyens	181,744	2,256	1.2	257,380	3,910	1.5
Employés	253,504	4,664	1.8	344,645	9,010	2.6
Skilled workers	298,224	32,860	11.0	310,920	47,170	13.2
OS + manoeuvres	373,624	91,068	19.6	367,085	113,845	23.7
Service Personnel	77,772	5,664	7.2	90,580	7,095	7.3
Grand total	1,266,040	138,084	10.9	1,494,360	183,715	12.3

[a]The table excludes a number of small "other" categories.
Source: Census tables.

ference is that extremely few North African women enter employment. For example, the 1975 census showed that in the
Rhône Department only 8 percent of Algerian women were
classed as "active" compared with 32 percent of Portuguese and
35 percent of French women.

Returning to the main sectors of economic activity, Table 2.8
shows that about one-quarter of all immigrant workers in the
Rhône Department in 1975 were employed in building and construction (sector 7) and that some 35 percent worked in the heav-
ier parts of industry (sectors 4 and 5 together). The figures for
French nationals are 6.5 percent and 20.1 percent, respectively.
We also see (Table 2.9) that the vast majority of foreigners are
employed as what the French call *ouvriers* (87.6 percent) and that
no fewer than 62 percent are semiskilled and manual workers.
The figures for French nationals are 67.2 percent and 29.5 percent, respectively. We shall next look more closely at this aspect of
the distribution of migrant workers in three industries: mechanical engineering, building and construction, and artificial textiles.

Mechanical engineering

This sector (*métallurgie*) covers a wide range of industries from
foundries, to the manufacture of consumer durables, to that of

precision instruments. The largest subgroup in Lyon is concerned
with vehicles, especially the production of heavy commercial vehicles and their components. *Métallurgie* has always been a big user
of immigrant labor, employing some ten thousand in 1968, for
example. Between 1970 and 1974 about a quarter of all ONI
entrants went to this sector for their first jobs. The sector does,
however, vary greatly in its reliance on foreign workers. For example, Delle-Alsthom, with a high proportion of skilled employees (see Bonnet 1975:104–5), takes on very few; Paris-Rhône
(starter motors), with large numbers of OS, recruits many. The
pattern of employment in two firms illustrates the variation that
occurs at the firm level.

La Société des Automobiles Berliet (which was described to me
as "*le grand morceau à Lyon*") produces heavy-goods vehicles. Originally a local business, it now forms part of the Renault-Saviem
group (see *Points d'Appui* No. 7, 1976). There are some 21,000
employees, about 15,000 at the main Vénissieux – Saint-Priest
complex. Between 1960 and 1975 the labor force grew by some 45
percent, although the largest increases were among white-collar
workers and technical staff (Employés, Techniciens, Dessinateurs,
Agents de Maîtrise – ETDA). Table 2.10 shows that in 1974
Berliet had 18.5 percent foreign workers among its employees,
but the proportion varies considerably among the four main categories. Thus, North Africans constituted 10.7 percent of the labor
force as a whole, but 25.5 percent of OS, and so forth. Detailed
figures for earlier years are not available, but it is possible (Table

Table 2.10. *The Berliet labor force, 1974, by nationality and category*

Category	French		North African		S. European		Total	% foreigners
	No.	%	No.	%	No.	%		
Cadres[a]	811	4.7	0	0	0	0	815	0.5
ETDA[b]	6,095	35.3	15	0.6	36	3.7	6,151	0.9
OP/JO[c]	4,935	28.5	207	8.3	160	16.2	5,346	7.7
OS/Man.[d]	5,445	31.5	2,270	91.1	790	80.1	8,885	38.7
Total	17,286	100.0	2,492	100.0	986	100.0	21,197	18.5

[a]Managerial.
[b]White collar and technical.
[c]Skilled.
[d]Semi- and unskilled.
Source: Berliet, annual reports.

Table 2.11. *Foreign workers and* ouvriers *at Berliet, 1968–75*

Year	Total *ouvriers*	Total foreigners	% foreigners
1968	11,949	1,850	15.5
1969	12,988	2,415	18.6
1970	13,994	2,555	18.3
1971	13,664	2,320	17.0
1972	12,747	2,198	17.2
1973	13,054	3,365	25.8
1974	14,231	3,911	27.5
1975	14,264	3,614	25.3

Source: Berliet, annual reports.

Table 2.12. *Foreign nationals employed at Berliet, 1968 and 1975*

	1968[a]		1975	
Nationality	No.	%	No.	%
Algerian	930	50.3	1,466	40.6
Moroccan	25	1.4	468	12.9
Tunisian	85	4.6	396	11.0
Italian	265	14.3	302	8.4
Portuguese	65	3.5	283	7.8
Spanish	335	18.1	315	8.7
Turk	n.a.	n.a.	80	2.2
Yugoslav	25	1.4	186	5.1
Others	120	6.5	118	3.3
Total	1,850	100.1	3,614	100.0

[a]1968 figures rounded to nearest 5.
Source: Berliet, annual reports.

2.11) to compare the numbers of *ouvriers* and the *total* number of foreigners employed by the firm over the period 1968–75. Given the small percentage of foreigners in the *cadres* and ETDA categories, Table 2.11 provides a reasonable guide to the increasing share of the *ouvriers* category taken up by foreign workers. Table 2.12, which compares the compositions of the foreign labor force in 1968 and 1975, shows that the additional workers taken on during this period came mainly from the "new" sending societies around the Mediterranean.

No figures are available for the distribution of foreign workers between the firm's *groupes de production,* but it was estimated that in two *groupes* (foundry and forge) they constituted some 80 percent of the *ouvriers* compared with 5–10 percent in the truck assembly and other *groupes* employing highly skilled labor. An internal study of the recruitment of Yugoslavs in 1973 found that 40 percent for whom tests predicted a "slow adaptation" to work were placed in the foundry. A similar type of concentration is found at another firm, the Société Nouvelle des Ateliers de Vénissieux (SNAV), which also now forms part of the Renault-Saviem group. At SNAV there are some 300 foreigners out of 580 *ouvriers,* but in one *groupe de production,* the container workshop, nearly 100 out of 106 employees were foreigners in 1975. At Berliet, SNAV, and other firms where foundries are involved, there has been an almost wholesale replacement of French by foreign workers.

Another important firm in the *métallurgie* sector is Câbles de Lyon, a subsidiary of the Compagnie Générale d'Electricité (CGE), which owns a considerable number of enterprises in the area. In Lyon itself, Câbles has some two thousand employees. Table 2.13 shows that as at Berliet, almost all of the firm's foreign workers are concentrated among the *ouvriers;* but the Câbles figures also show that the proportions differ significantly between male and female staff. A more detailed breakdown of the male *ouvriers* at Câble's Gerland factory (Table 2.14) shows that on the production line (i.e., the figures exclude the service departments) some 66 percent of OS 1, 2, and 3 were foreigners. At this level, North Africans form by far the largest group (more than 50 percent). As at Berliet and SNAV, however, foreign participation in the labor force varies among *groupes de production* or departments. No official figures are available, but one example may be cited,

Table 2.13. *Employment at Câbles de Lyon, 1975*

Category	French	Foreign	Total	% foreign
Cadres[a]	124	–	124	0
ETDA[a]	589	7	596	1.2
Ouvriers				
male	671	433	1104	39.2
female	211	26	237	11.0
Total	1595	466	2061	22.6

[a]See Table 2.10.
Source: Câbles de Lyon.

Table 2.14. *Nationality and level of skill, male* ouvriers, *Câbles de Lyon Gerland factory, 1976*

Category	Total	% French	% North African	% "European"	% others	% foreign
OS1/2	220	30.5	60.0	3.6	5.9	69.5
OS3	296	36.8	43.6	10.1	9.5	63.2
P1	182	70.9	19.8	7.1	2.2	29.1
P2	71	90.1	2.8	5.6	1.4	9.9
P3	55	96.4	3.6	–	–	3.6
All	824	51.3	36.4	6.7	5.6	48.7

Source: Câbles de Lyon.

that of the *caristes,* whose problems are discussed in Chapter 9. Of the twenty-four *caristes* (forklift–truck drivers), all OS2, only one is French.

Building and construction

The census figure (Table 2.8) for the foreigners employed in this sector in the Rhône Department (32.1 percent) may well be a serious underestimate. Table 2.15 contains figures supplied by the employers' federation for this sector that suggest that in 1973 the proportion of foreigners may have been close to half of all employees. Probably the missing element in the census is the adult male North African worker, whose presence in the population at large is severely underestimated. Because this is a highly mobile section of the labor force, underestimation is likely.

Foreign employment varies between the two main sections of the industry: the *grosses oeuvres,* concerned with preparatory and other heavy work, and the *secondes oeuvres,* with finishing or interior work (plastering, electrical fitting, etc.). In firms specializing in *grosses oeuvres,* immigrants may form 80 percent or more of the labor force. Their proportion is much lower among the more specialized and skilled trades. There is also some evidence of an ethno-occupational hierarchy. A Spanish crane driver remarked to me, "The Arabs do the work that is dirtiest; the Portuguese, that which is hardest; the Spanish neither one thing nor the other. The Italians [makes mincing gestures with his hands], the work that is very fine. Sweepers, cleaners are always Arabs." A director of a building firm commented, "The Portuguese are very skilled

Table 2.15. *Employment by nationality in building and construction, 1973* [a]

	French	Foreigners	Total	% foreign
France	1,149,409	491,798	1,641,207	30.0
Rhône-Alpes region	69,690	62,224	151,914	41.0
Rhône department	24,368	21,961	46,329	47.4

[a]Excluding self-employed.
Source: Fédération Nationale du Bâtiment.

and work as bricklayers, *coffreurs,* crane drivers. They want to become skilled because for them qualifications mean a high income, which they need to send home. Algerians have very little education and have a low level – not all. Some do become skilled and are even employed as *chef d'équipes.* [See Figure 2.1.] Almost all the bricklayers' mates are Algerian. Among the bricklayers one finds French, Portuguese, Italians, Moroccans. Tunisians enjoy working with cranes, perhaps because people recruit each other into this kind of work, perhaps it is work that isn't arduous – one sits in the crane – and perhaps because it suits their temperament of superiority. The crane driver is a key man on the site."

About half the employees of this informant's firm were foreigners, rather fewer, it was thought, than in other enterprises because of the firm's status as a cooperative. Although the majority are employed as OS and *manoeuvres,* a fair proportion achieve skilled status: Khalid, a Moroccan carpenter, had the high grade of OHQ (*ouvrier hautement qualifié*). He had been in France since 1968 and claimed to have worked in many places – the north, the Riviera, the Alpine resorts, and elsewhere – after working for eighteen years as a carpenter in Morocco. He once showed me two pay slips each for more than 5,000 francs (for the month), and a contract for a job that would give him 12 francs per hour plus bonuses. He often worked eleven hours a day. "The hours are long; but the work is not hard, and it is in the warm."

This man's job, like many occupations in the building industry, calls for his presence on a site only at certain stages of the construction process. Many workers are recruited by the firms for a particular *chantier* and then move on, to another site, another firm, another region. This mobility is taken into account in the industry's pay structure. Special bonuses are paid at the end of a

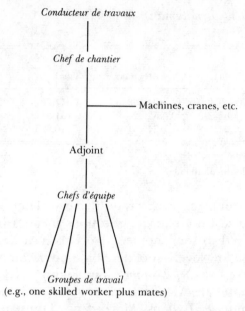

Conducteur de travaux

Chef de chantier

Machines, cranes, etc.

Adjoint

Chefs d'équipe

Groupes de travail
(e.g., one skilled worker plus mates)

Figure 2.1.   Organization of a large chantier *(about eighty workers) (From information supplied by* L'Avenir *[Entreprise Générale de Bâtiment et Travaux Publics]).*

chantier. These take the place of the *primes d'ancienneté,* stability bonuses, in the engineering factories. Mobility in the industry is one of the reasons why firms often supply accommodations for their workers – usually in chalets or "bungalows" on building sites. These bungalows may be carried by railway cars and are sometimes parked in railway yards, which for the duration of a job become small housing complexes.

Artificial textiles

Between 1962 and 1975, employment in the artificial-textile and clothing industries had fallen by about a third, while that in the (related) chemical sector had risen by some 12 percent (*Points d'Appui* No. 9, 1977). For example, at the four main Lyon factories of Rhône-Poulenc Textile, the labor force fell from 7,271 in 1972 to about 5,400 in 1977. One factory at Vaulx-en-Velin, where it was decided to end rayon production, was particularly badly hit. This factory had long relied heavily on foreign labor, including, before World War II, Spanish, Italians, and a large number of

Eastern Europeans. In 1975, when the labor force was cut from 1,400 to 800, about 60 percent of the employees were of more recent immigrant origin, mainly from North Africa and Portugal. Many of these were employed as OS in the rayon department, where on all sides (management and union) the working conditions were considered to be especially hard and difficult owing to the heat, fumes, and dirt. A very small number of these recent immigrants had skilled jobs, mainly in machine maintenance.

This example shows that the replacement of French by foreign workers in unskilled and semiskilled production-line employment, which is of fairly recent origin in mechanical and electrical engineering (see the figures for Berliet cited in Table 2.11), occurred much earlier in other industries. In Rhône-Poulenc's Vaulx-en-Velin factory, North Africans and Portuguese replaced an earlier wave of migrants. In these factories, and on building sites, in those departments where the working conditions are more difficult, immigrants often constitute the majority of workers; indeed, there may be hardly any French employees at all.

Pay

The complex way in which the pay structure in French industries is organized makes comparison (e.g., between what French and immigrant workers actually earn) difficult. It simplifies matters a little that few immigrants are employed other than as *ouvriers,* in that there is no need to discuss the pay of other categories of staff (white collar, technical, and managerial). Among *ouvriers* in general there is an established system of differential pay according to skill, which in any one industry, firm, or department is laid down by what is termed the *grille hiérarchique*. These *grilles* indicate a coefficient for each skill level. Thus, in the building industry in 1976 an OS1 had a coefficient of 130, an OS2 had one of 140, and so on up to OHQ, with 200. An actual basic monthly wage is calculated by multiplying the coefficients by a notional figure called the *valeur du point*. Hourly rates are then determined by dividing the monthly figure by the agreed number of working hours in a month. The *valeur du point,* a sum in francs (e.g., 10 francs in the building industry in 1976), is usually the figure actually discussed in salary negotiations. In the engineering and chemical industries the *valeur du point* was in 1975–6 about 10 percent higher than in the building industry. The basic *valeur du point* in an industry is determined centrally and nationally by a Commission Paritaire to which the trade unions make representations. Local agreements may increase this.

The basic rates are, of course, affected by overtime pay and bonuses for dirty work or, in the building industry, working away from the *chantier*. In that industry anyone prepared to work long hours in difficult conditions (e.g., in water) can, in fact, earn considerably more than the basic wage. Thus, an OS2 by working fifty hours a week could increase his pay by nearly a third. In one union office in the building industry, I heard a discussion about a man who had worked more than 320 hours in the month – roughly 70 hours a week.

Taking basic wages only, the average OS2 in a "good" firm in the building industry earned in early 1976 about 1,500 francs per month. In a "good" firm in mechanical engineering, such a worker might have earned 1,900 francs. A skilled worker (OQ2 or OP2) might have earned 2,000 or 2,300 francs, respectively. In each case actual pay might be enhanced by overtime (if available) and the agreed bonuses. For foreign workers who are legally and properly employed, the principal factor affecting their wage by comparison with that of French workers is the level of skill they have achieved, or the coefficient applied to the jobs they do. For example, the median wage of MTE hostel residents at the end of 1975 was given as 1,666 francs per month (MTE Annual Report 1976, Annex 2, section 27). This is about 10–15 percent lower than the average industrial wage at that time, a discrepancy that may be wholly explained by the workers' level of skill (84 percent *manoeuvres* and OS). For this and other reasons, "qualifications" loom large in the discussion of immigrants' employment problems, as we shall see in Chapter 9.

Finally, it should be noted that immigrants qualify on the same terms as French workers for a wide range of social-security benefits. There are, however, certain exceptions, including the rules applied to unemployment benefits. One of the most important exceptions is that relating to family allowances. Foreign workers in France whose children reside abroad are (unlike workers in Britain) entitled to receive family allowances for those children. In such cases, however, allowances are paid at the rate prevailing in the country of origin. Thus, for example, an Algerian with five children in France received in 1975 five times more in family allowances than one whose children resided in Algeria, although the social-security deduction was the same. A proportion of the money saved by the French exchequeur is paid into a fund (Fonds d'Action Sociale) that then subsidizes many of the French associations concerned with immigrants.

No account of immigrant employment can omit the fact that a considerable but unknown number of migrant workers are employed illegally. All foreigners resident in France must have valid residence permits and, if they are gainfully employed, work permits. In theory the Office National d'Immigration is the principal route to legal employment and residence in France for most national groups. (The legislation is complex and varies somewhat from one group to another.) In fact, the great majority of migrants have historically arrived by other means, often as "tourists," sometimes clandestinely. Juliette Minces (1973:13–25) provides a vivid account by one young Portuguese migrant of the trials and tribulations of the illegal passage, known as *o salto* in Portuguese (which is also the title of a film on this topic).

The French administrative system adopted a realistic attitude to this state of affairs. During the early 1970s it was customary to allow illegal entrants to apply to have their situation "regularized," and many took advantage of this. In 1973, for example, 56.5 percent of ONI entrants were in fact workers whose situations had been regularized after they had entered the country illegally (*Points d'Appui* No. 9, October 1975, *L'immigration etrangère dans la région Rhône-Alpes de 1970 à 1974*, p. 23). Many, however, remained employed illegally or subject to conditions that ignored their rights under French labor legislation, e.g., to the guaranteed minimum wage (Salarie Minimum Interprofessionnelle de Croissance, or SMIC).

IMMIGRATION AND THE "CRISIS"

This research was originally conceived at the height of the economic boom of 1973. It was undertaken in 1975–6 during the period of what the French called the "crisis" following the rise in oil prices. This new situation closed down certain lines of inquiry but opened others, although in fact the implications of the crisis were not apparent when I first visited Lyon in 1974 and did not become manifest until late in 1976.

The impact of the crisis was exceedingly complex and varied, and no attempt can be made here to provide a detailed assess-

Table 2.16. *Unfilled vacancies and demands for employment, 1973–7*

At year ending	Rhône-Alpes region		Rhône Department	
	Vacancies	Demands	Vacancies	Demands
1973	22,398	27,162	7,340	7,246
1974	11,674	47,573	3,334	12,522
1975	8,136	71,841	2,379	19,380
1976	9,213	75,482	2,385	21,599
1977 (Sept.)	11,484	90,803	3,011	25,209

ment. Some indication may be obtained from Table 2.16, which gives information on unfilled vacancies and registered demands for employment (which are not the same as "work seekers") during the period under discussion. In 1973, for example, notified vacancies outstripped the demands for employment. Anecdotal evidence indicates that in that year in the principal factories in Lyon, the "door was open" to anyone who wanted a job, irrespective of the applicant's legal situation. Between 1973 and 1976, however, vacancies fell to a third, whereas demands for employment tripled. In addition, many firms went over to short-time working. In 1973 in the Rhône Department, only 5,000 workers had been on short time; but in 1975 some 150,000 were involved – a substantial proportion of the department's industrial labor force.

Immigrants were directly affected in three ways. First, in July 1974, the French government called a "temporary" halt to immigration. For a time this applied to both workers and their families; but the ban on the entry of the latter, when the worker was already in France, was later lifted. Second, French policy for the recruitment of migrant workers had in the early 1970s been to encourage short-term employment contracts of one or two years' duration. Contracts (and work permits) would be renewed if employment was available. Thus, those most affected by the crisis were recent recruits, mainly young migrant workers, especially Moroccans and Yugoslavs employed in certain firms in the mechanical- and electrical-engineering sectors. In addition, in 1975–6 it became virtually impossible for those who had entered France unofficially to obtain regularization, a common procedure previously.

The third effect of the crisis is more difficult to document precisely. This, a worsening atmosphere of uncertainty and unease surrounding the situation of migrant workers and their relations with the French, was not ameliorated by a remark by the prime minister, Jacques Chirac, in early 1976 to the effect that a country with a million unemployed and 2 million foreign workers did not have a problem of unemployment (see Event 2 in Chapter 3). Later, after I left the field, the government instituted legislation to encourage the return of migrant workers to their homelands, establishing funds for this purpose.

Finally, mention must be made of the special position of Algerians. In the autumn of 1973, officially in response to a wave of attacks on its nationals in France, the Algerian government banned emigration. This ban did not affect those already overseas or those already in possession of an Algerian emigration and work permit from the Office National Algérien de la Main d'Oeuvre (the *carte d'ONAMO*). Neither these restrictions nor those introduced after 1974 by the French entirely prevented the continuing arrival in France of young *tourists* or *students* seeking jobs. At the same time, however, all of these events encouraged many Algerians to think seriously about returning permanently to Algeria.

CONCLUSION

Let me summarize the main points a reader might hold in mind for the moment. In the late 1960s and early 1970s, France as a whole – and the Rhône Department, including the city of Lyon, in particular – experienced a period in which there was substantial immigration. This was, in fact, the second major wave of immigration since World War II. The first had occurred in the late 1940s and early 1950s, with an influx of Italians, Algerians, and, later, Spaniards. This immigration, which in the case of Algerians consisted almost wholly of single men, reached a plateau in the mid-1950s. From then until the mid-1960s the North African population of Lyon increased very slowly; and indeed in 1963–4, after the end of the Algerian War, there was a net return of migrants to North Africa. With that war out of the way, and with the French economy growing at a spectacular rate, mass immigration recommenced drawing on a traditional source of labor power (Algeria) but also began involving "new" countries such as Portugal, Tunisia, Morocco, and Yugoslavia.

It has been suggested that a rough-and-ready contrast might be made between two main clusters of national groups among immigrants: the Southern Europeans and the North Africans. Certainly the contrast between the two in terms of the demographic structure of their populations is a marked one. We shall see later how such differences were perceived by the French, and why they were felt to pose quite different problems for French society.

In other ways, perhaps, the differences between the two groups are less marked. Almost irrespective of national origin, migrant workers have been employed in the same few sectors of the French economy, the old-style industries of the secondary sector, where in some firms they have almost entirely replaced the French. To that extent, one may agree with the view that they form a subproletariat in French society. For various reasons, however, certain nationalities (e.g., Italians and Spaniards) are more easily able to move up the ladder of industrial skills. Hence the majority group at the lowest level (the OS and the manual worker) is often formed by North Africans, who together in some situations with the Portuguese might be said to form a subgroup within a subproletariat.

As I have said, this book is about the French response to this population. Having set out what seem to be some of the key features of contemporary immigration to France, and having described some of the characteristics of the groups concerned, I shall proceed to examine the contrasting ways in which such people are conceptualized by the French, or rather by different elements in French society.

3

Two modes of discourse: *immigrés* and *étrangers*

Deux groupes s'expriment au nom de l'idée radicalement différente qu'ils se font de la patrie. Les slogans criés lors des affrontements de rue, des meetings ou des bagarres universitaires traduisent dans la langage des masses des oppositions longuement mûries ailleurs, les symboles opposent deux systèmes de valeur.   [Rebérioux 1975:22]

In this book, immigration provides an extended case study through which to examine the workings of the institutions and ideologies that characterize contemporary France. This chapter explores certain features of the *ideological* framework. It begins with two meetings. Event 1 took place at an international hotel in Lyon under the auspices of a club that supported the then president, Valéry Giscard d'Estaing, and was addressed by the minister responsible for immigrant affairs. Event 2 was a meeting of trade unionists held at the Bourse du Travail.

There is a threefold purpose in presenting these meetings and others (Events 3, 4, 5, and 9) in some detail: They illustrate one type of data collected during fieldwork; they enable some of those who became "informants" to be seen speaking directly, as it were, and in context; and they provide abundant evidence for the various ideas that informants held, the topics that exercised them, and the institutions in which they operated. These scenes will also, I hope, convey to the reader part of the complex "reality" with which the fieldworker is confronted and which analysis works over in a more discursive way. That reality is almost always multifaceted, and these Events provide material simultaneously for several different aspects of analysis, only some of which can be handled satisfactorily at any one time. The reader will find, therefore, that we return again and again to these Events and others in the course of the book.

For present purposes it is the predominant mood of the two meetings that is of interest, especially their contrasting ideological tenor. The two represent, at first sight, two ways of conceptualizing the population under discussion, two perspectives that in a simple way may be represented as those of right and left in political terms, and that, again in a simple way, permeate attitudes and ideas about immigrants in all aspects of their social situation.

Event 1: The Minister visits Lyon, October 1975

In October 1975 Monsieur Paul Dijoud, Secrétaire d'état chargé des travailleurs immigrés auprès de Monsieur Michel Durafour, ministre du Travail, came to Lyon. The principal object of his visit was to attend an "open day" at the new Centre d'Accueil, d'Information et d'Orientation des Travailleurs Etrangers (CAIO), one of a network of reception centers established by his ministry. In addition to fulfilling his official obligations, he took time off to address a private meeting – invitation only – of the Lyon branch of the Clubs Perspectives et Réalités. This is a national organization that groups the supporters of the president, Valéry Giscard d'Estaing. I received an invitation to attend the meeting through E, a town-planning consultant, who thought it would interest me. Though not himself a member, he knew a number of people in the club.

The meeting was held at the Hotel Tourinter in central Lyon. We assembled first in the bar, where punch was served. The minister was engaged in conversation with a Monsieur Paramelle, who was to share the platform. A burly attendant – a *gorille*, E called him – vetted our invitations at the door. Drinks consumed, we were ushered into the room where the meeting was to be held – a sort of lecture theater – cum-cinema with plush seating. There were several people in the audience whom I recognized. E introduced me to an acquaintance of his who is a prominent member of a Third World group in a suburb of the city.

The local club president opened the meeting by "presenting the table." The minister was introduced as thirty-seven years old and the mayor of Briançon. In the Messmer government he had been a junior minister concerned with environment. (E in a whispered reply to a question of mine assured me that he was certainly a Giscardian; otherwise he would not have been asked to address the club.) Also present on the platform were Madame Simone André, municipal councillor, and Monsieur Paramelle, who is involved with a number of associations in the region, including Logement et Accueil des Travailleurs et Familles de l'Ain (the adjacent department). The president also explained briefly about the clubs, which were founded in 1965. There are two hundred in France and abroad. He listed a number of these, including the branch in Guadeloupe (actually part of France) among those "*à l'étranger*" – as my Third World neighbor pointed out.

The minister now spoke for some forty minutes. It is not irrelevant to note that although now a member of the "majority" and very close to the French president in his general position, he was formerly a socialist. He began with a few words about government policy in general and referred to what had been achieved since the presidential elections of 1974 with the aim of transforming society – a point he stressed on several occasions. He referred to the office he held, which had been created by the president and which he had been asked to take on when his predecessor, the first occupant, had resigned after a few months. Valéry Giscard d'Estaing was the originator of the immigration policy. It was the will of the president, and its elaboration was in response to his desires.

The fundamental problem was this: A prosperous country that provides for its own subjects cannot leave aside 4 million foreigners. There must be "justice, assimilation, integration, living together." Of these 4 million, however, half rarely pose problems. But regarding the other half, if nothing were done, "we might have an *îlot de blocage social,* which might lead to the same situation as with the blacks in the United States." [The identity of this other half was never explicitly stated. But the examples cited and the images employed made it clear that the minister was thinking almost exclusively of North Africans and, in some circumstances, Portuguese.]

He had defined certain lines of pursuit. The policy demanded patience, and would need seven to ten years. The mobilization of personnel and means of finance, the building of administrative structures had all to be provided. The aim must be to transform the psychological condition of the migrant. There was danger if the migrant knew that integration was impossible and the opportunity to go home was also impossible. He referred to the man who came to find work in France. In Tunisia, Morocco, and Algeria one could hear such men exaggerating their gains, their wages, to people at home.

He then outlined a number of ideas. First he wanted to provide freedom of choice to individual foreigners: either naturalization and assimilation or the possibility of return if they wished. And to enable them to prepare to go back if they wished. Second, to develop relations with the sending countries. The problem of immigration was not just a problem of the receiving country. He conceived this as an international problem. Third, the phenomenon must be controlled. There could be no solution if the flow of immigration was anarchic. Now numbers were stabilizing. But it was the policy to allow the entry of families. The administration had taken matters into their own hands to ensure decent housing, to ensure a real "insertion" of the families. Fourth, the policy had to be coordinated with the work of the local authorities and associations. They bore the brunt of the work. In this connection he mentioned the education of children and the training of adults.

The problem of racial prejudice: He looked forward to a situation where people welcomed foreigners as their neighbors and were not concerned about too many foreign children in their schools. To this end he proposed a campaign to *"sensibiliser les Français aux problèmes d'immigration."* Hostels were being built. One must ensure that they were filled and that the dilapidated tenements were cleared out. The *"marchands de sommeil"* [exploiting landlords] must be tackled. Families must be dispersed in "social" accommodation. Small groups of dwellings must be constructed for difficult families. In the schools, *"classes d'initiation"* and *"cours de rattrapage"* [see Chapter 7] must be provided. Foreigners must be assured of the same opportunities as the French in skilled training. Illiteracy must be eliminated. He referred to the national campaign against illiteracy, which was aimed at both French and foreigners. Foreign women should be brought into the framework and provided with the minimum necessary – language and the like – to live in France. One must also attend to the leisure activities of children and their *"promotion culturelle."*

However, links with the country of origin had to be maintained. In this respect, courses in Arabic for young children were important. Religion was a basic factor in these cultures: Islam in the case of the Arabs, Catholicism in the case of the Portuguese. Facilities for the establishment of mosques and churches should be made available.

He remarked that government policy went against popular feeling. "Our fellow countrymen wish to remain unaware of these problems." He cited several examples of popular racist sentiment: "They eat our bread," and so forth. "Our ideas won't gain us many votes. But the ideas at the heart of the president's policy do not rest on electoral popularity. By following this policy we gain new enemies, but the president wants justice and progress in this sector as in others. We are engaged in a fight to transform French society. Let no one be mistaken about this." The policy was a sort of French socialism, social democracy. The policy on immigration had to be set in the perspective of the president's general policy. With a final flourish he sat down.

The president of the club now asked for questions, adding that the minister had to leave shortly.

Q1 says that he has had twenty years of experience working with immigrants, and he wishes to know where the money is coming from and how it will be allocated. (The speaker is from the Groupe d'Information et de Soutien des Travailleurs Immigrés [GISTI].)

Minister: "In the end it does not matter out of what pocket the money comes, what matters is is the amount. It doesn't matter whether the resources are provided nationally or locally."

Q2 identifies himself as the deputy mayor of the Ist Arrondissement of Lyon. He makes a lengthy intervention, which he himself says is not so much a question as a statement. He is concerned, principally, with the law and the legal penalties that should be exacted against the *"marchands de sommeil* who exploit their coreligionists."

Q2's somewhat rambling intervention is brought to a close by the president, who announces that the minister now has to leave, which he does after appropriate thanks. The president now calls up Monsieur Paramelle.

Monsieur Paramelle undertakes to explain the activities of his own association in the Ain. He first draws a distinction between two groups of foreigners: on the one hand, the North Africans; on the other, the Latins. He deals mostly with the former. There are three types of accommodations for foreigners: the hostels for the bachelors, the *cités de transit,* and the Habitation à Loyer Modéré (HLM) for the families. His association is concerned with the management and the *animation* of these types of accommodations. *Animation* includes "*animation culturelle*" For example, in the hostels there are libraries, what he describes as "seminar rooms," first-aid courses, driving schools. Half the residents of the M—— hostel passed their driving test via such a driving school. There are facilities to allow the foreigners to express themselves culturally – be they Pakistanis or whatever their origin. In the hostels there are management committees, residents' committees in both hostels and *cités de transit* whose members were elected. Through these committees a sort of *autogestion* [self-government] is achieved, especially with regard to matters concerned with *animation.* At first it was necessary to designate the representatives, but after a few years (and they have had experience for a few years) elections are now taking place.

He refers to their experience in the small town of B—— with a hostel and *cité de transit.* The occupants were marginals and they tried to integrate them. French *mères de famille* went in their cars to fetch the North African women to take them out to supermarkets, show them how the system worked, and take them home again. Thus one began to bring them out into the society. The children of Portuguese and North African families were helped by students to improve their French. He concludes that the aim was not to adapt the foreign family to the French way of life but to seek some intermediate solution.

The president again throws the meeting open for questions.

Q3 (a young man): "How far can the policy that works at B——, a small town, be adopted in Lyon?"

Simone André (brought in to answer this one) stresses the importance of restoring *animation* in each quartier of Lyon during the period of urban renewal. There are some areas of the town where the foreigners concentrate – at La Guillotière and at La Duchère. At this point she tries to bring into the discussion a venerable old gentleman with a white beard sitting in the body of the hall who, she says, is someone with many years' experience of working with immigrants – the local head of the Armée de Salut (Salvation Army). He half rises to speak but is anticipated by another member of the audience.

Père Arderius (head of the Portuguese Catholic Mission): "Would it not be preferable to have all the questions at once, and then for the platform to answer them all together?" Assent is granted, and he continues, "In the Sixth Arrondissement, where I live, many foreigners are losing their homes in the renovations. The old buildings are being replaced by apartment blocks where they cannot afford to live." He then alludes to the rue Olivier de Serres.

Q2: "The rue Olivier de Serres! When the fire brigade was called to an incident there, the fireman were stripped of their clothes."

Simone André, replying to Père Arderius, says that in the Part-Dieu scheme it was the policy to provide 28 percent of HLM among the new buildings.

Q3: "Is it not the case that sociological research has established that there is a threshold of tolerance of 5 percent?"

Q1, getting to his feet, begins to comment on sociologists but is interrupted by Q2.

Q2: "Have you any children?"

Q1: "Yes."

Q2: "Do they go to schools where 80 percent of the pupils are foreigners? When the level reaches 80 percent, the French leave, taking their children away and putting them in private schools."

Q3: "Unemployment. The policy of admitting families means that one is admitting groups of eight or ten people, at least two of whom would be youths looking for a job."

Q4 (hastily brought in by the president) asks about training for skilled work.

Simone André: "This is very important. In the building-and-construction industry 55 percent of the labor force is foreign. Among the cadres only 3 percent are foreigners. Mostly the foreigners are OS. Unless we take charge of the problem, the ghettos will increase."

Shout of "Too late!" from the back of the hall.

Q5: "I want to ask a question about a group of loyal French citizens who have been neglected by the government – the Harkis."

Q6 (standing next to Q5): "Le gouvernement a baissé leurs culottes devant les Algériens."

It is now evident that a group of some five or six people, placed around the hall, are acting in concert. The club president, recognizing this, invites them to come forward, which two do, including Q3. The president, however, immediately asks Monsieur Paramelle to sum up, which he does briefly, and the meeting is closed. On the way out the group of interrupters distribute a leaflet on behalf of an extreme right-wing organization called "Le Front de la Jeunesse" (the Youth Front).

Event 2: A CGT-Métallurgie meeting at the Bourse du Travail, April 1976

This Confédération Générale du Travail (CGT) discussion on immigrant workers was held at the Bourse du Travail in central Lyon. It had been advertised by poster and by word of mouth in the factories. When I arrived, several men were sitting in a group at the front of the room. They were Turks. One of them, younger than the rest, was standing with them but slightly apart. He later took a place on the platform. I sat down near the Turks. A European came in and asked me if Comrade Michel was coming. I replied that I did not know and in return asked him if I could stay. Was the meeting open? He said it was for workers in *métallurgie*. Just then Michel appeared, and my man, who turned out to be a Portuguese from the Union Départmentale of the CGT, (UDCGT), asked him if I could stay. Michel, whom I had met several times, agreed readily.

The room was decorated with a number of posters and slogans in a variety of languages – Arabic, Turkish, Portuguese, and so forth. Thus: "ALONE we can do nothing; UNITED we can do a great deal. The CGT is there to unite us and to help us in our struggle." "We need a strong, democratic trade union, open to all – it's the CGT!" "No to discrimination. Workers, French and immigrant, all united in the struggle." One poster dealt in graphic detail with discrimination against immigrants and women at one factory, Câbles de Lyon, showing the percentage of each group in each grade of the pay system compared with the percentage of French male workers. Another series of posters referred to CGT action in the hostels. While we were waiting for the meeting to begin, Michel handed out a leaflet. Some music was played and Michel announced, "We have discs in Algerian, Egyptian, and Turkish. If any Tunisian or Moroccan comrades have discs, bring them up."

Eventually some fifty people arrived. Most were North Africans, who appeared to sit in groups from their own firms. The Turks, all from Paris-Rhône, sat together, as did a group of North Africans from Câbles de Lyon. The platform – consisting of Michel, a French worker priest employed at Câbles de Lyon, the Portuguese from the Union Départementale, the young Turk, a young Algerian (Yusef), and Jean (a Frenchman) – assembled, and the meeting began.

Michel: "This is a meeting of workers in the *métallurgie* sector at Lyon to prepare together for the Fourth CGT Congress on the Problems of Immigration, problems that are very numerous. In all the departments, in all the big cities, workers are meeting together to prepare for the big meeting at Paris. In Paris four hundred delegates from all over France will assemble to discuss purchasing power, housing, classification, but above all the problems that particularly affect the immigrants – employment, racism – and to prepare a statement of claims for each nationality. There are bilateral agreements between France and a number of countries – for example, Portugal – which have been modified, thanks in part to the immigrant workers themselves, who together with the French workers have fought to modify the agreements. It is necessary to modify the agreements between the countries. To prepare for the congress, there will take place at Paris, on April fifteenth, a round table on racism – in the factories, in the cafés, in the streets, in housing. Racism must be denounced publicly. We must publicize the sort of racism we encounter every day. A point that affects you all, *all* workers – employment, unemployment. Note the statement the other day by the minister of labor, and another by the prime minister that was very similar, where he said that the way to solve the problem of unemployment was to expel the immigrants [quotes statement]. He even said that the immigrants earn too much! S——, the bosses' boss, in referring to the revaluation of manual work, has suggested a special bonus to encourage immigrant workers to return home. We are here to protest against this, to seek together – it is we, it is you who will have the say – to suggest what can be done to achieve security of employment."

Michel asks Yusef to translate into Arabic. He does this, using a large number of French words, simplifying the speech, employing homely phrases and personal terms. A translation into Turkish follows.

Michel: "Note the key claims, to secure the employment of all – French and immigrant workers. What are the special claims of immigrant workers?"

The discussion is thrown open. Several people speak, and as they make points, these are noted down on a blackboard.

Q1: "The *délégués du personnel* don't have the same power in regard to North Africans – Algerians, Moroccans, Tunisians – as in regard to European workers when they take up cases with management."

Jean: "There are agreements between certain countries – for example, Italy – that give a privileged position to certain workers. We in the CGT want the same thing for all."

Q1 comments on the *délégués du personnel* in the CGT and the Confédération Française Démocratique du Travail (CFDT). He then changes the subject: "About qualifications. There are workers employed in capacities below their qualifications."

Michel: "What about discrimination in salaries, in classification?"

Q1 starts to speak, but Michel shuts him up.

Michel: "What about Paris-Rhône?" He asks the young Turk to ask his compatriots. The Turk comes forward and goes into a huddle with his compatriots.

Turk: "Yes, the problems are the same for all."

Q2: "I know an Italian who speaks very poor French. His supervisor used his ignorance of the language to undergrade him."

Michel: "At Câbles de Lyon . . ." He pauses and calls up a young Moroccan (Q3) from the back of the room, where the group of Câbles de Lyon workers is sitting, and asks him to explain their poster. He does this succinctly and receives a round of applause. A photographer starts taking pictures while he speaks.

Michel: "To try to solve the problems of employment, the CGT – the CFDT as well – demands security of employment for *all*. We demand also the maintenance of purchasing power of salaries. Why? To ensure employment. To allow workers, French and immigrant, to buy more. If one buys more, one produces more and hence creates employment. For immigrant workers this is of interest. For all workers we demand a reduction in hours of work, a lowering in the rate of work, betterment of conditions of work, the institution of breaks during work. We have obtained one such break at Câbles de Lyon."

This remark provokes an intervention by the Câbles de Lyon workers, who say that what has been won is very little and not very important. At this point a diversion is caused by the entry of an old, fragile-looking French lady who sits down in the midst of the Turks. Michel asks her what she wants. It transpires that she is looking for a meeting of old-age pensioners. She leaves.

Michel: "For immigrant workers what is necessary in addition?"

Q3: "There is the problem of residence permits and work permits."

Michel signals to Yusef to answer this.

Yusef: "The CGT demands one year for the worker to remain in France [i.e., after losing his job]." He looks to Michel, as if for confirmation.

Q1: "There are the police controls in the cafés. If an immigrant doesn't find a job, he is expelled."

Michel: "The government's policy is to expel workers. The CGT demands that immigrant workers have the same rights as others. The Geneva Convention says that immigrant workers should be considered as national workers: no expulsions, a permanent residence permit."

Q4: "That's all very well, but guarantee of employment is needed also."

Q5: "There is the legal problem, which has been around for many years. Some people have permits valid for the whole of France, others for some areas only. It is said that they are going to change the Algerian permits so that they are the same as for other workers. Without a guarantee of employment the question of returning home is raised in many people's minds."

Michel: "What is the precise question you would like to raise for the congress?"

Q4: (An intervention I did not catch and that was ignored by the platform.)

Michel: "What other ideas do people have?"

Q5: "I work in a factory, a small *boîte* [colloquial term for place of work] with fifteen employees where there is no union."

Michel: "Does anyone have any experience of trying to start a union in a small enterprise?"

Q5 (a young man): "I asked someone, a CGT official at Saint-Priest [a suburb of Lyon] about this. He told me that immigrants don't have the right to be *délégués du personnel* until they are over twenty-five."

Michel: "There are several people here who can answer that."

Q3: "At Câbles de Lyon we don't have any CGT *délégués* who are immigrants, but four will be presented [at the next election], including myself, and I am under twenty-five."

Michel explains the law relating to trade unions and how it has changed in recent years, adding, "The CGT fought for twenty years for this."

Yusef: "In my factory there is even an eighteen-year-old who is involved."

Q4: "There is a problem of lack of French in *boîtes* where there are *only* immigrants." (Michel had mentioned the language requirement in his summary of the legal situation.)

Q1 intervenes to give a concise account of the procedure to be followed when setting up a trade-union branch.

Michel suggests to Q5 that he stay behind after the meeting. "Let us pass on to another problem. The CGT is for guaranteed employment, guaranteed residence. Let us pass on to the problem of racism, which hits us all."

Yusef: "At the moment there is a great deal of racism. Racism is an ideology the boss has put into the head to create divisions between French and immigrants. We mustn't blame French workers, mustn't say the French are racists. Racism is a means of dividing. Discrimination, that's the same. It creates ill feeling between immigrant and French workers. Nine-tenths of the bosses are unionized. They are well organized and use every means to divide us. Why Algerians especially? Because the Algerians have tried to build an economic order with a bit of justice. The same with the Portuguese comrades. For example, the Algerian oil-price increase is designed to take profits from the capitalists, to attack capitalism. There have been attacks on Algerian property. Dijoud [the minister responsible for immigrants] talked the other day [see Event 1] about the reception of immigrants. But he does nothing for the immigrants in the case of these attacks. Look at the hostels — three people living in one room. However, even among immigrants we find that the same ideology has entered their heads."

Michel calls for facts and mentions the notebooks that have been circulated in the factories in order to record instances of racism. Some of these are produced.

Q6: "At Câbles de Lyon a North African worker who had had to go home asked for special leave. The supervisor refused and said, 'If you're not happy here, get your cards, go back to Algeria.'"

Q3 produces what he calls a "bulletin," which had been compiled at Câbles de Lyon and which documents all such incidents.

Q7: "Each police post is a center of racism. Every policeman . . . I say ninety percent of policemen are racists."

Michel: "We must have facts."

Q7: "There are several forms of racism — between workers and bosses, in the streets, among the police. Racism is an enormous thing. We can eliminate certain types of racism — for example, when the boss sacks someone because of his nationality. This human gangrene that is racism . . . But there is also the problem of the CGT. I was sacked from a *boîte* where the CGT *délégué* was a friend of the personnel officer's. The CGT must impose itself. We must understand the role of the CGT, which is to mobilize the whole mass of workers — immigrant and French."

Q4: "The more unemployment rises, the more the patron tries to divide the workers. Take the saying 'They eat our bread' [a racist slogan]. It is an ideology the boss tries to insert into the heads of the workers. I have even seen racism among the ranks of foreigners because of differences of pay. When someone is given an HLM and told, 'Buy this, buy that' – TV, washing machine, and so on – he is captured, transformed."

Michel asks the young Turk to inquire about the experience of his compatriots. The Turks confer. It is announced that they agree: Racism is everywhere.

Q8: "I want to mention a case of racism in the mountains. The Commission d'Immigrés at Câbles de Lyon organized an outing to the mountains. Just when we were about to go up to the snow, to ski, someone called the police and all the immigrants had their papers checked."

Q9 (a Frenchman): "I know a case of a North African who had his papers checked in a café and was fined forty francs [on the spot] for no apparent reason."

Jean: "That was in the Place————, at Monchat" [in Lyon].

Michel: "At Câbles de Lyon there was a man, a North African, who turned up at work without shaving. Like me, he prefers sometimes to shave in the evening. The guard at the gate asked him, 'Haven't you got a razor? I suppose you shave with a stone over there.' The main said, 'No, I've got a razor, and we are as civilized as you are.' The guard replied, 'It takes twenty years to be as civilized as me.' The government wishes us to believe that immigrant workers are responsible for unemployment. Little by little we all become racists. That is why we must fight."

Jean: "At the day conference the CGT is organizing on racism doctors will be present. Why? Because people say the hospitals are full of immigrants. It is they who eat up the Sécurité Sociale's money. We say that the immigrant workers who have work have the hardest and most dangerous jobs. They are housed three, four, five to a room in bad conditions. For the most part they earn the minimum wage. This morning I was talking to a man who earns seven francs ninety per hour. The doctors will explain all this. There'll be lawyers there. Why? To describe the cases they get when they help people with legal problems. MRAP [Mouvement contre le Racisme et pour la Paix] will be there. All this will reveal the *anti*social policy of the government."

Q3: "The notebooks are not enough. We must mobilize foreign and French workers. At Câbles de Lyon, if a supervisor makes a racist remark, we inform everyone."

Q10 recounts in whispered Arabic a long and involved story of an incident in a post office to Q1 sitting next to him. Q1 offers a brief translation but confesses he does not understand the incident.

Q7: "We must unite the working class – French and immigrant – on the question of racism. One educates it [the working class] – everyone, immigrants, French."

Q8: "I wish to denounce how the management at Câbles de Lyon houses immigrants in huts."

Michel: "Before finishing I wish to remind you of certain dates. First, April fifteenth, the round table at Paris, which will invite all workers to fight. Second, April twenty-ninth to thirtieth, the Congress on the Problems of Immigration. Four or five delegates will represent the *métallos:* the Turk, Yusef, a comrade from Câbles de Lyon, and one from B——. Today the workers from B—— could not be present because they had their own meeting. Third, the May-first demonstration. A big effort will be made at Lyon to ensure that the immigrant workers participate fully in the demonstration that day. Come with your banners. The working class is international. With the banners one can give an international flavor to the demonstration. Finally, I call upon the comrade from the Union Départementale to say a few words."

Comrade from the UDCGT: "The immigrant workers have a difficult situation, but it is not isolated from the context of other workers. The crisis exists in all countries, and more and more the problems of employment, housing are subject to the crisis. We must struggle, all together, we must all respond to the attacks of the bosses. Regarding unemployment, the solution is to provide jobs in France. Increase consumption to increase production. We refer to the experience of 1968, when unemployment decreased after wages were increased. We must fight together – French and immigrant workers. It is mass action, by the totality of workers, that can resolve the problem. Racism is a tactic of the bourgeoisie to divide us, to hit at us. The CGT is not against racism for humanitarian reasons alone but because to fight against racism is to fight against the bosses. The immigrants must join a strong union. Fifteen workers alone can do nothing. But fifteen workers with the support of the CGT . . . Join the CGT; recruit for the CGT as a means of protecting the immigrant workers. May first, French workers, immigrant workers march together!"

This seems to signal the end of the meeting, and a recording of the "Internationale" is played, accompanied by some of us in a desultory fashion. At the last moment, however, Jean is reminded that he should say something about the hostels. He explains the CGT's criticisms of the organization of the hostels, and what had happened regarding the rent strike in Paris. At a meeting with the regional director of SONACOTRA [Société Nationale de Construction de Logements pour les Travailleurs], they had been authorized to go to the hostels to confer with the residents. He lists the demands, which he has some difficulty recalling. "There's the right to receive visits, the right to hold meetings, er, against the increase in rent, er . . . There's a whole load of things. We have distributed a leaflet."

Michel: "Residents' committees must be created."

Jean: "We went to the ALHTRAM [Association Lyonnaise pour l'Hébergement de Travailleurs Migrants] hostel at Gerland with Comrade Ch——. They have problems there with the showers, with the date the rent is due, with the *animation*. One must try to control the running of the hostels. The hostels were built with your money." He explains about the Fonds d'Action Sociale.

Q4: "Why just SONACOTRA? Why not the Maison du Travailleur Etranger?"

Comrade from the UDCGT: "We have had some success in Paris with SONACOTRA. It makes sense to proceed step by step."

This really is the end, and the proceedings are concluded with the playing of a revolutionary Algerian song, although the group from Câbles de Lyon calls for a record made by a popular Egyptian singer.

"IMMIGRANTS" AND "FOREIGNERS"

In Chapter 1 I suggested that no reader of these Events could fail to be struck by the constant references to the "problems" of immigration. The contrast in ideological perspective must be equally apparent. We may begin to understand this contrast, and obtain insight into its complexities, by focusing initially on two key terms, *immigré* and *étranger,* which under certain circumstances appear to signal two orientations toward the population so named.

The original project on which this book is based had the title "Ethnicity, class, and status among foreign immigrant workers in French industry." The SSRC suggested that either "foreign" or "immigrant" was redundant and should be dropped. From sheer perversity I declined, but on reflection it seems that even then I was unconsciously aware that both were important modifiers.

Long after returning from the field, I had great difficulty deciding how to describe in English the people whose situation I studied. It is partly a matter of translation: English has one set of terms; French, another; and the two do not coincide. It would not, however, help to use French, for I would then be faced with an even more difficult decision.

French has a number of general words available to describe the population whose characteristics were outlined in Chapter 2, just as there are a multiplicity of terms for specific groups of nationalities – for example, *Nord-Africains, Maghrébins, Arabes* – not to mention a variety of abusive words and phrases. The two most widely used general terms are *immigré* and *étranger,* as a glance at any bibliography would reveal. I was not consciously aware that there might be an important difference between these two until late in fieldwork. I knew, for example, that in 1970 Granotier had published his *Travailleurs immigrés en France* and in 1973 Minces her *Travailleurs étrangers en France,* but neither offered any explanation of its title. That there were also many organizations concerned with either *immigrés* or *étrangers* at first meant little.

After some five months of fieldwork it appeared that a significant difference might exist between the two terms. At first, when talking about the subjects of study, I had been giving and receiving the word *étranger.* A change in the direction of research produced a change of word to *immigré.* This led me to explore the two words more systematically, sometimes asking direct questions, sometimes leading the conversation around to what seemed an important topic. Two things emerged: Most speakers recognized a difference between the two but articulated it in a variety of ways; and many people, without prompting, applied the adjective "pejorative" to either *immigré* or *étranger.*

At this stage there seemed to be an observable pattern in usage, connected with the political orientation of the speaker. Putting it simply, those on the left talked about *immigrés,* while others talked of *étrangers.* Thus, the words seemed to signal an ideological orientation. This, it must be stressed, was a first approximation; but it helped explain how I became aware of the difference. During the first five months of fieldwork I was talking to former officers and NCOs in the French Army, now employed as directors of hostels, and with employees of a Catholic organization concerned with the rehousing of slum dwellers. The word *étranger* was quite natural in such contexts. Later I worked with informants from the trade unions and from three associations generally thought of as leftist. Here the word *immigré* was equally natural.

What do the two words signify?

This first approximation was inadequate, but for the moment it is not too misleading to say that the words have different ideological connotations. What, then, do they signify? Later I shall be examining the dictionaries, but for now let us see what informants reported. Here is a small sample of statements that provides some sense of what is involved:

Robert, a bricklayer and former union official: "The word *étranger* has a pejorative meaning. It's a bourgeois term. The word *immigré* is more internationalist. The bourgeoisie talk of *étrangers.* But a worker [*ouvrier*], he's a worker like the rest of us but his situation is that of an *immigré*. The phenomenon of immigration, the status of *immigré*, makes it very difficult to organize workers in the building industry."

A social worker: "For me the word *immigré* suggests a worker from the Third World who is, um, a proletarian. The word *étranger* is wider. An EEC [European Economic Community] worker, a teacher perhaps, might be a foreign worker. The Italians who are very well integrated are *étrangers*. I know a man whose father came to this country. He preserved his nationality. He is in management. An *immigré* – that's an Arab who lives in his shack."

Another social worker: "In ordinary speech *immigré* is more pejorative. I am an *ètranger* [a Belgian]. You and I are *étrangers*. We are not victims of racism. An *immigré* is someone who is forced to leave his country, the poor bloke – Arabs and so on."

From a conversation between a doctor and a social worker attached to a factory: At first they said they did not think there was much difference between the two words and in ordinary speech they were interchangeable. Then the doctor said, "All *immigrés* are *étrangers*, but not all *étrangers* are *immigrés*. You [i.e., the anthropologist] are an *étranger*, for example. *Étranger* refers to nationality; *immigré*, to socioprofessional position." The social worker added, "The word *immigré* is a bit more pejorative."

From statements such as these, and from examples of casual usage, we may in the first instance list some of the characteristics that appeared to be associated by various informants with these words. Thus:

Étrangers: Bourgeois term, nationality, past individual arrivals, North Africans, blacks, black French, Algerians, Vietnamese, Poles, Spanish, Harkis, Armenians, Italians (*not* Italian businessmen), Spanish supervisors, EEC workers, teachers, management workers, *co-opérants*, high social level.

Immigrés: Internationalist, socioprofessional positions, workers, proletarians, forced to leave country, retain attachment to country, recent collective arrivals, economic and political causes, Third World, underdeveloped world, victims of racism, here to install themselves, North Africans, covers all nationalities, can be French (e.g., *pied noir*).

These lists might seem to contain a somewhat heterogeneous collection of attributes and connotations. Some are, in fact, idiosyncratic, peculiar to a particular speaker. For that reason and others, it may be mistaken to assume that all the attributes listed under one heading can be subsumed under a single meaning or are unambiguously associated with a single word. What I will argue is that there are several loosely connected themes or points of reference that are much of the time conjured up, as it were, by the two words, and that individual speakers may (or may not) relate more or less consistently to adduce a contrast between two perspectives on the same population. Ultimately, the two words may be seen as connoting two "discursive formations" (Foucault 1972:115). This implies that the similarities and differences within and between the lists cannot be understood at the level of surface content. There is an underlying logic that allows a speaker to label an attribute as one belonging to that discourse within which one speaks of *étrangers* or to that within which one talks of *immigrés.*

Sometimes there may be no logic; but often there is, and it may help here to examine an instance where that logic is explicit, and where there is a reasonably consistent association of label and attribute.

IMMIGRÉS: THE VIEW FROM THE CGT

Let us look closely at the views of a French trade union, the CGT. There are three main groups of trade unions in France: the Force Ouvrière (FO or CGT-FO), a moderate body, particularly strong in the public sector; the Confédération Française Démocratique du Travail (CFDT), which is close politically to certain tendencies within the French Socialist Party; and the Confédération Générale du Travail (CGT), which certainly at the higher levels is closely associated with the French Communist Party (PCF). (See Hanley, Kerr, and Waites 1979:164, 178.)

In contemporary documents (books, leaflets, posters, and the like) and to a large extent in speech, the CGT and its militants employ almost exclusively the word *immigré.* In 1975–6, the CGT's position on immigration was expounded in the report of the IIIe Conference Nationale sur Les Problèmes de l'Immigration, held in 1972 (CGT 1973b). The CGT meeting reported in Event 2 was held to prepare for the Fourth conference, in 1976. In the 104 closely printed pages of the 1972 report there are several hundred instances of the word *immigré*, whereas *étranger* occurs only in quotations from non-CGT sources. A similar distribution is found in Vieuguet's outline of PFC policy toward immigrants (Vieuguet 1975).

This usage and the frequent use of associations of the kind that appear in the *immigré* list cited above must be understood in terms of the CGT's general theoretical orientation. That, in its turn, has to be set in the context of certain currents in French Marxism. These are the traditions the CGT brings to bear that lead it to the word *immigré*, and to a particular view of that word (cf. Freeman 1979:246).

Helpfully, the CGT sets out the principles underlying its position.

> La GCT considère que les travailleurs immigrés, constraints de quitter leur pays d'origine pour lequel ils manifestent naturellement des sentiments profonds, sont placés dans les mêmes rapports de production que les travailleurs français et, à ce titre, ils sont partie intégrante de la classe ouvrieré. . . . Travailleurs français et immigrés sont donc liés par une communauté d'intérêts.
>
> [CGT 1973a:1; see also other documents in a similar vein cited by Freeman, 1979:232.]

Any understanding of the CGT's view must begin with the concept of a "unity of interest" of French and immigrant workers, a point stressed by the written texts and also by many informants. Thus, the 1972 conference report states: "L'exploitation capitaliste n'établit pas de distinction de nationalité, de race ou de religion entre ses victimes. Elle s'exerce et se renforce sur l'ensemble des travailleurs. C'est de cette réalité de classe que découle la communauté d'intérêts des travailleurs français et immigrés" (CGT 1973b:9). As Georges Séguy (the general secretary) put it at the end of his speech to the conference, "Vive les nobles traditions de solidarité ouvrierè internationale du mouvement ouvrier français!"

It is frequently said that the CGT is a "mouvement de masse et de classe." Immigrant workers are *workers* and thus form part of the working class. The CGT's strategy is to incorporate them ideologically and physically within its ranks on a mass-class basis. *Immigrés*, with or without *travailleurs*, comes to have for the CGT, and for others on the left, a class connotation, it is a class term. Thus: "Les travailleurs italiens en France, constraints de s'expatrier et de se détacher de leur classe ouvrière d'origine, deviennent partie intégrante de la classe ouvrière du pays où ils vivent et travaillent, dans le sense qu'ils ont les mêmes intérêts et problèmes en tant que travailleurs" (CGT 1973b:101). All of this is summarized in the slogan "Travailleurs français-immigrés, même patron, même combat."

If, however, the essential unity of workers (French and immigrant) is the cornerstone of CGT doctrine, immigrants are still particular *kinds* of workers, whose distinctiveness derives from the fact of migration itself. At the time of the 1977 legislative elections, an organization that lobbies on behalf of immigrants asked each of the political parties to state its views on immigration. The PCF replied as follows:

> Le PCF considére que les travailleurs immigrés sont à la fois partie intégrante de la classe ouvrière de France par la place et le rôle qu'ils tiennent dans la production et partie de leur peuple d'origine auquel ils restent profondément attachés par les liens nationaux et culturels. Ils sont donc semblables et différents des travailleurs français et leur spécificité doit être sauvegardée.
> [Reproduced in *Regards sur l'immigration*, Accueil et Rencontre, Lyon, cyclostyled, no date]

As we shall see, the last part of that statement signals a slight shift in the position of this section of the left, but for the moment the point is that in this ideological perspective the word *immigré* signals both unity *and* diversity. But the meaning assigned to this diversity often leads back again to unity. For if at one level the fact of being an immigrant differentiates one worker from another, at another it unites them, and not simply by placing them in the same class.

This point requires some explanation. Consider, again, the general theoretical line regarding immigration. I once asked a CFDT militant what he thought about the then recent halt to immigration enforced by the government. "That raises a lot of questions. In order to understand that, you have to understand the whole system," that is, the place of immigration within the capitalist system as a whole. The CGT's view was summarized by Marius Apostolo, a member of the national executive, as follows: "Nous assistons, à une gigantesque accumulation du capital, à une concentration renforcée, au développement des sociétés multinationales. La main-d'oeuvre immigrée est une des catégories utilisée par les grandes sociétés comme un élément important de ce processus" (CGT 1973b:16). Immigration is seen as a product of the processes at work in contemporary capitalism. This further emphasizes the unity of French and immigrant workers. Both are constrained by this system, although they may be obliged to respond in different ways. The differences between them are explicable by reference to the *same* system. The CGT places difference at one level in the context of similarity at another.

A further point is that the CGT's model of immigration resembles "dependency theory," which sees highly developed "core" industrial areas positively *under*developing weak "peripheral" ones (cf. Grillo 1981a:14). Not surprisingly, therefore, *immigré* is often taken to imply "from the Third World," most commonly North Africa. In other ways, too, this framework enables the CGT to find explanations for the generally low status of immigrants in France. Figure 3.1 summarizes some of these themes.

The analysis shows that the attributes listed under *immigrés* may be linked by reference to a coherent ideological discourse. The word is polyvalent, but there is a central referent. The concept of *un immigré* also indicates certain problems of a fundamental nature for the CGT (class unity) and points to their resolution. To say *immigré* is to say this, in a way that "immigrant" in English does not. My own difficulty in discussing my research in French may now be appreciated. To say that this book is about *les problèmes des immigrés might* reveal an ideological view.

Let the *might*, the potential, be stressed, however, because

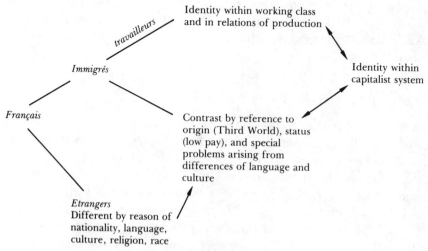

Figure 3.1. Français, immigrés, *and* étrangers.

whereas the word *immigré can* be given an ideological significance, it need not be. It is, after all, a perfectly ordinary French word. All the dictionaries deal briefly with it (in contrast with their detailed accounts of the word *étranger,* discussed later). First cited for 1769, and thus a relatively new word, it means someone who has moved from one country to settle in another. There is no guarantee that someone who utters it is aware of the ideological meaning it may have for others. There is no guarantee that when speakers use it in a stressed sense we are given access to their beliefs or provided with an index of their understanding of the issues involved. One does not have to be a card-carrying theoretician of the French Communist Party to use the word, although such a person is likely to use it in the way described.

The point is that the CGT's definition of *immigré* has not so totally captured the word that to say *immigré* is to imply that definition (cf. the English words "black" and "gay"). What the CGT is saying is: Here are these people. Their situation, their problems, and the solution to those problems must be located within our theoretical framework. We call them *immigrés.* Not everyone would be aware of this argument, and certainly no one is obliged to follow its logic. Nevertheless, within the left, and to a considerable extent outside it, the use of *immigré* is taken to imply a general reference to that ideological position, or at least aspects of it. A CFDT document, for example, comments, "Le simple fait de parler toujours globalement des 'immigrés' n'est pas encore les définir seulement par rapport au système social dominant?" (CFDT 1975:8; cf. Véronique and Tribollet 1981:36). Certainly many left associations concerned with immigration use the word *immigré* in their titles.

ETRANGERS

It was noted earlier that in texts the CGT avoids the word *étranger* except in direct quotations from other sources, as for example in a citation from the journal *L'Usine Nouvelle,* described as "organe du patronat de la métallurgie" (CGT 1973b:19). As my informant, Robert, said, *étranger* is a bourgeois term. Thus, of two words that refer to the same population, one (*immigrés*) signals a range of attributes that make it an appropriate word to be used by the left, while the other (*étrangers*) connotes a different set of attributes, which the left avoids. In certain respects, as we shall see, this is a misleading oversimplification. But first let us consider what the word *étranger* implies.

On the face of it, *étranger* should require less explication than *immigré*, since it is the ordinary word for "foreigner" and is frequently used where we would employ our word (e.g., in the title of the ministry concerned with foreign affairs). However, it obviously shares the same origins as the English "strange" and "stranger" and can also carry those meanings. And note that the title of Camus's novel *L'Etranger* is sometimes, correctly, rendered in English as *The Outsider*.

Whereas *immigré* (like the English "immigrant") is of relatively recent origin, *étranger* or its equivalent goes far back in the language. In medieval French, a primary meaning appears to have been "someone from outside a defined locality." Thus, a twelfth-century document says, "If any [foreigner] assaults a member of the commune his neighbour must come to his aid" (cited in Godefroy 1884:638). The etymologist also links the medieval French form *estraigne* with the verb *estraignier* or *estrangier* – to put out, distance, expel, and also alienate or sell off; compare the English "estranged" (Godefroy 1884; Huguet 1946; and principal dictionaries).

Nowadays, dictionaries cite the first meaning of *étranger* as "Qui est d'une autre nation" (Robert 1960:1766). Most modern usage reflects that definition; that is, it has something to do with nationality. Historically that meaning is secondary to the meaning conveyed by *estraigne* in early French, before the development of the nation-state. The word has always had something to do with defining "us" and "them," "insiders" and "outsiders," but at some stage the concept of the nation became the primary marker of "our" identity, and thus *étranger* became someone not of "our nation." This is certainly how the word is used in official publications and in law. For example, the census divides the population into three categories: *français par naissance, français par acquisition,* and *étrangers.* Avoidance of *étranger* must reflect an avoidance of the national characteristics of the population in question. As the CGT says, "L'exploitation capitaliste n'établit pas de distinction de nationalité" (1973b:9).

Nationality is not the only element, however. In a little book entitled *Les travailleurs immigrés dans la lutte de classe,* the author, Françoise Pinot, provides one of the few instances where some of these issues are discussed explicitly. (Cf. also Catani 1973:285–6.)

She begins with an examination of three perspectives on immigration: "La visée 'Tiers-mondiste'"; "le langage de la 'marginalité'"; and (pp. 14–17) "La pensée en termes de 'nationalité.'" She comments, "Pour un certain nombre de personnes et de groupes, parler de travailleurs migrants, ce n'est pas parler de Bretons venus travailler à Paris. . . . Les migrants seraient-ils d'abord définis comme 'nonfrançais'? La qualité 'd'étranger' peut se définir sur un double plan, juridique et culturel" (Pinot 1973:14). She points out that a strictly legal definition of migrants-as-foreigners would exclude those from the Overseas Territories – for example, the French West Indies – who are French nationals but whose general circumstances are similar to those of migrant workers from other parts of the world.

Pinot continues, "Si . . . on aborde le problème sous l'angle des différentes cultures, on se prête à deux préjugés successifs: faire du Français moyen . . . la 'norme' à partir de laquelle on raisonnera en termes d'adaptation ou d'assimilation, et diviser les courants migratoires selon une échelle qualitative de plus ou moins grande proximité avec le norme" (p. 15). She adds:

> Dès qu'on ne parle plus de "travailleurs," mais de "Français" et d'"étrangers," on se dispose à tomber dans le piège des raisonnements qui tentent de calculer ce "qu'ils nous coûtent," ou ce "qu'ils nous rapportent," comme s'il était possible de définir sans ambiguïté des "intérêts nationaux" homogènes ("ils" et "nous"), intégrant les intérêts de toutes classes sociales. Ces oppositions et divisions sont un des instruments utilisés depuis longtemps pour affaiblir la combativité de la classe ouvrière.   [pp. 15–16]

Pinot was trained as a sociologist but in 1975 was employed as a social worker in Lyon, where I met her. We did not, however, discuss the issues raised by this extract from her book, which I have cited at some length because it raises a number of issues to which we will have to return in this and later chapters. For the moment, all I wish to stress is that the concept of *étranger* refers to both nationality and culture. But it contains other referents, too. Consider the following remarks made by a housing official:

"I divide immigrants into two groups: those from the hot regions – Southern Europe, North Africa – and those from Northern Europe, the cold regions. Hungarians assimilate very quickly because their way of life is not very different from ours. People from the hot regions like to live out of doors. They have a family tradition that is very closed. They have a lot of children and make a lot of noise. If it were a question of you or me, there would be no problem; but the difficulties occur with the children. The Arabs, for example: Their children do what they want, run around damaging property, breaking mailboxes. With adults, well, sometimes they kill a sheep in the bath; but generally so long as people are clean, and the children. People suffer from the filth. The blacks are just the same, though they are few at the moment."

I asked if by "black" he meant African. He did. And what about the Antillais? "They pose fewer problems, unless there are too many. They speak French and are much more integrated." (The speaker was himself of Greek descent.)

The sentiments expressed by this informant provide an excellent illustration of the various elements (nationality, culture, language, race, and, obliquely, religion) employed in drawing a distinction between "us" and "them" by reference to *étrangeté*. They are also typical of the way many people in France talk about the population in question. There are, however, variants of this mode of discourse, in which difference is discussed in less emotive terms. There is, for example, as we shall see, considerable reference to differences of "culture," a word that has several meanings in French, one of which roughly coincides with anthropological usage. Statements such as "These Algerian girls are really between two cultures" are very common (cf. Watson 1978).

Étrangeté, then, is associated variously with differences of nationality, culture, language, religion, and race. In a loose sense it represents an "ethnic" ideological perspective, in the way that *immigré* represents, loosely speaking, a "class" perspective. I have also suggested that the former tends to accompany a right-wing political orientation, the latter a left-wing one. Both terms are concerned with hierarchical divisions in society (although the language of *étrangeté* can and sometimes does refer to vertical divisions: differences between groups otherwise considered of equal status). From the viewpoint of certain informants, the language of *étrangers* masks the division implied by the language of *immigrés* and vice versa. Each, from the perspective of the other, might be interpreted – indeed, is interpreted – as a kind of false consciousness. An example of that interpretation occurs in the discussion of racism at the CGT meeting (Event 2 in this chapter) when

Yusef, a young Algerian, says, "Racism is an ideology the boss has put into the head to create divisions between French and immigrants."

Although in CGT documents we find a conscious, highly elaborate application of a class perspective to the population in question – a systematized and systematic ideology that is avowedly of the left – it is much harder to locate in *contemporary* political discourse a similarly elaborate theoretical systematization of those elements that constitute an "ethnic" ideology, that is, one that links nation, language, culture, race, and religion in a coherent world view, although certain groups on the extreme right and perhaps in the so-called new right (see Hainsworth 1982:155) come close to providing one. Such a perspective is, however, implicit in much of French thought and is, indeed, central to it.

Briefly, early in the nineteenth century an emphasis on nation and nationality formed part of the radical tradition stemming from the French Revolution. It was only later in the century that nationalism came to be redefined as a phenomenon of the right, and it is to the later period that we owe the theorizing on the relationship between language, culture, race, nation, and religion as it appears within what is now the dominant tradition (Biddiss 1970; Brunschwig 1966; Rebérioux 1975; Shapiro 1962; Weber 1965, 1968).

To assert this, of course, is to compress and distort complex issues. The last point, in particular, skirts around controversies in the historical discussion of eighteenth- and nineteenth-century French thought. Much of this, however, centers on the specific question of the intellectual foundations of scientific racism. Cohen, for example, argues that the "systematic underpinning of racism was fully developed in eighteenth-century France" (1980: 97, cf. p. 262; also Hoffmann 1973:126, "Gobineau n'a rien inventé"). Poliakov, although allowing that ideas about racial difference had their roots in the eighteenth century, states that their *systematization* was a nineteenth-century phenomenon (1977).

But race is only one of the elements that may define *étrangeté* (and racism, only one way of evaluating difference). The knitting of race, nationality, language, culture, and religion into a systematic social and political theory of human difference was a distinctly nineteenth-century phenomenon (cf. Petitfils 1973:66). It may be linked with the ideas of men such as Renan (cf. Marrus 1971:10–12), and Barrès, of whom Sternhell (1977:118) writes, "Le nationalisme barrésien constitue une vision complète de l'homme et de la collectivité." (But see Anderson 1974:341.)

Such doctrines now form part of the unstated background to discourse, and I would agree with Cohen that in racial conflict in contemporary France "the role of earlier ideas was mainly that they were available to rationalize frictions that had developed" (Cohen 1980:289; cf. Anderson 1974:298).

Etrangeté *in left-wing discourse*

This account, it must be admitted, oversimplifies matters in a number of ways. The implication that "class" and "ethnicity" represent mutually exclusive, even antithetical, discourses may be true for the CGT-PCF spectrum of the left, but in practice avoidance of the word *étranger* and what it implies is not always as strong as has been suggested, certainly outside the CGT-PCF spectrum.

In the first place, to say that a language of ethnicity and a language of class constitute two distinct modes of discourse over-systematizes a contrast between what are in fact loosely knit collections of themes. What I have done is locate in the statements of informants and in written texts a number of elements (a, b, c, d, etc.) and suggested that elements a + b = a "class" ideology of the left, signaled by *immigré*, and elements c + d = an "ethnic" ideology of the right, signaled by *étranger*. Now, although we may construct two distinct discourses by reference to the elements that cohere to each, in actual statements the distinction may not be as clear-cut. Some elements are detachable, as it were, and usable in another discourse. And some speakers are veritable *bricoleurs* making do in ideological terms with whatever elements in the general repertoire come to hand. The result sometimes is an idiosyncratic ideological syncretism. For example, a metalworker from the Cameroon referred to *"immigrés étrangers"* – the only time I head such a phrase. He was referring to the Antillais, who, he said, "are not really *immigrés*."

Some of the variation that one finds, especially in speech, can be explained in a straightforward way. Take, for example, the following passage: "As a trainee social worker I did a project on the housing policies of the patrons. I was told by one firm that they cannot give the one percent to the HLM to house *étrangers*, because the HLM say they will accept it only if they do *not* [her emphasis] send *étrangers*. B puts its money either into hostels or into loans for people to buy their own houses – which hardly affects *immigrés*." Here the shift from *étrangers* to *immigrés* can be explained by the fact that the former appears in a kind of indirect speech: "One firm said . . .," "The HLM said . . .," and as like as not they did say *étrangers*.

In an important CFDT policy document issued in 1975, which is interesting in part precisely because of the relatively frequent use made of *étrangers*, we find the following sentence: "La mobilité plus grande des travailleurs étrangers par rapport à celle des travailleurs nationaux confirme la réalité de cette fonction de régulateur économique que le capitalisme assigne aux immigrés" (CFDT 1975:3). The word "national" attracts *étrangers;* "capitalism," *immigrés*. To an extent this confirms what has been argued but suggests also that usage may sometimes be contextual and situational. The two words may not always represent two distinct and exclusive ways of talking about the population as a whole but may refer to different aspects of its situation.

In a slightly different though related context, Soumille (1977: 252) notes a "hesitation" in the use of the words *Arabe* and *musulman* in late-nineteenth-century writing in Algeria. This, he says, reflects uncertainty as to whether the population in question should be categorized by race or religion. The frequent use of *étranger* in CFDT texts may reflect similar uncertainty, although it also suggests a greater sensitivity on the part of the CFDT, compared with the CGT, to those aspects that *étranger* connotes. Analysis of CFDT policy suggests that this is so.

A key statement says, "La classe ouvrière en France est aujourd'hui composée de multiples nationalités" (CFDT 1975:8). In an important passage it is argued:

> Le travailleur immigré se voit brutalement imposée une sèrie de comportements qui se présentent comme indispensable à sa survie dans notre système social. Mais ce conformisme imposé, exoge bien au delà d'une adaptation minima et traduit un refus d'accepter les différences ainsi que la dévalorisation systématique des autre cultures présentées comme "attardées." Leurs langues, civilisations, coutumes, traditions et modes de vie sont volontairement ignorés ou traités comme folklorique. Le simple fait de parler toujours globalement des "immigrés" n'est-ce pas encore les définir seulement par rapport au système social dominant? N'est-ce pas considérer comme qualtité négligeable ce qui dans la culture et la civilisation d'un travailleur marocain, le différencie d'un portugais comme d'un français?   [CFDT 1975:8]

Later the document argues:

> Pour que les immigrés trouvent toute leur place dans l'organisation syndicale, un problème-clé est celui du respect de leur identité. Il s'agit d'abord de connaître le contenu de l'étrangeté de ces travailleurs. . . . Tenir compte des différences, ce n'est pas une tactique, une méthode d'approche, c'est beaucoup plus, une des conditions même de la démocratique syndicale. [CFDT 1975:29]

These remarks are only comprehensible in the context of the debate between the CFDT and the CGT, and ultimately between the PCF and certain elements of the Parti Socialiste – the last sentence, for example, would require understanding of the concept of *autogestion*. Such debates ultimately reflect the different intellectual traditions to which the left in France is heir. Guiral (1977:37–8), for example, draws attention to divergences within the left between the Jacobin tradition, in which "la différence raciale ou mieux culturelle est appelée donc à disparaître," and what he calls the "liberal tradition," which "admet les divergences, accepte les faits minoritaires."

Briefly, at the level of ideology and practice, the CGT stresses the unity of immigrant workers *with* the working class of France, whereas the CFDT emphasizes the specificity of immigrants *within* the working class. CGT leaflets, for example, often contain sentences such as "The general situation of French workers and immigrants is more or less the same"; "Our interests are linked"; "We have common claims." The CGT often subsumes demands that concern immigrants within the context of the common claims: *les revendications.*

Two comments will illustrate the difference with the CFDT:

"Relations between the CGT and CFDT are not good," said a CFDT militant. "The CGT see the working class as one and try to get workers to express this by joining them and the PCF.

"The CFDT sees that there is an immigrant labor force with particular problems. The CGT analysis breaks down when confronted with situations in which there are conflicts between ordinary workers and the *chefs,* who are often Italian and in the CGT."

A CGT official said, "We – the CFDT and CGT – organize a common campaign insofar as the CFDT bases itself on a class position. The CFDT position is blurred, however, because in that organization there are some people – children, leftists – who believe that immigrants are a revolutionary class, like delinquents. The CFDT has a lot of special categories – the young, women, and so on. Of course, such groups have special problems; but they all form part of the working class."

These different ideological perspectives are reflected in – and perhaps arise from – the handling of day-to-day affairs at the workplace. Thus, as we shall see in Chapters 9 and 10, the CFDT is often found, if not stimulating then at least fostering independent industrial militancy on the part of the special groups such as immigrants, while the CGT often appears to "demobilize" such activity. To understand how and why this occurs, it would be necessary to examine the history of the two labor movements and their differential involvement in the industrial scene, a topic well beyond the scope of the present chapter.

There is, then, a difference in orientation toward immigrants within the left, which a comparison of the CGT and the CFDT illustrates. The contrast between the two is, however, perhaps less clear-cut than I have implied. Although the CGT stresses the formal unity of French and immigrant workers and attempts to subsume the two within a single entity – the working class – it does make special provision for immigrants in its organizational framework. First, there is a hierarchy of *commissions* (roughly "working parties") concerned with immigrant workers. These exist in factories, within particular industrial unions at the departmental level (e.g., metalworkers), within departments linking industrial unions, and nationally. Each has an official designated *responsable* for immigrants. At one time the CFDT had a similar structure, which was abolished because it was thought to place too much stress on differences within the working class. One has the paradox, therefore, that the CFDT, which emphasizes difference, abolished a form of organization, whereas the CGT, which plays down difference, promotes it. The CGT also organizes ad hoc meetings of workers from different language groups for *débats casse-croûte* (lunch-time discussions).

The CGT began in the mid-1970s to give some weight to the particular demands of immigrant workers and the needs of particular groups of immigrants. Formal links were also established with workers' organizations and parties in the countries from which immigrants came. The CGT line became, I was told, the following: "We are based on a class position. All are in the exploited class. But we think that the Algerians have more worries. There is a single working class, but immigrants have special problems." There was a recognition that the law distinguishd between

French and immigrants (e.g., in respect to rights to participate in trade-union affairs, rights to certain welfare benefits, and so forth) and, in complex ways, between immigrants from different countries. Thus the legal system generates particularistic claims. The CGT thinking in the mid-1970s went beyond that in two ways, however. First, it argued that while the capitalist system exploits everyone, some are more invidiously treated than others (e.g., with regard to pay, conditions of work, housing, and so forth). Second, it began to recognize a range of cultural claims, or rather claims to cultural specificity, as did the PCF (see statement cited in Chapter 8). This recognition was accorded especially to claims in the field of language (see Chapter 8), that is, the immigrants' mother tongue. The *débats casse-croûte* conducted by the language groups provided an outlet for this (cf. similar organizations in the PCF, Vieuguet 1975:185).

In the early and mid-1970s there was, then, a shift in the direction and scale of CGT action regarding immigrants, partly perhaps as a result of the relative success enjoyed by the CFDT in recruiting immigrants (the two unions are, after all, in competition), partly as a result of pressure from the CGT and PCF's international allies. But these shifts in orientation on the part of the CGT-PCF spectrum of the left, which were apparent at the time of my fieldwork, can be set in the context of the longer-term relationship between the trade unions and the political parties and immigrants in France. It is apparent, for example, that in the 1920s and 1930s the CGT (or, rather, its predecessor) was much more prone to use the language and connotations of *étrangeté* (see Gani 1972:9–26), as happened even more markedly after my fieldwork, when there was an apparent dramatic shift in PCF views on immigration during the run-up to the 1981 presidential election. It may also be noted that in the nineteenth century there was a strong strain of racism, or at any rate anti-Semitism, to be found among certain elements of the French left (Byrnes 1950: 114, 156; Guiral 1977:39; Marrus 1971:132). The adverse meaning of *étrangeté* is not always, or only, the property of the right.

MODES OF DISCOURSE AND THE REPRESENTATION OF PROBLEMS

Let me summarize what emerges from this chapter and state its implications for the rest of this book. In the first instance, what we

appear to have located are two ways of talking about similarity
and difference. (See Figure 3.1.) The language of *étranger* points
in the direction of cleavages (which may be either vertically or
hierarchically ordered) based on nationality, culture, language,
and race between both French and foreign peoples and between
foreigners themselves. The language of *immigré*, which is highly
theorized by certain groups in contemporary society, recognizes a
difference based on geographic origin but contains it within a
framework that suggests another kind of similarity between immigrants of all kinds and those of equivalent status in French society:
les travailleurs. In certain respects the two words signal distinct
ideological perspectives, but they may also be used situationally to
refer to different aspects of a population.

A slightly different way of regarding the material is to see
étrangers and *immigrés* as representing major ideological themes,
ethnicity and class, each comprising a set of elements. Specific
ideological statements on the part of individuals or collectivities
then constitute variations on these themes. If the data are sim-
plified sufficiently, we might expect to find three main variants,
depending on the "weight" given to the principal variables of
"ethnicity" and "class" (Figure 3.2).

Take, for example, the slogan "[Travailleurs] français-immigrés même patron, même combat." On the surface the juxtaposition of *français-immigrés* may seem odd. Pinot alludes to this when,
referring to the "ambiguity" of the "couple," she asks, "Les immigrés sont-ils des travailleurs à part entière, ou des travailleurs
entièrement à part?" (1973:16). Why, if there is a single working
class, is it necessary to make any distinction that in part at least,
refers to national origins? There is, in fact, a perspective in which
such distinctions are ignored completely, in which "workers" are
just that. In a series of leaflets a *groupuscule* called "L'Humanité
Rouge" issued during a strike in 1975 at the Lyon factory of the
firm Paris-Rhône, where a large number of Moroccans, among
others, were employed, there is only one reference to *immigrés,* in
a sentence where it is clearly attributed to an adversary speaker.

	V_1	V_2	V_3
"Ethnicity"	$0 \longleftrightarrow 1 \longleftrightarrow 1$		
"Class"	$1 \longleftrightarrow 1 \longleftrightarrow 0$		

Figure 3.2. Ideological variants.

"[Travailleurs] français-immigrés, même patron, même combat"

[class] + nation + class = class against class

+

nation

Figure 3.3. Decoding a slogan.

Neither the CGT nor the CFDT goes that far, and both attempt a resolution of the two themes, as does the slogan itself. There the juxtaposition *français-immigrés* heightens the ambiguity of *immigrés* as a class term that also has the sense of "from another country." The subsequent phrase resolves this by placing both in the same context (*patron, combat*). (See Figure 3.3 and Seidel 1975. For other ways of decoding slogans, see Calvet 1976.)

The resolutions favored by the CFDT and CGT are slightly different. Neither refers to race, and nationality is interpreted in mainly legal terms, although it is used to signal a wider range of attributes. Of these the CGT singles out language, while the CFDT stresses culture. The CFDT aim is, as it says, "connaître le contenu de l'étrangeté de ces travailleurs" (1975:29) – that is, rather than treat cultural difference as part of the boundary between "us" and "them," to redefine it as an attribute of "us."

The problem the two unions face in reconciling class and ethnicity may be put in a wider perspective. First, at some point in the past "our" identity began to be defined by reference to the nation-state, and variously to conceptions of cultural, linguistic, and biological distinctiveness. This formed part of the dominant tradition in Europe. In France during the nineteenth century there emerged a stable definition of "us" as French, although, as Eugen Weber (1976) points out, the incorporation of Frenchmen within that definition was not accomplished until World War I and perhaps was never fully accomplished.

Second, there have always been alternative ways of viewing human collective identity in Europe, one of which, it might be argued, was traditionally provided by the Catholic Church. During the nineteenth century, socialism provided a major alternative perspective with its emphasis on class ties' cutting across those of nation. This perspective, with varying success, was an attempt to counter the then dominant view. The Socialist International foundered on this very question in 1914.

It is important to see that, for example, the debate between the

CGT and the CFDT, and the ideological variants they and others propound, address questions that are not only of contemporary concern but are matters that have been faced in Europe for at least the last hundred years.

The contrasting efforts by the CFDT and CGT to come to terms with ethnic and cultural differences between immigrants and the French may also be placed in a wider contemporary context if we recall the growing support in the 1960s and 1970s for *regionalism* in France. (See, for example, Lovecy 1982, among many others.) Certainly, at the point on the spectrum represented by the CFDT, there was a systematic attempt to recapture *étrangeté* for the left, in respect to both immigrants and regional minorities.

If, at the levels of both theory and practice, we must distinguish two principal strands of the left, represented here by the CGT and CFDT, it must also be acknowledged that the right, too, is not undifferentiated. This has implications both for the way in which *étrangeté* is incorporated in discourse and for what we may identify as the "dominant ideology," or prevailing orthodoxy, during the period under study.

René Rémond, the great authority on this subject, in fact distinguishes three traditions in French right-wing thought (1963:22, 291): the Bonapartist (authoritarian, statist, nationalist), the Orleanist (élitist, liberal), and the Ultra. Gaullism was the heir to the Bonapartist tradition; the followers of Giscard d'Estaing (president 1974–81), to Orleanism (Rémond 1971:394; cf. Hanley, Kerr, and Waites 1979:137, 145). Monsieur Dijoud, the minister who appears in Event 1, and the members of the Clubs Perspectives et Réalités are in that vein, while groups such as Le Front de la Jeunesse, whose adherents also appear in Event 1, represent the third, Ultra, tradition.

Gaullism was undoubtedly the dominant ideology of France in the period 1958–74, and many of the policies enacted to deal with immigrants were influenced by that ideology (cf. Freeman 1979:115). The advent of Giscard d'Estaing to the presidency brought a change at least of style and emphasis, as the appointment of Dijoud and the policies he advocated perhaps indicate. The change in style was epitomized by a catchword of 1975, the very Giscardian *décrispation*, a neologism, I believe, meaning literally "unclenching," as of a fist, and reminiscent of the advertisers' word *décontracté* (relaxed, casual). It was Giscard's Orleanism, with its particular emphasis on technocratic solutions (cf. Freeman

1979:122), that can be described as the prevailing orthodoxy of the period during which I undertook fieldwork. The discussion in Chapter 4 of the policies of *animation* and *participation* in the hostels, and the response to them by hostel directors, will illustrate some of the differences between these two traditions.

The purpose of this chapter has been to indicate the range of ideological perspectives brought to bear on the social definition of immigrants and foreigners and the identification of their problems. We began with two perspectives, loosely of right and left, between which a major difference is the weight given to class and ethnicity as principles of ideological organization. Clearly, however, these are not the only principles shaping form and content, and in some respects it makes more sense to speak of *five* major ideological variants, each of which is voiced in some degree by speakers in Events 1 and 2. These variants represent five overlapping fields of discourse (see Seidel 1975) that cut across one another in complex ways: The liberalism of the extreme left and of the Orleanists, for example, can be contrasted with the Jacobinism of the Gaullists and the PCF.

The next step is to look more systematically at the application of at least some of these variants, paying greater attention to the context of variation. We will do so by examining a succession of institutional settings: housing, the social services, schoolwork, and so on. This has the advantage of enabling us to analyze these ideologies not as free-floating or decontextualized sets of ideas but as embodied in everyday practice.

4

Urban development and the problems of housing: the "bachelors"

Let us begin with housing, and in particular the problems of housing migrants the French describe as "bachelors," or at any rate as "living as bachelors." This means beginning with the city.

THE GROWTH AND DEVELOPMENT OF LYON

For most people, French and others, Lyon is a city they know only as a place seen in transit – to the Midi, Italy, Switzerland, or Spain. Historically it owes its importance to that fact. Its site, which has been continuously occupied since before the Roman era, made it a naturally defensible crossing point in the great river system floating north-south through this part of France. The area around the "Place du Pont" (the Place Gabriel Péri), now iron-ically one of the main Arab quarters and thus sometimes known as the "Place des Cons," was the location of one of the earliest bridges across the Rhône, built to take Richard the Lionheart to the Crusades. Lyonnais themselves sometimes suggest that this quality of the city accounts for the frequently observed *froideur* of the native inhabitants. (For the history of Lyon, see Bonnet 1975; Deriol 1971; Kleinclausz et al. 1924; Latreille et al. 1975; Lojkine 1974.)

What is now known as the *agglomération* of Lyon, the city and adjacent communes administered collectively as COURLY, has like many French cities experienced a rapid growth in the postwar years. Between 1954 and 1975 the population increased by some 50 percent during a period that roughly coincided with the may-oralty of the late Louis Pradel, one of the most formidable of French city bosses.

Table 4.1 traces the growth of this urban area over a rather longer period. The city itself probably reached its present size about the turn of the century. Apart from a period in the 1950s and 1960s when Lyon experienced some growth, the main locus

Table 4.1. *The growth of Lyon and the principal suburbs, 1830–1975*

Year	Lyon	Villeurbanne	22 main suburbs[a]	Other areas	Total
1830	170,000	n.a.[b]	n.a.[b]	n.a.[b]	n.a.[b]
1876	342,815	9,033	54,947	29,277	436,052
1901	459,099	11,176	71,189	48,594	590,058
1931	579,763	82,038	139,463	40,253	841,517[c]
1946	460,748	82,359	144,473	36,627	724,247
1954	466,471	80,905	159,454	43,149	749,989
1962	532,569	105,156	225,736	92,029	955,490[d]
1968	524,600	119,516	331,515	113,538	1,089,169[d]
1975	456,716	116,535	475,143	122,266	1,170,660[d]

[a]Namely: Bron, Caluire, Décines, Ecully, Feyzin, Fontaines-sur-Saône, Francheville, Irigny, La Mulatière, Meyzieux, Mions, Neuville, Oullins, Pierre-Bénite, Rillieux, Saint-Fons, Saint-Genis-Laval, Saint-Priest, Sainte-Foy, Tassin, Vaulx-en-Velin, Vénissieux. Each of these communes had a population of more than 5,000 in the 1975 census.
[b]Data not available.
[c]The 1931 census is now considered highly inaccurate; see Bienfait, 1970.
[d]The COURLY administrative area.
Sources: Bonnet 1975; censuses.

of population increase this century has been in the suburban communes. The first suburb seriously developed was Villeurbanne, immediately to the east of the VIth Arrondissement. Since about 1954, however, the other suburbs have taken over. Between 1954 and 1975 their population increased by more than 315,000 persons. The effect has been a shift in the balance of the population of the *agglomération* away from the central areas (Lyon and Villeurbanne). (See Table 4.2.)

This shift was one result of the massive program of construction and reconstruction undertaken by Pradel. Between 1962 and 1975 the number of principal residential units in the *agglomération* increased by approximately 100,000, about a third. Between 1968 and 1975, in fact, some 88,000 new housing units were completed, while some 36,000 were lost through demolition. Of the net gain of some 52,000 units, nearly 35,000, about two-thirds, were in the eastern suburbs along a belt running from Rillieux in the north to Saint-Fons in the south, an area known as the *ceinture sociale,* or sometimes less euphemistically as the "red belt." A substantial proportion of this new housing was in fact built in three ZUPs at Rillieux, Vaulx-en-Velin, and Vénissieux. In general terms the suburbs to the east are the main areas of working-class residence, those to the west are by and large middle class.

Table 4.2. *Percentage changes in urban population, 1901–75*

Period	Lyon	Villeurbanne	22 suburbs
1946/1901	+ 0.36	+ 637.29	+ 102.94
1962/1946	+ 15.59	+ 27.62	+ 56.25
1968/1962	− 1.50	+ 13.27	+ 46.86
1975/1968	− 12.94	− 2.49	+ 43.32
1975/1901	− 0.52	+ 942.27	+ 567.43
Pop. change, 1975/1968	− 67,884	− 2,981	+ 143,628

Table 4.3. *Percentage distribution of population between main urban areas*

Year	Lyon	Villeurbanne	22 suburbs	Population
1901	84.8	2.1	13.1	541,464
1946	67.0	12.0	21.0	687,620
1954	66.0	11.5	22.5	706,840
1962	61.7	12.2	26.1	863,461
1968	53.8	12.3	33.9	975,631
1975	43.6	11.1	45.3	1,048,394

This surge of residential construction was part of the determined effort throughout France to overcome the gross inade-
quacies of the existing housing stock. At the same time, Lyon, like
many French cities during the same period, underwent a major
reshaping. The 1960s and 1970s saw a radical restructuring of the
central urban area and its extension beyond its nineteenth-century focus in the Presqu'Ile (Ist and IInd Arrondissements) east-
ward across the Rhône to create what French planners call a "hy-
percenter" for the metropolitan region. Plans in progress or
completed in the mid-1970s included a transurban highway network (*Paris-Perpignan sans un feu rouge*), the commercial and administrative centers of the Part-Dieu and the Perrache, an under-
ground railway system, and a number of prestige office and
residential tower buildings. Pradel rejoiced in the nickname *le roi
du beton:* "They call me the king of concrete. Do you know in our
day another material? If marble had been cheaper, I would have
used it to build HLM. . . . Don't forget that when I succeeded
Edouard Herriot [a previous mayor] I found shantytowns. I suppressed them. There were slums. I demolished them." (Interview

on Radio Monte Carlo, reported in *Le Progrès de Lyon,* October 9, 1975.)

The implementation of these schemes entailed considerable physical and social disruption of the central urban area, especially the Ist, IInd, IIIrd, and VIth Arrondissements. Between 1968 and 1975 these four arrondissements lost some 20 percent of their population, or about 50,000 inhabitants. This was a net loss that underestimated the total population movement, as there was some new residential construction in this area. The new housing, however, consisted mainly of high-quality, high-cost apartments that replaced tenement buildings dating from the nineteenth century and earlier. There was consequently a significant change in the social composition of these areas. Not the least affected by these developments were immigrants.

THE GEOGRAPHIC DISTRIBUTION OF IMMIGRANTS IN THE LYON AREA

This section is in the first instance mainly descriptive. Table 4.4, which uses the evidence of the 1975 census, details the distribution of the foreign population of the *agglomération,* by arrondisse-

Table 4.4. *Distribution of foreign population in COURLY by commune, 1975 census*

Commune		Total pop.	Foreigners	% foreigners in pop.	% of all foreigners in area	IRC[a]
Lyon	I	31,455	5,100	16.2	3.67	137
	II	34,220	3,010	8.8	3.17	75
	III	73,745	7,755	10.5	5.59	89
	IV	33,410	2,825	8.5	2.04	72
	V	49,160	4,570	9.3	3.29	79
	VI	52,740	4,240	8.0	3.05	68
	VII	57,680	6,140	10.6	4.42	90
	VIII	71,240	6,450	9.1	4.65	76
	IX	53,760	5,195	9.7	3.74	82
Total Lyon		457,410	45,285	9.9	32.62	84
Décines		19,955	3,720	18.6	2.68	158
Meyzieux		19,350	2,705	14.0	1.95	119
Vaulx		38,155	10,985	28.8	7.91	244
V'banne		116,875	17,345	14.8	12.50	125

(*continued*)

Table 4.4 (*continued*)

Commune	Total pop.	Foreigners	% foreigners in pop.	% of all foreigners in area	IRC[a]
Total east	194,335	34,755	17.9	25.04	152
Bron	44,910	4,885	10.9	3.52	92
Feyzin	7,370	1,370	18.6	0.99	158
Mions	4,850	710	14.6	0.51	124
St.-Fons	16,395	3,060	18.7	2.20	158
St.-Priest	36,760	6,725	18.3	4.84	155
Vénissieux	75,040	13,775	18.4	9.92	156
Total southeast	185,325	30,525	16.5	21.99	140
Irigny	5,505	550	10.0	0.40	85
La Mulat.	7,730	650	8.4	0.47	71
Oullins	27,555	2,780	10.1	2.00	86
Pierre-B.	10,330	1,670	16.2	1.20	137
Total southwest	51,120	5,650	11.1	4.07	94
Chaponost	4,665	485	10.4	0.35	88
Ecully	17,680	855	4.8	0.62	41
Francheville	7,990	350	4.4	0.25	37
St.-Didier	4,670	355	7.6	0.26	64
Ste.-Foy	21,700	1,325	6.1	0.96	52
St.-Genis	12,820	900	7.0	0.65	59
Tassin	14,750	795	5.4	0.57	46
Total west	84,275	5,065	6.0	3.65	51
Caluire	43,545	2,425	5.6	1.75	47
Fontaines	6,415	305	4.9	0.22	40
Neuville	5,700	810	14.2	0.58	120
Rillieux	31,090	3,255	10.5	2.34	89
Total north	86,750	6,795	7.8	4.90	66
Rest of Agglomération	112,820	10,735	9.5	7.73	81
Agglomération	1,172,035	138,810	11.8	100.00	100

[a]IRC is an elementary Index of Relative Concentration, which is calculated as: Observed foreign pop. in commune/Expected for. pop. in commune × 100.

ment for Lyon itself, and by commune for the remainder of the urban area. It will be seen that in terms of numbers, the communes/arrondissements with the largest foreign population are, in descending order: Villeurbanne, Vénissieux, Vaulx-en-Velin,

Lyon III, Saint-Priest, Lyon VIII, and Lyon VII. These seven areas contain about half the foreign population. They are not, however, always the communes with the highest density of foreigners. Eight areas have 16 percent or more foreigners in their populations: Vaulx-en-Velin, Saint-Fons, Décines, Feyzin, Vénissieux, Saint-Priest, Lyon I, and Pierre-Bénite. Three areas appear on both lists (Vaulx-en-Velin, Vénissieux, and Saint-Priest), and these three areas alone hold some 23 percent of the total foreign population. Within those three communes, foreigners constitute 21 percent of the local population.

Amalgamating the communes into larger groups (Table 4.5) brings out more clearly the relative distribution of the foreign population between city and suburbs. In 1975 more than two-thirds of the foreign population resided in one or another of these suburban communes, a proportion higher than that among the population as a whole (Table 4.6). With the possible exception, at least until recently, of North African immigrants, the foreign population has since World War II tended to be drawn toward the suburbs. Between 1968 and 1975 the tendency increased, accelerated by the general shift toward the suburbs noted earlier. Between 1968 and 1975 the total foreign population recorded in the census increased by 40,000, but 88 percent of that net increase was located in suburban areas.

Table 4.5 also brings out very clearly the relative distribution of the foreign population between the suburban areas to the east and south and those to the north and west. Of significance here again is the *ceinture sociale,* in particular the belt of communes

Table 4.5. *Table 4.4 summarized by main areas*

Communes	Total Pop.	Foreign Pop.	% (a)	% (b)	IRC	% (c)
Lyon	457,410	45,285	9.9	32.6	84	39.9
East	194,335	34,755	17.9	25.0	152	15.4
S'East	185,325	30,525	16.5	22.0	140	15.0
S'West	51,120	5,650	11.1	4.1	94	4.4
West	84,275	5,065	6.0	3.7	51	7.7
North	86,750	6,795	7.8	4.9	66	7.7
Rest	112,820	10,735	·9.5	7.7	81	9.9
Total	1,172,035	138,810	11.8	100.0	100	100.0

% (a) = percentage of foreigners in area population; % (b) = percentage distribution of foreigners living in areas; % (c) = percentage distribution of French living in areas.

Table 4.6. *Percentage of foreign population of urban area living in suburbs (including Villleurbanne)*

Year	Algerians	All others	All foreigners	Total pop.
1954	n.a.[a]	49.14	n.a.	34.0
1968	54.02	61.18	58.84	46.2
1975	67.66	67.22	67.38	56.4

[a]Data not available.

Table 4.7. *Distribution of communes according to percentage of immigrants and* ouvriers *in their population*

	Under 50% *ouvriers*	Over 50% *ouvriers*	Total
10.5% + immigrants	4 (A)[a]	12 (B)	16
10.5% − immigrants	12 (C)	4 (D)	16
	16	16	32

[a]See text for communes listed in cells A, B, C, and D.

Table 4.8. *Percentages of immigrants and Algerians in communes with high, medium, and low proportions of* ouvriers

Communes with:	No.	Mean % immigrants	Mean % Algerians
High prop. of *ouvriers* (55%+)	11	17.3	6.2
Medium: 45%–55%	10	10.5	4.1
Low: under 45%	11	7.1	2.1
Ratio high : low		2.44 : 1	2.95 : 1
Ratio high : medium : low with low as base 100		100 : 148 : 244	100 : 195 : 295

running from Vaulx-en-Velin to Feyzin. The distribution of the foreign population in fact correlates fairly closely with the social composition of the districts (Tables 4.7 and 4.8). For future reference it will be useful to bear in mind the following general groupings:

(A) Middle-class communes with high foreign population: Lyon III, Lyon VII, Bron, Rillieux. (22,035 foreigners, 17.2 percent of foreign population).

(B) Working-class communes with high foreign population: Feyzin, Saint-Fons, Vaulx, Pierre-Bénite, Vénissieux, Saint-Priest,

Décines, Neuville, Meyzieux, Mions, Lyon I, Villeurbanne (77,745, 60.7 percent).

(C) Middle-class communes with low foreign population: Fontaines, Lyon IV, La Mulatière, Lyon V, Saint-Genis, Tassin, Francheville, Caluire, Lyon VI, Lyon II, Sainte-Foy, Ecully (12,375, 9.7 percent).

(D) Working-class communes with low foreign populations: Irigny, Lyon VIII, Lyon IX, Oullins (15,920, 12.4 percent).

CONCENTRATIONS

Relatively high concentrations of foreigners in some areas and not in others is, of course, a common feature of many European cities (see Rex and Moore 1967 and Rex and Tomlinson 1979 for a discussion of a British example), and one that deserves the closest attention. It would be well, first, to paint in the finer points of the picture. Table 4.5, which distinguishes in gross terms between large groups of geographically distinct communes, obscures certain important differences between communes within each area – Lyon Ist in Lyon, for example, or Pierre-Bénite in the southwest, each with densities of foreigners much higher than average for their general area. Similarly, a much more varied picture emerges when we examine the quartiers in each commune. Because each of the larger communes was divided into quartiers for census purposes, a relatively systematic examination is possible. (For some reason, Vaulx-en-Velin was left as a single district for census purposes.)

The relevant data are presented in Tables 4.9 and 4.10, which locate the quartiers in each commune and arrondissement that contain high relative concentrations of foreigners. Most of these quartiers, as might be expected, are in the eastern and southeastern suburbs. There are, however, certain quartiers in other areas with very high concentrations. Thus, in Oullins, in one quartier foreigners constitute as many as 41.8 percent of the population, compared with an average for the commune of 10 percent. Nearly half the foreigners in Oullins live in that quartier which contains a large *cité de transit*. On the other side of the *agglomération*, in Bron, nearly two-thirds of the commune's foreigners are found in two out of the eight quartiers in the commune.

Taking the urban area as a whole, and including the commune

Table 4.9. *Distribution of foreigners by quartier, commune, and area*

Area	Quartiers with . . . % foreigners						A[a]	B%[b]
	0–4.9%	5–9.9%	10–14.9%	15–19.9%	20–24.9%	25%+		
Lyon	0	2	1	3	0	0	0	0
I	0	6	0	1	0	0	0	0
II	3	5	1	2	2	0	2,005	25.9
III	1	3	2	0	0	0	0	0
IV	2	3	0	1	1	0	1,215	26.6
V	2	4	2	0	0	0	0	0
VI	1	2	4	1	0	0	0	0
VII	0	7	2	0	1	0	800	12.4
VIII	4	5	0	1	1	2	1,300	25.0
IX								
Décines	0	0	0	2	1	0	1,800	48.4
Meyzieux	0	0	1	1	0	0	0	0
V'banne	1	4	7	1	3	2	8,130	46.9
Bron	2	2	2	0	2	0	3,165	64.8
St.-Fons	0	1	2	0	3	0	2,410	78.8
St.-Priest	0	1	1	2	0	2	3,355	49.9
Vénissieux	0	2	0	5	2	1	3,635	26.4
Irigny	0	1	1	0	0	0	0	0
La Mul.	0	2	0	0	1	0	90	13.8
Oullins	2	4	1	0	0	1	1,270	45.7
Pierre-B.	0	1	0	0	1	0	1,430	85.6
Ecully	2	1	0	0	0	0	0	0
Francheville	1	1	0	0	0	0	0	0
Ste.-Foy	2	3	0	0	0	0	0	0
St.-Genis	0	1	1	0	0	0	0	0
Tassin	2	2	0	0	0	0	0	0
Caluire	5	2	2	0	0	0	0	0
Rillieux	0	3	2	0	0	0	0	0
Summary:								
Areas								
Lyon (18)	13	37	12	9	5	2	5,320	11.7
East (23)	1	4	8	4	4	2	9,930[c]	41.8[c]
S'east (30)	2	6	5	7	7	3	12,565	44.2
S'west (15)	2	8	2	0	2	1	2,790	49.4
West (16)	7	8	1	0	0	0	0	0
North (14)	5	5	4	0	0	0	0	0
Totals (176)	30	68	32	20	18	8	30,605[d]	27.2[d]

[a]Column A = foreign population of quartiers where density is 20% or more.
[b]Column B = percent of foreign population of area living in quartiers where density is 20% or more.
[c]If Vaulx is included, these figures read 20,915 and 60.2%.
[d]If Vaulx is included, these figures read 41,590 and 33.6%.

Table 4.10. *Foreign and French populations of high-density quartiers compared*

Commune		Quartier	% foreigners in quartier	% foreign pop. in quartier	% Fr. pop. in quartier	Ratio[a] foreign : French
Lyon	III	4	21.1	13.3	5.8	229
		8	20.4	12.5	4.2	298
	V	1	20.0	26.6	10.9	244
	VIII	9	20.5	28.8	19.7	146
	IX	3	26.4	2.3	0.7	329
		4	21.1	8.9	3.5	254
		9	43.5	13.9	1.9	732
Décines		3	20.6	48.4	42.7	113
V'banne		1	36.3	1.6	0.5	320
		5	27.6	7.9	3.6	219
		15	23.2	19.2	10.8	178
		17	20.0	7.7	5.3	145
		18	22.2	10.5	6.4	164
Bron		4	20.2	32.1	15.5	207
		8	20.2	32.7	15.6	210
St.-Fons		1	21.2	11.1	9.5	117
		2	22.8	42.2	32.8	129
		5	24.6	25.5	17.9	142
St.-Priest		1	27.5	10.2	6.0	170
		2	29.7	39.7	21.0	189
Vénissieux		3	20.0	4.0	3.6	111
		4	22.6	21.0	16.2	130
		6	29.9	1.5	0.8	188
La Mulatière		3	20.2	13.8	5.0	276
Oullins		3	41.8	45.7	7.1	644
Pierre-B.		1	20.4	85.6	35.6	240

[a]Ratio gives a rough index of the relative concentration of a commune's foreign population in a particular quartier when compared with the distribution of the French population.

of Vaulx-en-Velin, about one foreigner in three lives in a quartier in which they constitute over 20 percent of the population. In fact, along a belt of communes from Vaulx-en-Velin in the east, through the southeastern suburbs (the *ceinture sociale*), to the inner southwestern suburbs across the Rhône, about half the foreign population live in areas where they constitute at least 20 percent of the inhabitants.

What has been said so far concerns foreigners as a whole, and no attempt has been made to distinguish between different groups.

Briefly, at the level of the large areas represented in Tables 4.4 and 4.5, there appears to be a greater concentration of Algerians than other nationalities. Second, at quartier level Algerians appear to be more concentrated than do other groups. Third, whereas there are numerous quartiers that tend to specialize, as it were, in Algerians, there are relatively fewer – though there are some – that take in higher proportions of other groups, such as the Portuguese.

Although at first sight the relative distribution of the foreign population looks clear-cut (Table 4.5), when examined in detail what emerges is a pattern more akin to a patchwork or mosaic. To understand this pattern, we must look more carefully at the nature of the concentrations, for they occur in several different types of area for a variety of distinct, if connected, reasons.

First, and traditionally most significant, were and are those found in certain areas of the inner city, in parts of central Lyon and on the border between Lyon and Villeurbanne. At one time, and still to a degree at present, those areas presented a ghetto-like aspect. Parts of the Croix Rousse in the Ist Arrondissement, and around the Place du Pont, with their shops, cinemas, restaurants, lodging houses, and above all cafés have, as I suggested earlier, long been a pole of attraction for North Africans. To an extent these are ghettos, but the picture conjured up by that concept is perhaps misleading. There is nowhere an extensive connected stretch of territory occupied solely by foreigners. The layout of the city, especially east of the Rhône, has prevented this. The area was built in the nineteenth century on a grid pattern, crisscrossed by major boulevards of substantial bourgeois housing. Within the areas created by the intersection of these boulevards are grids of smaller streets with less substantial housing, and it is within these "islands" that concentrations of foreigners were traditionally located.

I say "traditionally" because these are the areas most affected by urban renewal. I suggested earlier that the restructuring of the inner city undertaken by Pradel had had important consequences for the population located therein. The effect was particularly marked in the VIth Arrondissement, which lost 22 percent of its total population, and 27 percent of its foreigners. The decline has been less marked, but no less significant, in parts of the Ist, IInd, and IIIrd arrondissements. A similar pattern may be seen in certain parts of western Villeurbanne adjacent to the VIth. Two areas in particular may be mentioned: that around the old cavalry barracks of the Part-Dieu in the VIth (now a major commercial center), and that on the lower slopes of the Croix Rousse in the Ist. Both of these were traditionally centers of immigrant implantation. Here were to be found the cafés, which offered cheap accommodation, and the tenements in which could be found dilapidated one- and two-room apartments at very low rents. It is ironic, again, that it was the boom in the construction industry that brought so many immigrants to Lyon in the 1960s and 1970s. Many of them found employment demolishing property they traditionally occupied to build new ones they could not afford. At the same time, other sources of accommodation disappeared when the *bidonvilles* around the central urban periphery, and farther afield, were swept away. They disappeared from Lyon in the 1960s for reasons of both social policy and economic necessity. Two of the principal *bidonvilles* were on sites required for development.

Beyond the inner urban area, similar traditional types of concentration may be found in the older, village-like cores of some of the adjacent suburbs, for example, at Oullins, or in Caluire in the latter's Saint-Clair quartier along the banks of the Rhône. In 1975–6 this area was scheduled for a road-widening scheme. Property under threat and left by the owners in a dilapidated state pending demolition could then be rented very cheaply.

Caluire also provides examples of two other ways in which concentrations of immigrants can arise: when a hostel for single men, or *cité de transit* (temporary-housing center) are located in an area. In the case of Caluire, therefore, a commune that has in terms of the *agglomération* a relatively low percentage of foreigners (5.6 percent in 1975) finds itself with three pockets or islands, centered on a hostel, a *cité de transit*, and an area earmarked for urban renewal, in which relatively large numbers of immigrants and their families are concentrated.

Two other types of concentration in suburban areas that mainly affect immigrant families may be mentioned. The first occurs when a private landlord or property company rents to foreigners. As we shall see, this is quite rare. The most famous (indeed notorious) example in the whole of the *agglomération* may be found in eastern Villeurbanne along the rue Olivier de Serres, where the "Régie Simon" houses several hundred North African families in a group of six large buildings. The second, and numerically far more important, type of concentration occurs mainly in the eastern suburbs, in particular on the ZUPs at Vaulx-en-Velin and

Vénissieux. There the concentration is the result of the workings of the system of public-housing allocation, which is discussed in detail later.

THE HOUSING MARKET AND THE "INSTITUTIONALIZATION" OF IMMIGRANT ACCOMMODATIONS

Several related factors help account for the geographical distribution of immigrants. One of these is the process of urban development, in particular the restructuring of the inner-urban area. This process, which reflects other forces – economic, social, political – at work in the society at large, has affected many sections of the population, including, of course, the French themselves. However, partly for reasons already indicated, and partly for reasons yet to be discussed, immigrants have been particularly affected, and affected in particular ways. As we saw, the demolition of inner-urban tenements with cheap if substandard accommodation is destroying traditionally key areas of immigrant implantation, areas that had long been used by newcomers to the city even before the mass immigration of the postwar era.

Another factor that is linked with urban renewal but that may be distinguished from it is the changing nature of the housing stock and the operation of the housing market. This in turn may be linked to the demand for accommodation, or rather accommodation of certain types, on the part of immigrants, and the relationship between that demand and the changing ethnic and demographic composition of the immigrant population. Especially important is the "fit" that exists (or rather, does not exist) between housing demand and the housing stock. This relationship must also be set in the context of public policy, national and local, toward what is termed "social" housing, and in particular toward the housing of groups such as immigrants. This policy has affected the provision of such housing in both quantitative and qualitative terms, in its location, and in the mode of access to it.

We may begin by looking generally at the nature of the housing stock and the urban-housing market. Here my approach has been influenced by, though it does not follow entirely, the pioneering work of Rex and Moore (1967) in Sparkbrook (Birmingham), and their much discussed concept of "housing class." In a more recent work, which somewhat modifies the original notion, Rex comments that the basis of the concept was the idea that "in any city there was a stock of housing of varying degrees of desirability to which different groups of people having different characteristics had differing degrees of access" (Rex and Tomlinson 1979:127).

Leaving aside for the moment the difficult question of desirability, and the extent to which among an ethnically heterogeneous urban population there are likely to be universally agreed criteria of what constitutes "good" housing (see Dahya 1974; Rex and Tomlinson 1979:128), it is obvious that any urban study must look seriously at the categories into which a city's housing stock may be divided, and at the way in which access to different types of housing is organized. In doing so, we must recognize that, in the first instance at least, we are probably dealing with "official" categories, or perhaps the urban planner's conceptualization of the housing system. I would, in fact, argue that in any urban system, especially perhaps that which characterizes modern French cities, the official conceptualization and organization are of primary importance. They provide the "dominant" framework in which all else must be set.

Census and other data for the mid-1970s point to a figure of just over 400,000 *résidences principales* in the Lyon *agglomération*. Less than one-third of these units were owner-occupied; that is, the great bulk of the housing stock is rented. Owner occupation is much lower than in Britain, though the rate of owner occupation in France has increased considerably since the war. The vast majority of rented units are apartments (in fact there are relatively few even privately owned houses in Lyon). Of the rented apartments some 75 percent are owned privately by individual landlords or property companies. The remaining properties come mostly within the public housing sector where they are owned and rented out by the *offices* or *sociétés* HLM.*

The HLM (Habitation à Loyer Modéré) are subsidized housing offering, as their title implies, what is in theory accommodation at a "moderate" rent. The HLM have roughly the same function as, but are no means the equivalent of, council housing in Britain.

*The principal sources of information for the Lyon housing market include the 1975 and earlier censuses. For Lyon, see the relevant tables of series LOG/54C, 55/C and 56/C. For the region as a whole see Deschamps 1976. Note also "Le parc H.L.M. régional," pp. 2–5 of *Points d'Appui* No. 1, January 1978. In addition, see Bonnet 1975, Lojkine 1974, and Michaud 1975. Information has also been obtained from the prefecture, and from the *offices* and *sociétés* HLM.

Although HLM represent approximately 16 percent of the total housing stock, they form a somewhat higher proportion of more recently built housing. Perhaps as much as 30 percent of accommodation coming onto the market in the late 1960s and early 1970s in Lyon was provided by the HLM. Although in earlier years HLM had been built at least around the periphery of the inner-urban area (in the eastern districts of the IIIrd and VIIth Arrondissements, and in the VIIIth, and to the west in the IXth), more recent developments have been located mainly in the suburbs, for example on the ZUPs at Rillieux, Vénissieux, and Vaulx-en-Velin. Some 43 percent of all residential units in those suburbs were constructed between 1968 and 1975.

All accommodation, whether privately or publicly owned, consists of relatively small units. According to the 1975 census, some 60 percent of all principal residences consisted of one to three rooms, and only 6 percent comprised six or more. In the HLM sector in the region as a whole, nearly 70 percent of all units are composed of three or four rooms. Six-room apartments form just 1 percent of the stock (*Points d'appui* No. 1, January 1978). About 26 percent of all apartments in the Rhône Department in 1975 were considered subject to overcrowding.

In sum, then, if we look at the housing market from the viewpoint of families in the poorer section of the community – and immigrants by and large come into that category because the vast majority are in unskilled or semiskilled occupations – the situation would appear as follows: Most are faced with the prospect of renting rather than buying. Mortgages are generally more difficult to obtain in France compared with Britain, where in addition the tax system encourages owner-occupation. If renting, tenants have a choice between an HLM, most probably located on a suburban ZUP, and a privately owned apartment. The private sector is very difficult to characterize briefly, because of the range of accommodations, in terms of both quality and cost, found within it. It caters, of course, for the whole social scale. However, two general points may be made. New *cheap* apartments are very scarce – I would be inclined to say nonexistent. To find low-rent private housing, one has to search among the tenements of the inner-city areas or in the village cores of some of the older suburbs, which are precisely the areas most frequently threatened by demolition. Second, outside such areas there is considerable evidence that landlords (whether individuals or corporations) discriminate against immigrants, especially those from North Africa.

If the nature of the housing stock, and the structure of the housing market, obliges immigrants to look for accommodations in certain areas, which accounts in part for their distribution in the urban area, it also has a number of social consequences. One of these is quite simply the relatively high concentration of immigrants in certain communes and quartiers where as a proportion of the population their numbers exceed what is called the "threshold of tolerance" (see Chapter 5). Another is that increasingly immigrants (both those with families and those living alone in France) are forced to seek accommodations in "institutional" housing: in *cités de transit* and in HLM in the case of families, and in hostels in the case of single men. A third is that this process, and the process of urban development as a whole, increasingly brings individuals and their families under the aegis of institutional control both in the field of housing and in that of social relations generally. A fourth consequence, to which this "institutionalization" is in part a response, is that the housing and rehousing of immigrants constitute a "problem" for French society. It is, of course, also a problem for the immigrants themselves, though perhaps one of a different kind. For the French it is a problem that has been generated in large part by the processes of urban development. And the solutions proposed are those according with, and reflecting, the necessities of that process.

In general terms, the consequences outlined above have been similar for all immigrants. They have, however, been rather more marked for those who originate outside Europe, especially those from North Africa. French society is particularly sensitive to the housing situation of North African immigrants, and accordingly, in this chapter and the next, greater attention will be paid to their problems.

Where North Africans and certain other groups are concerned, a distinction may also be drawn between those living as "bachelors" and those living with their families because their problems and the solutions proposed are somewhat different. By and large, the bachelors compete in a different sector of the housing market, though there is some overlap in that within the tenements of the older areas families and bachelors (often in multi-occupied rooms) live side by side. It is in institutionally provided accommodations that the main difference resides.

At this point the "housing class" concept, which enables fine distinctions to be drawn between the situation in the housing market of several distinct social categories (see Rex and Tomlinson

1979:132), begins to lose some of its attractiveness. It is certainly important to indicate the relationship between categories of *housing* and categories of *people*, but the conflation of the two has its dangers if it leads us to forget the kind of overlap in competition for housing that we find in this case. Moreover, although it does enable us to make a necessary distinction between families and bachelors with regard to institutional housing, it would be difficult to contend that this places the two categories in a different class, at least in the more general sense of that term.

The rest of this chapter is, then, concerned with immigrant bachelors as, in a loose sense, a housing class. The situation of families is considered in detail in Chapter 5.

THE "ISOLATED" MALE

In Chapter 2 we saw that there is a significant difference in the ratio of adult males to adult females in the two main groups of nationalities constituting the population of migrant workers, those from Southern Europe and those from North Africa. Although family migration has been increasing, North African immigration in the mid-1970s still consisted predominantly of adult males living in France without their families. These migrants are referred to in administrative circles as *célibataires,* or *vivants en célibataire,* or simply *les isolés.* The fact that this phenomenon exists on a large scale is well established. How many there are, and where they are located in the urban area, is something that is not known with any degree of precision.

Inspection of Tables 2.1 through 2.4 will show a considerable discrepancy between the figures of the foreign population derived from the census and those derived from the prefecture. In general, prefecture figures are based on information contained in the dossiers held on each foreigner, which are not always up-to-date. There is a tendency, for example, to underestimate the child population, and perhaps to overestimate the *isolés,* for example, by counting those who have left the area in search of employment elsewhere or to return home. This discrepancy matters insofar as prefecture estimates play a part in determining official policy. Applying his own methods of calculation to the prefecture figures, the sociologist Pierre Michaud has estimated that there were roughly 66,500 *isolés* in the Rhône Department in 1973, of whom about 50,000 were North African (Michaud 1975). A similar method applied to census data for 1975 suggests a figure of about 40,000, of whom about about 35,000 might reside in the Lyon area (perhaps 43,000, using prefecture figures). (For further discussion, see Crétaine 1974 and Dubreuil 1975.)

There is no firm systematic evidence for the distribution of these "isolated" males within the urban area, but a rough indication can be garnered from the 1975 census. For example, the ratio of males : females in the Algerian population of the *agglomération* as a whole is 1.9 : 1. Areas where that ratio is one and a half times the average (i.e., 2.8 : 1 or more) include the Ist, IInd, IIIrd, VIth, VIIth, and IXth arrondissements of Lyon, and the suburb of Tassin. The suburbs of Caluire and Saint-Fons are the only other places where the ratio is significantly above average. On the whole, it is the central urban areas that attract and house the isolated male migrant. For it is in these areas that are found the lodging houses and cafés.

If the lodging houses still provide accommodations for the majority of male migrants, and others are housed by their employers (for example, the prefecture estimates that 3,000 workers are housed in cabins on building sites), increasing numbers find rooms in two other types of accommodations: the *garnis agréés* and the hostels. The *garnis agréés* are in fact no more than lodging houses that have been inspected by the prefecture and given its seal of approval. In the mid-1970s there were in the Rhône 750 such *garnis* offering room to some 11,800 people; 560 of these *garnis* were in Lyon city itself. The prefecture has the power to close this type of lodging house, and in fact between 1966 and 1975 some 330 were so treated. Of the 5,600 occupants, 4,100 were then found accommodations in hostels.

There are some seventy-six hostels in the department with a total capacity of about 17,000 beds. Fifty-nine cater exclusively for migrant workers, and a substantial proportion of male North Africans have had experience of hostel life. The hostels are run both by national organizations such as SONACOTRA (thirty hostels in the Rhône) and by private local associations, notably the Maison du Travailleur Etranger (sixteen hostels). These and other organizations date from the early 1950s and were a charitable response to the needs of Arab workers arriving at that time. Some of the oldest hostels, which are still in use, were converted factory buildings. In these – what the MTE director calls their "first generation" of hostels – residents are housed in dormitories with up to forty beds in a room. The most recently built hostels – the "third generation" – are large and modern, and house up to four hundred residents in single rooms, with communal kitchens, common rooms, a bar, and so on. While the older hostels are located around the periphery of the inner-urban area, the new hostels have been built in the suburbs – there are six at Vénissieux, five at Vaulx-en-Velin. Of all hostels, 70 percent are now in the eastern suburbs. It is intended that the older hostels be gradually phased out, but up to 1976 the only major closure had occurred in the early 1960s, when the Part-Dieu barracks, which housed 1,500 North Africans, a substantial proportion of the Arab population at that time, was cleared prior to demolition.

The hostels are seen by the French as a necessary replacement for the lodging houses as these are closed or demolished. In the early 1970s, hostels acquired an additional significance when all new immigrants were required to have a limited contract of employment, which also carried with it an offer of accommodations. To this end, employers were able to reserve places, and indeed some hostels were constructed to cater for the projected arrival of workers recruited by some of the larger firms.

Some fifty hostels were opened during the late 1960s and early 1970s, their development and location reflecting the urban-area changes described earlier. They functioned in ways that gave greater institutional control over migrants and migration, by directing workers toward certain types of areas and accommodations. The hostels also exercised considerable control over the lifestyles of their residents. For example, MTE rules state that political activities, such as distributing leaflets in the hostel, will lead to immediate expulsion. Other, more informal, means of control are also exerted, as when directors advise their unemployed residents to return home. Hostels do not as yet dominate the housing market for the *isolés*. In the long run, however, as the areas in which the lodging houses are located are renovated, the hostels may provide the main source of their accommodations.

THE HOSTELS AND THEIR RESIDENTS

Only one group of hostels (MTE) publishes systematic information on the social backgrounds of their residents. The relevant information, summarized in Table 4.11, concerns some 3,500 persons (all male) residing in their hostels at the end of 1974.

Table 4.11. *A profile of the residents of MTE hostels, 1974–5*

a) *Nationality*	%	b) *Age range*	%
Algerian	58.0	Under 25	14.0
Moroccan	9.4	25–35	42.3
Tunisian	25.4	35+	43.3
Portuguese	0.6		
Turkish	2.8		
Yugoslav	1.7		
Others	2.0		

c) *Marital status:* Married 73.6%, unmarried 26.4%

d) *Length of stay in France*		e) *Sector of employment*	
	%		%
Less than 1 year	1.9	Building and	
1–3 yrs.	27.5	construction	38.4
4–6 yrs.	22.1	Factories	43.8
6–10 yrs.	21.8	Other	17.8
10+ yrs.	26.8		

f) *Level of skill*		g) *Monthly pay*	
	%		%
Manual worker	41.0	Under 1,300 frs.	5.8
OS	45.7	1,300–1,500	43.6
OQ or OP	12.9	1,500–1,800	33.1
Retired	0.5	1,800+	17.5

Note: All totals add to 100%, except for rounding.
Source: MTE Annual Report 1975.

What stands out at once is the high proportion of North Africans, of those in unskilled and semiskilled occupations, and of those who have been working in France for ten years or more.

The MTE hostel population does not differ significantly from that of the other organizations. There is, however, some considerable variation *between* hostels in each group. For example, one of the MTE's newer hostels houses substantial numbers of recently recruited young factory workers from such areas as Morocco, Yugoslavia, and Turkey. The older hostels are dominated by Algerians and to a lesser extent Tunisians. One fact not presented in Table 4.11 is that although there may be a high turnover of residents in some, if not all, hostels, there is also a core of long-term residents. In one hostel I met two Algerians who had stayed there since 1954, returning each summer to visit their families back home.

As we saw earlier, the hostels are the main alternative to the lodging houses. In fact, the hostel directors themselves see the lodging houses as their competition for custom: "The *garnis* are our *bête noir*. We have been pushing the prefecture to close down all the hovels [*taudis*]." One reason for this is that although the various hostel organizations receive subsidies from the state and from various parastatal bodies, it is expected that they should recover their costs. This puts pressure on their rents. It is difficult to estimate the average rent in lodging houses, but information from both French and immigrant sources would suggest a figure of between 100 and 200 francs per month in 1974–5. The hostel rents (or what SONACOTRA prefers to call the residents' "share of the running costs") vary according to their generation, and only in the oldest hostels is the rent at or below the level of the lodging houses.

Hostel directors, many of whom are ex-army ("I was given my job because of my knowledge of dealing with foreigners, acquired during my military service"), comment that North Africans are not used to spending large amounts of money on housing (i.e. back home), and in any event do not wish to do so: "The residents of the older hostels wish to pay the least possible rent, and send as much money home as possible." The director of one group of small hostels run by NDSA, the Notre-Dame des Sans-Abri (see Chapter 5), commented: "The standing of my hostels is less than those of other organizations, but they correspond with what the workers are looking for. They are not prepared to pay out a lot of money and wish to send home as much as possible." This desire to save, it is argued, obliges them to "go into the *garnis* where they are exploited by dishonest elements, the *marchands de sommeil*." (See remarks in Event 1.)

Another reason offered for what is generally accepted as a preference for the *garnis* is the relative freedom (to come and go, to receive visitors) that they offer, and their location: "Most Arabs love the city center." The NDSA hostel director stressed the advantage his own hostels gained from being in the Ist Arrondissement, in a *tissu urbain*. Others, however, comment on the positive advantages seen in the "calm" of the hostel environment, and the absence of "disturbances."

Many North Africans of my own acquaintance adopted a pragmatic attitude to the hostels. The rent was important, but so too was the location, especially its convenience in getting to and from work. The most frequent complaints I heard about hostels concerned their rules about guests, and the attitudes of the directors. It is certainly also true that saving money is of paramount importance, especially for those with families in Algeria. The hostel director who said of his residents "If a man earns fourteen hundred francs per month, he sends a thousand home to his family, and if he could, he'd send twelve hundred," may have exaggerated, but another was perhaps closer to the mark when he claimed: "They divide their salaries into three parts. One-third for their expenses here, one-third for their own expenditure, and one-third for their families over there."

This propensity to save means that many North Africans, especially the older married men, appear to live a life of grim self-denial: "They do not go out much in the evening or at weekends. They sit in the hall, or in their rooms, drinking coffee and playing cards. There are some residents I have never even seen watching television. There's one man who earns two thousand francs per month who refused to pay one franc for the film show." "My residents work eight or nine hours a day; they sleep eight hours. That's sixteen or seventeen hours. The other seven or eight hours they spend in the hostel." This brings us to the question of what is perceived to be the quality of life in the hostels and of hostel residents. It also brings us to a concept of some significance in modern French urban planning, which appears in the concluding remark of the director who added up the time spent in hostels: "That's why *animation* is of fundamental importance."

ANIMATING THE HOSTELS

"My hostel is clean but soulless," said one director. To combat this state of affairs, the hostels have introduced a policy of *action socioculturelle,* or *animation.* As this concept is relevant also to the next chapter, it is worth examining in some detail. *Animation* may mean, literally, "endowing with life," and was several times glossed by informants as *donner l'âme* (soul). I discussed the concept with a sociologist who worked with an urban-planning group attached to the ZUP at Vaulx-en-Velin. He had been a proponent of *animation* for a number of years and had written an (unpublished) paper on the subject. *Animation* in his view was concerned with "leadership," and with "communication" and *concertation.* It was to do with consciousness-raising and mobilization through the medium of social groups. "L'animateur a une fonction socialisatrice du groupe." There was need for the *animateur* in all kinds of collectivities. He made a comparison between life in the town and life in the village, "where the structure remains strong." *Animation* is directed to restoring life in the urban milieu. A young man working as an *animateur* in a *cité de transit* said: "It is a vast concept, but I have a very simple idea of it – to instill a sense of human relations, to go into a situation and find out people's needs, to help them orgranize themselves."

In 1973–4 there were national discussions initiated by the Ministère du Travail from which emerged a policy for "animating" the hostels and their residents, based on the following principles:

> L'objectif: faire en sorte que l'étranger se plaise dans le foyer, qu'il s'y trouve chez lui. Les méthodes: un accueil chaleureux, une connaissance réelle des aspirations des résidents, une large participation des intéressés à l'action, une imagination constructive. Les moyens: une équipe de direction de foyer responsable, consciente et compétente, un minimum de moyens matériels et financiers, une aide technique d'animateurs spécialistes, un milieu d'accueil largement ouvert.
>
> [MTE Annual Report 1975:14]

Toward this end a number of hostel administrators were sent on training courses at the Institut National de Formation des Animateurs des Collectivitiés (INFAC).

By the time these policies reach the level of the hostels, however, they are presented in a somewhat less grandiose fashion. In practical terms, the kinds of activities that have been encouraged include language classes (basic literacy and other courses; see Chapter 8), provision of a library, film shows, television sets, discussion groups, outings, and above all, football (soccer). In theory these activities are seen as the starting point – the young *animateur* mentioned above had talked of *animation globale à partir de foot* – but usually they amount to no more than what they are, a way of passing the time. And even then there are problems: "We had a very successful lecture on India, with slides, which provoked discussion, comparison with Algeria, and so on. But the main interest is in the TV, and I regret having only one set. Two or three at least are needed. Otherwise, billiards, baby foot [pinball machines], and the Tiercé [the French off-course betting system] are what animate people the most." The absence of enthusiasm for sport was something that worried this hostel director, because his superior had placed a great deal of stress on its value: "You can find fifteen people [i.e., out of 250] who express an interest until the time comes to pay the subscription. You can find eleven people for a game, but only half the team turn up."

Very few of the activities actually work in the way intended. The language classes are poorly attended, the trips to Switzerland turn into smuggling expeditions, and on films the annual report of the MTE says this:

> Outre son intérêt sur le plan de la distraction et de la formation, le cinéma représente l'avantage de réunir un nombre important de résidents. Plus que le sport ou les voyages, c'est une activité de "masse." Ces réunions permettent aux responsables de l'animation . . . de s'addresser à beaucoup, d'établir un dialogue très fructueux. . . . A l'issue du film une discussion est engagée. Elle m'intéresse malheureusement que peu de spectateurs . . . Malgré le prix modique, les spectateurs sont plus nombreux aux séances gratuites. [1975:27]

The directors of the hostels embark on *animation* with varying degrees of enthusiasm: "The government required us to animate the hostels, the residents didn't. We asked the residents to give us some ideas. Nothing." Some directors, especially those in charge of the older, smaller hostels, averred that *animation* was not needed. In one case a director remarked: "*Animation* takes care of itself." This was partly because of the hostel's location in an inner-city area "where *animation* is available locally," partly because of what he called the "collective, group, tribal structure" of the hostel's Arab residents.

If there are differences of opinion as to the need for *animation,* there are also differences about its aims, or rather about what kind of social environment it is intended to encourage. Thus, should one aim to improve the milieu *within* the hostel, or should the purpose be to establish links *between* the hostel residents and the inhabitants of the quartiers in which they are located? An official of the SONACOTRA organization (which had commissioned an internal report on "Perception des foyers-hôtels SONA-COTRA par la population environnante") averred that it was their policy to "get away from shutting the residents up inside the hostel. We welcome them, house them, orient them toward the oustide society." One MTE director likewise wished to encourage closer relations with the quartier, and talked of getting the boys from his son's school along to play soccer. Even those who see no virtue in *animation* as such may feel that such contacts are useful: "I encourage literacy classes less for the result, which is not great, than for the human contact. When a young students comes in and talks for an hour, contact is established. An exchange takes place."

ANIMATION AND PARTICIPATION

In connection with the programme of *animation*, the government also encouraged the hostel organizations to establish a greater dialogue with their residents. The whole question of "representation" is discussed in Chapter 11, but some remarks are in order here. Each of the main hostel organizations now has some system of joint committees involving directors and residents. In SONACOTRA hostels they tend to be quite small (six to ten members) who are in theory chosen informally by the residents themselves. MTE *conseils de maison* tend to be larger. In one case the director asked for two representatives from each corridor of twenty rooms – making thirty in all. He then sifted the delegates to ensure an ethnic balance. He also ensured that the one Turkish resident who could speak French came forward, and also a Moroccan whose cousin was vice-consul at Lyon ("for diplomatic reasons"). In other cases directors claimed to have had to search out representatives, and one chose those he considered to "express themselves well, the *avant-garde de la vie moderne*."

Although national policy has pushed the hostels toward forming these committees, local events have also given the movement impetus. In one group of hostels, the need for such bodies emerged as follows: In 1973–4 there was considerable disquiet in one hostel about the behavior of the director, who was said to show favoritism toward his Yugoslav residents at the expense of his Moroccans. One evening at about 9:30 he discovered three Moroccans about to begin a game of billiards, and ordered them to stop. They said it was not yet 10:00, when the light would be put out. Words of abuse flowed. The director then slapped one of the Moroccans, who happened to be a devotee of karate. The director was hospitalized. His assistant, who now took over, decided that the assailant would have to leave but in the meantime should apologize to the director. He did so, and all seemed forgotten; but when the man came to collect his things, he found he had a summons from the police to answer a complaint from the director. The Moroccan residents at once sent a delegation to the director general of the organization to explain the affair, and mentioned the possibility of a rent strike. The director was suspended from duty, and I believe the case did not come to court.

Such behavior on the part of directors is, by the way, not infrequent, as the following saga shows. In 1974 a major firm in the

Lyon area recruited seventy-four Sardinians on contract via the Office Nationale d'Immigration. The whole operation was a disaster. The Sardinians first received their fare to Milan, but twenty of them never arrived. Of those who got to Lyon, about half left their jobs after a month or so, and the number was reduced to twenty-two at the end of the first six months, and only one after a year. One problem had been that in Lyon they were found accommodations in hostels where, according to my informant, an official of the firm concerned, they found the military-style attitude of the director intolerable. The final straw had been the director entering one of the (private) bedrooms to discover "a homosexual scene." "To my surprise," said my informant, "the Sardinians were more upset by the inopportune intervention of the director than they were by the homosexuality."

The primary concern of these representative groups is with the disposition of the *animation* budget. The MTE, as I say, calls them *conseils de maison,* and the term *comité* was specifically rejected: "We could have had a committee, but that would not have been prudent. They would have tried to impose the law on the directors. We said no to *co-gestion.* A meeting of the hostel association was almost unanimously in agreement on that point." Items on the agenda of one of these *conseils* included changing the bed linen, ventilation in the showers, the provision of hot-water taps in washbasins, and the purchase of a color TV. They do not meet frequently.

In one small group of hostels no committee structure was evolved. The director explained it thus: "These are small units where everyone can express himself. And I have personal knowledge of each resident. There is a direct democracy. In addition each ethnic group and subgroup has its own customary leader – customary chiefs, as we used to call them in Africa – who owes his position to his personal qualities or the position of his family in the village. They are the *sages de leur collectivités.*" However, a year or so earlier there had been difficulties at one of the hostels when some students involved in a language class had tried to mobilize the residents, especially over the question of rent. "This attempt at *autogestion* . . . The Arab understood nothing, was absolutely not ripe for it." Since then the hostel had caused a lot of trouble. In the annual report on this hostel the director commented: "Population composite, souvent antagoniste. Le Foyer se ressent ͻurtout d'une experience d'autogestion qui fut entreprise au début, sous la houlette d'étudiants gauchistes. L'expérience n'a pas duré" (*L'Arche sous l'Arc-en-ciel* No. 88, June 15, 1975:13).

This discussion of the committees – and the reference to the *gauchistes* – raises the question of whether there was opposition to the hostel regime on the part of their residents, and whether groups on the left concerned themselves with the hostels. As to the first question, my impression was of widespread disgruntlement, especially at the attitude of the directors and at the high rents in the larger hostels. Most of the time this did not translate into action. Residents could, after all, still find rooms elsewhere, and in fact there was considerable concern on the part of the authorities at the inability to fill the larger, newer hostels, which were in consequence running at a loss. The program of hostel building led to the opening of several new hostels just as immigration was halted. The "crisis" that led to the return home of some immigrants meant also that there was less pressure on the *garnis*.

In 1975–6, however, there was an important strike movement based on the SONACOTRA hostels in the Paris region that spread in a limited way to the rest of the country. At the height of the dispute a number of strike leaders were deported – literally in the middle of the night (see *Le Monde*, April 18–19, 1976, et seq.). These "expulsions" provoked widespread opposition among both French and immigrant organizations, including those of the left. The Lyon area was affected only slightly. A list of hostels on strike on April 7, 1976, did not include any in the Rhône-Alpes region.* However, as the remarks made at the end of the *métallos'* meeting testify (Event 2), the local CGT, and the PCF, did take up the issues involved, as did a number of *gauchistes* groups who put out a leaflet in French and Arabic entitled "Solidarité avec les travailleurs résidants dans les foyers en lutte."

The strikers' demands, which all groups supported – even if their militants could not always recall them (see Chapter 3, Event 2) – included lowering of rents by 50 percent, and a rent freeze; the legal status of "tenant" for hostel residents (which would give them more protection); freedom for visitors, without regard to

*See "Liste des foyers en grève," p. 7 of "Dossier de Presse," Comité de Co-ordination des Foyers SONACOTRA en Grève, Paris, cyclostyled. See also documents issued by the same organization's *conference de presse* of June 14, 1976, and "Immigration," a supplement to the March–April 1976 issue of ACFAL-CIMADE (Comité Inter-Mouvements auprès des Evacués) *bulletin commun*, Lyon; cyclostyled.

sex; freedom of expression and the right to hold meetings; dismissal of racist directors; and official recognition of the strike coordinating committee.

As I say, the strike made relatively little impression in Lyon, and the action was firmly in the hands of the CGT, through which organization close contact with the dispute was also maintained by the PCF and the Amicale des Algérians en Europe (see references to "Comrade Ch——" in Events 3 and 4). In effect, the CGT intervened on the part of the residents and conducted negotiations at a fairly high level with the hostel administrations. The significance of this material will emerge in later chapters.

CONCLUSION

Let me summarize briefly some of the issues raised by this chapter. First there is the nature of the geographic distribution of immigrants through the urban area. That distribution is not random, and must be understood in large part as a product of the interaction between a housing market affected by urban renewal and local and national policies toward social housing, and a migrant population with a certain ethnic and demographic structure.

Second, because of their relatively different "housing class" situations it was useful to distinguish among migrants between those with families and those without. Regarding the latter, various factors – perhaps above all the needs of urban renewal – have obliged the powers that be to intervene extensively in their housing. The medium chosen for intervention has been organizations such as SONACOTRA and the MTE, both of which represent several elements of the established order, from which they draw their funds and their authority. Included in the foundation of the MTE, for example, were representatives of the central state (prefecture, other government departments), local government (the mayor, the Conseil Général), and local businesses in the engineering and construction industries.

The preferred solution to the problem of the accommodations of the *isolés* is an "institutionalization" of such workers, especially those from North Africa, in organizations the structure and structural situation of which generate further problems. Their relatively high rents provoke pressure for closure of their competitors, the *garnis*. They may also lead to opposition by residents committed to the lowest possible expenditure. Their internal organization and relationship with the surrounding society leads to attempts, more or less unsuccessful, to foster their *animation*. There are also questions of how to control residents' behavior, of whether or not to allow their participation in decision making, and of what form their participation should take.

Responses to these questions illustrate the variant ideological perspectives brought to bear by different groups among the French and among immigrants themselves. *Animation* was a central plank of government policy for hostels and *cités de transit*, as we saw in the meeting reported in Event 1. It reflected the prevailing orthodoxy of liberal-minded intervention based on technical, quasi-scientific, and socioscientific criteria and evidence. The frequently skeptical response of hostel directors to *animation*, and to policies encouraging participation and representation, represents in many ways an older orthodoxy in which the handling of hostel residents is believed to require firmness and authority. Directors' conceptions of immigrant life, and of the social and cultural organization of North Africans in particular, with its emphasis on their "tribal" structure, is part of this. (See further in Chapter 11.)

The situation in the hostels also leads to intervention from the left. The CGT and the *gauchistes* both seek to "act on" the relationship between the hostel management and the residents, but in ways that reflect markedly different conceptions of the form that intervention should take, and what its goals should be. The nature of these differences, and their implications, will emerge more clearly in later chapters.

Having considered the housing of "isolated" males, I turn now to look more closely at the housing problems of families.

5

Housing and the "problems" of immigrant families

IMMIGRANT FAMILIES IN LYON

It is impossible to be precise, but it is indisputable that between 1968 and 1975 there was a significant increase in the numbers of immigrant families in the Lyon area. A comparison of prefecture data for 1969 and 1975 would suggest that the child population of Algerians, Moroccans, Tunisians, and Portuguese rose by more than 50 percent in that period. It is probable, in fact, that the prefecture's count of North African children seriously underestimates the true picture, as does the official figure of about 8,000 North African families in the Rhône for the mid-1970s.

My own best guess of up to 10,500 North African families takes into account marriages established in France between French citizens and foreign spouses – almost all of which involve North African *men* marrying or establishing conjugal households with French *women*. Zehraoui (1971) has estimated that one in six households where the head is an Algerian male were formed by such unions, and this accords reasonably well with census data available for one commune in Lyon (Table 5.1).

Taking together all the available information, including that supplied by the Office National d'Immigration relating to members of Moroccan, Tunisian, and Portuguese families admitted to France, or "regularized" after unofficial entry, it seems likely that between 1968 and 1975 North African families were entering the Rhône at a rate of about a thousand per annum. In addition, in each year some five hundred Portuguese families entered the area. To put this in slightly longer prespective, Mathieu (1961) estimated that there were about 4,500 North African children (mainly Algerian) in the department at the time he wrote. By 1975 there were likely to have been in excess of 35,000.*

*The prefecture provides a figure of 25,883 North African children under sixteen for 1975, in the Rhône (see Table 2.5). The education authorities, however, counted 25,216 children *at school* in September 1975. My own figure of

Table 5.1. *Nationality and domestic status of foreign adult males, commune of "X," Lyon, 1975 (percentage figures across rows, all rows adding to 100.0 percent)*

Nationality	"Bachelors"	Married, wife at "home"	Married, wife in France	Married, wife French	Other[a]
Algerian	14.1	53.7	25.3	5.6	1.3
Moroccan	23.1	38.5	38.5	0.0	0.0
Tunisian	39.5	49.5	11.0	0.0	0.0
All North African	19.4	52.0	23.3	4.2	1.1
Italian	2.5	3.6	50.8	25.4	17.8
Portuguese	0.0	9.1	72.7	9.1	9.1
Spanish	5.9	10.1	67.2	12.6	4.2
All "European"	2.8	6.8	61.0	17.6	11.7
All	11.6	30.5	41.0	10.6	6.2

[a]E.g., mostly adult males living with parental family. However, 5% of Italians (2.3% of all "Europeans") are widowers.
Source: Based on a sample drawn from the 1975 census (unpublished data).

For the purposes of this and the following chapter it will be useful to know how the buildup of the family, in particular the child population, occurs. Typically, the wife and children follow the husband some years after his initial installation in France. Various sources (apart from my own qualitative evidence, see two internal reports by the Service Social Familial Nord-Africain (SSFNA), "L'introduction des familles algériennes dans le département de la Loire," and "Enquête jeunes ménages," both dating from 1971–2) suggest that the North African worker who brings over his family is one who has achieved a measure of social mobility in France, who has, in particular gained stable employment in a factory (as opposed to the construction industry). This is not necessarily decisive, however. I knew many people who had worked in Lyon for fifteen or twenty years with the same firm who had not transferred their families. Leaving aside national and local economic and political factors, in both the receiving society and the sending areas, the domestic situation of the individual may be important. There is often, as it were, a "launch window" for family migration. Two examples may illustrate this.

35,000 includes those at school, those under school age, and those over sixteen who have left school but live with their parents.

Chabanne, a highly skilled, well-paid metalworker, in France since 1961, said: "If I'd known at the beginning that I was going to be in France as long as this, I'd moved my family. But now it's too late." Why too late? Boujema, a Tunisian waiter, suggested a reason. Now in his fifties, he reached France in 1969 after holding a variety of jobs in Tunisia. He has seven children aged between ten and twenty-two, all but the eldest at school. If he now brought his family to France, the children would lose their education, especially in Arabic, which they are acquiring at home.

In the case of Boujema, the timing of his migration in relation to the ages of his children was wrong. In the census data for the commune cited in Table 5.1, half the North African couples had *no* children when they arrived in France, and a further 18 percent had only one or two children under six years of age. The larger, more "mature" families with, for example, two to four children aged six or over on arrival, formed just over a quarter of the total.

If, then, a substantial minority of North African families arrive with children already of school age (six or over), perhaps two-thirds arrive with one or two small children in the preschool age group. Once families are in France, however, the birth rate is high. Nearly three-quarters of all North African children in the commune from which these figures are drawn were actually born in the country. Information from *cités de transit* (Lapraz 1972) suggests that one additional child per family per year is not unusual in the period after arrival. In the commune mentioned previously, there was found a mean of 3.6 children for each North African family, compared with 1.4 in the families of immigrants from Southern Europe.

FAMILIES AND THE HOUSING MARKET

What are the housing prospects of these families? And what part does the French administrative system play in their housing? In the previous chapter we saw that for those with modest incomes the housing market offers a limited choice both of type of accommodation and of its location. The relatively large size of the North African family, in many cases at entry, in most cases subsequently, compared with the French working-class counterpart (with one or two children on average) further restricts choice. As often as not, the solution open to such families is to accept overcrowding. In the old quartier Saint-Clair in the commune of Caluire, the typical household occupied apartments with one or two principal rooms – irrespective of household size. The shortage of suitable accommodations for North African families is itself one of the reasons cited by French sources to explain why migrant workers from North Africa leave their families at home.

Given these circumstances, it is not surprising that *bidonvilles* have flourished around many French cities. As I indicated in Chapter 4, however, there have been no *bidonvilles* proper in Lyon since the late 1960s, though they existed then around the periphery of Lyon city and the suburb of Villeurbanne, for example, on the site of what is now the science-faculty campus of one of the universities.

So, then, if a North African migrant decides to bring his wife and children to France, and succeeds in doing so (itself no mean feat, as we shall see), where can they live? It is theoretically possible, but highly unlikely, for him to secure an HLM apartment before they leave home. In most cases, therefore, recourse must be had to the private sector, initially perhaps to a one- or two-room flat in an inner-city tenement, or suburban village "core." There are also, as I mentioned earlier, a handful of property companies with developments in the eastern suburbs who let to immigrants.

No study of Lyon would be complete without an account of one of these, the "Régie Simon,"* a company owning a development of six large apartment buildings along the rue Olivier de Serres in eastern Villeurbanne. There are some three hundred apartments, almost all let to North Africans, with a total population estimated at up to two thousand people. These apartments were built in the early 1960s with government aid to house *pied noir* families returning from North Africa. To say that Simon skimped on their construction would be more than generous. In any event, the *pied noir* families began to leave almost as soon as they arrived, and as Simon could find no other takers he opened his door to Algerians. Their arrival accelerated the departure of the original residents, and in a short time the buildings were occupied almost

---

*There is a large local literature on the Simon properties. See, in particular, a series of articles in the *Le Progrès de Lyon*, March 1975 and August 1976, and in *Le Point*, December 15, 1975. Also "Olivier de Serres" in *Immigration*, No. 7, November 1977, and, for the earlier events, "Histoire des Immeubles Simon," a cyclostyled tract of May 1972 by Le Comité de Défense des Travailleurs Immigrés de Villeurbanne.

entirely by Arabs. The local primary school has a 100 percent Arab intake. It may be noted that the SONACOTRA organization decided in 1974–5 to build a large hostel with several hundred beds on an adjacent site.

I discuss conditions at the rue Olivier de Serres elsewhere (Grillo 1979) – both the physical state of the buildings and the tenancy conditions imposed on the residents: the high rents, the large sums required as rent in advance, the substantial *caution* (deposit) that is demanded, and so on. It was put to me by a French social worker familiar with the area that the problem for the tenants was not to get into the Régie Simon (as it might be with other private-property companies who turn away Arabs), but to get out. Families desperate for accommodations have found the money, but having done so, for that and other reasons are trapped.

The best chance that most immigrant families have of obtaining reasonably priced decent accommodations is to secure an HLM apartment. One way of doing this is to be rehoused by the authorities because one's home has been demolished or because one can demonstrate an urgent social need. A Tunisian factory worker: "In order to bring your family in, you have to have a decent apartment [see below], but in order to get a decent apartment, you have to have your family here. I came in 1969. I put my name down with the *commission d'habitat* [in his factory], but waited in vain. At first I lived near the Bourse du Travail [IIIrd Arrondissement] with an Algerian. I wouldn't have got a flat if they hadn't knocked a hole in the wall during demolition work. I live at Les Minguettes now [on the ZUP at Vénissieux], in a tower building on the fifteenth floor."

However, direct relocation into an HLM is rare – at least for Arabs. Many first go to a *cité de transit*, settlements providing temporary accommodations for homeless or badly housed families. In Lyon these *cités* are run by three private associations, of which the most important is the Notre-Dame des Sans-Abri (NDSA), which also runs a number of small hostels for single people. The NDSA was founded in the early 1950s by Gabriel Rosset, a teacher, and was originally concerned with homeless men (tramps especially). It now houses some 1,500 families of whom about 600 to 700 are North African, on several dozen sites. The size of the *cités* varies considerably – anything up to a hundred units – as do the conditions: from chalets or Nissen huts to apartment houses of HLM standard.

The NDSA draws its inspiration from the Catholic Church, as perhaps the following comment from a director of one of the *cités* suggests: "The caretaker is a Portuguese. His family and another family came here because they were noticed by two volunteer workers living in appalling conditions. They reported them to Monsieur Rosset, who said take them to ———. A lorry transported their belongings. When they arrived, their eyes opened in wonder. They had moved from hell to paradise. Well, not paradise exactly, because they are only here for a provisional period."

In fact, sojourn in these *cités* may indeed be more than provisional. A survey (Lapraz 1972) discovered that half the families had been in their *cité* for five or more years, and in one site, ten years old, 35 percent had been there since the foundation. NDSA's own figures, as reported annually in their journal, *L'Arche sous l'Arc-en-ciel,* suggest a fifth of the families leave each year, rather fewer than those who enter. There are, however, differences between national groups, for two reasons. First, since chances of being rehoused depend on the availability of suitable accommodations, there is slower movement out on the part of the larger North African families. Second, for reasons to be discussed, families who enter the *cités* from the tenements are considered to need preparation for living in HLM. This applies in particular to those from North Africa. The result is a gradual buildup of large Arab families in the *cités.*

A fairly good *cité de transit* was located at number 83, Avenue de Böhlen in Vaulx Sud, a part of the commune of Vaulx-en-Velin that, as we have seen (Table 4.4), contains a very high proportion of immigrants, many of whom live on the recently constructed ZUP. Avenue de Böhlen is, however, off the ZUP, though it does include a number of HLM buildings, one of which (numbers 85–7) is next door to the *cité de transit.*

The following account (Event 3) is of a meeting of a cell of the PCF, the ruling party in the commune. In the course of the meeting several points emerge concerning conditions in the *cité* and relations between the mainly North African residents and the *cité* management. The meeting also provides evidence for a number of other matters which will be discussed subsequently in this and later chapters.

Event 3: A meeting with the PCF at Vaulx-en-Velin, February 1976

This was a meeting of a local cell of the PCF held jointly with a number of Algerian residents of the *quartier* – the Avenue de Böhlen, in Vaulx Sud.

Participants: Local PCF secretary, plus members; Ch——, K——; one out-sider. Two groups of Algerians: one group of five from HLM (numbers 85–7) and one group from the NDSA *Cité de Transit* (number 83). The meeting was held in a public room in the LOGIREL (Société d'HLM de Logement, Région Lyonnaise) group at number 85–7.

I was among the first to turn up at the meeting. Only two Frenchwomen were present when I arrived. They asked who I was, and I explained that Ch—— had suggested I come. They were not certain they knew him under that name. "Is he of our tendency?" asked the older of the two, who I learned later was a nursing teacher. "I think so." "Is he a Communist?" Again, I thought so, I replied. They asked what I was doing and I explained briefly about the research. They expressed great interest and asked a lot of questions about Britain. "What sort of jobs do *immigrés* in Britain do?" Thinking of West Indians in London, I mentioned bus conductors, gar-bagemen . . . "So they are a subproletariat, then?" I agreed they might be so described.

At this point the nursing teacher suggested preparing the room. "We had better sit here" – indicating a long table – "more like a family." She pulled up additional chairs. Several Algerians began to drift in, and eventually Ch—— made his entrance. "We were expecting Comrade K——," said the nursing teacher. "Well, I'm here," said Ch——. Another Frenchman ar-rived and was introduced to me. He was the cell secretary. A fourth Frenchman was introduced as the secretary of the Fédération des Locataires des Cités de Transit. Altogether, seventeen people attended the meeting, dive Europeans, including the anthropologist, twelve Arabs. Several of the latter sat silent throughout the meeting until the very end.

The secretary opened the meeting by referring to several investigations that had been made at the *cité* (number 83) into damp in the chalets, and into the heating. This had been followed by some correspondence to which he referred, including a letter from the deputy mayor of Vaulx to the director of the NDSA. He read out the reply from NDSA. This letter referred to the preceding correspondence and expressed surprise that anyone should com-plain about the heating being insufficient. This had not been reported by "my inspectors," who had visited the *cité.*

Ch——: "Did anyone see them?" Several interjections of "NO!"

At this point Ch—— translates the gist of the opening remarks and the correspondence into Arabic.

The secretary continues with the NDSA letter: "I myself visited the *cité* once or twice, and seeing that the heating was insufficient, had it repaired. A check was made and it was found that the level of temperature varied between twenty degrees Celsius and twenty-three degrees Celsius, which is a level a little above the legal requirement. However, the temperature at night was not checked." The secretary interpolates some comments on the problems of insulation and ventilation. He returns to the letter, which goes on to refer to the specific problems of particular chalets – a broken radiator, "an accidental, localized failure," which has been repaired, condensation in chalet 9, ventilation in 25 and 26. The letter ends: "The chalets were built in conformity with the regulations in force at the time of their construction."

The secretary then says that a petition has been organized and signed by all, and that the PC has written in reply to the NDSA. He quotes the letter, which refers to the problems of humidity and to the distribution of heating through the chalets. The temperature is normal in the sitting rooms, but not in the other rooms. Their letter also refers to a 10 percent increase in heating costs and concludes that "we Communists" find all this intolerable and support all initiatives taken by the residents.

Comrade K—— (speaking in French) (K—— is an Algerian born in France who is believed by Ch—— to speak poor Arabic. In fact, very occasionally at the meeting he gives some signs of understanding the remarks that are made in Arabic. This surprises one of the Algerians present, who says he thought K—— spoke no Arabic at all. K—— protests that he does): "Regarding the heating, we must continue the battle. They say that the *immigrés* don't know how to use the housing like other people. We must reply to that. All this with the French comrades. But it is up to you to continue to press for improvements."

At this point several of the Algerians intervene to list a number of other matters that need attention at both number 83 and numbers 85–7, including the children's play area.

Secretary: "We have mended the seesaw."

K——: "We must send a delegation to the *société*, to NDSA."

Nursing teacher: "Gabriel Rosset!"

K——: "All the people must go, with the elected representatives."

Ch——: "The residents are being blackmailed. There is a lie in this letter about the inspector who didn't come. Was it not said: 'If you're not happy, go back to Algeria!' The residents now know which are the municipal authorities and the party that really defends the *immigrés*. Take the article in today's *Minute* [an extreme right-wing newspaper]. I was in fact pleased to see that. There has been a certain amelioration with regard to heating and ventilation. The delegation must be prepared immediately among all, or at least the majority of residents. The matter must be noted in the municipal newsletter so that the population know what has been done, what has already been obtained."

Nursing teacher: "It is already done."

Secretary: "There is the matter of the charges for water, two francs seventy-five per cubic meter. I propose that we check the meters at the time the next reading is taken to make sure that the readings are accurate."

Nursing teacher: "It [the water] is very expensive."

K——: "Are there apartment buildings around the house? We must integrate the battle with that concerned with charges [for utilities] and rent. We must unite the population in solidarity. The Commission d'Immigrés has things in hand. What must be discussed is whether later the matter should be passed to a tenants' committee.

Secretary: "What about this proposal to set up a committee?"

Ch——: "As Commissar for Immigration, I think it is premature to hand it over – but nothing should hinder the formation of a committee."

Secretary of the Fédération des Locataires: "There is a problem about creating an association that would be regulated by the law of 1901 and which would be refused registration if it were headed by *étrangers.*"

Ch——: "There is nothing to prevent a committee being formed. One can get around the law."

Nursing teacher: "Why is the water more expensive in the *cité* than in the urban area [COURLY]? Regarding an association, that has some authority in a quartier. Look at our experience in the LOGIREL group at La Balme."

Secretary of the Fédération des Locataires: "But the problem [there] is not the same."

K——: "The best means of defense is to form a Communist Party cell. It is regulated by no law. One has the support of the elected representatives. A committee, it's nothing but that. It's on its own. The cell – one has comrades – French, Portuguese if there are any. And one can take action wherever it is necessary to go. Behind the cell, there's the section, behind the section, the federation. One has brothers."

At this point one of the Algerians intervenes to draw attention to a different matter, which concerns the residents of numbers 85–7: a letter in which certain Algerian residents of the HLM LOGIREL have been attacked. Three anonymous letters have been sent to the police saying that certain Algerians are responsible for breaking trees and causing damage to the grounds, that their children create trouble, that women have been attacked, and that the men possess guns. Four Algerians living in the HLM have been summoned to the police station, where they signed statements denying all this . . . and no arms have been found.

Secretary: "There should be a meeting with the residents."

The nursing teacher reads out a letter from the party cell referring to the contents of these letters. It notes that Algerian children make up only 25 of the 125 in the block – 4 families out of a 100. The letter ends by calling for the *rassemblement de tous les travailleurs.* The letter is to be distributed on Friday.

One of the Algerian residents in the HLM, an old friend of Ch——'s, tells him in Arabic of an incident in which a CRS patrol demanded to see his sixteen-year-old son's papers. The boy was standing on the road not far from the HLM. He had left his papers at home and was fined 60 francs on the spot for not carrying his papers on his person. The patrol was later seen drinking in a café till 1:00 A.M. "Did you get the number of the car?" Ch—— asks. "No, we were afraid."

The secretary tries to bring the discussion back to the letter.

Ch——: "This letter is like the 1940s, when Jews were denounced to the Gestapo."

K——: "You must take your affairs in hand yourselves. One can form a cell that is linked to the section and to the federatiòn. One mustn't think that because the party has the matter in hand, that's enough. The party is not a thing, it is men. How to defend for the future, that's the problem. There are twenty-five percent *immigrés* in the Rhône. You are not alone. We are lucky to have a strong Communist Party in France. Take your affairs in your hands, within the Communist Party."

HLM resident: "But the mayor here even has said: 'Shut the door to immigrants.'" [This is a Communist municipality.]

Ch——: (A lengthy and apparently impressive intervention in Arabic in which he explains the position of the PCF and the situation at Vaulx.)

A resident of the cité: "If one is a Communist, won't the police make trouble? Won't one risk expulsion?"

K——: "They can – but if the mayor says: this man works, he pays his rent . . . I'm not saying that if a man is stopped by the police, he should produce his party card, but if he hands out leaflets at a market with other comrades, the police can't do anything. And then an expulsion order has to be signed by the minister of the interior. One is allowed fifteen days, and a lot can be done in fifteen days."

Ch—— translates into Arabic, concluding in French: "Liberty, that is one of the Communist Party's demands. Of course, you mustn't shout your membership of the Communist Party from the rooftops, but in the Communist Party you have the support of [your] class. You shouldn't say simply: 'I am an *immigré.*'"

Resident of the cité: "But we don't have the right to take part in politics."

Ch——: (fiercely): "Who says that?"

Resident: "Weren't people expelled at the time of the oil crisis?"

Ch——: "Not a single Communist was expelled."

K——: "The capitalists want to divide the immigrant workers from the French workers."

About now the meeting starts to break up into small groups who continue discussing with one another. The secretary produces some application forms for membership of the PCF and lays them on the table. Two elderly men sitting near the secretary show him some pink slips of paper – their latest bills for water. The secretary looks at them and announces, "It's beginning all over again." Ch—— explains in Arabic about the previous decision to check the water meters.

Secretary: "The Communist Party will not leave the matter as it is. We should send the cell's letter regarding LOGIREL to the mayor and to the public prosecutor."

K—— puts in another plea for the Communist Party, repeating his earlier remarks. Three or four of the application forms are picked up and signed.

About a fortnight later, when I revisited the area, I saw the following poster issued by the PCF. Protesting against a recent bomb attack on the Air Algérie office in Lyon, and a statement on unemployment by the prime minister, it continued:

> Il est nécessaire de lutter ensemble pour les revendications et contre le pouvoir, pour le renforcement et de la communauté d'intérêts. La Fédération du Rhône renouvelle aux travailleurs algériens, à l'Amicale des Algériens en Europe et au gouvernement algégrien sa solidarité pour mettre en échec avec tous les démocrates, les forces de la réaction nationale et internationale qui veulent s'opposer aux progrès de nos deux peuples, de notre classe ouvrière en France et en Algérie. Contre le racisme, pour une politique démocratique de l'immigration, j'adhère au PCF.

THE "INTRODUCTION" OF IMMIGRANT FAMILIES

It is often said on all sides that the ideal solution to the housing problems of an immigrant family is an HLM apartment. To obtain such an apartment entails a complex process. Before we consider that process, however, it is necessary to say something about the role of accommodations in the system by which families are legally admitted to France.

The procedure to be followed if a worker wishes legally to "introduce" his family into France, or to have an unauthorized family entry retrospectively "regularized," involves at various points the prefecture, the police, the local authorities and social services, and the ONI. The worker who is in France applies first to the Action Sociale branch of the Direction Départementale de l'Action Sanitaire et Sociale (universally known as the DDASS), producing a residence permit, a work permit, a marriage certificate, a *livret de famille*, proof of resources (e.g., pay slip), and proof of accommodations. The application is then subject to inquiries on the part of the DDASS, undertaken by the *assistant[e]s de secteur* and the police. If reports are favorable, the dossier is now (since 1974) sent to ONI in Paris, from where further inquiries are undertaken in the home country. Medical checks and the issuing of documents is the responsibility of ONI bureaus in the country concerned. There is a special procedure for Algerians and black Africans, who apply directly to the mayor of the commune in which they wish to reside. The mayor gives his opinion and passes the dossier to the prefecture, whence it is passed to the DDASS, and so on.

The DDASS inquiries establish the "utility" of allowing the entry of the family, and its "adaptive capacity": Can the family live in France as other families of the same ethnic group, or even as the French? The inquiry verifies the relationship of the applicant to his family (in polygamous households only the senior wife would be admitted), and only direct dependents are permitted to enter. The "professional stability" of the applicant is assessed. The proposed accommodation is vetted: Is it clean, not too expensive, and so on?

The DDASS social workers unanimously dislike undertaking these inquiries, which some informants likened to police work that "warps the relations with the clients." Some suggested that they never provided an unfavorable opinion, though if the apartment was obviously unsatisfactory, they might "block the dossier" until the applicant found something better. Others, while maintaining their reservations, do go further: "I try to see how far the husband understands the problem and how far he will help the adaptation of his wife to French life. I try to get him to think about the future of his wife in France, and consider whether his wife might adapt badly. In my sector, three or four years ago, we had an influx of young Moroccan wives who stay in their own homes and are completely isolated." After "introduction," families are systematically followed up by the social workers "to help with adaptation."

Social workers are also involved in applications for HLM. Anyone who fulfils certain (minimum) income requirements is entitled to apply for an HLM. French families apply directly to one or another of the *sociétés* or *offices;* all applications from foreigners in the Rhône Department, however, go through the prefecture and in addition have to be made via one of two private social welfare organizations – the Service Social Familial Nord Africain (SSFNA) for Algerians and the Service Social d'Aide aux Emigrants (SSAE) for others. At the prefectures successful applications are placed on a waiting list, from which persons are nominated when the HLM notify a vacancy.

In 1973–4 the SSFNA in the Rhône handled 950 applications and complained that "consulting hours have become housing-application sessions." Each application may require several meetings if it is to be fully vetted. In one sector, of 290 applications, 56 were found to be inadmissible (family not in France, or in France clandestinely), 14 were forwarded to the prefecture as urgent cases, and 35 were directed toward the associations running the *cités de transit*. Overwhelmed by this work, the SSFNA withdrew from the procedure, claiming it was outside their terms of reference (SSFNA Rhône Report 1974).

Despite the centralization of applications, the ordinary DDASS social workers also find much of their time taken up with housing applications, as do the *cités de transit*, who forward applications on behalf of their residents directly to the prefecture. One *cité* director remarked, commenting on the attitude of the HLM, who also undertake their own inquiries: "The HLM control property. That means they choose families because they will pose few problems for them: regular salary, sufficient salary, sufficient furniture in the existing apartment, apartment well-maintained. Morality of the family: good payers at the shops, no history of quarrels with neighbors or in the quartier, husband and wife married, not living in concubinage. I think sometimes the HLM are too demanding. When we propose a family to an HLM, we provide a guarantee." What sort of guarantee that is, we shall see.

Even if an applicant successfully negotiates all the bureaucratic hurdles, and also finds a suitable apartment, or is placed high on the HLM waiting list, there is no certainty that he and his family will be permitted to enter his chosen area.

THE *SEUIL DE TOLERANCE*

We saw earlier that the process of urban development and the operations of the housing market have produced areas in which there is a high density of immigrants. For the French the significance of these areas of concentration varies according to the nationality of the groups involved and their demographic structure, but in the first instance their very existence is considered a matter of concern (see remarks made at the minister's meeting in Event 1 and at the PCF cell meeting in Event 3).

Justification for this concern was found in what was frequently cited to me as the "sociological law of the threshold of tolerance" (with which it was sometimes assumed I would be familiar). This "law" had wide currency in official and unofficial circles, and though some skeptics could be found, many people accepted its validity. It states that beyond a certain "threshold" (which was put variously by informants at anything between 5 percent and 20 percent of the population) the French react against a foreign presence in their midst. The basis for this "law" was a study published in 1971 by the highly respected social scientist Alain Girard (Girard 1971; cf. Girard and Stoetzel 1953), which explored attitudes toward foreigners in a small French town. The main findings, detached from the original context, were set out in an interdepartmental government bulletin as follows:

> Seuils de tolérance: les seuils moyens sont de 15% d'étrangers dans une ville de 5,000 habitants, et 18% dans un ensemble de 100 logements. Mais la moitié des personnes (médiane) indique un seuil inférieur (respectivement 9 et 10%). Pour l'école, on considère que la classe serait gênée a partir de 8 élèves sur 30. On retirerait l'enfant de l'école à partir d'un effectif du tiers.   [Fleury 1972]

It was this recension of a serious psychological study that entered official circles and the public arena, in particular through the speeches of Monsieur Michel Massenet, a senior government member (Freeman 1979:157–60; Silber 1973). By 1975, references to this so-called law abounded.

I am not concerned here with the validity of these propositions. For our purposes it is sufficient that they were widely held to be true and were employed as a justification for policy. In official circles the key figure was held to be 15 percent foreigners in a population, though a supplementary figure of 5 percent for North Africans was also used. Table 5.2 indicates the numbers of quartiers in each area of the *agglomération* that had passed the general threshold.

One way in which the prefecture uses the 15 percent figure is to insist that those HLM with low proportions of foreigners should take more. Levels should generally be brought *up* to the threshold – the maximum has become the norm. The second is in a procedure, which in 1975, at least, was, I believe, unique to the Rhône, whereby the prefecture, in conjunction with the commune authorities, can forbid the introduction of families into certain areas. The prefecture had in fact begun to do this as early as 1970 (Arrêté of June 15, 1970) by designating certain quartiers defined by reference to the school catchment areas. The first area so defined was that around the rue Olivier de Serres in Villeurbanne, but fairly rapidly other streets and whole quartiers, and

Table 5.2. *Proportion of quartiers with 15%+ foreigners,*
by main urban areas

Area	(Total) Quartiers	Quartiers with 15%+ foreigners	% quartiers with 15%+ foreigners
Lyon	78	16	20.5
East	23	10	43.5
S'east	30	17	56.7
S'west	15	3	20.0
West	16	0	0
North	14	0	0
Total	176	46	26.1

eventually whole communes, were added. By 1975–6 there was a race among local politicians to ensure that one's own bailiwick was on the list, with the result that extremely few places remained where an immigrant could obtain accommodations for the introduction of his family.

It should be emphasized that these regulations apply to the *introduction* of families in France. Their movements after arrival in the country are controlled only indirectly, through the processing of HLM applications. It was in the distribution of the successful applicants that the communes, particularly those in the eastern areas, where the ZUPs are located, exerted political pressure in 1975–6. In an article entitled "SOS ZUP" that appeared in the *Le Progrès de Lyon* (December 18, 1975), the communist mayor and parliamentary deputy of Vénissieux, Monsieur Houël, referring to the large numbers of foreigners in his commune, was reported as saying: "Quant à nous, la solution réside dans une meilleure et plus équitable répartition de ces familles. Il n'y a pas que Les Minguettes ou les ZUP! Pourquoi ne pas en loger ailleurs, mais décemment." Other local politicians and officials at Vénissieux and at Vaulx-en-Velin (see Event 3) supported this argument: "One of the things we have had to struggle against was the wave of *étrangers*. This is not because we are against foreigners. It is against their own interests for the percentage to go above a certain point. When this happens, the French move out, more *immigrés* move in, and the result is a ghetto." But, this informant added, "It was the prefecture that forbade us to introduce families. The government, yours and mine, brings workers here to be pro-

ducers, to create surplus value. Families don't interest the capitalists. If the families are here, they are a charge on the state. The
government has no interest in letting families flourish."

Thus the communes deflect responsibility to the prefecture (or
the government or the capitalist system), and the prefecture
pleads pressure from local politicians. And immigrants make the
round of the offices: "C'est toujours la même musique," commented one weary applicant.

THE "PROBLEMS" OF IMMIGRANTS IN THE RESIDENTIAL CONTEXT

Discussion of the *seuil de tolérance* indicated a major problem
posed for the French by the presence in their midst of immigrant
families, especially those from North Africa: the possibility of
what is often termed "ghettoization." There is also concern at
what is generally called the "adaptability" (or "integrative" or "as-
similative" or "evolutionary" capacity) of such families. As we
have already observed, this is something social workers are required to evaluate in their assessment of applications for family
admission. The two phenomena are often linked, as we shall see.
First, however, let us take ghettoization.

The use of the term *isolés* for single male migrants refers, of
course, to the fact that they are in France on their own, without
families. But it may also imply standing aloof from the receiving
society. As we saw, for some people the aims of *animation* included
the establishment of links between hostel residents and the
(French) residents of the local quartiers. Many informants, in fact,
had views on the "separateness" of immigrants from French society that at times seemed to amount to an obsession. Such views are
found both on the right and on the left – for example in the CGT
(and PCF) emphasis on the "community of interest" of French
and immigrant workers. The imagery of the vocabulary employed, especially by social workers, contains many terms referring to "openness" and "closedness": *ouverture* (understand, *d'esprit*), *sortir* (used in both a physical and social sense), *enfermé, repli
sur soi*. An *éducateur* (see Chapter 6) talking about North African
youths used *épanouir*, which means "cause to open out like a
flower."

So far as the single migrants are concerned, the majority of
hostel directors would probably accept that the North Africans
"like to enclose themselves in tribal structures" (hostel director) or

"like to live in tribal groups" (prefecture official), and leave it at that. With families it is different. The fear of creating enclosed, self-contained concentrations of North African families – ghettoization – was one of the factors that led the prefecture, and through the prefecture the communes and the HLM, to attempt a greater dispersal of the foreign population and to prevent the creation of more areas like the rue Olivier de Serres:

> Des immeubles où aurait passé la guerre: vitres cassées, volets arrachés, fenêtres aveugles ou béantes . . . Mais les draps pendent au balcon et claquent joyeusement au vent clair du mois d'août. Ce sont des ruines modernes. On y campe. C'est un camp d'immigrés. Trois mille personnes. Ou deux mille, on ne sait: il y a tant de va-et-vient! Bien sûr les enfants grouillent dans les ruelles. Ils sortent des couloirs comme une nuée de mouches. Quelques jeunes, muets, l'épaule contre un mur montent la garde. C'est un ghetto. [*Le Progrès de Lyon*, August 9, 1976]

In this article (which was entitled, correctly in my view, "Ces ghettos que *nous* frabriquons" – my emphasis), the author, Paul Gravillon, lays great stress on the physical degradation of the area, and on the violence associated with the quartier. ("Quant aux policiers, ils ne se hasardent pas la nuit, sauf evidemment en cas d'urgence. 'C'est Chicago,' dit-on.") The local authorities, especially the communist ones, emphasize the costs that a high proportion of immigrants forces the communes to meet: "Foreign families are the most deprived, with the lowest wages. They call on financial aid more than other families." Thus the areas with "ghettos," mainly themselves working class, have to bear a disproportionate amount of the financing of immigration.

If one consequence of concentration is seen to be the creation of degraded (and administratively costly) "no-go" areas, another is thought to be the additional problems posed for the "adaptation" of the families. This theme runs through many SSFNA reports. It is one of long standing. Thus the SSFNA Annual Report for 1958–9 referred to the grouping of families of Algerian origin as "un obstacle direct à l'évolution des jeunes femmes." In 1967–8 a report on a *cité de transit* noted that family members

> ont resserré les liens entre elles et avec la communauté musulmane du bidonville, y retrouvant tout un ensemble de traditions, un mode de vie patriarcal avec des chefs de clan responsables, une vie en circuit fermé, même sur le plan économique. . . . Il est important de faire remarquer à quel point les regroupements de cette sorte reduisent ou détruisent même les possibilités d'adaptation.

This at once raises the question of what is meant by "adaptation": to what and from what? An understanding of this and allied terms must begin with the contrast – or rather the perception of a contrast – between the "traditional" life of immigrants in their countries of origin, and the life-style of the receiving society. This contrast is a central element in the discourse within which the problems of immigrant families are discussed. The opening statement in the ACFAL debate on "cultural identity" (see Chapter 8, Event 4) and other remarks in the course of that debate illustrate this quite clearly. If the distinction is widely made, however, its evaluation varies considerably: "The type of person one gets in a *cité de transit* is a manual worker – intellectuals don't come to us – who is not cultivated, who is simple. For example, the Portuguese worker from a farm, a peasant, from a situation where people live very differently from the way one does in large apartment blocks in a big city. There are some from cities, but there is no comparison between a city in North Africa and a city in France. It is necessary, therefore, to give them support, to teach them neighborly relations. This is not racism. It is only a question of personality. The aim is to round out the men morally, and teach the women to cook and sew. It is necessary to prepare people for cohabitation, to train them so that they can be admitted into an HLM. Regarding the *aides familiales,* the main area of their intervention is in regard to the female role, so that the mother fulfills her role as mistress of the house. One is trying to get them to the stage where they can live in France. The residents are manual workers, at the level of beginners in the culture. They are still primary, primitive even. The ones that give most difficulty are those who arrive directly in France. My wife tells me that fifteen years ago it was the Italians and Spanish who gave most difficulty. Now they speak French, they look like Frenchmen. These days it is the Portuguese and the North Africans. But the Arab, with the typical Arab features, remains an Arab" (a director of NDSA).

The SSFNA Rhône Report for 1974 (p. 4) commented on:

> Visites à domiciles, à ces femmes maghrébines traditionellement tenues à rester au foyer sans contact avec l'extérieur. . . . S'il est moins fréquent actuellement de rencontrer les situations extrêmes d'ignorance et de claustration des femmes courantes il y a 20 ans, s'il est vrai que la population féminine primo-arrivant plus jeune semble plus rapidement adaptable, il n'en demeure pas moins que la majorité des familles quittent sans transition un mode de vie traditionnel et presque toujours

rural, pour passer dans un monde "étrange" que ni leur mentalité, ni leur éducation, ni leur entourage immédiat ne les incitent à affronter directement. De plus la plupart ne parlent pas français n'ont pas été scolarisées, et ont la tendance à se replier sur elles-mêmes.

Leaving aside the remarks specifically concerning women, to which we return subsequently, concern about "adaptation" focuses on three areas: adherence to what are sometimes seen as shocking customary practices; hygiene; and noise, especially the noise of children. All three elements were contained in the sentiments of the housing official cited in Chapter 3. The "sheep in the bath" is an often quoted example: "Que dire aussi de certains comportement?! Le 26 janvier dernier, à l'occasion de l'Aid-el-kebir, n'avons-nous pas encore appris que des moutons avaient été sacrifié en pleine ville au grand scandale du voisinage indigne et écoeuré" (SSFNA Loire Report 1971–2). The contrasting styles of bringing up children also provoke comment. They are at once too severe ("Leurs sanctions nous paraîtront barbares – frotter les lèvres d'un enfant au piment. Elles n'imaginent ni la cruauté, ni les conséquences"), and not strict enough ("absence de discipline, un bébé pleure, il se trouve toujours des bras pour le bercer"). Both comments may be found in the same paragraph of Annex 1 to the SSFNA Annual Report of 1972–3.

Popular opinion frequently associates Arab families with dirt. A Spanish immigrant woman remarked to my wife when they were passing through the Place du Pont area: "I wouldn't come here alone, I'm frightened of them. They're dirty. My parents brought me up to consider them dirty and have nothing to do with them. They don't know how to live properly. My daughter had Arab friends at school, but I didn't like it. I've seen the women come to the school. They are incredibly fat and dirty. Never comb their hair. The children too are dirty and unkempt. I apologize for my attitude, but that's the way I was brought up." Comrade Ch—— (from Event 3), himself an Algerian, referred to the problems of "Women straight from a *douar,* used to doing her business in the fields, who does not know how to keep a bathroom or toilet clean."

The lack of discipline among these large North African families is often thought to be the cause of one frequent source of complaint: their noisiness. "There is a family living in my quartier whose children make a lot of noise. People complain, and who could blame them? Their complaints are not racist, they're directed at the noise. The social workers tell me that they have tried to give advice to Arab parents, but it's ignored." Sometimes their noisiness is associated with the idea that they "like to live out of doors." Often the noise is said to be particularly marked at the time of Ramadan or on the occasion of annual religious feasts.

For these and other reasons, then, the unrestricted admission of large numbers of immigrant – especially North African – families to a quartier is believed to create focuses for potentially hostile relations with the French, or leads to the rapid withdrawal of the French from the area, creating ghettos in the true sense. The physical and social environment of the ZUPs (Les Minguettes at Vénissieux consists mainly of large fifteen-story tower buildings with sixty apartments in a building) is thought to be difficult enough as it is. Therefore immigrant families must, as the NDSA director put it, "be prepared for cohabitation," trained to live in an HLM. Such preparation is the objective of what is termed "action socio-educative."

"*ACTION SOCIO-EDUCATIVE*" AMONG IMMIGRANT FAMILIES

"Notre but dans cette Cité est aussi de faciliter à nos locataires 'temporaires' leur passage dans un logement définitif, en essayant de leur inculquer les principes de l'habitation en immeuble collectif" (Gabriel Rosset in *L'Arche sous l'Arc-en-Ciel* No. 84, May 15, 1974, p. 6).

Faced with the perceived problems outlined in the previous section, a number of organizations undertake a sort of remedial action. This takes a number of forms, which differ somewhat according to the organization involved. I will refer to the work of three associations: the NDSA and PACT (Centre de Propagande de l'Action Contre le Taudis), both of which run *cités de transit*, and the SSFNA.

The remark of Gabriel Rosset, and the comments of the NDSA director cited earlier, indicate what the NDSA sees as its goal – the training and preparation of families for living in French apartment buildings. In fact, this is the goal assigned to such organizations by government: "Cités de Transit peuvent être définies comme des ensembles d'habitation affectées au logement provisoire des familles, occupantes à titre précaire, dont l'accès en habitat definitif ne peut être envisagé sans une action socio-educative destinée à favoriser leur insertion sociale et leur promotion" (*Journal Officiel*, July 20, 1972; circular of April 19, 1972). Such families, it is argued, will have spent years in substandard accommodations before entering a *cité*. Therefore, "Il est impossible d'estimer le temps nécessaire pour une remise en condition de 'santé' physique et psychique de ces familles que ne sont pas a considérer commes des simples 'mal logés' à reloger, mais comme des familles gravement perturbées par leurs années passée" (Lapraz 1972:28). Later, Lapraz refers to them as "convalescents."

In his study, which was a report on and for the NDSA, Lapraz contrasts two sample Algerian families of roughly the same size and condition. The first: "Présente un logement propre, bien rangé: lits avec draps propres, appartement decoré, plantes vertes, fleurs artificielles, TV, mobiliers de salle à manger... chambre à coucher... en contre-plaqué avec enjolivures. Le ménage est organisé, les enfants contrôlés: une pièce est affectée à leurs jeux. La cuisine est restée algérienne, mais le foyer dispose d'une voiture avec laquelle homme et femme vont faire ensemble les achats dans les supermarchés." The second:

> Présentait déjà après 4 mois d'occupation un appartement très dégradé: murs sales et tâchés de graisse sur les tapisseries, sol non nettoyé. Quelques essais de décoration cependant: gravures de fleurs sur les murs. Un mobilier très sommaire: presque pas de meubles, un buffet en formica dans la cuisine. Literie très sommaire, à même le sol, avec des parasites. Les enfants ont été plusieurs fois renvoyé de l'école pour désinfection de la téte; ils jouissent d'une totale liberté et ont causé plusieurs blessures par jet de cailloux; les escaliers, caves, couloirs leur tiennent lieu de WC.   [Lapraz 1972:130]

The objective is to encourage families of the first kind, and not just in matters of hygiene. A whole life-style is involved. The NDSA journal lists the kind of "intervention" made by their socio-educative service (*L'Arche sous l'arc-en-Ciel* No. 84, May 15, 1974, pp. 9–10): *Household:* arrangement of furnishings, cleaning, airing, disinfection, making the home "agreeable." Making up bedcovers and curtains. *Budget:* sorting out family expenditure. "L'aide familiale... engage la grande fille indolente à chercher un emploi." *Child care and upbringing. Harmony in family relations:* "Les filles maghrébines se révoltent contre les projets que nourrit leur père de les marier. L'aide familiale essaie de raisonner les uns et les autres. . . . Un père étant parti seul depuis deux mois en Algérie, elle lui ècrit de rentrer." *Relations with neighbors* and *Helping with administrative matters* also engage their attention.

Lapraz (1972:145–8) suggests that there are three "thresholds of evolution" of such families:

1. *Apprentissages matériels:* learning about housing, household equipment and tasks, the payment of rent regularly, and the organization of budgets. Then about school, the rhythm of work and of urban life. Then about the administrative system.

2. *Ouverture culturelle:* literacy, education, and skilled training.

3. *Participation sociale:* relations with groups in the quartier, participation in parent-teacher associations and trade unions. This is described as *l'indice le plus parlant de* l'INSERTION *dans une communauté.*

In this style of approach a whole process of cultural transformation may be effected. One thing leads to another: "L'apprentissage matériels peuvent être des acheminements à une ouverture culturelle." The end result allows families "s'enraciner et de s'épanouir dans un univers culturel qui sera le leur." (Note once again the image of "opening up.")

The idea that something grand emerges from something simple appeared in the material on *animation* discussed in Chapter 4. The director of a PACT *cité* put it this way: "For us a contract [i.e., for the apartment] is not just a means of getting a key. It is a means of dialogue. To create an apartment building, to run it, that's the job of the property company. Our task is to run the *cité* in such a way as to be a sort of link between the families and the 'social equipment.' Running the *cité* provides a privileged contact with families – through the collection of rent, discipline, imposing respect for the buildings. This is a means of contact with the families. A property company puts people out. We get people to respect their contracts, pay rent, observe discipline. But at the same time we can discuss with families why they have difficulty with the rent, why the apartment is badly looked after. We can give them advice on how to look after their money and belongings, telling them that the next landlord will be different. These are people who lack understanding of how to budget. They are badly prepared for living in a consumer society."

Although social work in a *cité de transit* is aimed at a specific clientele whose problems are thought to be especially acute, organizations such as the SSFNA – who undertake socio-educative action alongside their usual activity of "following difficult family situations" – entertain similar goals when dealing with the more general run of North African clients. In theory, the SSFNA distinguishes three sorts of collective action: *action socio-éducative en groupe, cours d'économie sociale et familiale,* and *regroupement à domicile.* In practice the first two are the same and the third scarcely exists in Lyon. The *regroupements* (small meetings involving two or three women in the home) are said to be difficult to organize, and the equipment (e.g., sewing machines) awkward to move from house to house. The "courses" therefore tend to involve largish groups of women and are held in public halls.

The subject matter of these courses is similar to that encountered in the work of the NDSA: household tasks (cooking and sewing etc.), and family organization. The SSFNA describes these as "basic techniques and knowledge that allow the participants to have access to a real autonomy." The courses touch relatively few people – the average attendance in one quartier of Vaulx-en-Velin was put at nine, with thirteen or so attending in another quartier. It is, however, their aim and content that are of interest here.

The SSFNA is less concerned with preparing families to move to an HLM (as is the NDSA) than with helping them once in situ. In 1971–2, when the ZUP at Vaulx-en-Velin took in its first residents, the SSFNA was assigned a role in the reception of North African families: "The reception of families is the first step in a good *insertion*." The SSFNA *monitrices* "rat-tatted on every door" where they were informed that a North African family lived. About two hundred families were contacted in this way, and others made direct contact on their own initiative.

The SSFNA assistant responsible for the operation described their task: "In the first stage the families faced a break with the old milieu [in the city center] in which they lived. The conditions were better in the ZUP, they had a smashing apartment, but in the old quartiers they had contact with their neighbors, shopkeepers, and so on. They were afraid of the much more parcellated (*cloisonné*) milieu of the ZUP. There was also at that stage a lack of facilities. The first step, then, was to make contact. The second stage was more materially based. It was a stage of learning, of finding out what existed, of the structure of the services. We also gave help with household equipment, advice on choice of materials for furnishing, on hire purchase. Help also with establishing contacts with other people. The third stage involved a collective response, group socio-educative action, to allow the women as quickly as possible to participate in collective activities [i.e. in the community at large]."

The advice provided by the SSFNA to North African families is available to others (French and immigrant) from specialist organizations such as the Groupement Social de l'Hygiène et de l'Habitat (GSHH). At Vénissieux, Vaulx-en-Velin, and Décines the GSHH operates six units in apartments offering courses concerned with household decoration and cooking. Very few foreigners attend their sessions, apart from Italians ("But they are French"). The GSHH felt that Arab families were more demanding and required a special type of training. They therefore left them to the SSFNA. "After a few years, when they become more *évoluées*, they try to join in."

From the SSFNA's point of view, the three types of socio-educative action listed earlier represent progressive stages (just as the three stages in the reception of families on the ZUP were said to "follow on one from another"). For example, in 1975 the SSFNA assistant at Vénissieux was proposing for the following season one course for older women, age thirty through forty, "who want only dressmaking, knitting, and cooking," and one for younger women who are "much more *evoluées* and educated and who want and need more structured courses." She proposed for them anatomy, sexual education, and pregnancy ("They know absolutely nothing about the growth of a fetus. It is a mystery to them"). She also drew a distinction between those who actually come to courses, and the "serious cases" with whom they have contact because they are "signaled" by another service. The following example illustrates what may happen then.

In the Ière Tranche at Vénissieux there lived a North African family of Berber origin. The wife was about twenty-five and had five children. Neighbors in their building had complained to the *société* HLM, and, at the HLM's suggestion, to a DDASS social worker, about the filthy conditions in which the family lived. The apartment stank, the children "not brought up at all did their business all over the place, slept on mattresses on the floor, wet their beds, and so on." The DDASS social worker said that the "filth was appalling, without parallel." When it was discovered that the wife knew no French (and little Arabic), the DDASS "signaled" the SSFNA, who sent their Arabic-speaking nurse to explain to the woman that she should keep the apartment clean. It was reported that the wife thought the house was clean. At that point the school intervened. The school nurse rang the SSFNA to say that the children could not be kept at school. They were in the corridor now, but they could not stay at school. The DDASS social worker now visited the father, who had two jobs and was not often at home. There was no problem of money or lack of affection, it was considered, and moreover "the father was in agreement with us. He thought the house filthy too." The various assistants felt they had to obtain the agreement of the wife, "so as not to damage her self-respect." The SSFNA and DDASS assistants planned their campaign: "Our mission was to transform the woman, to make her suitable to live in France in an HLM." The father was given a list of cleaning materials, which he agreed to purchase, and the assistants assembled at the apartment to help the woman clean it. The husband was described as "very likable, very clean in his person." The wife: "She was overcome by events. She had come straight from the *bled* [countryside] to Lyon and had never acquired the habit of taking herself into her own hands."

With such a woman the next step might be to bring her together with others in a *regroupement à domicile,* and eventually bring her out of the home to the courses. These courses are for those "éléments ayant atteints un premier palier et désirant poursuivre, et jeunes femmes récemment arrivées, plus ouvertes. . . . Le cours est l'étape de mise a l'aise pour approcher la structure prévue pour les mères de familles françaises du quartier" (SSFNA Rhone Report 1974, p. 6). The aim is to make the woman, and the family, "autonomous, beyond the need for our service," and able to present their own problems in residents' committees, parent-teacher associations, and the other institutions that make up the life of the quartier. That is what *insertion* means.

SOME PRELIMINARY CONCLUSIONS

At the risk of repetition, let me summarize what has emerged so far. The economic growth of Lyon has required a substantial immigrant labor force. A major factor in economic growth has been urban renewal, which has entailed the reconstruction of inner-city areas and a movement of population to the suburbs. Immigrants, especially North Africans, have been affected in that the housing market has forced them to seek accommodations in precisely those areas most touched by urban renewal. As these areas are closed, they have been forced into various kinds of institutional accommodations: hostels, *cités de transit*, HLM, ZUPs. At both ends of the chain the process creates concentrations of population that are "abnormal" from the viewpoint of the receiving society. Concentrations of families, ultimately ghettoization, pose special problems because of pressure on welfare resources, schools, and so on, and because of the social environment they are believed to create (noise, dirt, obnoxious customs, and so on). In large numbers they push the French over the "threshold of tolerance," a concept that in origin is a descriptive one but that has "trickled down" into administrative and political circles in a prescriptive form.

The difficult, if not impossible, housing situation of many immigrant families very rarely, in Lyon, gives rise to the kind of local political mobilization that Castells (1976c) and Olives (1976) report as occurring in Paris. The one major exception to this was a campaign by a consortium of leftist groups in the rue Olivier de Serres in the early 1970s (see Grillo 1979). It does, however, pose a serious political problem for the French.

The dilemma of the PCF is particularly acute. In Communist Party strongholds the local authorities often express the view that immigrants and others have been foisted on them, to their political embarrassment. For example, a senior official at Vénissieux remarked: "Since 1968, we and Vaulx-en-Velin have received large numbers of people rejected by the big city in the urban-renewal program. These were not people we would have chosen to come: large families, foreigners, social cases – single-parent families and other categories of people with problems – the poor. These people are marginal." Insofar as ordinary French people are hostile to immigrants, that is to say, express racist attitudes, PCF politicians are caught between the demands of their ideals and the realities of their constituents, in the same way that CGT activists are squeezed by what is felt to be the racism of their members in the factories (see Event 2 and Chapter 9). Meetings of the kind held by the PCF cell at Vaulx Sud (Event 3) represent one kind of attempt to resolve this dilemma. The position taken by the PCF during the 1981 presidential election, when in effect it succumbed to racism, represented the other side of the same coin.

To combat the problems associated with concentrations of immigrants and their life-styles, the authorities have intervened to a considerable extent in the allocation of housing. They have also attempted through *animation* and *action socio-éducative* to intervene in the life-styles of both "isolated" males and families, often through the auspices of specialized private associations such as the Catholic NDSAA and the SSFNA, whose work is supported out of public funds.

Critics of NDSA and SSFNA characterize them as "paternalist," though it may be added that "at the base" a number of their workers are "very motivated, very politicized," and exempt from this criticism. There are some avowedly radical groupings who also participate in socio-educative action, but it cannot be said that on the surface their practices differ markedly from those of the NDSA and the SSFNA, even if the aims are subtly different. One such group, attached to a social center, located in a PACT *cité de transit*, explained these as follows. "The women must gain a certain autonomy through the courses. We refuse to be a place where people just consume. There must be possibilities for autonomy. We stress quality of presence rather than amount. At the center is a reception desk. We could just fill in their forms and so on, but we give them an outline of the structure that exists. It is not up to *us* to do things for them. The important thing is that we make people conscious of their exploitation, of the fact that there are means. There is now a tenants' association that is beginning to ask questions. It is very active in the running of the center. The aim is that people take charge of their own *animation;* that they themselves become responsible for the *quartier*. *Animation* is not the *crèche*, not the services. Behind this is the chance for women to express their actual situation. In the literacy class the *monitrice* [an Algerian] directs the women's attention toward the female condition, so that they take control of themselves, become aware of this condition."

Another person involved with this center put it this way: "One tries to animate the group so that at the end of 240 hours' [course time] there is a progressive autonomy of the women. Among immigrants in their own country there is a collective organization that is important. Here life does not blossom, it degenerates. The immigrant woman has a double alienation, as woman and as immigrant. She is the wife in a Mediterranean couple. This may work over there, with the support of other relatives, but in France all that remains is repression. They liberate themselves through prostitution. One starts with dressmaking and so on, which is what the women demand. The immigrant women don't want to become militants of women's lib. They want to make clothes for their kids to save money. One tries to exploit that to the maximum. From then on, one tries to find a way for them to become mistresses of their own situation, to become conscious."

In this discourse what is sometimes called *ouverture d'esprit* (or *ouverture culturelle*) is termed *prise de conscience*. Both concepts, however, are applied to the same segment of the population – North African women – and indicate a potential resolution of what are considered to be their special problems. The next chapter explores this in more detail.

6

North African women and the French social services

In Chapter 5 we began to focus on French perceptions of the situation of the wife and of the children in immigrant households. This chapter continues that discussion, paying particular attention to the part played by the French social services in the management of what are conceived to be the problems of the North African woman in France. The first part of the chapter provides an outline account of the structure of the social services. The second part looks at what are termed the "problems of the couple" and is concerned with the North African woman in her roles as wife and mother. The third part focuses on younger women, particularly those in their midteens, and is concerned especially with the father-daughter relationship. The discussion in that section will lead on to Chapter 7, which deals more generally with children, including the position of immigrant children within the school system.

IMMIGRANTS AND THE SOCIAL SERVICES

We have seen already how heavily various branches of the social services are involved with immigrants, in the administrative processes of introduction and regularization, and in applications for an HLM. Although the social services may be marginal in the lives of ordinary French families, for immigrants they play a central part. In many respects the services are one of the principal instruments through which immigrants, especially immigrant families, are monitored by French society.

An ordinary French family's contact with the services would be confined, probably, to dealings with the pre- and postnatal facilities that are available in medical-social centers, and perhaps with the social assistants in the schools. A much smaller number of "problem" families – "difficult family situations," as they are called – would be subject to much greater contact. It is no exaggeration to say that from the viewpoint of the services and, to some extent, of French society as a whole, the majority of immigrant families, especially those from North Africa, would fall into the "difficult" category. Thus, steady contact with the services is "normal" for such families. As a remark cited in Chapter 1 shows, the presence of a social assistant in a quartier is considered as convenient as that of a supermarket.

It is impossible to estimate the overall extent to which the social services devote their time and resources to immigrants. The following figures are simply illustrative. In Vaulx-en-Velin, I was told that in the Sector Nord, 65.2 percent of all consultations concerning babies involved foreigners; in the ZUP, 63 percent. In the Sector Sud, 90 percent of all "interventions" pertained to foreigners. On the ZUP at Vénissieux, 50 percent of all children seen by the psychiatric service were foreign, and 90 percent of the clients of a group of *éducateurs* were North African. In the southeast sector of Villeurbanne, 54 percent of all consultations concerned North Africans from the rue Olivier de Serres. Two specialized services dealing with children in danger reported that one-third of all children placed in their care were foreigners. All these figures, except the last, relate to local areas with high concentrations of foreigners, but in each case the involvement with the services is much higher than might otherwise be expected. This is not to suggest that immigrants as a whole command a disproportionate share of the social budget. In fact, the reverse is probably true (see Cavard, Cordiero, and Verhaeren, 1973). Still less is it intended to suggest that immigrants cost more than they add to the value of the national product.

Before going any further, I will give an overview of the services provided in a French city. I include in the social services a very wide range of activities, organizations, groups, and people, since besides the *travailleurs sociaux* – a term that is broader than the English "social worker" – there are many individuals and institutions engaged in parasocial work, often in a voluntary capacity. The term *travailleur social* would include the following categories: social workers proper, that is, those described, trained, and employed as *assistant[e]s social[e]s* in organizations such as the DDASS, the SSFNA, and the SSAE; *éducateurs*, for example, the *éducateurs de rue* (see below); *animateurs*, that is, those professionally engaged in *animation* (see Chapter 4); and a variety of people engaged in, for example, socio-educative action, who might be described as *aides ménagères*, *aides familiales*, or *moniteurs*.

The range and diversity of personnel found on the ground may be illustrated by reference to the commune of Vaulx-en-Velin. In this commune the DDASS runs eight social-medical centers with eleven general social assistants, eight specialist child nurses, a psychiatric medical team, and other specialist medical units. There are also representatives of several of the specialized social work departments of the DDASS (e.g., the Service de Prevention). A number of other government bodies (e.g., the Caisse d'Allocations Familiales) also have social assistants working in the area. There are also *assistantes scolaires* in the schools. These are all from the *public* service. *Private* associations provide a team from the SSFNA, an assistant of the SSAE, a group of *éducateurs* of the Sauvegarde d'Enfance, another of an organization called Société Lyonnaise pour l'Enfance et Adolescence (SLEA), the *animateurs* of the Association pour l'Animation Culturelle et Sociale (APACS), the socio-educative teams of the NDSA, and, finally, a number of social assistants employed by certain large firms with factories in the area. The SSFNA once discovered that in the Régie Simon in Villeurbanne, where it had contacts with 150 North African families, 7 percent of those families were being "followed" by it alone; 34 percent, by two services; 38 percent, by three; 21 percent, by four; and one family was being followed simultaneously by five separate services.

By far the most important of all the services is the DDASS, which is a vast organization, almost exactly the equivalent of the Department of Health and Social Security (DHSS) in Britain. Of the numerous DDASS sections, those that have the greatest relevance for this study are: Actions Sociales, concerned with the introduction of families; Santé Scolaire, which controls the *assistantes scolaires;* and Protection Maternelle et Infantile. It is within the latter section that the social assistants are placed so far as organization at local level is concerned.*

On the ground, social assistants are allocated to a *secteur* and several *secteurs* form a *circonscription,* of which there are fifteen in the Rhône. In few cases does the boundary of a *circonscription* coincide with any other administrative boundary, though it does so at Vaulx-en-Velin. The work undertaken in the *secteur* by the

---

*The organization is more complex than this in that for administrative purposes the assistants belong to a separate section at the department level. Currently, the personnel of different sections within a *secteur* are being grouped in multidisciplinary teams based on the medical-social centers.

personnel de base is both medical (care of mother and child, pre-
and postnatal care, etc.) and social (financial distress, conjugal
difficulties, family breakdown, children in danger, etc.). Then
there are the innumerable tasks that come their way – "whatever
help the family wants," for example, help with bureaucratic problems ("retranslation into everyday language of administrative language," "unblocking dossiers"). Contact with "clients" may be
made directly and independently, or a case may be "signaled" by
another service, for example, the *assistante scolaire*.

We have already met the two principal private associations concerned with social work among immigrants. The SSFNA was
founded in 1952 at Paris and has *implantations* (each service has its
own special jargon) in ten departments. In Lyon there are three
assistants, each responsible for various communes, and part-time
helpers called *monitrices d'enseignement ménager*. The SSAE, founded in 1924, is the French branch of the Service Social International. The headquarters is in Paris, and there are *antennes* in ten
regions, with bureaus in the Rhône-Alpes in Lyon, Grenoble,
Saint-Etienne, and four other centers. In Lyon there are a regional *assistante chef* and five social assistants, of whom four are allotted
to sectors. In theory they do not deal with Algerians but are responsible for all other foreigners, including refugees. They are
mainly concerned with administrative problems and difficulties
they regard as deriving directly from the migration experience.
Both SSFNA and SSAE receive substantial financial support from
the authorities.

Anyone described as a "social assistant," wherever that person is
employed, will have undergone similar training at one of the thir-
ty-six schools offering courses leading to a state diploma. There
are three of these schools in Lyon, each with an enrollment of
thirty to forty. Many, but by no means all, social assistants employed in the city were trained locally and maintain a network of
relationships derived from their schools, or the joint school
courses they may have taken. The vast majority of entrants to the
profession are women who have left high school with the *baccalauréat* (*bac*). Until recently, when scholarships became available,
most were of middle-class origin.

There is a uniform syllabus at all these training schools in
France, which includes theoretical work in medicine, law, sociology, and psychology, and practical work when the trainee is
assigned to established social workers. The practical work is as-

sessed by means of a short dissertation. Sometimes the practical work undertaken in an area with many immigrants attracts the trainee to specialist organizations like the SSFNA. Otherwise there is no formal preparation for such work. Many assistants complained that they had to learn on the job about, for example, Muslim culture. Recently, however, there have been attempts to rectify this by means of short joint-school courses addressed by social workers and others with some direct knowledge of immigrants. Some assistants attempt to learn Arabic at evening classes (see Chapter 8), but few claim more than a rudimentary knowledge of the language.

To the best of my knowledge there are no immigrant, and certainly no North African, social assistants in Lyon. There is a legal barrier in that those employed by the DDASS must be French citizens, although this rule does not apply to the private associations. A small number of North Africans work in such associations, but as *éducateurs* or *animateurs* rather than as social assistants.

Professional *éducateurs* and *animateurs* also receive training at specialist schools, of which there are two for *éducateurs* in Lyon. They appear to be a less homogeneous group in terms of background, sex, and nationality compared with the social assistants. The role of *éducateurs* was created originally to deal with the problem of institutionally housed parentless children after World War II. Since then their "clientele" has expanded to include problem children generally, especially those assigned to their care by the *juges d'enfants*. In the late 1950s and early 1960s they began to operate in an "open milieu" in the quartiers where such children were to be found: hence the designation applied to some groups, *educateurs de rue*. Some are employed by the DDASS, but most are organized by private associations. Based on a street or in an apartment building or a café, they aim to make contact with young people, mostly young male teen-agers, in their own environment. They try to assess the youngsters' needs and develop activities based on these.

Educateurs say that whereas they work through individuals, *animateurs* organize collective activities. In fact, as we saw in Chapter 4, *animation* has as its objective the creation of "community" (*communitas*, even). Outside of the hostels and the *cités de transit*, *animateurs* may be found in various quartiers, particularly in the new suburban-housing estates and on the ZUPs, attached to a club that in fact they run. At Vaulx-en-Velin, for example, APACS was created by the housing authorities to centralize the running of the social facilities that the law now requires on ZUPs. APACS has a group of *animateurs* to organize activities for young people, and it is in the context of the club on which these activities are based that the *animateurs* come into contact with immigrants. At this level, their work and that of the *éducateurs* tends to be similar.

This by no means exhausts the range of social work undertaken in Lyon, but I hope the description has clarified some of the material discussed in earlier chapters and provided some essential background for what follows in this chapter and the next.

THE PROBLEMS OF THE NORTH AFRICAN COUPLE

We saw in the last chapter, and in the discussion in Chapter 4 of the attitudes of hostel directors, that a contrast is frequently made between the "traditional" society of the immigrants' culture and country of origin, and that of the receiving society – France in general and urban France in particular. For many social workers this contrast is exemplified, in the case of North African immigrants, by two aspects of Arab culture: the role of the wife, and relationships within the conjugal couple; and the relationships between parents and children. It is difficult to separate the two, but in the first instance I am concerned with the husband-wife relationship.

Lapraz (1972:122) refers to "les familles étrangères qui ne nous semblent marginales que parce qu'elles sont plongées dans un univers culturel différent du leur, mais qui dans leur univers original seraient parfaitement intégrées." On the one hand, the difference between the two "universes" is seen to reside in the absence in France of the extended family believed to characterize the kinship structure in North Africa – and in Southern Europe. On the other hand, there is seen to be a sharp difference in the husband-wife relationship, and in the position of women generally.

Many social assistants would agree with another remark of Lapraz's that the majority of North African women remain *rivées au statut ancien de la femme maghrébine* (1972:137). I have described the assistants' conception of that traditional status elsewhere (Grillo 1980b). The following comment illustrates this, and also the connection that is made with the absence of the extended family in France: "In Algeria there is practically no life as a couple. There is a world of women, their life, their own world. Not everywhere, of course. In some milieus that's changing. Here the woman finds herself in a nuclear family, and eight children on one's own are more difficult to bring up than twenty-five children shared between three. And the women are called on to do more things. The husband here sees his authority diminishing. He is devalued" (an assistant of the DDASS).

The image of the North African woman is of a person "crushed by events." She has to cope not only with a segregated and subordinate status in the household, which derives from traditional values, but also with the consequences of the changed environment found on migration to France: poor housing, low wages, the urban system. There are also the changes forced on her family by living in France: "Traditionally the North African woman was forced to remain on her own, in the house. Now she has to go out, to get the children from the school, do the shopping, and so on." "Most of the women feel bypassed by the evolution of their children in French society and are aware of the gulf that separates them."

The point about relationships with children made in the last statement is taken up later, but an example will illustrate some of the difficulties that occur. An *assistante scolaire* reported that the mother of a fifteen-and-a-half-year-old girl in her school had sent a letter to the head teacher (it had been dictated to her oldest son) complaining about the sexual education that the daughter was receiving in a course on child care. The letter was passed to the assistant, who tried to see the mother. She decided that there was a problem of education and contacted the SSFNA, who visited the home and now follows the family. The mother never went out, so they persuaded her to go to the school, visit the classes, and so on. "It was important for her to see all this." The *assistante scolaire*, who had brought in the SSFNA because there was a language problem, believed long-term work was required. The mother did not want the child to go out, go on school trips, take part in sports. "She had not been able to situate herself [i.e., in France]. The mother said that the child was upset by sexual education, but really it was she who was upset. Then there were nine children in the family. What worried me was that there was a whole gang of kids following on behind [the girl]."

The weight of social service activity is in effect placed behind such women urging them toward *adaptation, intégration,* or *évolution,* as it is variously called. The traditional status of the North African woman is compared unfavorably with that of French society, where the working mother (own pay packet, children at the *écoles maternelles,* at *colonies de vacances* during the holidays) is believed to have an independent role.

Pressure to change in that direction is believed also to come from the surrounding society (from the example of neighbors, and from the images projected by the media). This leads to conflict with the husband, and consultations about conjugal problems take up much of the assistants' time. "When a couple come to me I talk to them, get them to explain what the problem is. I then try to help them make a choice. Often – not always, but frequently – the problem arises because one partner wishes to live in a European style, a modern style . . . the woman, that is. It is the man who holds back the *évolution* of the woman, who wants the woman to live in a more traditional fashion. If his wife evolves, he loses prestige."

I have argued elsewhere that with certain exceptions the production of the "evolved" North African woman is the goal of the social assistants, and that this involves becoming like a certain kind of French woman (see Grillo 1980b). I was once taken by a housing official at Vénissieux to visit an Algerian resident. She was introduced as more evolved than the others, partly because she spoke French – though it was also remarked that "she dresses in trousers." The immaculate state of her apartment and of her children was also noted as an example of her *évolution.* Other French persons in the area also cited her as an example of an evolved woman, said to be "different from the rest."

Tension in the conjugal relationship caused by the evolution of the woman is believed to account for the increase in demands for divorce that all assistants report they now have to handle. The result is, of course, not always as dramatic as that, but husbands are under considerable pressure, at least to change their life-style and allow changes in that of their wives. The social assistants' interventions often stress this: "In the end, the problems with which we deal are caused by uprooting. Their resolution often involves the husband having to be more tolerant toward his wife." Sometimes the assistants then have to face the men's anger: "Algerian men are very aggressive. On Mondays I am alone in the office and would prefer not to be. I am sometimes glad there is a desk between me and them."

In order to examine the role of social assistants and others in the "evolutionary" process, I will take, as an extended example, their work in one field of considerable importance.

Birth control

We have seen that there is a major difference between French and North African families in terms of their average size. For many assistants the subordinate reproductive role of the North African woman is the central problem. "For many women the pill is a symbol of *évolution*," said Laïd, a young Algerian teacher of Arabic. Many social assistants would agree with that, even if they then rejected the conclusions Laïd wished to draw. The following remarks illustrate their views:

"The social assistant is an emancipating factor. The husband doesn't like this, and it is often the husband who needs support. For this I often resort to an *éducateur*, to provide an explanation man-to-man. There are often aspirations that are difficult to realize in this context. The wife asks for contraception, the husband doesn't want it. He sees it as an attack on his manhood. One discusses the problem with them, using the services of the *éducateur*. One leads them to the consultations [at the clinic]." "Yes, there is a demand. One helps. Among the mothers there is agreement in principle, after having had a certain number of children. But there are cultural difficulties. Some do take the pill. The husband, that's another matter. With some, one takes the opportunity to broach the subject. It's very, ah . . . It depends on the individual. For some there is no question, the religion forbids it. Others pay lip service to the idea, but as for acting on it . . . Some have given permission for their wives to have their tubes tied."

The comment is most often made that the demands come from the wives. In a discussion among a group of *éducatrices* at Vaulx-en-Velin, someone asserted that many North African women want birth control ("All women do," interjected another), but then it was pointed out that when this group had organized a stall at Vaulx market ("You remember, when the mayor intervened"), large numbers of North African men had come up to inform themselves. The director of a *cité de transit* also reported that the men discussed the matter with him and that he encouraged them, despite the fact that birth control was contrary to the rules of his own Catholicism.

Another assistant employed by a factory described how she broached the subject. "It is well known that family planning is not well understood. They are unwilling to undertake it. 'We have children, *Inshallah!*' The religion may have been abandoned, but it is still considered a blessing to have children. A barren woman is rejected, divorced. The husband says, 'My wife can't have children. I am going to Algeria to find another.' The women, although they live secluded lives, despite it all, begin little by little to discuss it. They begin to react a little bit. The husbands who discuss it are very rare. One tries to discuss it with them, to make them understand their wives are worn out with having a child every year. And perhaps after the eighth or ninth child, they will agree to an operation to tie the tubes. At the ———— Hospital is a group who try to 'sensibilize' people, especially immigrants. The gynecologists try to orient them toward family planning. The women, to find a support, turn to the DDASS, which then tries to put pressure on the husband. I myself have tried. I've broached the question, but it's not easy. Among the *évolués,* one can always approach them easily. As for the others, its more hidden. If I mention the subject, they ask, 'Why are you talking about that?' It is easier to talk to the wife. The DDASS does not call on me to talk to the husbands, but I enter on the personnel records details of all births. When a new child arrives, I try to raise the matter when I see the husband. It's not always easy. The husband takes it for an insult. They are proud of their virility. Among Arabs that's important. Among them virility, sexuality, are related to the number of children they have. Sterility is never the fault of the woman. There is a fantastic stress on virility."

An assistant of the SSFNA explained her response: "I have frequent individual demands from women saying, 'I'm fed up, my husband wants more children, I don't.' Often these demands are camouflaged, not direct. They talk about the expense of bringing up children and ask, 'You French, what do you do?' When we finally get around to talking about birth control, I try to find out what the husband thinks. If the husband is against, if there is a problem of the couple, I proceed very cautiously. If both are agreed, I send them to a family-planning clinic or a doctor. I remember one case where the wife said the husband did not want her to take the pill. The husband said it was his wife who wanted

more children. When I saw them both together, the wife admitted
this. At the collective level, in conjunction with the *enseignement
ménager* courses, there have been two types of intervention. Last
year we had a meeting addressed by a doctor. . . . But it was very
technical and didn't go down well. Second, we tried to give out
information via the *monitrices*. We found we had to be very careful. For example, the women speak dialect Arabic in which all the
sexual terms are vulgar. Literary Arabic has scientific terms, but
these are not known. I put in a lot of work, getting vocabulary
together and so on, to prepare a presentation in French. We had
to use simple vocabulary. The word 'spermatozoa' was not understood and had to be repeated several times. So there was a language problem. There was also difficulty with the diagrams.
There is a lack of knowledge of how we are made, but a real thirst
for knowledge.

"At the ZUP we decided to work jointly with a former DDASS
assistant and a nurse who knows the milieu, about taboos and so
on. We set up a course of five sessions dealing with anatomy,
physiology, the menstrual cycle, conception, birth, and contraception. There was an enormous amount of preparatory work. We
got the help of an Arab woman who speaks literary Arabic and of
her brother, who is a fourth-year medical student. One of our
monitrices who speaks Arabic prepared the translation, and we got
together the audiovisual material. About twenty women attended,
ten regularly. This added to the difficulty because some of the
women missed sessions and got behind. It was a difficult job.
Pictures don't necessarily talk, and one of the films was too technical. Some of the young women did not want to come. They were
interested, but ashamed to participate in such discussions in front
of older women. But at the end the women said they hadn't realized before that women react in a psychologically different way
from men, that they hadn't known about the physical differences
between men and women, that other women, too, had problems,
for example, with menstruation. So they discovered they were like
others. They discovered that the sex of a child did not depend on
them. 'Why do our husbands reproach us with bearing only
daughters?' they asked. They said they'd talk to their husbands
about this. One woman said that she had had ten children and
would have carried them better if she had known about the physical side of it.

"Regarding contraception, there was no great enthusiasm in

the group. All methods were discussed. They were willing to listen, but not react. Individually some asked for help with the temperature method. They were not sufficiently *évoluées* to use the pill. There is a psychosomatic reaction to that – they're not sure it's in accordance with the religion – and against sterilization, use of the diaphragm, and so on. One girl who used the temperature method rang me at four in the morning saying she was pregnant. She was."

This account refers to a number of matters, for example, the language problem, to which we shall return subsequently, and later in the chapter I will try to draw together the themes that emerge from the material presented here and in earlier sections. For the moment, let us concentrate on the tension in the North African household that the process of *évolution* is considered to generate. So far, we have been concerned with tension in the conjugal relationship, and the sense that one is given of the North African male, as husband, under siege, so to speak, by the receiving society. This sense will be reinforced when we look at the father-daughter relationship.

THE PROBLEMS OF ADOLESCENT GIRLS

There is frequently said to be a *décalage* (lack of alignment) between North African parents and children – see Sherif's speech in Event 4. Implied is something more than "generation gap": "Portuguese children pose a problem, but not for the same reasons as North African children. They are attached to Islam, which is very hard. The children are influenced by France, and this leads to a *décalage* between parents and children. The parents have been brought up in a different society. There are problems, especially for the women. The girls have a need for a different way of life, seeing liberty here in France. In school they mix with others and embrace an opening toward others that is not found in the family." The SSFNA Rhône Report for 1974 (p. 6) refers to "l'effrontement de modèles culturels à la discordance dans le rythme et le sens de l'évolution des époux, à la distorsion des niveaux d'instruction entre parents et enfants, à l'ampleur que prend la crise d'adolescence dans un tel contexte."

The situation of young North Africans was put in a general perspective by one *animatrice* working at a *cité de transit*. The door of her office had been smashed. How did she explain that and other examples of violence at the center? After some thought she provided a number of reasons:

"The center represents a power that the people do not have. Break, break, ransack, is the only language that remains to them. Previously it was the Centre Medico-Social that was attacked. There and here the workers are *women*. A particular problem of the young in these families is the *mother*. They attack the center as a substitute. [The local social assistant reported that *Maman et Papa* had been scrawled on her door.] Many of these adolescents are split between two cultures. Their parents are very North African, while they are brought up in a culture that is very French. They are proletarian, French *immigrés*. There is a process of marginalization that begins at school. There is a failure at school, social failure at school. They are parked in a *cité* like this. School, TV, express a culture that is not theirs, a bourgeois culture. The boys have a chance to play the two cultures. They can go out. The girls are shut in at home, so one gets an enormous amount of running away, suicide attempts."

Some of the issues raised by that comment, and by the material presented below, will make more sense when the school system is discussed in the next chapter. For the moment I wish to concentrate specifically on the situation of the young girls. As with their mothers, immersion in French society is believed to produce a desire for *évolution* that creates conflicts with the adult male in his role, this time as father:

"The most difficult problem for North African families is the upbringing of children. The parents say, 'Our children are not like us. We have done everything for them, but . . .' The children say, 'We are in the twentieth century, but our parents are in the Middle Ages.' The girl who goes out may be contrasted with the girl who stays in. If a girl is serious, she may be allowed to stay on at school, the parents may allow her to find a job. She can fulfill what her parents expect of her. She can aspire to the model of an average French girl, and at the same time be a model girl in the eyes of her parents. . . . On the other hand, the girl who goes out is seen to take part in antisocial activities. She is seen as a prostitute, a bad girl. I have heard a father say, 'If we weren't in France, I'd kill you.' "

A particularly difficult time for the girl is the period around her sixteenth birthday. Until then she must stay at school, but at that point a decision must be made: Should she stay on at school, or get a job, like other (French) adolescents? Or should she marry? North African tradition ("We fight to preserve the girl's virginity until marriage. The earlier one marries, the better") runs counter to the French conception of the evolved woman, and the image presented via the school, the media, and the child's classmates. It is often said that such girls are "squeezed" (*coincées*) between these conflicting demands. The following cases document this and show what happens.

1. A group of social assistants at Vaulx-en-Velin followed a case involving a girl of seventeen who had come to see them. She had had "real possibilities" at school, but the father had made her leave at sixteen "because there were four grown lads at home who had to be looked after." The girl took this very badly. The assistant in charge of the case asked the father to come to see her, but he did not, so she visited him at home, argued with him and persuaded him to allow the girl to go out one afternoon a week to visit an *éducateur*. Later the girl returned to the assistant, saying she was really fed up and had packed her bags ready to leave home. The assistant argued her out of this. She had not seen the girl for a year but believed she was still at home.

2. An *assistante scolaire* at Vénissieux, referring to the "problems of young girls between two cultures who aspire to get out," mentioned the case of an Algerian girl who was somewhat backward educationally. She had seen the father several times over this and other matters. The girl had been involved with a petty theft and generally had difficulties at school. The father's reaction had been that he would marry the girl off. This did not happen, however. (Several assistants reported that they had had to remind North African parents of their legal obligation to keep the children in school until age sixteen.) Subsequently the girl discussed with the assistant what to do when she left school. She herself wanted to work in a jewelry shop, and hoped to take a training course. The father disagreed, but the assistant persuaded him to go with her to visit the training center. Among other things, the father objected to the cost of the course, for although the training was free, materials had to be bought, and then there was the fare. However, the girl failed the entrance exam. She then wanted to take a secretarial course. Her father agreed to pay out 200 francs a term for this. When the father had first mentioned marrying the girl off, he had withdrawn his threat provided the child worked hard at

school and did not go out. If she began to go out, to "evolve," as the assistant put it, he would insist on her marriage.

The assistants are fully aware of the cultural conflict involved, and sometimes this leads them to disagree with the occasional North African who is also engaged in social work.

3. An *éducateur* at Villeurbanne: "It is after adolescence that the problem arises. They are surrounded by French life. Things have begun to evolve a bit. If the girls get on well at school, if they work hard, they have a chance to get out. We have girls come to us and say 'I'm getting out. Find me a hostel.' When we talk, we find that the family want them to marry, or stop them getting a job as a hairdresser or something. We've discussed what to do in these circumstances, and the team is divided. The family is important. The girl is at risk especially if they go back home and she is 'francisized.' The Moroccan *éducateur* thinks we should leave the customs alone. Even if people have lived in France a long time, at bottom they remain the same. The Tunisian *éducatrice* has a more subtle position. She thinks the girl should remain Algerian, but *évoluée*. Back home, in North Africa, that's possible, but here ... We worry that if the girl doesn't give in to her parents she will get into prostitution."

4. An *éducatrice* at Vaulx: "A lot of girls want to continue their studies against the opposition of their father. We try to get the parents to understand that in France things are different, that girls do get jobs. When we talk to the mothers about this, if they have been in France for some time, they understand things are different here. I spoke at a girl's request to her father. He was reluctant but allowed his daughter to seek a job. I disagree with [the Moroccan *éducateur*]. Changes are taking place, the position of women in Algeria is changing. If a girl wants to follow the customs, fine. But if she wants to oppose her father, to get out, then we'll help her. I understand what [the Moroccan] wants, but these girls are really between two cultures."

5. Another assistant referred to this dilemma: "There was an Algerian girl, now age fifteen and a half, who had been signaled by the primary-school psychologist as someone with difficulties. She cried all the time. This carried on at secondary school. Every Wednesday she goes and cries to Madame Y. The girl has been promised in marriage to someone from her tribe living in Lyon. She can't accept marriage with a barbarian. The marriage is supposed to take place this summer. I don't know what one can do.

She could be taken in charge by the *aide sociale,* by the *juge d'en-fants.* We have the right to use that procedure, and it is used a great deal. But should one do this when what is involved is the parents' ethic, in which they believe? Why should we force them not to marry off their daughter? The *juges* place such children in the care of an *éducateur.* When they return home, sometimes the family gives in. But more and more the *juges* don't want to be involved, saying: 'Let the North African families sort themselves out.' Getting back to the girl. Madame Y. signaled the SSFNA, who tried to open discussions in the family. But in these families there is no discussion. The fiancé is twice as old as the girl. In fact, the girl's father was twice as old as her mother. The two have nothing in common. Bit by bit one talks to the parents. Meantime, the girl shuts herself in her bedroom. She feels that the school is there to help her. She has to choose between freedom and the family. She is squeezed."

There are in fact three ways in which a child can be placed under legal protection, but the most important from our point of view is the procedure by which a *juge* orders a child to be placed in the care of the Aide Social à l'Enfance, a process that entails a DDASS inquiry. A child so placed is sent to a *cité d'enfance,* and then perhaps to a family or an institution. The DDASS Service de Prévention is concerned with cases before they reach the courts, and undertake "educative action to prevent the worst, the inter-vention of the *juge.*" Cases are signaled to them by other services, and very occasionally the police. Of 5,660 cases passing through the hands of this service in Lyon in 1974, some 35 percent in-volved immigrant children.

Many social assistants receive requests from the children them-selves to be placed in care ("Find me a hostel"). The eagerness on the part of the DDASS to place children was criticized by one social worker attached to a factory in Vaulx Sud, who mentioned the following case:

6. "The father had worked at the factory for sixteen years. He had nine children. One little girl had been sickly since birth, in and out of hospital. Several assistants and medical staff reported that the child was very happy in hospital, but very miserable when at home. Eventually the *juge* ordered the Sauvegarde d'Enfance to see the child. We went with the woman from the Sauvegarde to the child's home. We came to the conclusion that the child was unhappy because the rest of the family spoke Arabic, but she,

because of her long absences in hospital, did not. The DDASS had urged that the child be placed because it was 'rejected.' But it wasn't that at all."

Mostly, however, the placing of a child requires the demonstration of physical danger from the father (as in one case where the girl was locked in a cupboard "because she went out with boys"), or moral danger from prostitution. Or it may follow flight from home, or a suicide attempt. An Algerian who taught language described two such cases known to him: "The first involved a girl who had asked to be placed. She had gone to the police and declared, 'My parents beat me.' The police, being racists, find this easy to accept, and so does the *juge,* who places the child automatically. When this happens, the child moves from a very traditional system of upbringing in the home into another style of life that is also a form of constraint, the hostel. The family is strict, but the hostel is also strict. The child slips backward and wants to return to the family. The hostel leads to prostitution, to the streets. In the second case, the parents withdrew their daughter from school. She found work not far from home. She thought that the job would enable her to free herself. The parents, being poor, insisted that she contribute almost all her pay to the household. If she refused, she knew she would be married. They reached a compromise. Half her pay was placed in a savings bank. This continued for a year, and then the parents wanted her to marry. She supposed she could meet a young man of her choice and marry him, but it is very hard to meet a suitable young man like that. The Arab man is alienated in relationships with a woman. A woman who walks about is a good woman to go around with, but bad for marriage. This girl tried several times to kill herself. She is squeezed. She withdraws into herself. She becomes submissive. She becomes depressed. Hence the suicide attempts."

That was the view of a young radicalized Algerian who had spent several years in France. Many of the issues he mentions, as well as those cited by previous informants, are touched on in the following lengthy statement from an assistant employed by the SSFNA, who in the summer of 1976 told me about seven "difficult family situations" involving girls aged fifteen and a half. "This is the critical age. Will they return to school after the holidays? What will happen to them when they go on holiday? The social services are squeezed between the trust of the families and the wishes of the young girls. One can, of course, send the girls to the *juges*. But they do not all react in the same way. Some are easy, but others say that if they cut the child off from the North African milieu, she will be removed from her psychological roots. For the girls there is a problem of the structuring of their personality, coupled with the problem of acculturation. The girls feel that they are devalued compared with their young French friends who go out, go to work, and so on. They are very uncertain as to their future, overburdened with heavy tasks in the home. The family does not understand their ambitions. What I do is give them the chance to express themselves, and the chats are sometimes very helpful. If they allow me, I act the part of the devil's advocate, to explain their parents' reactions. I try to make them aware that they are between two stools, to make them aware of how they want to live. So my priority is to allow the girls to structure themselves.

"Another point. In the school system, in the family, in the quartier, these girls feel themselves to be abnormal. I encourage them to meet and talk with one another, to allow them to find a solution that they have worked out together. At these discussions the girls will ridicule another's threat of suicide, though this might have been in their own minds. I listen to them individually and mirror the picture of their parents, without aggression. Faced with that, the girl can structure herself.

"The *juges* have been getting harder, but I think sometimes it is better to cut the girl off from her family for a while. I have had two suicide attempts in the seven cases. The girls themselves ask to be placed. They come saying that their parents want them to marry. They know that this is a good argument when talking to social workers. You also get suicide attempts, simulations of suicide, absenteeism from school, which are all cries for help: 'My parents don't understand me.' If a girl tells me that she is going to commit suicide, I say 'Okay, if you wish.'

"In many of these cases I notice envy on the part of the mothers. They have had a hard life themselves, married at thirteen, a child at fifteen, a child dead at seventeen. Unconsciously the mothers envy the girls who go to school, who don't have to do anything. I find it easier to work with the fathers. Their view is that they have to protect the girls' virginity, to preserve the honor of the family. I see the father if the girl wishes, but I try to get the girl to tell the father herself that she is coming to the consultations, without giving the reasons. This in itself establishes a form of dialogue.

"There was one case of a girl who was supposed to marry who ran away, who talked of suicide. She didn't want me to see her father, but finally told him herself. We talked with the father and in the end he agreed that his daughter could attend an SSFNA course. The mother was seen by one of the *monitrices*, who got her interested in sewing. And now there is no more talk of marriage in the family. We lead the parents to allow the girls to undertake something. What they want is training for a job. But it is important not to rush matters. The social service is in an extremely perilous situation.

"Regarding the cases. The girls are very much afraid of being married off during the holidays. I have given them the addresses of certain hostels and introduced them to the *juges*. But I'm just as worried if the family doesn't go home to North Africa on holiday and the girl stays in the house for two months. They don't agree to camps for their children, to *colonies de vacances*. At the end of the school year there is the *orientation scolaire*, so the question is always: 'What am I going to do after the holidays?' Three of these cases were signaled to me by the *assistante scolaire*, two by the DDASS, two by other services. Madame ——— [the *assistante scolaire*] signaled one of the cases because of the girl's absences from school. She was ashamed to be in the class because she couldn't dress like the others. She was ashamed vis-à-vis the school."

CONCLUSION

Let me summarize what has emerged here and in the previous chapter concerning the relationship between social workers and their immigrant clients. First, let it be clear that for the most part I have been examining *statements* (even the "cases" are based on informants' descriptions) that contain evidence for the perceptions of their work and their clients. Although I have attempted to "contextualize" those statements by reference to social processes that appear significant to the observer as well as (sometimes) the informants, for the moment the perceptions themselves are the principal focus of interest. A number of points may be made.

First, most French informants, and many North Africans too,

draw two kinds of contrast: between the traditional/rural milieu of the sending society and the modern/urban milieu of France; and the (related) *décalage* between parents and children. It is also generally agreed that the transition from one milieu to the other is especially difficult for North African women, wives/mothers and adolescent daughters, though certain differences *between* the three North African nationalities are frequently mentioned in this context. Tunisian and sometimes Moroccan women, and men, are often said to be more "evolved" than those from Algeria. However, it is believed that a certain change may occur in the status of these females undergoing this transition, which has important consequences for relationships with husbands/fathers. These changes are called by some *évolution*. Social work aids this *évolution* by helping North African women "get out" in both a physical and a social sense. Such women are seen as enclosed in the ghetto of their status, so to speak, just as they are sometimes seen as enclosed in a residential ghetto in the true sense.

These perceptions draw on several kinds of knowledge. First, there is intercultural knowledge (see Grillo 1982), which is a kind of anthropology in that it deals with the cultural norms and values of the people concerned. This knowledge is founded partly on direct and indirect personal experience (acquired on the job or learned from colleagues). It is also informed by general "public" knowledge of North African Muslim society, knowledge that in a sense forms part of French culture. It also draws on (esoteric) social scientific knowledge acquired through training and reading. Social work, in fact, represents the application of such knowledge that has trickled down into popular discourse.*

In these respects, the views of many different social workers are similar. There are differences, however. For if the aim of social work – articulated with greater or lesser sophistication – is "autonomy" of the clients ("Je travail à ma propre disparition," said one *animateur*), getting them to take themselves in hand, it might well be asked: To what end? Here we may distinguish broadly two aims. Consider the following: "The *éducateurs* are implanted in problem quartiers to establish a relationship and lead young people to reflect. The authorities often see the police as the stick and

---

*It is often very difficult to disentangle "scientific" and "folk" knowledge. *Décalage*, for example, is a term used by Piaget, but I am not certain whether popular usage reflects Piaget's, or vice versa.

the *éducateurs* as the carrot. Petty crime is a means of expression, a way of life. The people distance themselves from the law. One must cause their personality to blossom. If you allow someone to blossom, so that he can express himself, he can then return to the system."

The aim of getting people to take their place in "the system" means their behaving like law-abiding "French" citizens, taking their place in, and manifesting behavior appropriate to, the housing market and the systems of production and consumption. I will term this the predominant ideology of social work in that it reflects the views of the majority engaged in such work and also represents the "dominant ideology" of the society. (See further the discussion of *insertion* in Chapter 8.) There is, however, another goal that, for example, leads the *animatrices* at one center to create a tenants' association that "begins to ask questions" of a more fundamental nature concerning the basis of the system. This view, in this case a leftist one, shares with the dominant ideology an acceptance of a traditional/modern dichotomy and of the fact of the subordinate status of North African women. The point of departure is in the kind of awareness pursued – glossed as *ouverture d'esprit* on the one hand, and *prise de conscience* on the other. They are opening the door to different conceptions of reality.

There is also another viewpoint, that of immigrants themselves. More often than not they have a strictly pragmatic view of the social assistant as someone whose help may be sought with the system. Social workers frequently suspect that they are being used. A social assistant reflecting on her past experience commented: "One was too interventionist. The women came to us, put on a big act, showed us knife wounds they had inflicted on themselves. *Tout un cinéma!* It is their psychodrama. An intervention here is a false route. We are being used by them."

Some North Africans adopt a more critical stance. "Pour combattre la misère dans le Tiers monde, les spécialistes occidentaux ne propose comme solution que les plans familiaux de contrôle de naissance," commented *L'Algerien en Europe* (No. 231, April 1, 1976, p. 8). I cited earlier in this chapter a remark of one Algerian informant about the pill. It was taken out of context: "In relation to sexuality, the problems are posed within the framework of another culture. When the question is put to the families, it is seen as forming all part of the attack on the culture. So one refuses the pill. Sometimes people put on the appearance of seeking contraception. For many the pill is the symbol of evolution. But it is more a symbol of malaise. For young girls, work, the pill, are the signs of the *femme évoluée,* in inverted commas. There is a striving to become like the other person. They respect us if we're like them. If we are not like them, they reject us."

To return to the French, however. It is not unusual for assistants to talk of the shock they feel when confronted with their clients' behavior: "I didn't think I'd have such cases when I started." Straightforward disapproval is rare, and more often reference is made to "my own problems of understanding, and the sense of shock I feel when confronted with the rites of a different people. I was upset to see how certain Spanish families live, in a fashion very different from us. The North Africans more so – children running around with bare feet . . ." Occasionally they admit to feeling threatened: "Most of the young North African men want a submissive wife. They have a certain idea of the woman and of sexuality. They were horrified by a film on abortion they saw. Their attitude to French women, me, for example, is to view them as sexual objects. For that reason I don't go into the café on my own." (The café was where her group of *éducateurs* was based.)

If this sense of culture shock cuts right across ideological orientation, so does the problem of the rights and wrongs of the social worker's intervention. While recognizing that there is an ethical dilemma at the individual level, some argue that at a more general level the question of whether one is aiding and abetting a particular kind of cultural change is irrelevant (see Grillo 1980b:81–2), in that change is occurring in both France and North Africa. Confronted with this, and the intrinsic difficulty of many of the problems they face, a sense of powerlessness is evoked: "In France there is a transformation of the material and psychological condition of the individual – just as I was transformed when living in Algeria. Thus, one's interventions affect very little." As a psychiatric social worker said of the cases with which they deal on the ZUP at Vénissieux: "These are symptoms of problems arising out of the conditions of life that are linked to psychiatric disorder. We are occupied with the symptoms without tackling the real problems. We only limit the consequences. Our aim? To help some kid to grow up without being crushed."

7

In the schools and on the streets

This chapter continues the discussion of the relationship between the French and immigrant families by focusing on young people, especially those of North African origin, in the school system and on the job market. It tells a melancholy story but one that will contain no surprises for anyone familiar with similar milieus in Britain or America (see, for example, Rex and Tomlinson 1979, Chapter 6). The chapter also continues the ideological analysis undertaken in previous chapters by examining French views on what are thought of as the educational problems of young people. First, however, it is necessary to comment briefly on the general structural situation of young North Africans, in particular North African males. This requires an understanding of their legal situation.

THE LEGAL STATUS OF YOUNG NORTH AFRICANS

"The prospects for a return to Algeria are difficult for the young. The Algerians born and brought up in France, or who have lived here for a long time, are treated in Algeria rather like the *pied noir* is treated here in France. Until the age of eighteen they are neither one thing nor the other, but then they can choose [nationality]. It is possible for someone at age eighteen to end up without work and no prospect of obtaining any" (an *éducateur* at Vénissieux).

"The children of the North African families in this area were born in France, but they have difficulty in finding an identity. They are rejected by the French but have no thought of returning home. They can become French at age eighteen, but sixteen-year-olds don't formulate the question of nationality. They don't think about the future" (an *animateur* at Vaulx-en-Velin).

The legal situation of young North Africans is not easy to untangle and indeed in the case of Algerians is contentious. The basic official position (cf. de Mauroy 1979:10) is that foreign children may acquire French nationality either by decree (if they are unmarried minors when their parents are naturalized) or by *declaration acquisitive* if born in France of foreign parents. The parents themselves may make this declaration on behalf of their children, but where this is not done, the child, if born in France, may opt for citizenship at age eighteen, or if born outside France, may qualify for citizenship through residence. Some authorities, however, offer a different interpretation of the status of young Algerians, based on the fact that before independence Algeria was a French department (see Pinot 1976).

There were some 47,000 naturalized persons in the Rhône in 1975 (3.3 percent of the population). In the Rhône-Alpes region as a whole between 1948 and 1977, Italians, Spaniards, and Poles made up 80 percent of naturalizations, North Africans only 3 percent (de Mauroy 1979:15). Few North Africans, therefore, aspire to French citizenship. This is partly because the immediate consequence of becoming French at age eighteen, say, is that a young man has to undertake military service. The advantages are considered minimal. He could, of course, enter a number of occupations reserved for citizens, but many of these (teaching, civil service) require educational standards he might not possess, or have undesirable characteristics. ("Why should I become a French citizen? In order to become a cop?") Such advantages would, however, be offset by identification on the part of the Algerian community with the despised Harkis.

For the most part, North African children born and brought up in France take no action and thus retain their parents' citizenship. But they usually wish to avoid military service in their "home" country and stay in France with the status of what is in effect a permanent immigrant. A young man cannot return to Algeria, for example, because there he is thought to have evaded national service. He cannot, therefore, obtain a passport or a travel document. This status of permanent immigrant and all that it implies has important consequences for young North African males during their later years in the school system and subsequently in the job market.

THE DISTRIBUTION OF IMMIGRANT
CHILDREN IN SCHOOLS

For the moment we will concern ourselves specifically with the school system. The arrival during the 1970s of large numbers of North African and Portuguese families posed a number of problems for the French. Of particular concern was the concentration of such families in certain areas of Lyon where their numbers passed the "threshold of tolerance." Among the indexes cited to demonstrate this is the percentage of immigrant children in schools. (Those unfamiliar with the organization of the French school system may consult the Appendix.)

Already by 1970 a prefecture report (SLPM 1970a) voicing concern at the educational problems, cited some "eloquent percentages" showing that in 12 schools in the Rhône Department more than 50 percent of pupils were foreigners. At that time, there were, in all, 46 schools with 25 percent or more immigrants on their books. By 1973, according to a paper by the primary-school teachers' union, the Syndicat National des Instituteurs (SNI), there were 157 such schools, including 52 with more than 50 percent immigrant pupils. In fact, by the early 1970s there was a significant "bulge" about to move through the school system, with roughly twice as many immigrant children in first-year primary classes as in the fifth (final) year.

The general picture for 1975–6 is shown in Table 7.1. The private schools attract very few immigrants (some 2 percent only of Algerian children), so there is first a relative concentration in the state sector. Within the state system, however, there is a pattern of concentration that follows closely the pattern of residential concentration described in earlier chapters. Some examples will

Table 7.1. *Numbers and percentages of pupils of foreign origin in Rhône Department schools, 1975–6*

	State schools	Private schools	Total
Preschool and primary	182,207 (17.33)	31,866 (3.35)	214,073 (15.25)
Secondary	93,815 (12.04)	33,540 (2.36)	127,355 (9.49)

Note: Figures in parentheses represent % of foreign pupils in sector.
Source: Tables 7.1, 7.2, 7.3, 7.4 and 7.5, and some figures cited in the text, from the Administration Académique de Lyon.

illustrate this. In the suburb of Caluire 9.6 percent of nursery-
and primary-school children are foreigners, 6.3 percent are
North African. Of the eleven schools in the suburb, *one* school
enrolls 46 percent of all foreign children, and 64 percent of all
North African children. In fact, 75 percent of all Algerian children attend just two of the eleven schools. In the suburb of
Oullins, one out of thirteen nursery/primary schools contains 60
percent of all immigrant children. Two schools contain 78 percent
of all North African children. In these schools, North Africans
form 45.5 percent of the pupils. In the other eleven, they form
2.2 percent. In Villeurbanne Sud, six out of twenty-five nur-
sery/primary schools form two adjacent *groupes scolaires*. Algerian
children constitute 67 percent of their pupils. In the other nineteen schools they form 4.7 percent. The history of one of these
groupes repays attention.

A number of schools in Lyon have more than 90 percent immigrant pupils. The Groupe Scolaire Jules Ferry in Villeurbanne
Sud, which consists of one *maternelle* and two primary schools, is
one of these. Out of 424 pupils, 409 are foreign. In one of the
primary schools there are 113 Algerian children, 8 Tunisian, 6
Portuguese, 5 Moroccan, and 1 Spanish: 133 foreign children out
of 133 enrolled. Several of the non–North African children attend the school because it has a special French-language class
attached to it. The *groupe* is, therefore, an "Arab" school and is
referred to as such by French residents.

The history of this *groupe* is related to that of the quartier – the
rue Olivier de Serres – it serves (see Chapter 5). According to the
director of one of the schools, who arrived in 1964, about 70
percent of the pupils were at that time French, but the numbers
fell as the Arab population of the Régie Simon increased, and as
French families from other parts of the quartier withdrew their
children. In the early 1970s an area adjacent to the rue Olivier de
Serres, within the catchment area of the *groupe*, was redeveloped
with large blocks of modern luxury flats. In order to meet the
expected demand for school places, a new *groupe scolaire* was
planned, but not completed, before the new apartments were
occupied. For a period the French children from the new houses
were taught in separate classes in temporary accommodations
within the grounds of the Groupes Jules Ferry. Let the director
take up the story: "When the new school opened, the parents of
the French children still at this school came to me and said they

Table 7.2. *Length of service of staff in 12* maternelles *and primary schools with a high proportion of immigrant pupils*

	Year started	No.	%
Less than 1 year	(1975)	50	52.6
1–2 years	(1974)	15	15.8
2–3 years	(1973)	6	6.3
3–4 years	(1972)	4	4.2
4–5 years	(1971)	0	0
5–6 years	(1970)	6	6.3
More than 6 years	(1969, etc.)	14	14.7
Total		95	99.9

wanted to remove their children because there were too many Arabs at the school and their kids were getting bad habits. I told them that each school had a precisely defined catchment area, and they couldn't move. They replied that they would put their children into private schools. I warned my superior, who said we couldn't force the parents to keep their children at the school. Within a fortnight all the French children had been removed. I spent the whole time filling in forms. After all, what's a catchment area to a parent? Later, a family from Toulouse moved into the quartier and came to see me. I thought I had better warn them in advance, so I explained the situation. At first the father said that the other parents were stupid – a school, it's only a school. But then the mother and father looked at each other and said, 'We'll think about it. We'll let you know tomorrow.' I didn't see them again."

Partly, then, as a result of patterns of residence that derive from the position of immigrants within the housing market, partly as a result of the response of French parents, a number of schools contain very high concentrations of immigrant children. Many of these schools are located either in run-down inner-city areas or on the ZUPs. One consequence of this location is that the schools have difficulty attracting and keeping staff (see Table 7.2). The *directrice* of one primary school, where eight out of twelve staff members had left the previous year, commented: "Well, the ZUP, it has a bad reputation. The teaching is difficult, in fact, very difficult. Teachers are in transit here. A year or two and then off to the countryside, which is certainly more pleasant." Another remarked: "We are beginning to get some stability. Last year only two of the six teachers left. There are teachers who stay up to four or five years. But a lot are young and inexperienced. Their posts are allocated by the education authorities" (i.e., they are obliged to take them).

The schools in these areas are generally short of resources, which is something that affects French and immigrant children alike. In 1976, Monsieur Houel, MP and mayor of Vénissieux, asked the minister of education to undertake special measures to help with the education of children on the ZUP Les Minguettes (*Le Progrès de Lyon,* March 18, 1976). His request reflected a concern partly about the general lack of resources in eastern Lyon (cf. *Le Progrès de Lyon,* March 6, 1976; April 22, 1976), partly about the extra costs borne by the commune in providing additional educational support for foreign children. However, there was another reason for his and others' interest, as is revealed by a reported discussion at the Conseil Général in 1975: "Un autre débat et toujours le même: la répartition des familles de travailleurs migrants. Délicate question. Pour M Desgrand (PCF, Villeurbanne) la concentration dans certaines villes de banlieue aboutit à susciter des sentiments racistes regrettables" (*Le Progrès, de Lyon,* October 9, 1975; cf. February 20, 1976). The passion this "delicate question" arouses can be seen in the comments of the deputy mayor of the 1st Arrondissement at the minister's meeting described in Chapter 3, Event 1.

IMMIGRANT CHILDREN WITHIN THE SCHOOL SYSTEM

If the concentration of immigrant children in schools poses problems of a political nature, it also poses problems of a more specifically pedagogic kind, as we shall see. First, however, let us see how immigrant children fare at school, in particular how they rate by reference to the standards of success and failure set by the schools themselves.

What is the relative distribution of immigrants between the various streams (or ability levels) of which the school system is composed? In principle it should be relatively easy to perceive any pattern. For example, where schools or classes are graded or streamed, or where success is defined by examination passes – and where the nationality of pupils is known – a comparison of the situation of different national groups should be straightforward. Unfortunately, the relevant data for the Rhône Depart-

Table 7.3. *Foreign pupils in secondary education, by school type,
Rhône Department, 1975–6 (state schools only)*

Type of school	% foreigners	% North African	S.E. school sector % foreigners	% North African
CES/CEG[a]	12.6	6.7	16.2	8.4
CET	14.6	7.6	17.9	9.5
Lycées	6.4	2.5	7.5	2.4
All secondary	12.0	5.9		

[a]Collège d'Enseignement Général.

ment are not readily available. Such evidence I have, however, is
consistent with that reported elsewhere in France.

Ouvrier, fils d'ouvrier, began a *Le Monde* article (March 14–15,
1976) commenting on official figures showing that in 1973–4
more than half the pupils enrolled in Certificat d'Aptitude Professionnelle (CAP) courses in technical colleges were children of
workers, while the latter formed only a quarter of those in lycées.
A poster display at a CGT fête in Lyon made the same point by
graphically portraying the careers from nursery school to employment of a working-class child and a middle-class child. The
relationship between class and school achievement has been well
established both in France and in Britain, where the issue has
been central to educational debate at least since the war. The
point made by *Le Monde* with reference to French working-class
children applies equally if not more so to the children of immigrants.

The evidence for this is scattered but nonetheless definite. To
begin with the secondary schools, it is clear that there is a very
significant difference between the participation rates of foreign
and French children in the different types of secondary education
(see Table 7.3). For example, there are proportionately three
times as many North African pupils in technical colleges (Collèges
d'Enseignement Technique, or CETs) than in the lycées (four
times as many in the southeastern suburbs). Thus, when immigrant children, especially North Africans, go on from the basic
secondary school (Collège d'Enseignement Secondaire, or CES),
three times as many go into technical training, leading to skilled
jobs, as into institutions that lead to professional careers or higher
education.

To understand this, we need to look back a stage, to what happens in the CES. Despite reforms, there still exists a considerable element of streaming in secondary schools, with children placed, more or less at entry, into either the "normal" (traditional) classes or into the *classes à programme allégé*. Once in the latter, it is difficult to escape. I was told that at one CES, at the end of the 5ème year, when important decisions are made about a child's future, some 7 percent of the *allégé* stream would transfer to the 4ème normal class, and perhaps go eventually to a *lycée;* about 60 percent would go on to a CET; and about one-third would continue at the CES in the Classes Préprofessionnelles de Niveau (CPPN) and the Classes Préparatoires à l'Apprentissage (CPA). The low percentage of immigrants at lycées suggests that relatively few are allocated to the upper streams in the CES. Data from outside Lyon confirm this. Figures for the Department of the Isère suggest that foreign pupils constitute 18–20 percent of the *allégé/* CPPN classes against 5–6 percent of normal classes (cf. also similar figures for Nanterre, in Meury 1975). Global figures for Lyon are not available, but at two schools where immigrants form 23 percent and 30 percent of the school population, the immigrant population of the lower streams was of the order of 70 percent. At one of these schools, where 12.5 percent of the 1975–6 intake were children with Arab names, such children constituted 17 percent of the three *allégé* classes.

Although individuals may not conform to the general pattern and indeed may go on to a *lycée,* the great majority of immigrant children, especially North African ones, enter the CES in the lower streams and proceed either to a technical college, if they are relatively successful, or into the CPPN. This streaming is based in large part on what happens before the child arrives at the CES, that is, in the primary school. The stream in which the child is placed in the CES depends on the result of examinations taken in the last primary year and on teachers' reports on progress made during that year. Some information obtained from primary schools is relevant here.

The following data are drawn from three primary schools and refer to the final year class of 1975–6. They were obtained in May 1976, when decisions for the following year were being made.

1. Out of fourteen North African children, eight would enter the normal class, the rest the *allégé* class (or would repeat the

Table 7.4. *Results of tests administered to 39 North African pupils (percentage distribution)*

Result	Verbal	Nonverbal	"Normal" distribution
Good	15.4	33.3	27
Average	53.8	43.6	46
Weak	30.8	23.1	27
Total	100.0	100.0	100.0

Source: School authorities.

year). Thus, in an area where about 86 percent of children usually enter the normal stream, 57 percent of the North African children from this school would do so.

2. Out of fifteen children (thirteen of them North African), four would enter the normal class. At the adjacent school in this *groupe* no child had entered the "normal" class at the normal age this year or last.

3. At this school I obtained the results of tests taken by one class of nineteen pupils (ten French, five North Africans, four Southern Europeans). The average score out of 20 obtained by the class was 13.4. Only one of the five North Africans obtained a mark above the average. If entry to the *allégé* were based solely on these tests, then, given the proportion of pupils in the area who enter such classes, we might expect the bottom five pupils to be so streamed. If that were the case, four out of five North Africans and one Italian would be placed in the *allégé* stream.

These examples reveal a general trend, even if there are variations between schools. In fact, the selection process is more complicated than has been suggested, because not all secondary schools stream immediately on arrival and some do not accept without question the primary schools' assessments of children's abilities. For example, the director of the secondary school receiving pupils from primary school (1) above regarded only one in eight of the North African children as suitable for the normal class, compared with the primary school's assessment of 57 percent. The secondary schools themselves also carry out further tests. Table 7.4 shows the results of these tests taken by thirty-nine North African children who entered one secondary school in 1975–6 and who had already been streamed.

Table 7.5. *Percentages of immigrants and Algerians in school populations of CES and SES schools in certain communes*

Commune	Immigrants		Algerians	
	% CES	% SES	% CES	% SES
Vaulx	33	44	19	35
Vénissieux	20	33	10	19
Villeurbanne	20	47	10	30

These tests would be used to "redress the inequalities," as the CES *directrice* put it, of the initial streaming. In this sample the relatively better performance of the North African children in the nonverbal tests is self-evident. Yet great reliance is put on the verbal tests both in secondary and primary schools. For example, the scores obtained in the tests administered in primary school (3) mentioned above would be based on results of tests in composition, dictation, vocabulary, comprehension of a text, grammar, conjugation, writing, and mathematics. The tests (Table 7.4) include numerical series, sets, two diagrammatic "differences" tests, verbal analogy, meaning of proverbs, vocabulary, and verbal classification involving both meaning and grammar. All of this suggests the need for considerable agility in the French language.

A final piece of evidence for the streaming of immigrants concerns the Sections d'Education Spécialisée, or SES. These special sections, usually attached to a CES, originated in 1909 to handle children with an "intellectual deficit." A very high percentage of children in these sections are immigrants (see Table 7.5). In 1975–6, in the Rhône Department as a whole, 546 out of 2,147 SES pupils (25.4 percent) were North African, proportionately four times as many as are found in the state secondary-school system as a whole (5.9 percent). To put this in another perspective, if we take the southeastern suburbs as a whole, we find that North Africans form 2.4 percent of the highest educational echelon – the lycées population – but 24.1 percent of the lowest, the SESs, that is, proportionately ten times as many are classified as subnormal, in terms of the French system, as are classified as bright.

Most people associated with the school system, or with immigrant children, are aware of this. "At school, the children know they are in the *classe poubelle* [the trash-can class]," said an *ani-*

mateur at Vaulx-en-Velin. The *directrice* of a CES in Vaulx, describing how at the end of the 5ème year the children go either to a technical college or into the CPPN, remarked, "It's in this last group that one finds many foreigners, especially North Africans or Portuguese. There are some foreigners who get on, the girls more than the boys. The Spanish and Italians can compete with the French. One mustn't exaggerate. In the 6ème and 5ème *allégés,* one has a good bunch that includes some who go on to the CET. It's the CPPN, that's the *poubelle.* Those in the CPPN can leave when they reach sixteen. Many can't wait to reach sixteen to leave, and we can't wait until they are sixteen to get rid of them." One social assistant commented that it was in the CPPN and SES classes with their high proportion of immigrants that most of her "interventions" occur. The *directrice* of one of the schools where she worked added: "There are three streams at this school: the best, the average, and the weak. The foreigners, the real foreigners, are found mainly in the latter. Spaniards and Italians escape this."

The facts about the distribution of immigrant children are widely known, at least in educational circles, and not disputed; what the facts mean is something that is much debated. I wish now to examine various views expressed on the causes of the "educational backwardness" (*retard scolaire*) of immigrant children.

BELIEFS ABOUT CAUSES

Consider, first, the following comments of a *conseiller d'éducation:* "The children who pose no problems, their parents come to see us. But the children who pose problems, we never see the parents. And everything comes from that. The children are left to their own devices, the parents speak poor French, they have large families. One understands that with thirteen brothers and sisters the parents can't occupy themselves with the children, and the children know it. They are out until eleven o'clock at night, left to themselves. But the fact that the parents speak poor French is no excuse, because others in the same position come to see us. Another problem is lack of respect for the buildings. There is a total lack of respect for all material things. Of course, the French children are like this too, but a friend of mine who teaches at a CES in the center of Lyon in a quartier that is, well, very good, there they have no problems of this kind whatsoever. But in the ZUP, where they have put all the foreigners, which consists of HLM and has a French population that is very very average. . . . So one has degradation. Not serious – broken doors, chairs, the caretaker's rosebush deliberately trampled down. You've seen how small the playground is. One has to be behind them all the time. One has the impression, it's difficult to explain, that they think they have the right to break everythng. They've got a lovely building, lawns, everything. That doesn't affect them. There's a lack of respect."

In the following discussion I will use this and other texts to illustrate a variety of themes that appear in statements taken from informants in the educational world, all of which concern the causes of *retard scolaire*. Each statement usually contains several themes or ideas, sometimes strung together in a rather haphazard fashion, though the ideas may be distinguished from each other analytically.

One major theme locates the cause of educational failure outside the school system. Frequently, as the statement recorded above illustrates, it is the family environment of immigrants that is treated as a primary cause. The *directrice* of a CES at Vaulx-en-Velins: "Why do the Portuguese and North Africans have such a low standard? The family environment is poor. The mother speaks very little French. The father speaks more but is always at work. They don't check the *carnet scolaire* because they can't read, and if the social assistant doesn't help . . . The children are absent from school, fool their parents, write their own excuse notes. Sometimes the mother and children have come to France after their father, having lived on their own over there. The children have lacked a father. But often the fathers are too brutal. The parents allow the children a great deal of freedom, letting them out of doors, but react too severely. There is a gap [*décalage*] between their customs and ours. On n'est pas raciste, mais peut-être ils sont plus facilement voleurs et menteurs."

A primary teacher in Villeurbanne: "Before discussing teaching problems, I want to mention first the social problems – the offensive remarks made about the quartier. But the educational standard *is* low. The children are in the streets always. When they leave school, they don't talk French in the home. One never sees the parents here asking after their children's results. The parents are afraid, they go out very little. At one time we held meetings jointly with the other school in the *groupe* about entry to the CES. For about forty pupils, three or four parents came. Take language. These children were all born here, they have always spoken French. But the standard is very low. They are bilingual. The mother has no *culture*, the father is unemployed or off sick. The parents never ask about the child's progress. The child leaves school with his hands in his pockets – no satchel, no books, no homework. One gets letters signed by the child himself. I once got into my car and went down to see a parent myself, but one can't do that all the time. If a child is absent, one asks for a note and gets the reply 'My father can't write.' The child himself might write the note, 'Please excuse X, he had a headache.' In fact, we have few problems of absenteeism. The children feel very comfortable here: ten absences in a class per month maximum. And even if children have the morning off to go for an injection, they come in the afternoon. The parents know the director will signal the Allocations Familiales, and school, for them, means the family allowance."

In these examples the problem is seen partly as one of lack of parental control over the children (an idea we saw at work in earlier chapters), and partly as one of lack of parental participation in the school system. The family environment is also thought to fail to prepare children for the school regime. The *directrice* of a *maternelle* receiving children from a *cité de transit:* "It was necessary to teach the families about the school, that there are rules to be respected, that the children should be brought to school at specific times. Then hygiene. It was virtually an education in itself among the families."

The first cause, then, is the family environment, or rather the gap between immigrant families and the French school system. This, in turn, may be attributed to the immigrants' culture of origin: "The big difficulty for me is with the Portuguese. They are very poor, from a very poor country, still very much country bumpkins. A social assistant told me that they live in one room even if the apartment has four or five. They save all their money to return home, and buy secondhand furniture at the flea market. I have children who don't even know how to use the toilet. They are a long way from being integrated. They are practically not civilized. Still *sauvages*. Their parents have hardly any contact with the school. They seek any job to get money to build their house at home and return there. They're not interested in installing themselves" (*directrice*, primary school).

The reference to Portuguese children here is important. Within the school system, though rarely in other contexts, Portuguese as well as North Africans are believed to constitute a problem group. Indeed, the *directrice* just cited compared the Portuguese un-favorably with Algerians, whose "parents concern themselves much more with the children: they are much better integrated." The following comment from an *orientation* assistant in Villeur-banne draws an interesting cultural distinction between the two groups. "The main problem groups now are the North Africans and to some extent the Portuguese. Portugal is a country quite far away from France. The families go home during the year to the house they are building there. The children follow the family – too bad for the children. Thus, Portuguese children pose a prob-lem, but not for the same reasons as North Africans. They are attached to a tradition, Islam, which is very hard." Another pri-mary teacher referred to the position of women in that tradition: "Among them there is a different role of the woman. Their sys-tem of discipline is different from ours. Ours is more gentle. Among them the father is the paterfamilias, the mother has no authority at all. So among them there is a great contempt for women. They class a woman as someone one dominates. All this leads to great problems with women teachers."

Another factor, of great significance, is language, as a number of remarks in comments previously cited will have shown. A pri-mary teacher: "The children don't speak the language, and when they do they have very little vocabulary. . . . They are behind, especially in French, in all aspects of language – writing, spelling, grammar." Another primary teacher referred to the problem of "false bilingualism, true bilingualism being one in which a person talks with another when both understand each other's language. The parents often can't read or write French or their own lan-guage. The children must undertake all the *démarches*. They have the status of adult. The parents have the status of a minor vis-à-vis the children. Because of this the child is often busy with the *dé-marches* at the town hall."

There will be more to say about language below and in the next chapter. The next comment, however, begins again with lan-guage: "Most of the children who come to the primary school have been in the *maternelle* since they were very young. But the 'cultural' situation is very low. These children don't have a mother tongue – neither French nor Arabic. Those who come direct from their country of origin have their language. Some of these families have sixteen children. They can't help each other because they speak French badly, and the mother can't help them. The mother speaks to the children in Arabic. They do not reply in Arabic, the children speak a mixture to their parents. The father, because of his work, speaks a bit more French. . . . But language is not really the heart of the matter. Language, yes, but more important is culture, and more important still are social reasons. These children have a social handicap like others – the French – from deprived backgrounds. Thus they are just like the French. But in addition they have a cultural handicap. There is nothing in common between the two cultures. The teacher can help a bit, but one should start in the *maternelle*. If you saw how they lived! These Arab ladies, they marry when young, have ten to fifteen children. They don't really bring them up. Among the North Africans the boys have no training. They are always in the streets. The mothers have no authority over their children."

The last part of that statement would seem to take us back to where we started this section, with the family environment. In fact, the priority given to "social reasons" over "culture" and "language" suggests a rather different ideological orientation in this speaker. A primary teacher employed on the ZUP at Vaulx-en-Velin put it thus: "The families on the ZUP are not from the highest social stock, and there are financial problems. The children, the French as well, are from very poor families. They are poorly nourished at home and often come to school hungry. They are poorly clothed. They lack material things." A *conseiller d'orientation* put it more bluntly: "There are very few French children in the CPPN at Les Minguettes [the ZUP]. This is because of the socioeconomic level of the families. The same applies to the French from the most deprived backgrounds. These are class schools."

Running through these statements, then, are various notions concerning the causes of *retard scolaire*, of which the principal ones are the family environment and the gap between family and school, the cultural background of origin, language, and a range of socioeconomic factors including class position. Occasionally, other notions appear, including those concerning national character (*Plus facilement voleurs . . .*). Individual speakers usually proffer several of these notions as explanations for educational, failure: sometimes simply listing them (with or without according one or another priority), sometimes establishing connections between them, for example, culture-family, environment-language. Occasionally, as we have seen previously, one notion may be accorded ideological supremacy, that is, it has the status of a controlling ideological principle within a discourse. The following statement by an official of the primary-teachers' trade union (SNI) illustrates a contrast between two such ideological principles: class and culture. "The basic view of immigrants [held by member of the union] depends on the political tendency [to which they adhere]. The general debate has focused on the weight attached to natural gifts as opposed to conditions of life and culture. Some teachers see the situation of *immigrés* in terms of culture, and only see a problem of culture. This view ignores the social causes. They ignore social and economic problems that are the same for French children, but aggravated in the case of *immigrés* by cultural differences. In our view, that of the tendency I follow, the problem is political and economic at root, and the other pedagogic problems are secondary. The majority tendency thinks the reverse. They concentrate on the pedagogic problems. Their view is narrower. Some people think of school as the liberator, but one has to deal with the society first."

It is obvious that the conceptualization of what constitutes a problem and of its cause(s) will have implications for the remedial action, if any, that is thought appropriate. The possibilities are also clearly limited by the context. Whatever view they might hold, teachers operating from within the school system are constrained by that fact. Official and unofficial action on the part of teachers as such in fact occurs on two fronts. First, in a general way, there are attempts to close the gap between school and family. Either the teachers themselves undertake these ("It was virtually an education in itself among the families") or more usually they signal another service, for example, the *assistantes scolaires* attached to the schools, or the assistants of the DDASS or one of the private services. These services then mediate between the family and the school and/or try to encourage a more favorable orientation toward the school system. Second, there are a variety of solutions of a more specifically pedagogic nature.

TACKLING "PEDAGOGIC" PROBLEMS

French schools provide a number of special course or classes aimed at foreign pupils. These include: (1) full-time courses

Table 7.6. *Distribution of special classes in the Rhône Department, November 1975*

Area	Primary	Secondary
Lyon	3	1
Villeurbanne	2	2
Eastern suburbs	8	3
Western suburbs	4	1
Northern suburbs	2	1
Outside *agglo.*	4	2
Total	23	10

(*classes d'initiation* in primary schools, *classes de soutien* in secondary schools) involving classes of fifteen to twenty pupils who either speak no French or whose knowledge of French is insufficient. The course lasts one year. (2) Part-time courses (*cours de rattrapage*) in both primary and secondary schools, involving groups of a dozen children who receive extra tuition in French in school hours. Table 7.6 shows the distribution of these classes in the Rhône Department in 1975, when there was approximately one class for every 1,400 foreign pupils.

Nationally, there were more than 500 *classes d'initiation* in 1974–5 compared with 33 in 1968–9 (Grange and Cherel, 1975:11). They are therefore a recent phenomenon. An informant involved in their development said: "In the mid-sixties a number of teachers faced with young Algerian children in their primary schools who did not speak French appealed for help to the minister of education." A typewritten report of April 1967 prepared by two local social workers refers to this problem. They note the arrival of some five hundred foreign children in Lyon in 1965 and record the difficulties faced by teachers (and French pupils) in classes where there is a significant number of foreign pupils. They comment: "Dans la grande majorité des cas, quelque soit son âge [l'enfant] est admis au cours préparatoire [first-year primary]. La présence de presque adolescents dans une classe d'enfants de 6 ans est un facteur de perturbation certain." They go on to suggest the opening of what they call *recyclage* classes for children arriving from overseas without any knowledge of French. My informant continued: "The matter went the rounds of the ministries. Education passed it to Foreign Affairs who passed it to Cooperation.

They defined the problem as one of language, learning the language, and passed it to the Ecole Supérieure de Saint-Cloud and to CREDIF [an educational research unit]." CREDIF (Centre de Recherche et d'Etude pour la Diffusion du Français) developed an experimental method that was first implemented in Paris, and the courses were formally instituted by a ministerial circular (No. 9, 70–73, January 13, 1970).

Classes d'initiation are separate classes located in an ordinary primary school. They are aimed at newly arrived children, who receive a full-time education with special emphasis on the rapid acquisition of the French language to a standard that will enable them to enter the ordinary classes. The *cours de rattrapage* are for children who have been in France for two or three years, though occasionally children born in France of foreign parents are assigned to them. A number of people, especially on the left, were critical of the poor provision of these classes, especially in the city of Lyon, where there are only three for the entire primary school population. In fact, with the tailing off of immigration, and the smaller numbers of children of school age arriving in the area, demand for places in *classes d'initiation* was thought to be falling. Indeed, two such classes (at Oullins and Vaulx-en-Velin) closed during the mid-1970s.

The emphasis in these classes is on language, and there is little additional aid specifically for foreign pupils. Most schools, however, do provide for all pupils a number of supplementary classes (the *études*) outside school hours. The cost of their provision falls on the commune, as the municipal authorities in working-class areas frequently point out. Special provision is sometimes made by private associations, and two different approaches to this may be contrasted.

At an NDSA *cité de transit*, the director and his wife, both retired teachers, organize *aide scolaire* for the families. For primary-school children signaled to them by the teachers, there are one or two hours a week extra work in French and arithmetic. For secondary-age children a room is set aside each evening with "tables, chairs, dictionaries, and silence." Help is provided with several subjects. The director saw this as a pilot project that would provide an example for the education of immigrants of the kind that Monsieur Rosset, the founder of NDSA, had provided for their housing.

Such *aide scolaire* has a mixed reception from teachers. Some feel that children are supposed to do their homework on their own, others that just this type of support is necessary. One CES *directrice* was enthusiastic: "I have told the inspector that there should be *répétiteurs*, even for the French children, one for ten or fifteen pupils to reinforce the work of the school, supervise the children's homework. The mother is often out at work. We have to replace the family."

A different sort of *rattrapage scolaire* was provided by the *animateurs* at another *cité*. "We don't want to be a safety net for the Ministry of Education. We work with the parent-teacher association and the teaching unions. On Wednesday afternoons we hold classes for children with serious psychological problems, and in the early evening we provide an *aide scolaire*. This has no relationship with the *études*. We work with small groups, getting the children to prepare theatrical performances or texts concerned with their culture – as proletarians, as immigrants, as people from another country." This speaker described the work of the NDSA as being "without political analysis."

If there is relatively little provision for foreign pupils, there is less for their teachers, who often feel unprepared for the problems of immigrant children. This applies both to the ordinary teacher and to those assigned to the special classes. One of the latter, who had training as a teacher, received her present job after attending a fifteen-day course organized by CREDIF. Later she took a one-year course: "The Ministry of Education didn't know where to put special training for teachers of immigrant children, so the course formed part of a general course on maladjusted children with some hours each week for my speciality." According to this informant, some thirty-five teachers passed through this course, which was subsequently disbanded.

In 1975, a new venture in special training was inaugurated at Lyon by Pierre Grange, director of CEFISEM (Centre d'Information et de Formation des Personnels Concernés par la Scolarisation des Enfants de Travailleurs Migrants). In 1975–6 the center organized four courses, each lasting six weeks, for practicing teachers, a course for primary-school inspectors, and a series of day courses for trainee teachers. This is the only center of its kind in France, and the full-length courses attracted one hundred teachers from all over the country. The content of these courses stresses the socioeconomic and political background to migration in both the sending and receiving societies, the social and "psycholinguistic" background to the education of foreign children, and the relationship between educational institutions and other institutional systems in the society.

The orthodox approach to the educational problems of immigrant children favors measures (language training, *aide scolaire*) that would, in theory, allow such children to catch up with their French counterparts and thus participate fully in the ordinary school system. In the mid-1970s, however, a number of proposals of a more radical nature were under discussion by educationalists attached to institutes such as CEFISEM. These suggested, a fulfledged bilingual and *bicultural* curriculum and would also involve teachers from the immigrants' countries of origin. ("In a school with a hundred percent immigrants, it is idiotic that the children should be taught by French teachers.") These proposals were still at the embryo stage in 1975–6, but the basic idea was that children should learn two languages (French and their mother tongue) in equal part. The curriculum would reflect this dual orientation, though it was also argued that it would not matter whether the rest of the curriculum (e.g., arithmetic) was followed in one language or the other. (See, for example, Colin 1976 and other papers prepared for a CEFISEM study course on educational problems.)

These proposals are quite radical in the French context, where the emphasis has always been on the integration of ethnic minorities by means of their "francisization." They emerged at a time when there were widespread demands among migrants for mother-tongue teaching. A researcher at CEFISEM: "On Saturday I attended the opening of the first Spanish school in Lyon. It is a pity because it shows that the French school system has failed, has been unable to respond to the demands of the parents. Soon there will be schools in Portuguese, Turkish, and so on. It will be regrettable, but they will be right." There will be more to say about language teaching and demands for courses in the mother tongue in Chapter 8. For the moment, let us return to the educational system, or rather to what happens after schooling is completed.

THE AFTERMATH

The following comments are from secondary-school teachers and advisers on careers:

"There is a great deal of difficulty at the moment in finding employers for pupils in [sandwich] classes. The big factories will not take them, so we have to hunt around the small artisans. A further problem for North Africans is that employers frequently refuse to accept North African children from these courses. For example, hairdressers don't want North African girls."

"The problem of employers who refuse to take North Africans affects the girls particularly. The sort of jobs they can get are as salesgirls or hairdressers. The *patrons* may be willing to take them, but the customers won't have it. . . . Schoolchildren can stay on until the end of the academic year in which they reach sixteen, but many leave on their sixteenth birthday even though they can't get jobs. I don't know what happens to them. They don't say. I suppose they get work as manual laborers."

"Immigrant children also suffer – not to mention unemployment – from certain employers who shut the door in their faces. They say to me, 'We want Europeans only.' They have become a bit cleverer. They used to say 'No North Africans!' Many different types of industry have said this, though not the building trades, which are still open. I remember the boss of a small metal workshop who told one young North African, 'I'll take you, but you promise me that you'll go at once to the prefecture to ask for French nationality.' The boy discussed it with me, but he didn't want to lose Algerian citizenship. Yesterday I was on the phone to a center where they take apprentices and they said, 'No foreigners.' They had 50 percent already. Young immigrants have to overcome a whole succession of barriers. A young man said to me, 'The French take us for slaves.' To be introduced to an employer by a social assistant means to be seen as a difficult case. There is always that inference. One employer said, 'I don't want delinquents!'"

These statements were made in the middle of 1976 at a time when the post-1973 "crisis" was beginning to take shape, but before unemployment, especially youth unemployment, became a matter of widespread concern. The job market was, however, becoming difficult, particularly for foreigners in search of work. It was the time of the widely publicized ministerial statement comparing the numbers of unemployed and the numbers of foreign workers in France (see Chapter 2 and Chapter 3, Event 2). In addition to a difficult job market and direct or indirect discrimination, North African youths are often faced with the fact that the system, especially the school system, labels them as "difficult."

Two comments by young Algerians engaged in the teaching of Arabic to North African children are pertinent here.

"I took on a class of children at ———. I was told that they were 'predelinquents.' After I'd met the children, I questioned this concept of 'delinquent.' I came to the conclusion that a delinquent was really thought of as someone who did not have the same values as the French."

"The system by which children are placed in care is very arbitrary. On the child's record card is marked his nationality and place of residence. If you come from a certain quartier, for example, the rue Olivier de Serres, the courts take that into account. Take the son of a friend of my father's. This boy was twelve years old and at primary school at the time of the oil crisis. His teacher made some racist remarks about Arabs and the boy had a fit and struck her. The police were called and he ended up in a center for the moderately mentally defective. But this aggravated his situation. He is squeezed and becomes more delinquent than ever."

"THE FIRE NEXT TIME"?

"These young people experience constant failure. They are always surprised when something works. At school they know they are in the *classe poubelle*. Soccer only interests them a little; they get tired of it very rapidly. Karate and kung fu are very popular, but it is the choreography of the movements that they imitate. They never have the means to express what's in their hearts. They are always aggressive, for example, in language." This is how an *animateur* at Vaulx-en-Velin characterized the groups of young North Africans who frequented the ZUP. A housing official at Vénissieux described such groups as "gangs of youths, layabouts, professional unemployed, professional sick." To many French people, such youths (indeed, North African men in general) appear threatening and potentially violent. A number of statements cited in this and previous chapters from teachers and social workers illustrate this. Real violence, however, is relatively rare. The following comments come from discussions with a group of *éducateurs* at the rue Olivier de Serres.

"Recently we have been led to take up educational problems. These kids leave school at sixteen without a trade. They think, well, one can get a job as a laborer, but we went to school and at the end have no more than our parents who didn't. One day about twenty kids came to the door crying, literally crying, about their schools, the teachers. Many of them enter the CES unable to read. The teachers are overwhelmed. Three or four years ago we tried to have a club. We were squeezed by the structure and the administration. We got one going for a certain age group. The younger ones also wanted to have a club, but the equipment didn't arrive, and the younger kids destroyed the other club. There were fights, they broke up the chairs. There was a soccer team, but it had such a bad reputation that no one played against it. The SONACOTRA hostel took three years to build. The kids broke everything, smashed windows. The firms employed a private security guard, and then asked for CRS [Compagnie Républicaine de Sécurité, the riot police] patrols."

"I understand that the police union has asked that ordinary police patrols not be used here because it's too dangerous. And then these are ten- to thirteen-year-olds, so what sort of intervention can the police make? There is a psychosis of fear. One day a CRS car was parked outside the buildings. Some youngsters – it was a game, they were amusing themselves – threw bottles down on the CRS from the top of the building. The police went to look for them leaving one of their number on guard. The kids distracted him and stole the car key and locked it up. You know the CRS vehicles [built so no one can break into them]. They were frantic. They spent three or four hours searching for the keys, not daring to go home for fear of their superiors. Eventually the car had to be towed away. These people are permanently devalued. School doesn't work, they are rejected in the streets, at work, because they are Arabs. They react, not to exist, but because through aggression, theft, they try to be consumers like the rest of the world. For a short time in the sixties we had *blousons noirs*, gangs of youths who joined together for a particular task. They burned a car once, rolling it over for a game. But in contrast with the situation in the United States, Harlem, the people here are in the position of being immigrants. They can be chucked out. The social situation here is also against revolt. They're really crushed. They are a subproletariat. In addition, they have no time to politicize themselves. Trying to earn a living is hard enough. And the Amicale [des Algériens en Europe] and the consulate tries to maintain good relations with the prefecture." The implication of that last remark, as we shall see, is that such organizations attempt to defuse what they see as potentially dangerous situations.

CONCLUSION

Let me summarize briefly what seems to emerge from this chapter. The influx of families has led to the existence in Lyon of a large and growing number of young people born in or brought up in France. Structurally they are "marginal" in French terms, as their position is that of permanent immigrants, unassimilated and in certain respects unassimilable. For a variety of reasons (subject of much discussion) the school system "doesn't work" for them, and they emerge from it with few if any qualifications. The job market is such that they are unemployed or employed only in manual work. Culturally, they are often said to be *entre deux chaises*. They are Frenchlike (in language, ideas, expectations), but can never be fully accepted as such. On the other hand, they are North African, even if they are losing their language and culture of origin (see Chapter 8, Event 4).

Within the schools, the principal sign that the system "doesn't work" for immigrant pupils is taken to be their "educational backwardness," and it is the reasons for this that exercise educationists and others.

In Britain too, of course, the relative lack of success of immigrant children at school has been the subject of much discussion. Here, and in the United States, however, debates about this have frequently become entangled with the question of the relationship, if any, between educational success, "intelligence," and race.

I do not believe that race has any bearing whatsoever on intelligence or on school success as the system defines it. Nor did most of my informants, though some came close to suggesting it. However, as in Britain, the vast majority of teachers would attribute educational failure to two sorts of factors, both external to the school system and therefore in large part outside their immediate control.

The first of these is the material basis of immigrant life – the social and economic conditions in which they live – or, in more political language, their class position. Thus: "One has to deal with the society first." The second is their culture, and the gap between it and that of the French school. It is on this factor that the official view places the greatest weight. Immigrant culture is seen as an obstacle to participation in the school system. Official policy, however, concentrates on one aspect only of the cultural gap: language (see the minister's remarks in Event 1). Ignorance of French, which creates severe practical difficulties for both teachers and taught, is perhaps the one problem open to practical solution. It can be seen as a technical matter with which the administration can cope.

That this is insufficient is beginning to be recognized by groups such as CEFISEM, and more generally by those on the left who believe that there are cultural as well as social and economic problems to be resolved. The view that immigrant culture, so far from being an obstacle, represents a positive force that is to be encouraged, is one that is slowly gaining ground, as we shall see in the next chapter. There is, however, another difficulty with a solution that emphasizes the acquisition of French as a solution to *retard scolaire*.

In the orthodox, dominant French view the school system exerts an homogenizing influence. Education and the acquisition of the French language break down old identities and create a new, French one. So far as North African immigrants are concerned, there are two contradictions in this ideology. First, the educational system in theory stresses equality of opportunity. It allows the best to emerge irrespective of background. In practice, its results mirror very accurately the class structure of the wider society. To that extent the experience of immigrants within it is quite normal. Through the school system they "find" their class position. Thus, although the schools make French men and women out of Arabs or Portuguese, they do not do so on the basis of equality. At best the system creates working-class French men and women. But, second, it does not, and cannot, do the job thoroughly. North Africans who go through the schools remain, in many different ways, North African – partly through their own volition, partly through their rejection by French society. Given their socioeconomic position, therefore, it is not inaccurate to describe the final product as a culturally and ethnically defined "underclass."

8

Language

In earlier chapters remarks were cited suggesting that in various ways language is an important issue for both French and immigrant informants. There are, in fact, several issues, depending in part on *what* language is under discussion and in what contexts.

It will be apparent from accounts of the education system, the social services, and the housing institutions that one focus of concern is the immigrants' lack of command of *French*, especially of the standard language. First, a poor grasp of French on the part of children and adult females is connected with incomplete or unsuccessful participation in the French system: schools, employment, the community at large. Second, it leads to difficulties for the personnel of French institutions. Their clients often have to be dealt with at one remove, for example, by way of interpreters or intermediaries, a point discussed further in Chapter 11. Third, there is concern at the differential knowledge of French displayed by different categories of the immigrant population (adult male workers, housewives, children). Fourth, this is thought to be associated with tension between members of North African families. Differential linguistic ability is part of the gap between parents and children and between husbands and wives. This is linked to the second point in that access to the institutions on the part of North African families (and vice versa) is frequently via children, not parents. This is believed to place the latter in a "minority status" vis-à-vis the former.

Discussion of the immigrants' own languages – their mother tongues – raises a different set of problems. Here the focus is the provision of instruction in such languages, mainly for immigrant children, both inside and outside the school system (see Event 4). The principal issues here include the extent to which there should be institutional support for such instruction, by whom it should be provided, and for what purpose.

A third problem area, relating directly to the first two, is French ignorance of the languages and cultures of immigrants. As we have seen, this was a matter of some concern to social workers, and to teachers for whom organizations such as CEFISEM now provide instruction, at least in the socioeconomic and cultural background of migrant populations. A number of professional workers go further and many attend courses in migrants' languages, especially in Arabic (see Event 5).

These various problem areas are linked in three ways. First, at their core are, ultimately the critical questions of the present and future status of immigrant cultures: Under what conditions are immigrants and their culture to exist in France, and in what form, and what is to be their relationship to both French culture and society and that of their home country? Specifically, is it envisaged that immigrants will *settle* in France, and if so on what terms? Or is it thought that sooner or later they will go back whence they originally came? There is a complex set of issues here, sometimes referred to elliptically as *le retour*.

The second link is the various ideological themes that cut across discussions of each problem area. I should perhaps stress that this chapter is principally concerned with ideologies of language knowledge and language learning and their institutional enactment, and the intention is to use material relating to language to illuminate certain wider ideological and institutional questions, in particular the meaning of terms such as *intégration* and *insertion*. The chapter is thus only indirectly concerned with language *behavior,* for example, the facts of bilingualism.

The third link is that solutions to the problems generated by the debates are in each case implemented through formal, institutionalized systems of instruction, that is, language courses. In fact, formal instruction is usually seen as the primary means of language acquisition. Interestingly enough there has until very recently been almost no discussion or study of informal language acquisition among migrant workers in France, in contrast to Germany (see Klein and Dittmar 1979, Heidelberger Forschungsprojekt "Pidgin-Deutsch" 1978). Some of the contributors to a recent publication (GRECO 13, 1981) remedy this, though many in fact reject a distinction between formal (*dirigé*) and informal (*naturel*) language learning (see Catani 1981:79; Descayrac and Dubois 1981:108).

This chapter is in two parts. The first three sections describe the institutions involved in language instruction, including instruction in French to adult learners, and instruction in one of the major immigrant languages: Arabic. In the course of that description I present accounts of two meetings (Events 4 and 5) at which a number of issues connected with language teaching and learning were debated. The second part of the chapter examines the ideological themes that emerge from such debates and from other discussions that impinge on language.

A final point: Various statements by informants cited in this chapter bear on matters (e.g., the significance of bilingualism or, more distantly, linguistic relativism) that are the subject of academic discussion. In fact, those informants may well be influenced by that discussion. For example, edited extracts (Philippe 1973) of Catani's important book (1973) on *alphabétisation* were in circulation in Lyon and clearly influenced a number of people I met. Such "academic" discussion must be treated as part of the datum of inquiry and not accorded a special, privileged status. The issues raised by this trickling down of social scientific ideas, which we have encountered elsewhere, will be discussed in the final chapter.

THE ORGANIZED TEACHING OF FRENCH

In debates about the teaching of French (and here, of course, I am concerned solely with the teaching of French to immigrants) a distinction may be made according to the category of immigrant presumed to be the target for instruction. These categories are principally those of age and gender: adult males, adult females, children. Concerning each of these there are somewhat different debates, often involving different personnel and institutions. The content of debate may also differ according to the contexts of language use to which reference is made – language in work, in the process of learning, in institutional relationships (e.g., social services, hospitals), in relationships in the community at large, and in relationships with commercial enterprises (personal consumption).

The teaching of French to foreign children is almost wholly the province of the schools, though occasionally private tuition may be secured by concerned parents. The organization of such teaching was described in Chapter 7. The teaching of French to adult immigrants is known as *alphabétisation,* or simply *alpha,* that is, literacy, and it may be noted that training in language and in literacy are not organizationally distinguished in this context.

Three sorts of organization are involved in *alpha,* the most important being the Amicale pour l'Enseignement des Etrangers (AEE), formally a private association but one that is backed and financed by the government. A national organization with a regional and departmental structure, it employs various categories of full-time and part-time teachers (for which it has its own jargon terms), almost all French, some on secondment from schools. The AEE runs French-language classes at various levels (beginners, second year, etc.) separately for men and women. Classes are mostly held outside working hours in social centers, *cités de transit,* hostels, and sometimes school premises. A certain number of classes are offered to employees at their places of work. The extent to which such classes should be provided is a subject of much discussion. The AEE's local branch, the Délégation de Lyon, employed in 1975 some 150 teachers and enrolled about 2,400 pupils (known as *stagiaires*) in approximately 150 ongoing courses. The *stagiaires* are mostly North African but also include a number of Portuguese, Turks, and Yugoslavs.

The AEE is the most important of the organizations in terms of numbers, but also very active in Lyon are several private welfare-type associations that engage in *alpha.* They are formally much less dependent on the state than is the AEE, except insofar as their activities in this field qualify them for government aid, which they receive from the Fonds d'Action Sociale. There are four of these. One is a relative newcomer to this scene, the Association pour l'Alphabétisation et l'Enseignement du Français aux Travailleurs Immigrés (AEFTI), which has links with the CGT. Of the others, CIMADE and Accueil et Rencontre are not as heavily involved in *alpha* as they were previously, but the Association de Coopération Franco-Algérienne du Lyonnais remains one of the most important private organizations in this field in France.

ACFAL, CIMADE, and Accueil et Rencontre were all initially concerned with the welfare of foreigners. CIMADE is a national organization, with its roots in Protestantism, that originally worked with refugees but subsequently extended its activities to include immigrants. The Lyon branch, however, was in 1975–6 more involved with the effects of urban renewal in the Ier Arrondissement, where its office was located. Accueil et Rencontre was formed in the 1950s by a group of Catholics interested in Africa and, by extension, black Africans in Lyon. Later this interest broadened to include North Africans and other immigrant workers such as the Portuguese (relatively numerous in the quartier where the association has its office). ACFAL, as its name implies, has always been concerned with Algerians, and during the 1950s was a focus of local French support for the FLN. Throughout its history it has also been engaged in *alpha*.

Each of these three organizations has changed considerably over the last decade. It is said that each has become increasingly politicized, and each has the reputation for being on the extreme left. ACFAL organizes courses roughly of the same scope as those offered by the AEE, though it depends much more heavily on volunteer teachers who are unpaid and largely untrained. This again is an issue that is much debated.

The third type of organization involved in *alpha* is the private profit-making language school. Normally such schools have directed their attention to the lucrative business market (e.g., in the teaching of English), but with the availability of financial support from the government, they have entered the literacy field, providing courses mainly to firms who have agreed to offer facilities for their foreign workers during the hours of employment. One organization that does this is the Association pour la Diffusion de l'Enseignement Linguistique (ADIF), which is backed by various chambers of commerce in Lyon, and by certain banks. Finally, various private social work organizations, such as the SSFNA, also undertake what is in effect language teaching in other courses that they offer (see, for example, Chapter 5), but their formal contribution in this field is not great.

Many of these associations participate at the national and regional levels in the Comité de Liaison pour l'Alphabétisation et de la Promotion (CLAP), which publishes a journal (*Alphabétisation et Promotion*), and provides information and documentation for member associations. CLAP is beginning to specialize in the training of *alpha* teachers by providing courses of its own.

MOTHER-TONGUE TEACHING:
ARABIC FOR THE ARABS

By the mid-1970s, ACFAL and Accueil et Rencontre were both becoming involved in the teaching of Arabic to North African children. The principal contribution, however, came from the three North African governments, especially those of Tunisia and Algeria. The Algerian government organized this contribution through the Amicale des Algériens en Europe, a body that comes closest of any to being a North African immigrant association. The Tunisian and Moroccan governments also have what are popularly called *amicales* in Lyon, but they are widely regarded as little more than extensions of the consulates, if not the political police, of the countries concerned. The Algerian Amicale is indeed closely connected with the Algerian government, and also the local consulate, but because of the greater popularity of the Algerian regime, its activities tend to be viewed more favorably, except by those on the extreme left.

The Amicale des Algériens employs students (often Tunisians) to give courses in literary and modern Arabic to school-age children. In 1976 the Amicale had fourteen teachers working in Lyon holding weekly classes in various social centers and at some schools (outside normal school hours). Each year it organized a *Fête scolaire* in a Lyon theater, at which prizes were presented for those children who had done well.

An organizer of the Amicale offered the following rationale for their involvement in the provision of Arabic language courses: "In Algeria the children are Arabs in an Arab milieu. Here the milieu is French. Even if the children speak Arabic at home, in school, on the streets, on TV they hear French. . . . The children born in France are in a completely different milieu. They do not know the cultural value of their country. They integrate in this milieu. The immigrant child is a bit deprived. He feels a stranger in school, and then on holidays over there he doesn't speak Arabic. His cousins treat him as French. The teaching of Arabic helps him to identify himself within a culture, gives him a means to get a grip on the strains in his culture. It gives the child a chance to express himself."

A number of other national groups were at this time engaged in the provision of mother-tongue teaching, including the Italian and Portuguese Catholic missions. Spanish, too, was being offered (see Chapter 7). The demand for these courses came variously from the governments concerned, from the parents, and from the children. It was supported by numerous French organizations such as the CGT and PCF. I was told by a representative of the latter: "Many North African children are born here and cannot speak Arabic. They are wounded, amputated. The PCF is fighting for language classes during the free course time at schools to allow them to retain their cultural patrimony. Algerians have a *perspective de retour,* always thinking of returning."

This was also at a time when the EEC was considering legislation to promote the compulsory provision of mother-tongue teaching in schools for the children of migrant workers. The prospect was not viewed with great enthusiasm by either the French government or the teachers: "I am in favor of Arabic classes. It is good to learn the mother tongue, preserve the culture. But that poses a problem. This could end up as an Arab school. This school is already rejected by the French. We have postponed the question [of introducing Arabic teaching] for a year. There does not appear to be a demand from the parents, though the mothers would like their children to speak Arabic. Another question is, what teachers? There already exists an Arabic course on Wednesdays and Saturdays put on by the Amicale or by some students. They use a very authoritarian method. One should teach the spoken language first. We don't want this to become an Arab school" (primary teacher, Oullins).

The teaching methods used in the Amicale's courses were often criticized by French teachers, but this statement raises a number of fundamental questions about attitudes toward multilingualism and multiculturalism, to which we return.

Although the bulk of mother-tongue teaching in Arabic is undertaken by the Amicale des Algériens en Europe, and the Algerian government is a major proponent of such teaching, both the French left and, in a different way, the French government, have become increasingly engaged in debating this issue. In Lyon, the private "leftist" associations such as ACFAL and Accueil et Rencontre provided in the mid-1970s a major forum for this debate, which under their auspices drew together a number of French teachers and social workers and some of the young North African students employed in Arabic-language training. Event 4 is a record of one such meeting, at which a principal theme was the close connection between language and ethnicity, and the desirability of fostering an awareness of cultural identity. Although situated in this chapter, where the emphasis is on language, the Event may also be read as a commentary on the general situation of young North Africans in France that was discussed in Chapter 7.

Event 4: A debate on cultural identity, April 1976

The following discussion took place at a study group which met as part of the proceedings of the Assemblée Générale of ACFAL. The principal participants were Sherif, Belkacem, Mohammed – all three Algerian students;

Jean-Paul, a French worker priest, teacher of Arabic, and sociologist; and the association's president. Some two-dozen people participated in the study group, including the above, of whom five were Arabs, the rest French, for the most part teachers and social workers.

During the Assemblée Générale, Belkacem reported on activities concerned with *identité culturelle:* "This refers to Arabic language courses for children. I began work in February at ——— [a suburb of Lyon]. About thirty children are taught literary Arabic by two *moniteurs.* The children are divided into two groups: six- to twelve-year-olds, and the CES [secondary] age group. Those kids are very motivated. It was at their request that the courses were organized. One is beginning to get some results, to make some progress. The method I employ is to try to create awareness among the people. The courses are oriented toward cultural identity, at the practical level, toward their cultural, national identity. However, although I am in favor of these courses, I don't think they should be run by ACFAL but by the governments concerned. The kids have a right to learn Arabic. We fill a gap." A question elicited the fact that thirty children at ——— and twenty in Villeurbanne follow these courses.

After the main meeting the participants divided into several study groups, one of which considered the question of cultural identity. Jean-Paul took the chair and Sherif opened the discussion.

Sherif: "The cultural problem is linked to the problem of immigration. People come here because they have to leave their countries to come here to work. The immigrant has a certain culture. He comes to France, to another ambience, to a different economic situation with strange forms of economic organization and cultural organization and ideological organization. There are problems as a consequence of his being in a new situation – for example in the organization of work. Industrial society has different customs from those found in underdeveloped countries. A first problem is language, when he steps off the boat. There are effects on his own language, there is an impoverishment of his own language. He uses very common French words at work – *usine,* for example. Outside work, in the streets, it's a life to which he is not accustomed. There is harassment by the police, the attitude of people who stare at him. All these changes create certain problems. So then he sends for his family. Over there [in North Africa] there is a highly defined organization of the family, of the traditional type. It is that type of family that comes here. We can contrast the family we describe as 'traditional' with the family one describes as *évoluée,* what one calls the modern type. In Algeria the family has the opportunity to evolve in its natural milieu, but they are parachuted into another milieu. The effect is to halt its evolution. A traditional Algerian family coming here remains a traditional Algerian family *in France,* with very little opportunity to modernize. The organization of the family is affected. The father has some elements of French vocabulary; the mother does not speak French. The children have much greater chance of contact with the society – they have their friends in the street, the TV, the school. Little by little a gap is created between parents and children. The child is distanced from his parents. He enters French society much more than his parents. Thus there arise more and more acute conflicts, which the parents try to resolve. They try to do this through the Arabic classes. These signify for the parents a means of recovering their children, of maintaining contact with their original milieu. From that moment there are conflicts. I apologize for making such a long speech."

Q1: "How do the children respond to their parents' demands?"

Q2: "These are the children's demands as well. The little ones feel they are not French."

Q3: "One gets a lot of requests like this in the primary schools, from among the parents. It is a recall to a society. The Arabic that is taught is literary Arabic, which the parents themselves don't understand. In the VIIIth Arrondissement the children go to extra classes."

Sherif: "There has been a permanent devaluation of all that belongs to these people. When he knows that the word 'Arab' is an insult [in French], that the name Mohammed is an insult, or the name Ali is an insult. In Arab culture Mohammed is the name of the Prophet. The children respond by saying: 'Reject everything that says we are Arabs.'"

Q4: "It is easier for them to speak the language they learned at school than their mother tongue."

Sherif: "There is scientific research that shows the ease with which the child can learn two languages, the one helping the other."

Belkacem: "The uprooting is at the origin of this. The way of life is different. There is the parachuting of the family. There is the blocking of the natural evolution of the family toward modernization. This comes from the children themselves. These children . . . French society is a consumer society. This encourages a sort of abscondment and leads to a sort of 'orgy,' in inverted commas, which is intellectual, and spontaneous in reaction. This leads to a cleavage between parents and children. The children learn about and wish to participate in all aspects of the society. The children wish to reach the same point as those in French society. Take, for example, a young girl. She sees French girls go to school, to university even, come home late at night. She wants the same freedom, the same way of life as these young people. Parents see their children going far away from them. The parents' response is to learn French. That's one way through which they can vet schoolwork. But they also want to put themselves in a position regarding a return to the culture of origin. There are two actions here that converge [Belkacem conveys the sense of 'from opposite directions' by a gesture of his hands]. The parents acquire a knowledge of the French world, the children, of the Arab world. Rejection of Arabic courses, yes, that occurs – but the courses are outside the regular school hours. The children are at the point of saturation. This diminishes their facilities of perception. If they have to attend an Arabic class on Wednesdays [a holiday or half day in French schools] they ask: 'Why are other children allowed out to play; why do we have to go to an Arabic class?' " Belkacem ends by saying that he stresses two points: saturation and a "pre-indisposition" not to go.

Q5: "There are three Arabic classes at Lyon in school hours with Tunisian teachers."

This intervention leads to a question about the activities of the Amicale des Algériens en Europe.

Belkacem: "The Amicale employs mostly students and mostly Tunisians, partly because Arabization has not gone so far in Algeria as in Tunisia, and partly because there is a cleavage between young Algerian students and the Amicale. The Amicale tried to organize classes at ———, but they didn't work. However, I repeat what I said earlier. It is not ACFAL's job, but that of the governments involved."

There follows a discussion of the law that allows instruction in the language of origin of foreigners in France if a certain number of pupils are available. Jean-Paul stresses that proper, fully trained teachers are required and remarks that at one place, in another department, there are five. One participant suggests that such teaching could replace the second language [usually English] in the secondary schools, as happens at one CES in Villeurbanne. Another recalls: "A year or two ago the Amicale talked about a large sum of money to be devoted to this task. Where did the money go?"

Sherif: "It is for the families to ask that!"

Jean-Paul: "Regarding the Arabic classes. There are children who prefer to speak French at home, and there are teachers who tell the children and their parents to speak French at home."

Q6: "I wish to question the benefit to the child of speaking French with parents who speak French badly."

Q7: "I know a family with six children. The two eldest speak Arabic, but the two youngest refuse to speak Arabic."

This intervention brings in a third Algerian, whose name, as Sherif notes rather hesitantly a little later, is Mohammed.

Mohammed: "There is a similar problem in Algeria with the Arabic and Kabyle languages. There are children in Algeria who understand Kabyle but don't speak it. The parents didn't learn Arabic at school, except perhaps in Koranic schools, where it was learned like Latin. The question is, what can the parent give the child in return. For us, Mohammed is the greatest of first names, here it is a term of abuse. Fatima as well. There are young girls who don't like to be called Fatima. The child is seated between two chairs."

Sherif: "What are the aims regarding the child? To get on in the world – *promotion sociale.* Here the only *promotion sociale* comes through the school. This is the only way to rise up the levels of French society."

Fourth Algerian: "Schools, yes, but after school, at work, the child gets his *carte d'in-intégrable."*

Sherif: "The school is the best means of entering and getting on [in French society]."

Mohammed: "I disagree with that. Look what happens to the Algerian child in school, going into the lowest streams . . ."

Sherif: "True, but if one wishes to get on, the best way is to proceed through the school system. I agree that the child of a worker has very little chance of becoming an engineer or a manager, but . . . In our society the teacher is highly valued, for example, in the Koranic schools. When I was a child at school [in Algeria], my father told the teacher that if his children don't learn: 'You can kill them. I give them to you!'"

Q6 refers to the "two-speed school" proposed by the recent Haby reforms: "Algerian children inevitably become unskilled workers. Some aspects of the Haby reforms look very liberal on paper . . . for example the opportunities for classes in the language of origin . . . but in practice . . ."

Q8: "What can ACFAL do about it with regard to the parents? I myself am in favor of literacy classes in Arabic. One always comes back to the knowledge of French. Why not use the network of literacy classes for teaching Arabic?"

Sherif: "It is a question of immigrant consciousness. Certain organizations are now demanding literacy classes in French *and* in the language of origin – Arabic, Turkish, and so on."

Q8: "This raises the problem of courses outside the hours of work. We have experience of courses in French and Arabic. These actions must be taken in liaison with other actions."

Jean-Paul: "I was recently in Constantine and all the notices were in Arabic only. A person who doesn't read Arabic doesn't feel at home. Regarding the devaluation of Arabic in France. In Grenoble, French children are learning Arabic; in Paris, they learn Portuguese. One must avoid a sort of ghetto. These courses must be really integrated in the school structure. We need a revaluation of Arabic culture. There are now certain Algerian and Egyptian films – good ones, not the pseudo-Hollywood of the kind that are generally shown – that the French now have the chance to see. We need a revaluation of Arabic culture in the eyes of the French."

Sherif: "What is really needed is the revaluation of the Algerian as a worker. There is an inequality between the French and the Algerian worker that is at the basis of it all. He is a person with some things to learn, but with plenty to give in exchange. We need equality of rights."

Belkacem: "The courses are only of value if there is an *explication*." He repeats his views about who should organize these courses and when, that is, during school hours.

Jean-Paul: "But hold on. That deprives the child of other activities."

Q9: "I have the sense that the demand for these courses comes from the desire for an eventual return [to North Africa]. Otherwise they find themselves like foreigners in Algeria. The children go home and find that they don't understand their cousins."

Sherif and Mohammed exchange words, disagreeing on the extent to which a child can make himself understood in French in Algeria. *Sherif* ends by stressing that: "Down there, there is an Arab environment."

Q3: "These demands are made to social assistants, to neighbors, to *parents-élèves* [the equivalent of parent-teacher associations]. There is a willingness among Algerian families to have courses in Arabic. But this consciousness doesn't exist among us. I advocate a raising of consciousness among French families in the local areas with films, cultural activities that present the Arab world."

Fifth Algerian: "Someone in my area [a suburb of Lyon] tried to organize a North African week. The organizer received an anonymous letter saying: 'If you do this, we'll blow it up."

The president of ACFAL: "At the Iraqi evening [held recently in the center of Lyon] there were a large number of North Africans. There is a demand for this type of activity."

Jean-Paul: "The play *Mohammed, prend ta valise* attracted great interest among French and North Africans. Next month the Familia Cinema in my own neighborhood is showing a series of Arabic films."

Q10: "There is the problem of delinquency among Algerians, especially the girls. There are judges who I feel are inclined to solve the problem by sending people to Algeria. I know a case of an Algerian girl who ran away several times and who was placed with an Algerian family in Algeria."

Mohammed: "I wonder whether that might not have been the best solution in that particular case."

Jean-Paul: "I knew the case very well and that was the only thing to do."

Sherif starts to talk about the problem of unemployment but gives way to:

Q3: "There are an enormous number of expulsions in the seventeen-to-twenty-two age group in Lyon. Of the order of one thousand a year."

Sherif: "The problem of young girls is more serious than that of young boys, but I disagree with Jean-Paul."

Jean-Paul: "What's your solution?"

Sherif: "You want me to give a recipe?"

The president: "But how do the children respond to these courses?"

Fifth Algerian: "I have the impression . . . in my area there are twelve percent North African families. The parents push the children. One risks putting them off."

The president asks for further information regarding the children's attitudes.

Q11: "In my area about twenty young children wanted these courses."

Belkacem: "In my courses the twelve- to fourteen-year-olds asked for them, wanting a knowledge of the Arab world before going there. Before I took the class, I was told that the children were predelinquents. I suspected that they were being labeled in this way because they were difficult to handle. And in fact I found my suspicions were justified. They were not predelinquents. I had no trouble with them."

Q11: "There is a difference between the young children and the adolescents. The young children do not have, as yet, a strong sense of rejection. But they want reassurance about their culture."

At this juncture a question is raised about the lack of a mosque at Lyon and the difficulties this poses for organizing religious festivals. The point is not followed up, and the session ends with some brief remarks on the practical problems of organizing courses at Lyon and on the training of teachers.

THE ORGANIZED TEACHING OF ARABIC – FOR THE FRENCH

Aside from a small amount of Arabic available as a school subject in certain lycées, the teaching of Arabic for French-speakers is provided mainly by the extramural department of Lyon II University, and by private associations such as ACFAL and Accueil et Rencontre. There is a considerable overlap in the teaching personnel. ACFAL courses are taught by the same small group of Arab students, coordinated by a French worker-priest with considerable North African experience (he appears in Events 4, 5, and 9 as "Jean-Paul"), who are also employed by the university. The students are undergraduates and postgraduates from Tunisia and Algeria who are enrolled in local universities and who undertake the teaching to help pay their way.

The courses at both the university and ACFAL are based on small weekly discussion classes, but ACFAL also organizes a three-week intensive Session d'Arabe each summer. I participated in both the annual and weekly courses. My fellow *stagiaires* included a wide range of people who for personal or professional reasons wished to learn the language. My weekly class, for example, contained a medical student who hoped to work in Morocco; two *alpha* teachers, one of whom was a woman employed as a driving instructor; a trade-union official in the building industry; and a woman who went to North Africa for her holidays but who was also associated with a youth club in an immigrant area of Lyon. Another class consisted mainly of social assistants. Other pupils had had their fees paid by employers who had been persuaded of the value of their employees' learning some Arabic.

The Session d'Arabe in July 1976 was attended by some sixty people of whom twenty-four came from the Lyon area, three from abroad, and thirty-three from the rest of France, representing twenty-one different departments. About a third were engaged in social work in the broad sense of the term, and a further third were teachers of one kind or another. Nurses, priests, nuns, and students made up the bulk of the remainder. Ages ranged from twenty-one to sixty-six with some 60 percent in the twenty-six- to forty-year-old group. The typical *stagiaire*, therefore, was the youngish professional worker whose job brought him (or more often her) into frequent contact with North Africans.

The language taught in these classes is a kind of modernized or upgraded dialect Arabic (or a modified standard modern Arabic, to put it the other way around). The question of which type of Arabic to teach in these and other courses (for example, those put on by the Amicale des Algériens en Europe) was the subject of much discussion among both the Arab teachers and the French students, as the debate at the following meeting will show.

Event 5: *Réunion des stagiaires* at ACFAL, November 1975

> Ahmed – student, Arab teacher
> Sherif – student, Arab teacher
> Pierre – medical student
> André – ACFAL organizer
> Jean-Paul – worker-priest, teacher of Arabic
> Elaine – literacy teacher

This was an evening meeting of students and teachers involved in Arabic classes organized by ACFAL. It was held in a room at the premises that ACFAL leases in the VIIth Arrondissement. Some thirty persons were present, mostly those from the beginners' and second-year classes. The meeting was opened by Ahmed, one of the teachers, who outlined the points we were to discuss: principally the question of the type of Arabic that should be studied, but also the organization and financing of the courses. "Regarding the language, the choice is between dialect Arabic [A.D.], which is important for those working with the immigrés, such as social assistants and future social assistants, and literary Arabic [A.L.], which is not widely understood."

Into the silence that followed this statement, he then added: "I suppose everyone is in favor of A.D.?"

Sherif: "There are many French words in A.D. One must get closer to modern Arabic [A.M.]."

Question from the floor: "Is there a lot of difference?"

Sherif: "A.M. is *Arabe relevée* [raised, corrected, exalted, noble]." As an example he cites the correct Arabic word for "factory," stating that the French word *usine* is used in A.D.

Ahmed: "The vocabulary of A.D. contains a lot of European words – French, Spanish, Italian – that have been Arabized."

Sherif: "An *immigré* is impoverished when he comes to France. He uses many loan words. This may be considered a form of colonization. We must make an effort to achieve a *décolonisation spirituelle*."

Pierre: "What Arabic is taught over there [i.e., in North Africa]? Is it not A.M.?"

Ahmed: "Yes, and perhaps A.M. will be used in the future."

Pierre emphasizes the importance of taking the long-term view.

Ahmed: "Are you intending to go to North Africa?"

Pierre: "Yes."

Ahmed: "Well, in that case perhaps your situation is a bit different."

Second question from floor: "Is the difference between A.M. and A.D. at the level of vocabulary or of structure? For example, in French we have *Qui est-ce* and *Qui c'est*?"

Sherif: "There is no difference in Arabic on that score. The difference is mainly one of vocabulary."

André: "The contrast is one between an Arabic that is practically useful and that will not separate the speaker from the *immigrés,* and an Arabic that is ideologically in accord with certain viewpoints."

Jean-Paul (addressing Sherif): "Do they [the *immigrés*] understand what is said on the radio?"

Elaine (interrupting): "I don't want to learn a very polished Arabic, but the Algerian dialect is not the only Arabic. What does one do when talking to Moroccans?"

Ahmed: "We should say we are talking about *Maghrébin* [North African] Arabic. There are differences of accent, but the vocabulary is the same." He mentions the Egyptian dialect, Syrian and Lebanese. "The Egyptians speak in dialect. Not everyone understands A.L."

Elaine mentions certain differences between A.L. and A.M. that Laïd (another teacher, not present) had told her about.

Ahmed: "In general the *immigrés* come from the countryside. A.D. corresponds eighty percent of the time with A.M., but *in France* loan words are incorporated." To Sherif, he says: "When deciding what to teach, one must take into account the demand."

Sherif: "You must orient the demand. What's all this fear about not being understood? The immigrant workers understand Arabic. I don't think the Arabic spoken by *immigrés* is Arabic. I won't teach it. Why communicate? Why understand? What is the point of it? The speaking of A.D. contributes to continuing a situation I consider as domination, as colonization. To refuse to accept it is to contribute to decolonialization."

Jean-Paul: "First, the country dialects have nothing to do with A.M. They are very beautiful languages in their own right. Second, A.M. contains many words that are not understood by the *immigrés*. Why should I teach someone to say the A.M. word for 'pay slip' when I know that everyone uses the French word *fiche de paie?* Third, if a Frenchman uses A.M., he risks being thought to speak Arabic better than 'us' – which creates another complex."

Sherif dismisses what he refers to as a supposed "complex" created in Arabs by the use of A.M. "A.M. is A.D. with the foreign words suppressed."

André: "I wish to compare the situation of the *immigrés* with that of the Ardèche peasant" [titters from the audience] "or the Breton in Paris."

Sherif rejects the comparison. "These people [*ces gens-là*] are a people from a different world, a different culture from that of the occident."

Third question from floor: "Isn't it best to learn the structure of the language first to be able to talk, and then pick up the A.M. vocabulary later?"

Jean-Paul: "I learn much from the *immigrés*. I learn their language. . . ."

Elaine raises again the question of local variation of dialects. "I was talking to a Moroccan woman and used a word and she said, 'That is not a Moroccan word, it is Algerian.'"

Jean-Paul: "There are many variants of A.D. at the level of countries – Moroccan, Algerian, Tunisian – and within countries, for example, Oran, Constantine. A.M., which the *immigrés* do not understand perfectly, is used on the radio. It is used on the TV and in newspapers. It is not just a matter of vocabulary. There is a different grammar. If you listen to Boumedienne, you will hear him speak different levels of dialect. When he addresses the UN, he speaks a very elevated Arabic that I don't understand. When he talks to peasants, he uses A.D." (Sherif interjects: "But no French words!") "Yes, true. Its [A.M.'s] use may be good for speaking with *gens cultivés* from different countries, but it won't help when talking to *immigrés*."

Sherif: "The *immigrés* are going to return home. One must take a long-term view. You claim to help them [*immigrés*]. In A.D. one uses the term *sidi* [sir; master], which is used by wives to address husbands, children to address fathers. You help the oppressors by continuing with this. I won't teach a false Arabic. It is a question of cultural emancipation. If you don't understand this effort . . . You must sustain this effort."

André: "Most people have a practical rather than an ideological interest. Anyway, eighty to eighty-five percent of *immigrés* speak better French than I speak Arabic."

Fourth intervention from floor: "The ideological issue is not our problem."

Sherif: "The ideological issue is our task. If there is a line that is considered right by those who are affected . . ."

Fifth intervention from floor: "I propose we strike out all English words from the French language so as to undermine American domination!"

Sixth intervention from floor: A student who says she has studied linguistics claims that linguists argue that there are no "bad" languages. "Do you use the same language when speaking to an *ouvrier* and *ingénieur?*" (Several shouts of "But that's the point!")

Elaine: "Is it possible to find a language intermediary between A.M. and A.D.?"

André: "Does one learn a language to have a pedagogic relationship with the person to whom one is speaking – or to be able to do something practical?"

Sherif: "A.M. is understood by the maximum number of people. Once the *immigrés* arrive here, they are deprived of all their cultural apparatus. By talking A.D., you assist in this *stade de régression.*"

Jean-Paul: "I wish to put a question to Sherif. When you say, 'The boss sacked me,' what do you use?"

Sherif: "*Atradani.*" [A.L. or A.M.]

Jean-Paul: "Yes, but the *immigré* would say *herrejni.*" [A.D.].

Sherif: "But he would say *renfwoyni* – an Arabized form of [the French] *renvoyer.*"

There are a number of issues raised by this debate, to which we will return. For the moment let me simply clarify the point about language variant. Informants identified three, if not four, kinds of Arabic: the classical literary language of the Koran; the modern standard language, which is a modified version of the classical language; and the dialects, the spoken languages of North Africa between which there are considerable differences of grammar and vocabulary. Within that last category some would distinguish "francisized Arabic," dialect spoken principally by Algerians that in terms of vocabulary has been heavily influenced ("impoverished," some would say) by the colonial relationship with France. As Event 5 shows, students and teachers of ACFAL were engaged in a hot debate on the type of language that should be taught: dialect, and if so, which dialect, or the modern language? And, more fundamentally, what does the learning of a language (or particular variant) mean for the relationship between French and North African immigrants?

AN IDEOLOGY OF LANGUAGE TEACHING: THE HEIGHTENING OF AWARENESS

One of the purposes of this chapter is to examine the various ideological perspectives that underlie debates about language teaching and learning, and the language problems of immigrants. I concentrate first on a perspective that may be associated with elements of the left.

In Event 5, one of the participants (Sherif) uttered the heartfelt cry "Why communicate? Why understand? What is the point of it?" This led André, the ACFAL organizer, to inquire: "Does one learn a language to have a pedagogic relationship to the person to whom one is speaking, or to be able to do something practical?" Running through the debate was a contrast between two views of language learning (and teaching and, indeed, speaking) that were characterized by André himself as "ideological" and "practical." I will follow his usage although according to my definition, pragmatism itself must be considered an ideology.

The distinction is between a perspective that sees language learning and teaching as a means to some elementary and specific end (e.g., a social assistant learning Arabic in order to be able to deal directly with her North African women clients, a migrant worker learning French in order to get on at work), and one that sees such teaching and learning as a total phenomenon thoroughly embedded in the social and cultural framework with a considerable array of social and psychological implications, individual and collective. I have elsewhere (Grillo 1982) described this as the "global view" of language.

These are ideal-type contrasts and should not be seen as simple labels to be pinned on individuals. For example, André, who adopted a pragmatic ideology in Event 5 when discussing the teaching of Arabic to the French, expressed a more "ideological" perspective on other occasions (for example, when discussing the teaching of French to Arabs).

I have referred to a tendency among many informants to see a connection between something small and simple and something great and complex ("the global animation of a quartier begins with soccer"). This tendency also appears in the discussion of language learning. On one occasion my ACFAL Arabic class talked about adult education. The driving instructor mentioned a friend of hers who spoke very good French but was illiterate in Arabic. He wanted to learn the writing, but where? "Ah, that's the difficulty," said our tutor (Amar, who appears in Event 9), and went on to explain about a course he was giving to some fifteen to twenty workers in a SONACOTRA hostel. The idea for the course originated with some friends of his. One of these, a Lebanese student, wanted to find a test group on whom to experiment with a new method of teaching. Existing methods for *alpha* were useless, especially from the viewpoint of the content they employed: "This is a cat," and so on. Instead they had compiled a vocabulary of the most common words found in the immigrants' life – work permit, trade union, and so on – and built the lessons around these words and phrases associated with them. They also encouraged discussion about these words. Thus, "army" led on to political discussion, for example, about the class struggle. This allowed the workers themselves to come to some conclusions about the nature of capitalist society without saying, "Marx said this, Marx said that." Amar hoped that next year the course would be subsidized by the hostel's *animation* budget, because at the moment he was receiving only traveling expenses and no salary.

We followed a similar method in our own Arabic class. Thus, I learned to say, in highly polished language, phrases such as "Unemployment is one of the aspects of the crisis of capitalism."

This example touches on the question of text content and teaching methods, to be discussed shortly. For the moment, however, let us consider the idea, expressed by many other informants, especially those of the left, that language teaching should cultivate critical awareness about what is thought to be the nature of the society in which the pupil is located – in other words, political consciousness. We may recall here the view held by some social workers that starting with sewing classes for women, for example, the *monitrices* try to get them to see "how they can become mistresses of their own situation, to become conscious." In a generally similar vein, one organization (AEFTI) describes itself as "la seule association pour l'alphabétisation qui se place délibérement du côté des forces démocratique," the style of the statement immediately identifying the association's political links (CGT, PCF).

An unpublished (and anonymous) cyclostyled paper entitled "Alphabétisation et analyse de classe," which was on sale in Lyon, identified four types of motivation among those engaged in *alpha*, of which the fourth and highest is described as follows: "Par rapport aux immigrés et à eux-mêmes, pour informer et se former politiquement, pour informer et former politiquement les travailleurs, en se situant clairement dans la lutte des classes. C'est à dire d'une part en participant et en soutenant les luttes que mènent les travailleurs immigrés sur leurs propres bases . . . et d'autre part en informant les travailleurs immigrés de la situation de classe des animateurs français et de leurs luttes."

Those who adopt this approach are extremely critical of the texts and methods employed in the conventional courses. The cyclostyled ACFAL *Bulletin* for September 1976, a special number on *alpha,* contained an article (Duriez 1976) that questioned the "neutrality" of texts, and cited two used in different *alpha* courses as illustrations.

First example: "Tous les matins, Manolo va travailler à 35 km de son hôtel. Il part à 5h ½. Il prend l'autobus. . . . Diallo est jeune, il travaille vite; c'est un ouvrier sérieux. . . . Jacques et Diallo ont beaucoup travaillé toute la semaine. Hier samedi, ils ont touché une bonne paye. Jacques met son pantalon neuf et sa veste neuve. Diallo met ses propres habits."

Second example: "Mohammed ne comprend pas: il est toujours manoeuvre, et pourtant il y a treize mois qu'il est chez le même patron. Normalement, il doit être OS après six mois. Doit-il aller voir le syndicat? . . . Paulo travaille dans le bâtiment. Les ourvriers de son chantier sont portugais, algériens, marocains. . . . Samedi dernier, ils ont eu leur paye. Il manquait de l'argent: 30F. Achour, un Algérien qui parle le français, est allé voir le chef de chantier pour réclamer. Le chef a répondu: je ne peux rien faire. Le lundi matin, personne n'a voulu travailler. Paulo a dit: allons voir le patron! Ils sont allés devant les bureaux, ils ont dit: on arrête de travailler si tu ne nous payes pas. Le patron a promis de tout payer l'après-midi." The same issue of the *Bulletin* (p. 10) contains a little cartoon that is illuminating. It is based on a simple language lesson that also involves some arithmetic. It shows a series of hands: "Un doigt, deux doigts, cinq doigts. Cinq doigts font un poing [clenched fist]."

The critique formulated by Duriez and others extends also to teaching methods, the classroom context, and the teacher-taught relationship. Thus the pamphlet "Alphabétisation et añalyse de classe" (p. 6) notes that among the basic objeçtives of *alpha* is "la transmission d'un certain savoir, principalement d'un groupe à l'autre. Remarquons que là encore il apparaît une autre dif-férence, à savoir l'instauration inéluctable . . . de rapports de domination des 'moniteurs' français sur les 'élèves' immigrés." (Cf. Catani 1973.)

This critique of *alpha* (more or less elaborately expressed) is not only supported by private left-wing associations such as ACFAL, it is shared by many of the teachers in the government-backed AEE who have on several occasions taken industrial action in support of reforms. Thus the CFDT section of the AEE comments in a vein similar to that of the statement just cited that "Les téchniques pédagogiques choisies ne doivent pas imposer le savoir du seul formateur, mais permettre de partager toutes les expériences, tous les acquis des membres du groupe en formation" (p. 19).

This ideology of language teaching, which embraces a thoroughgoing critique of aims, content, and method, is a global view of language learning that I will describe as the "radical" one. I have suggested elsewhere that it is a distant descendant of the eighteenth-century French conception of French as the language of intellectual liberation (Grillo 1982). It may be contrasted with another global view that is also partly rooted in eighteenth- (and nineteenth-) century French thought.

ANOTHER IDEOLOGY OF LANGUAGE: THE CREATION OF IDENTITY

The radical perspective sees in language learning a vehicle for the creation of political (i.e., class) consciousness. Another perspective also concerns itself with political consciousness, albeit of a different kind. I cited earlier the view of an organizer of the Amicale des Algériens en Europe that the "teaching of Arabic helps [the child] to identify himself within a culture." Here the aim of language teaching is in part the formation and maintenance of an ethnic identity. A comment from Belkacem, an Algerian student employed by ACFAL, illustrates this (see also Belkacem's remarks in Event 4):

"In my teaching of North African children I use material related to reality, which maintains links with the return to the source. Early on, I begin with a question like 'What is your fatherland?' expecting the answer 'Algeria.' In this way I give the child a self-image. Recently I took a poem written by a Tunisian during the Algerian War, which goes: 'The Algerian people are Muslims and of Arab origin. He who says that they have lost their Arabness or even that it [the people] is dead is a liar.'"

The link between aim and content could not be clearer. And the aim is both cultural and political. The two are inextricably linked in the Arabic language movement, promoted by the Amicale. However, the specific political aims of that movement (at one level, the unity of all Arabs; at another, the reintegration of the people of Algeria; at another, support for the Algerian revolution and thence the regime in power in Algiers) would not all be supported by a teacher like Belkacem. He had previously worked for the Amicale, but had quarreled with them over the methods used in their courses. His disagreement with the Amicale ran deeper than that, however, for the specific political goals of the Amicale's language program would not include the creation of the kind of political awareness that is the aim of ACFAL teachers. The Amicale's objective is "retribalization," to use Cohen's term (1969), though the French term favored by North African sources is *réinsertion*.

Amicale conference and discussion documents frequently portray the situation of young Algerians in France in terms similar to that employed by the Amicale organizer cited earlier in this chapter. Many of their comments are highly relevant to debates about cultural pluralism in that country, which we will discuss shortly (see especially an article on "Misère de la culture arabe en France" in *L'Algérien en Europe* No. 231, April 1, 1976). The learning of Arabic is central to their attempts to solve the problems of these young people.

The draft Algerian "National Charter," published as a discussion document in 1976, contained the declaration: "La langue arabe est un élément essentiel de l'identité culturelle du peuple algérien" (Section III (I). See "Avante-projet de Charte Nationale" in a special supplement to *El Moudjahid*, May 1976). This sentiment entails the promotion of the classical and standard modern language as part of a policy of linguistic integration of Algeria. This Arabic is accorded high official status compared with the dialects and, indeed, the non-Arabic minority languages such as Kabyle. The Amicale has a special role to play in fostering this Arabic among Algerian migrants.

The Amicale operates in two milieus: among North Africans in France, and among those who return to Algeria or at least may hope to return. Accounts of the structure, organization, and distribution of their language courses in France may be found in a number of Amicale documents (see Amicale des Algériens en Europe 1973:96–101, 1974b, 1974c). In describing the network of courses and ancillary activities, one paper refers to the goal of combating *l'assimilation de notre jeunesse* (1974b:12). It later mentions theatrical and musical troups that have received prizes "tant pour récompenser la qualité de leur prèsentation, que pour encourager à travers les participants la jeunesse émigré à s'algérianiser'" (1974b:13).

For those who hope to return to Algeria, the Amicale proposes a "politique globale et efficace de réinsertion a la fois économique, sociale et culturelle" (1974b:1). For the children of returning migrants, for example, there are *classes de rattrapage* provided for them to catch up on the language (Amicale des Algériens en Europe 1974a:10–13). There is also a planned network of reception centers in Algeria. An article in *L'Algérien en Europe* (No. 232, April 15, 1976) described the opening of the first of these at Oran. It was termed in French a *centre d'accueil et de réinsertion*, a curious echo of the French CAIO (Centres d'Accueil, d'Information et d'Orientation des Travailleurs Etrangers).

The Algerian view of language as a device for stimulating ethnic homogeneity and solidarity is, of course, derived from the same source as the traditional French view of the role of their language in the cultural and political integration of France (see Grillo 1982 for a discussion of the background). This latter view traditionally informed the aims of French language teaching: "In France there are two schools of thought. One, government policy, which I myself support, favors integration, dispensing French culture. The second, which is supported by some Christians, stresses respect for the personality and the person's culture. The consulates and certain religious organizations also support this line" (NDSA hostel director). The French language courses influenced by the first of these two schools of thought, and the Arabic language classes influenced by the Arabic language movement, in effect work toward similar ends that in the context are diametrically opposed: One orients the learner toward France and integration with French culture, the other away from France and toward North Africa.

In fact, in the mid-1970s, French policy toward the language and culture of immigrants was less clear-cut than the NDSA director's statement might suggest, as certain remarks of the then minister (Event 1) illustrate (cf. Dijoud 1976). Room was being made for the maintenance of the culture of origin (see Hessel 1976), including the mother tongue. But the minister's statement (Event 1) that he "wanted to provide freedom of choice to the individual foreigner" in fact suggests that the toleration of cultural difference reflected a policy of encouraging some people to return to source. It would thus have a function in allowing the freer movement of labor between sending and receiving societies. The official French view that cultural difference should be seen in the context of "the return" was in fact similar to the view of the Algerian government and the Amicale, whose ultimate aim was the *physical* reintegration of the Algerian people. Neither side really envisaged the permanent establishment of culturally distinct groups *within* France.

LANGUAGE, *ASSIMILATION, INTEGRATION,* AND *INSERTION*

Historically it is undoubtedly the case that the global aim of French language instruction was *assimilation* and *intégration*. This was the dominant ideology. But what precisely does *intégration* mean? An editorial (p. 31) in the ACFAL *Bulletin* cited earlier in this chapter opens a debate in its columns by citing a frequently expressed criticism of ACFAL's "line":

> Ce que doit être notre action c'est: alphabétisation essentiellement; aider les immigrés à s'adapter au mieux chez nous sans perdre leurs coutûmes; favoriser l'intégration des immigrés dans notre ville. Ce que ne doit pas être l'alpha c'est: actions revendicatives (grèves, manifestations); renseigner les immigrés sur les syndicats; distribuer les tracts. Si l'ACFAL n'est pas cela: elle devie de son but; elle manipule; elle trahit la confiance des immigrés. [A short following article developed a counter-critique asking, "S'intégrer au mieux chez nous . . . c'est quoi?"] [p. 33]

Intégration in the fullest sense of the term comes close to meaning *assimilation,* and might be linked with *évolution* (see Grillo 1981b, and above, Chapter 6), in that it is concerned with the production of Frenchness. Although this might once have been the dominant ideology underlying *alpha* courses, by the mid-1970s the perspective had shifted. *Alpha* courses now reflected not so much a policy of *intégration* as of *insertion*.

Consider the following two comments, which refer to *alpha* in an industrial context:

"Our organization first became interested in language courses for foreign workers when it was discovered [about 1969] that there were serious problems relating to understanding in the workshops" (a teacher at a private school). "With regard to *alpha* classes, tests are administered to identify the level of competence, and depending on this there are various solutions – for example language labs, or, what I myself prefer, at the building-industry training school where the person can learn the language and the *gestes du métier* at the same time" (director of a building firm).

It can be argued that many of the courses provided for migrant *workers*, especially the courses located in the firms themselves, aim at the *insertion* (the AEE's own term) of the workers in the production process and are designed, at least in part, to solve essentially managerial problems: "In Renault where I used to work, they had people in the factories to teach French. But what kind of French! They would write on a blackboard 'Ali gets up to go to work. Ali is never late for work.' They might as well have written 'Ali never goes on strike.' That sort of approach trains people for work. What is needed is a true training in literacy. The question is, does a man know how to fill in a money order, buy a loaf of bread" (Algerian factory worker and CGT representative).

Managers are, of course, not the only ones with language problems in industry. French trade unionists, too, see the immigrants' ignorance of French as a stumbling block to their own activities (see Chapter 9): "With the Turkish workers there is a problem of language. I could go and talk to the Turks. I want to. But I don't know the language." As we have already seen, a similar problem is encountered by teachers and social assistants: "During my office hours it is usually the Arab father who comes to see me. With him there is no language difficulty. With the mother, if I make a home visit, a neighbor has to be called in, or the child translates. There is not enough time on the social work course for training in Arabic. Perhaps afterward. But the tendency is to train the mother in French" (social assistant in the education sector).

An assessment of these remarks, and of the content of the texts that are most frequently used, leads to the conclusion that the orthodox courses deal primarily with the language of, and behavior appropriate to, situations that reflect roles basic to processes of production and consumption in French society. By "consumption," it may be recalled, is meant both private and collective consumption: buying a loaf of bread, getting a *mandat* (money order), visiting the social-security office or the hospital, talking to a teacher about a child's progress. By "role in production" is meant not just the job a person does (learning the *gestes du métier*), but the total culture of the industrial milieu: getting up, going to work, working seriously, getting paid at the end of the week.

The courses are also, to an extent, gender specific in an obvious way. For men they deal with work, for women they deal with home, shops, and the market. For both, however, they cover relationships with the institutions, albeit different ones. They also portray a highly conventional image of the sexual division of labor, as in this example from an AEE handbook:

> Un soir chez Pédro et Maria. Pédro habite près du poste, à droite, dans la rue du Bois. Son nom est écrit sur la porte. Pédro est marié avec Maria. Ils ont un joli bébé: José. José est petit: il ne marche pas et il ne parle pas. Toute la journée, Maria est près de José. Elle passe son doigt sur la joue. José rit. Pour jouer, il tire sur les boutons de la robe de sa mère. Pédro a fini sa journée. Il ouvre la porte. Il dit bonsoir à Maria. Après le repas, Maria couche le petit José. Pédro lit le journal. Maria tricote un bonnet pour le bébé et elle écoute la radio. [Text employed by AEE in 1972]

The tenor of such courses, when aimed at women, recalls the structure and content of courses provided by organizations such as the SSFNA, and the "socio-educative action" undertaken in NDSA *cités de transit*. All of these courses aim at producing particular kinds of French – like persons with a basic competence in certain aspects of French society. In like manner, the French courses for immigrant children prepare them specifically for the school system. Undoubtedly they hope to give the immigrant a chance to deal with situations where those with no knowledge of the language must experience great difficulties. But such situations are also ones in which ignorance of French on the part of immigrants creates problems of other kinds for the French.

There is criticism of these types of courses that is not quite as radical as that put forward by those who advocate the use of *alpha* to promote political consciousness. The argument is that the courses do not reflect "real life":

"*Alpha* courses have been put on during working hours organized by the comité d'établissement, who got teachers from the education ministry. The object is to improve everyday life. The boss who will teach them what a *bobine* means does not provide a real training" (French trade unionist). This point, which is often made by CGT/PCF militants, seems to suggest that such courses should deal, even more than they do, specifically with roles in production and consumption. It is also frequently argued that the content of the courses should be linked directly with training for skilled work (*formation professionelle*): "If they don't know French, they cannot get promotion at work" (CGT official). This view was supported in a comment made at a conference of the Algerian Amicale: "Il faut bien constater que nos travailleurs sont souvent déçus . . . par le fait que le contenu pédagogique de cette alpha-bétisation vise plutôt à favoriser leur intégration sociale que leur promotion professionnelle" (Amicale des Algériens en Europe 1974a:2).

As a result of such criticisms, both inside and outside the teaching profession, there has been some movement away from the type of lesson illustrated by "Un soir chez Pédro et Maria" (cf. Descayrac and Dubois 1981:107). This does not, however, answer the objections of the more radical critics either nationally (e.g., Catani 1973) or locally. A CFDT militant in adult education: "There is a crisis in the capitalist system. A certain quantity of foreign labor must be retained, but it must be one that must be kept in hand, that is pliant. Dijoud's policy is to organize this labor in a more coercive fashion. . . . Training is not always necessary. In some ways it is necessary to have a labor force that is illiterate. But some training is useful. And there are protests against the conditions of life of the foreigners that must be considered. In factories, training is necessary because of the social costs, acci-dents at work and so on. We can see delinquency in this context. These things are a serious cost to French society. So one fixes things up. Dijoud wants to have all this in his hands. He is in the course of taking over the AEE. He will liquidate the old team. Transferring the AEE to Dijoud will mean transferring it [from the Ministry of Education] to the Ministry of Labor in effect, which means the bosses."

Those working in adult education and *alpha* who espouse such views are faced with a problem similar to that encountered by the radical social workers. For them, language training (or social work) ought to provide a means of awakening people and trans-forming them, but they also admit to its elementary, practical value. The CFDT militant cited in the previous paragraph put it: "One can't avoid the written code living in France. Women in the quartiers throughout their life struggle against the written code, in the shops, in schools." That is to say, even if the courses only rarely achieve their ultimate aim, the creating of political aware-ness, they have their value in that they help people to survive and make out for themselves in their roles as producers and con-sumers in French society.

CONCLUSION

In this chapter I have located four perspectives on language teaching and learning. Two of these I have described as "global" – some of my informants would call them "ideological": that which views language learning as a device for raising political (class) consciousness; and that which sees language as a crucial instrument of national and ethnic consciousness. The other two have more limited, "practical" aims: the view, which in the mid-1970s was the dominant one, that language training should provide an *insertion* in French society, and that which considers the *insertion* perspective too narrow, and advocates courses in greater accord with the "real" needs of immigrants. Each of these perspectives, to pick up a phrase used in Chapter 6, attempts to provide the learner with an entry to a different conception of "reality." And it is in fact interesting to observe how frequently the word "reality" occurs in debates about language, particularly in CGT/PCF discourse.

I have suggested that the traditional dominant ideology of France, in which language is, so to speak, the cement of the nation, is one shared by proponents of the Arabic language with regard to their own tongue. In theory, demands for French and demands for, say, Arabic, might conjoin in support for *bilingualism*, associated perhaps with some form of cultural pluralism. In fact they are often seen ultimately as alternatives: French for those who stay, Arabic or another mother tongue for those who will ultimately return. Nevertheless, it is agreed on all sides that at least some knowledge of French is necessary for those who reside in the country. An Algerian *animateur* in Grenoble put it this way: "The main problem is to allow the foreigner to maintain his culture of origin, and at the same time allow him to have reasonable contacts with the host society." However, this begs the question of what "reasonable contact" means.

The contemporary orthodoxy is that language courses should provide for a minimum *insertion* in French society, meaning by that basic competence in the fields of production and consumption. However, it is often argued (cf. the exponents of the CGT/PCF position) that they scarcely achieve that aim. A director of the AEE suggested to me that 720 hours of course work was needed for an adult learner of the language. The practical chances of a migrant worker having the time and energy for this after work are very low – hence demands for courses during working hours.

I should perhaps interject here that this chapter has not specifically been concerned with assessing the actual progress made by those attending such courses, nor with estimating the amount of language learned outside the courses, for example, at work.

If, however, we accept the validity of the criticism that the orthodox courses do not accomplish their objectives, then there are two structural consequences. The first emerges from a point made by Catani (1973:232), who argues that immigrants really need French only in relations with the administrative system, or in such unforeseen circumstances as accidents, and so on. Then, however, "La connaissance réelle qu'il faudrait du français demande un trés haut niveau d'aisance verbale." Without this, there is inevitably a recourse to intermediaries, persons literate in French and familiar with the intricacies of the French administrative system, who help their compatriots negotiate a path through that system, writing letters, filling in forms, or explaining the rules of, say, social security. In some circumstances they may indeed become *intermédiaires . . . qui les exploitent* (Catani 1973: 232), for example when they build up good relations with officials who are then in a position to engage in an exchange of favors.

The second consequence is that there exists a substantial mass of persons who are relatively poor speakers of French, or speakers of "poor" French by exacting French standards. Some of these people (especially the children) may also become increasingly distant from their mother tongue, and it may be noted that no amount of teaching of literary Arabic will help here because that language is far removed from the dialects spoken in most homes. They thus constitute a *linguistic* underclass, and this reinforces their subordinate position in economic, social, and cultural terms.

9

Work

A la sortie de l'usine chacun prend sa masque bourgeoise.

[A CGT militant]

One of the themes of earlier chapters has been the differences and similarities between two main streams of French thought regarding foreigners/immigrants, which may be roughly identified with the right and the left. I have also referred to differences *within* the left that are characteristic of two contrasting strands in French socialism. This chapter looks more closely at these differences as they emerge in the context of organized labor's attempts to grapple with the problems of immigrants at work.

The chapter is centered around three industrial disputes (Events 6–8). A fourth (Event 9) will be considered at somewhat greater length in Chapter 10. These disputes enable us to see how the two main trade-union groups, the CGT and the CFDT, handle the problems of immigrants in employment, and the problems posed for the unions by immigrant participation in the labor force. The material also throws light on the general relationship between French and immigrant workers in industry. Before looking at the case material, however, two somewhat technical points must be made.

The first concerns the organization of French trade unions. Earlier, in Chapter 3, I noted that there are several different groups of trade unions in France, of which the most important are the CGT and CFDT. Both are active in the main industrial sectors in Lyon, and both are organized in a similar fashion with separate unions for each industrial sector (building, engineering, etc.). These industrial unions generally have a central office at the Bourse du Travail staffed by one or more *permanents*, and branches (*sections*) that elect their own representatives (*délégués syndicaux*). In addition, within a firm, employees elect a committee of *délégués du personnel,* usually on the basis of proportional representations of the votes received by slates of candidates proposed by the unions. In the larger firms there are also other committees (e.g., the *comités d'établissement*) for which representatives are elected. After legislation was enacted in the early 1970s, foreigners were eligible for election to almost all offices of trade unions and consultative committees (see Event 2 in Chapter 3).

The second point, which is particularly important for an understanding of Event 6, relates to the grading system that prevails throughout French industry. In Chapter 2 it was suggested tha a major reason for the relatively low basic pay received by immigrants is simply that most of them hold jobs at the lower levels of the industrial hierarchy. Many are in fact poorly qualified at entry, in terms of both their basic education and industrial training. Others, with trade qualifications obtained in their country of origin, sometimes find that these are not recognized in France. This often leads to the belief on the part of the individual that he or she has been undergraded, assigned to a job at a lower level than their qualifications warrant.

A further difficulty is that the grading of the jobs themselves is not absolute. They are subject to continual review and, within certain limits, there is a constant "reclassification" of jobs in French industry. The most notable example of this has been the virtual disappearance in many firms of the category *manoeuvre* and its replacement by OS1/2, a cosmetic change which means very little so far as the job itself is concerned. At Berliet in 1974–5 there was a wholesale reclassification in which several hundred jobs were moved from OS to a skilled category. (In the course of this, the label *ouvrier* was replaced by the phrase *agents de réalisation.*) Some of these problems of classification are illustrated in the following dispute at the Gerland factory of Câbles de Lyon.

Event 6: The *caristes* dispute at Câbles de Lyon

Caristes are men who drive forklift trucks and other internal transport vehicles within a factory. It may be recalled (Chapter 2) that of the two-dozen workers employed as *caristes* at Câbles de Lyon's Gerland plant, only one was French. In many factories in the engineering sector immigrants form the majority of *caristes.*

I first heard about their difficulties during a general discussion on problems at work with one of their number, a Tunisian named Sassi who was a

CFDT *délégué du personnel*. Sassi cited three problems faced by immigrants: "They are the first to be sacked, they're underpaid, and they're undergraded." As an example: "We *caristes* think our job is skilled and should be graded as such. We have been trying for years to get the job graded P1. Workers in other factories in the engineering industry — Renault, Berliet — have achieved this." He compared the situations at Câbles unfavorably with that at Berliet, where he had had a temporary job for a month when he first arrived in Lyon. At Berliet he had found the workers as a whole more welcoming. And at Berliet, "the *cariste* had his own place, his own round. Here you have to move all over the factory."

About a week after I first encountered Sassi, I went to meet him at the factory and quite unexpectedly found a meeting of the *caristes* in progress. This meeting was held in the CGT office in the presence of two officials from the CGT (Michel and Guillaume) and two from the CFDT (Georges and Arlette), and thirteen *caristes*, of whom ten were North African, two Spanish, and one, François, French. The meeting was conducted entirely in French.

There were two phases to the discussion. The first concerned strike action in support of the claim for P1 (i.e., skilled) status and ended with a vote to strike if necessary. The second was concerned with tactics. The meeting had been called because the *délégués du personnel* had asked the management to receive a delegation of *caristes* at discussions scheduled to be held with management the following day. It had been agreed that ten *caristes* should attend, "nearly half the section," said Georges. But what was to be done if, as was expected, the management rejected the proposal to reclassify the jobs? François, supported by others, spoke strongly in favor of a strike. Miguel, one of the two Spaniards, was against. "If we strike, the management won't let us back into the factory. That would mean an occupation. Won't the management bring in the CRS to get us out?" Georges reassured him that if that happened, the other workers would be conscious of this and support them. Georges intervened in the discussion on several occasions to bring out a number of practical points: "If you strike, it will have to be an occupation, otherwise the supervisor will get hold of the cars and restock the section overnight." Michel's interventions were many fewer, though he attempted to calm François when he became very agitated and shouted: "They refuse to make me a P1. They pay that lot [another group] as skilled men, but they say I am not a skilled man. Very well, I won't act like a skilled man. I'll drive my car into the wall. I'll not care who's behind me. I'll toss cyclists in the air." In similar fashion, when Sanchez, disgusted by a remark of Miguel's, rose gesticulating, Georges restored order.

Despite Miguel's arguments, the meeting agreed to support a strike, with occupation, should the negotiations fail. When put to the vote, the resolution was carried unanimously, even Miguel slowly, reluctantly raising his hand. An Arab, who had spoken in favor, said excitedly to Michel: "Note down the names, so that no one can say afterward we didn't vote." "No", said Georges, "write nothing down."

The meeting now considered tactics. How was the occupation to be organized, how was the management to be prevented from freeing *the cars*? Georges, however, still asked: "Is this really the only course of action? Is there nothing else to be done?" Sassi replied: "We have tried everything else." It was eventually decided that each night a number of men would stay in the garage. Most of those present volunteered their services and names of others who would be willing were mentioned. Miguel declined. "My child is sick and I can't leave my wife overnight on her own." "Not even for one night?" "No, not even one." An Arab: "Never mind, wife, sister or what. Just provide some blankets and some food." Michel asked if they could rely on all these others not present at the meeting and elicited the names of some who might be hesitant. "You must talk with them tomorrow." He also advised the distribution of a leaflet to the workers in other departments so that they should be aware of what was happening. The CGT or CFDT office would duplicate it.

There followed a discussion about how to arrange the *cars,* which led to a complicated proposal from François involving locking their *cars* without the keys in a certain part of the garage and using other *cars* to block the entrance – "They won't be able to get them out in a fortnight." "That I like," said another *cariste*. It only remained to agree the date: Friday or Monday? Eventually, Monday was chosen. It was finally accepted that after the discussions with management all the *caristes* would meet to assess the situation.

Subsequent events did not develop as rapidly or as dramatically as anticipated. The crucial meeting with management did not take place until the following week. As expected, the regrading proposal was rejected, but the other *caristes* were less enthusiastic than those present at the meeting described above. As a compromise, it was agreed that there should be sporadic stoppages for one or two hours, especially during busy periods. To prevent the movement of loads by night, there was a modified form of occupation with three or four workers sleeping in. The action continued for some days, during which the unions issued a press statement:

Les organisations syndicales CGT-CFDT des Câbles de Lyon annoncent que . . . le service des "caristes" . . . est en grève tournant (4 heures par jour) pour la reconnaissance de leur profession par la classification en P1 et pour un salaire de base de 2,000F. La fixation d'un salaire minimum à 2,000F est de loin la revendication la plus importante du personnel. C'est sur la base de cette revendication qui devrait se traduire par une augmentation de 300F minimum à tous, que l'ensemble du personnel se joignant à l'action des ouvriers caristes a cessé le travail . . . pendant deux heures. Ces arrêts de travail ont eu aussi pour but de protester contre l'application faite dans l'entreprise des nouvelles grilles de classifications imposées dans la métallurgie par la signature d'organisations syndicales minoritaires. Cette application se traduit par des déclassements indirects, la dévalorisation des métiers et fonctions, la sous-qualification du personnel féminin. De plus ces nouvelles classifications n'ont aucun lien direct avec les rémunérations. Ces arrêts de travail largement suivis par le personnel ouvrier montrent le réel mécontentement existant dans l'entreprise. [Quoted in *Le Progrès de Lyon*, March 27, 1976]

After this the action ceased, but not before one Spaniard was sacked after receiving a warning for being fifteen minutes late and Sassi had been given four separate warnings about his activities. Four or five of the *caristes* working on the large five-ton *cars* were, however, promised promotion to P1, and eventually the sacked Spaniard was reinstated.

Besides illustrating the depth of feeling about "classification," the material raises a number of other issues, some of which are discussed later. Of particular interest is the role of the unions. As we shall see, there was in this dispute an unusual degree of cooperation between the CFDT and the CGT, though ultimately the position adopted by the latter came closer to that which it took elsewhere. CFDT informants suggested that the CGT was opposed to the *caristes* strike but was unable to prevent their action. Later it generalized their grievance by incorporating their dispute about grading into the wider issue of classification within the industry as a whole (see press statement) and linking it with the question of pay (not mentioned at the *caristes* meeting) and the current wage demand. One of the *caristes* (not a union member) in fact claimed that "the unions told us to stop," and Arlette (of the CFDT), that "the unions broke the strike." To understand these accusations and what lay behind them, we must look more fully at the views and policies of the two unions.

IMMIGRANTS AT WORK: THE PERSPECTIVE OF ORGANIZED LABOR

At the meeting described earlier as Event 2, in which Michel, the CGT militant at Câbles de Lyon, played a prominent part, we saw the CGT preparing for a major conference on the problems of immigrants. The organizational procedure whereby the CGT arrived at its conclusions will be discussed in Chapter 11. Here our focus will be the content of those conclusions: the CGT (and CFDT) views on what constitutes the problems of immigrants.

As we saw in Chapter 3, such views must be set in the context of their wider ideological perspective. In the first instance, trade unionists in both the CGT and the CFDT are generally reluctant to isolate the problems of migrant workers from those faced by the working class as a whole. "One fights for all the workers, for the entire working class" (Michel of the CGT); "One must not isolate the immigrants from the mass of workers" (CFDT *permanent*). The "isolation" referred to is both conceptual and organizational. Another CFDT *permanent* in the engineering section put it this way: "For the CFDT in the *factory* [his emphasis], the problems of immigrants are the same as for all the workers: qualifications, pay, unemployment. Perhaps a bit more for the immigrants the conditions of work, but that comes down to pay. Immigrant workers have arduous jobs, but that's one criterion among others and it all comes down to pay. Life outside the factory, however, poses special problems. Regarding the *commissions d' immigrés*, in my view to group immigrants apart is to create a ghetto. Their problems are the same as those of the French. All workers' problems are the same. We don't want to act the part of a social assistant, as the CGT does. The CGT wishes to act as a social assistant for immigrants, to obtain for them certain material benefits. We do that too, but our fight is to give them the same rights as French workers. They should be able to participate on the same basis as any other worker. In the firms special problems do not exist."

Several of the points made by that informant will be discussed later. Here I am concerned with the view that the problems of immigrant workers cannot be isolated from their situation as *workers*, that is, as participants in a labor market and in a particular form of industrial organization. Although this is the starting point for many trade unionists, and indeed many of those on the left, it is widely recognized that there are problems specific to migrant workers or particular groups of immigrants, and that their situation cannot be wholly identified with that of the French working class. Michel, again, who begins by discussing racism: "Unemployment is a cause. They say 'If the immigrants went home, there would be jobs for all.' Then bad conditions and pay are said to be caused by the fact that foreigners accept low salaries. I blame ourselves for not fighting enough on the part of the immigrants. Another example. We all know that the social security system is in crisis. They even blame immigrant workers for the bad conditions in the hospitals, which are full of immigrants. It is true that many are in the hospital. Why? Because they suffer more from work accidents. Ninety-five percent of workers in the building industry are immigrants. People in that industry 'normally' – in inverted commas – suffer more accidents than others. Immigrant workers suffer from chest complaints and fill the sanitoriums. Why? Because they live in bad housing, they are not accustomed to the climate, to conditions of work – in the cold and wet in the metro excavations, for example. This leads to rheumatism, headaches, lung complaints, and so on."

In this perspective, which is characteristic of that of the CGT (see Event 2), the special problems of immigrants are a function of their particular situation in the labor market. A CFDT *permanent,* however, touched on a different range of factors that create differences between immigrants and the French, and among immigrants themselves. He is discussing recruitment to the unions. "The North Africans have a history of colonialism and of attachment to France with the result that they do not react in the same manner as Southern Europeans. For example, the North Africans join trade unions more often than do the Southern European immigrants. They have a more developed collective consciousness. I suppose this is a cultural phenomenon – the concept of the village, of the family in the broad sense that is relatively extended, the war of liberation. It is noticeable that one finds many more outbursts in the building industry among North Africans, compared with the Portuguese. The Portuguese are less often *manoeuvres* and OS than are the North Africans. And the Portuguese worker is often here to maximize his capital. They are thus much more integrable in the employer's policy."

These last two statements from CGT and CFDT militants respectively illustrate differences between the two unions that were noted in Chapter 3 – the CGT's materialism compared with the CFDT's references to culture. They also contain allusions to the issues most frequently cited as those that concern trade unions as *unions* in relations with immigrants. There are four of these, and they are linked: racism, union recruitment, immigrant representation in unions, and language.

In 1975–6 the CGT was deeply concerned about racism in factories, not, as the speaker in Event 2 makes clear, "for humanitarian reasons alone." It is the divisive nature of racism that is critical, divisive, that is, within the working class. What is meant here is usually not the institutional racism of the kind that has perhaps been documented in early chapters in this book and that is endemic in French society, but racism at a more personal level, that in fact of person-to-person. It is possible that such racism is less intense in factories and other places of work than it is outside work. A CGT representative at Berliet regretted that the solidarity that sometimes existed on the production line did not extend to the housing estates: "In the factory one finds camaraderie which one does not find elsewhere. At the factory gate everyone puts on his bourgeois mask. One realizes that the immigrant is alone." An Algerian CGT militant, however, disputed this: "Racism is everywhere – in factories, on the streets. But in the factories people are sometimes forced to accept one. If you're face-to-face with me, you pretend to accept me, though in your heart you may not."

An example of the result of such racism that is often cited is the failure of immigrants, especially those from North Africa, to be elected as representatives. One such instance occurred at Câbles de Lyon, where the CGT in 1975 included two immigrants (a Tunisian and an Algerian) on its slate of candidates for election as *délégués du personnel*. Michel: "Normally the voters simply put the list into the ballot box. The workers are disciplined to vote for the list. When the votes were counted, it was found that the two immigrants had not been elected. When we discussed the problem, we concluded the racism was the only reason. The voting slips showed that some fourteen voters had struck off the names concerned." Another CGT militant accounted for the result as follows: "About a year and a half ago, Câbles was penetrated by leftists. They got hold of some immigrant workers and got them to go on a hunger strike. They were manipulated, led on by the leftists. The hunger-strikers occupied their hostel, the police intervened and withdrew their residence permits. This episode led to a racist campaign against immigrant workers that was orchestrated. Immigrants risk being maneuvered, and some are easy to manipulate. These leftists join the CFDT. The immigrant feels the need to struggle. One must not divert the struggle. That's very good for the *patron* and gives the police the opportunity to intervene." It is reasoning such as this that lies behind the CGT's opposition to isolated strke action on the part of small groups of immigrants such as the *caristes* at Câbles de Lyon, or the container men at SNAV (as discussed in Event 8).

The divisiveness seen as both a consequence and a cause of racism can, it is argued, be overcome by recruiting immigrants to the unions. The election of immigrant representatives encourages such recruitment: "The CGT wants to get the Arabs into the unions. Having Arab representatives draws the customers – like a bar owner wishing to attract Arabs who takes on an Arab waiter" (Algerian CGT militant). This informant added that while election of immigrants to posts as *délégués du personnel* was encouraged, election to posts on the *comités d'établissement* was not. "Whether the argument is valid or not, it is said that the French know the laws better and are better able to discuss with management. He, the Arab, hasn't the head for that."

For the CGT, the recruitment and incorporation of immigrants is also necessary for the successful implementation of an industrial strategy that normally involves the mobilization of the greatest possible number of workers for highly organized demonstrations and stoppages in support of limited, centrally agreed claims (*les revendications*). This incorporation is hindered by differences of language. "With the Turkish workers there is a problem of language. I could go and talk to the Turks. I want to, but I can't speak the language" (CGT official at Berliet). All the unions issue a variety of publications in foreign languages (including, in the CGT's case, a regular newsletter). They also provide translations of the inevitable leaflets. "However, many Arabs don't read Arabic. If you hand out a leaflet, people don't read it. So the way in which information is passed is not the same. Much more falls on the *délégué* to explain by word of mouth. Then there are problems of translation, of interpretation, of conveying the meaning from one language to another" (CFDT *permanent* in the building industry).

As that official said, immigrant *délégués* are needed to convey information. Sassi: "Very few Arabs read Arabic, apart from the Moroccans and Tunisians. Previously there was only schooling in French in Algeria. But one always finds one or two people like myself who read French a bit and explain to other workers what a leaflet is about." In some cases it has proved exceedingly difficult to find such interpreters. To approach a small group of Pakistanis employed at Câbles de Lyon, an English student was used (and English translations of leaflets had to be provided). At Berliet, an Algerian representative attempted to discuss union affairs with the Turks via classical Arabic, although eventually they had recourse to a Frenchman of Armenian descent.

It is not enough, or course, to communicate with immigrant workers. They must be recruited as members and persuaded to support union action. When that happens, the militants express their pleasure, as did this CGT official: "Yesterday's stoppage was supported by ninety-eight percent in my shop while it was eighty percent in Berliet as a whole. The movement was well supported by immigrants because some of the claims coincided with their own claims. . . . Did you see the demo yesterday? No? That was a pity. There were a lot of immigrants. Why? Because they were acting within the enterprise, they were protected and not in danger. When there is a demo outside the firm, they are in danger and they demonstrate very little. In 1973 a demo was called by an obscure organization concerned with Penarroya at the Place du Pont. The police charged the demo and arrested some people. The immigrants try not to be known to the police." The reference here is to a famous strike at the Penarroya factory in Lyon (see Anselme 1972 and, for an earlier reference to the factory, Michel 1955:38).

The distinction drawn in that statement between action over industrial issues *within the firm* and action *in the streets* (often over "political" issues) is an important one: "I personally support the trade unions, but I never go on demonstrations. There is often trouble and when the Forces of Order go in they generally grab the Arabs. And an Arab risks imprisonment and expulsion. The French, what do they risk? Twenty-four hours inside, that's all. Not even a fine" (Algerian metal worker). Michel of the CGT: "When a demonstration is political, very few immigrant workers participate because they are afraid of being spotted by the police and expelled. But if the demonstration is industrial, then they participate heavily. I visited ——— during the recent strike, not every day, and I had the impression that the immigrant workers are very interested in what happens. Especially the Algerian, who have behind them the revolution and a certain sense of *combat*. But workers other than Algerians are afraid because they are not protected by the Evian Agreement. Especially Tunisians and Moroccans. There is repression in France of Tunisians and Moroccans. The consulates have informers who spy on militants and report them. People have disappeared. Previously the Portuguese were afraid, but since the April revolution there has been a liberation of the Portuguese. They have become freer, more dynamic. There is a priest with their mission who has links with the consulate. He was also the official translator and kept a close watch on Portuguese families. Now he has changed a bit, swung with the changes in Portugal. I don't know about the other missions. With the Portuguese it was very visible. With the others it is less clear. Immigrants bring another dimension to the working class, an international dimension. They bring something extra. And once they come into the unions, they are among the most militant of workers. They have already an international consciousness."

Other trade unionists, such as this CGT official of Rhône-Poulenc, are not so enthusiastic: "The immigrants hold us back. The *patron*, he makes use of that. Look at the building industry. Up until 1948–9 the building unions were very strong, but gradually the labor force became more and more immigrant as the French avoided that type of work. Now the unions are very weak." It should be pointed out that in terms of *membership* French trade unions generally are much weaker than their British counterparts, and indeed membership in the building industry is perhaps the lowest of all the principal sectors. The structure of the industry itself – a large number of relatively small firms, a work force scattered on numerous sites, high rates of mobility between jobs – makes union organization a difficult task. There is also the fact that management certainly does not encourage militancy on the part of migrant workers.

A personnel officer at Berliet described to me the ideal type of (Moroccan) worker sought by the firm when recruiting via the ONI: "Young men with a knowledge of French, from a small town, *not* from Casablanca where the people are, in inverted commas, 'corrupted by civilization.' We want people who are more naïve, not too accustomed to urban life. Those who are too urbanized are too demanding. We want people who are not too *revendicative*."

Neither the failure to join a union, however, nor indeed national and cultural origin, should be equated with passivity in industrial relations, as Events 7, 8, and 9 will show. This is perhaps particularly true of the building industry where, as I said, union organization is very weak.

Event 7: The strike at Léon Grosse

"Léon Grosse" is a construction firm with, in 1976, a number of sites in the Lyon area including the Perrache (Lyon IIeme) and Tassin, a western suburb where, at a *chantier* known as "La Marée Verte" the firm was engaged in the construction of an office building. La Marée Verte was a medium-sized site with, at the time of the events to be described, a labor force of about forty. It was at the stage where most of the workers were bricklayers, together with some crane drivers. All but three of the employees were foreign: three French, two Italians, one Portuguese, nine Turks, and about eight each of Algerians, Moroccans, and Tunisians. As is not unusual on such a site, the *chefs d'équipe* were either from France or Southern Europe. One of the Frenchmen, Raymond, a bricklayer by trade, was formerly a *permanent* of the CFDT Bâtiment union. Prior to the strike the CFDT was not formally represented on the site. There was a CGT "representative," but according to one of the Moroccans, who subsequently became the CFDT *délégué du personnel,* this man "was always on the side of the *patron,* and did nothing." The CFDT in a subsequent discussion of the strike contained in a cyclostyled *Analyse* of a number of disputes with which it had recently been involved, mentions the existence of a third union (Force Ouvriére) in the firm, but this organization does not figure in the events that follow.

I first heard of the dispute at Léon Grosse from Raymond, who was following the same ACFAL Arabic course as myself. In early May 1976 he missed several sessions. The reason I learned from Raymond himself when I chanced to meet him during a trade union Day of Action march in which he participated with a group of workers from Léon Grosse. "I can't come to the Arabic classes at the moment," he said. "We're on strike and I'm exhausted."

The strike had begun on May 11. The initial cause was a dispute with an Italian supervisor, but in the course of events a number of claims were made. These were listed in a leaflet of May 15 printed in French, Arabic, and Turkish:

> CFDT. A Tassin, grève des Travailleurs au Bâtiment du chantier "La Marée Verte." Mes chers amis. Nous sommes des travailleurs immigrés (en majorité) et français. Nous travaillons sur le chantier de la "Marée Verte." Nous sommes presque tous logés en bungalows sur le chantier. Nous sommes une quarantaine d'ouvriers en grève depuis le 11 Mai. Nous luttons d'abord pour: le paiement des heures supplémentaires; le respect des ouvriers par le chef de chantier; l'autorisation d'absence de 2 mois pour retourner au pays, par an; l'augmentation du panier de 13 à 20F; la revision des classifications. Nous vous demandons de nous rejoindre dans notre lutte. Venez nous voir et parler avec nous. Nous vous expliquerons ce qui se passe sur notre chantier et dans le Bâtiment.

A subsequent leaflet elaborated some of these points:

> C'était trop, on en avait marre. . . . On veut être respectés – On nous commande comme à des bêtes: "Va rentrer dans ton pays," ou bien, "si tu n'es pas content ici va travailler ailleurs." Qu'on nous paye au moins toutes les heures travaillées! [The leaflet explains their working hours.] Toutes ces heures s'accumulent, d'une pays à l'autre et on s'est rendu compte qu'elles n'étaient pas toutes payées: "On nous coupait des heures." Notre cahier

de revendications: Rappel immédiat des heures non payées . . . ; respect des ouvriers; remise en ordre des classifications et augmentations minimum de 1F par heure; indemnités de déplacement de 13F à 20F; prime d'outillage de 0.75%; bleus et chaussures de sécuritié; autorisation de 2 mois par an pour retourner au pays; paiement des journées de grève. On ne veut pas vivre comme des clochards. "On veut monter." Soutenez notre lutte. Venez discuter avec nous sur le chantier.

The dispute received no coverage in the press until, at the end of the first week, seventy men at the much more important Perrache *chantier* associated themselves with the demands of the Tassin workers and came out on strike. The CFDT thought this was the crucial development, because the Perrache site had to be completed rapidly and was subject to time penalties. On May 19 after a "marathon session" (*Le Progrès de Lyon,* May 26, 1976) the CFDT negotiators, supported by a large crowd of strikers, reached an agreement in which most of the claims were met.

The day after the men returned to work, the CFDT held a *gala de soutien* that had been organized to rally support for them and for another group of workers whose dispute had also been recently settled. The gala therefore became a victory celebration. Finally, three weeks later, the workers at Tassin held a *meshwi* (with four roasted sheep) on the *chantier* to thank CFDT officials and people from the locality who had backed them during the strike.

Three aspects of the dispute require consideration. The initial cause was the behavior of an Italian foreman. Raymond described this as "very insulting to the immigrants," and numerous strikers to whom I talked referred to this. It was said that "the Italians are always like that. They push the workers in order to get promotion." The claims subsequently added to the list reflected a general discontent in the *chantier,* and a search for conditions comparable to those found elsewhere. An example of this was a demand for the provision of individual refrigerator boxes in the bungalows where twenty-six of the workers were housed, which was granted in the final round of negotiations. Other claims were highly technical – many of them refer to customary payments in the industry. Their presence in the list, and indeed the progress of the strike to its successful conclusion, needs to be placed in the context of the unionization of the dispute.

At the outset, the CFDT did not exist on the *chantier,* indeed there seems to have been little trade-union activity or interest at all. The CFDT in its *Analyse* claims that the choice of union was made "after long discussion among the workers." But although the CFDT had no official section, there was a CFDT presence (Raymond). Several of the strikers contrasted him with the CGT man "who did nothing" and praised Raymond as the only French-man who really sided with them. Raymond helped the strikers to set down their grievances in writing and to present them as a set of claims. His influence manifestly affected the choice of union, and his knowledge of union structure (and the "language" of disputes), as well as his contacts at the Bourse du Travail, were obviously crucial factors in the development of the conflict.

During the strike a CFDT *section syndicale* was formed and a representative elected. The man, who was chosen unanimously, was a twenty-six-year-old Moroccan who had been in France for four years working as a *maçon coffreur*. He was married with four children in Morocco, and had a good command of French. Four representatives were chosen to attend the negotiations on the workers' behalf, one from each of the main nationalities on the site. I was told that there was "100 percent support" for the strike, with no divergence on the part of any nationality or grade of employee.

The third aspect of the strike worth noting is the support received from the locality. A considerable number of French and Arab residents of Tassin attended the *meshwi*. The Arabs on the *chantier* maintained good relations with others (single men and families) living nearby, partly through common use of a café opposite the worksite. This link with the café, whose French *patron* was presented with a choice cut of meat from the *meshwi*, also provided contact with local French residents. Support from other French residents came via the commune's Comité Français-Immi-grés (CFI).

The CFIs, which exist in a number of areas and bring together local, mostly *gauchistes*, militants, sprang up about 1972, inspired by the Penarroya strike. They were particularly active in 1973–4 organizing opposition to a government directive (the Circulaire Marcellin-Fontanet) that tightened the link between work and residence permits. The Tassin CFI organized its own *meshwi* a week after the one at La Marée Verte, which was attended by the Léon Grosse strikers, among many others. It was in fact held on the grounds of a social center not far from the *chantier*. One of the organizers, a French woman married to an Algerian who himself took a prominent role in the festivities there and at the *chantier*, explained to me that the *comité* met from time to time and consist-ed of local people who gave help and support to immigrants in difficulties (e.g., the unemployed) or involved in conflicts such as the Léon Grosse strike. The complexion of the group may be judged from the banner displayed at the entrance to the *meshwi*: "Comité Français-Immigrés: Unity of the working class. All united." There was some overlap between this group and another grouping that also gave support, the local CFDT militants from other unions linked by the Union Interprofessionnelle de Base (see Event 9A).

The broadening of support by an appeal to the quartier is not untypical of CFDT strikes outside the large factories (see Event 9). So is the attention they pay to the particular grievances of immigrants. Also typical, however, is what I will refer to as the "incorporation" of the dispute by the CFDT. Through this incorporation in the union's organization and ideological framework, inchoate grievances became recognizable "claims" that were then negotiated with employers. We return to this later.

I have referred frequently to differences in the ideologies of the CFDT and CGT in regard to industrial relations in general and disputes involving immigrants in particular. One Algerian CGT militant (Comrade Ch—— of Event 3) put it thus: "The CGT is a mass organization, a class organization. The CFDT has a number of leftist tendencies. The fundamental difference is that the CGT advocates mass action, while the CFDT advocates action by agitating minorities" (cf. Freeman 1979:250n). This attitude is reflected in the remarks cited earlier that linked the CFDT with "leftists" at Penarroya and Câbles de Lyon. It also emerged during a strike at the Vénissieux factory of the SNAV in the spring of 1976.

Event 8: The CFDT versus the CGT: the container strike at the SNAV

The SNAV manufactures heavy wagons of various kinds, including containers. In 1976 there were about 930 employees, of whom 400 were OS, 260 were skilled workers, and 270 were white-collar and technical staff. During the previous year some 300 employees had been made redundant, partly because of the "crisis" and partly because of a major reorganization of the heavy foundry sector in the region as a whole. A number of immigrants employed on contract at the firm had lost their jobs, but there remained over 300 in 1976, almost all OS. The majority (about 60 percent) were from North Africa, many of them young unmarried men or men living apart from their families. They tended to live in SONACOTRA hostels where the SNAV had reserved places.

Both the CFDT and CGT had sections in the factory, about a quarter of the labor force being enrolled in a union: 80 in the CFDT, 160 in the CGT. Of the eight *délégués du personnel*, two were CFDT and six were CGT, a distribution that reflected the relative support for the two unions in the factory as a whole. One of the CFDT representatives was from West Africa, where he had been a railway clerk. Since coming to France in 1958 he had worked in Paris and Grenoble in various car and tractor plants. The CFDT elected section delegate, who played a prominent part in the strike, was a Frenchman (Marcel) from the Beaujolais who described himself as of "peasant origins."

According to the CFDT there had been a history of dissatisfaction in one of the three deparments at the factory, the container workshop. Salaries were said to be lower than in other departments, and in May 1975 shiftwork had been discontinued and hours of work reduced from forty-three to forty a week, with a consequent lowering of take-home pay. There were also complaints about conditions of work and about the attitude of supervisors. The workshop employed 106 *ouvriers*, the vast majority immigrants, especially from Morocco, and a number of supervisors and office staff.

It was said within the workshop that the CGT had never really discussed their grievances. In late 1975 an approach was made to the two unions. The CFDT urged a vote to gauge support for a strike, the CGT said they would only give support in the event of dismissals. At the first of a series of general assemblies convened by Marcel in December 1975, a majority had voted for a strike. First, however, certain proposals were put to the management. These were rejected and a further meeting of workers in February 1976 decided to hold a series of work stoppages. The result was a substantial loss of production. A letter from the chief personnel officer, dated March 5, to one of the workers states: that whereas the norm in his section for just under 8 hours work by 25 men was 17 containers "ce matin, pour 2h 33 de travail, vous avez rendu 1 seul container au lieu de 5." The letter warns: "Si vous n'apportiez pas, de suite, une amélioration à votre attitude, nous serions dans l'obligation de prendre toute autre sanction que votre comportement aurait rendu nécessaire."

This letter also threatened to pay according to the results of production. This threat was in fact implemented on March 6. Although there were precedents for this in other factories, payment *sur rendement* was not recent practice at the SNAV. At the end of the period February 24 – March 9, characterized by the CFDT as one of "great combativity" on the workers' part, but one during which all attempts to negotiate with management had failed, a further general assembly decided to occupy the workshop. This decision was taken because despite the cut in production, the management had been able to supply its customers from stocks accumulated during the previous poor trading year. At 4:00 A.M. on March 9, then, the gates of the workshop were blocked to begin a three-and-a half-week occupation of the premises.

At first some fifty of the workers took turns at the occupation. Marcel himself slept in the workshop for whole weeks, though N'Dongo (the West African *délégué*) attended less frequently. Other employees at the workshop not directly involved in the occupation either called in sick or were redeployed in the factory.

The management response was to seek an injunction against Marcel, N'Dongo and two other CFDT militants. They argued that a customer urgently required the delivery of two hundred containers and by preventing this "une minorité . . . prenait la lourde responsabilité d'aggraver la situation de l'entreprise, déjà rendue précaire par la crise économique." (Reported in *Le Progrès de Lyon*, March 13, 1976.) The decision of the tribunal before which the case was heard was that the four militants, "et toutes autres personnes agissant de leur chef" (*Le Progrès de Lyon*, March 16, 1976), must allow management free access to the workshop. Failing that, recourse might be had to the police.

The same day, a further meeting of strikers decided to continue the occupation and used a major trade-union demonstration that took place on March 17 to distribute a leaflet publicizing their stand. In fact, despite the passing of a deadline, the police were not called. It is not entirely clear what occurred, but a CGT leaflet of March 16 had stated: "Halte à la provocation . . . Nous mettons immédiatement le Deputé Maire de Vénissieux au courant de la situation, afin qu'il intervienne auprès du Prefet pour denoncer le mauvais coup qui se prepare contre l'ensemble des Travailleurs. Nous sommes également intervenus auprès de la Direction pour l'avertir que JAMAIS les Travailleurs de la SNAV ne travaillerons avec les flics dans l'entreprise. TENEZ VOUS PRETS, A LA MOINDRE ALERTE." The *Progrès de Lyon,* (March 17) in fact reported that the mayor of Vénissieux (Monsieur Houel of the PCF) had telephoned the *Préfet,* who had replied that no request for the use of police had been received.

Thus the occupation continued, albeit with a diminishing number of active supporters. At this time, collections of money were made to sustain the strikers. Then, on March 24, some seventeen strikers were sacked. On the following day a leaflet issued in the name of the strike committee reported this, and stated: "2 solutions s'offre à nous: SOIT rentre, la tête basse, et accepter les licentiements. SOIT s'engager fermement dans la voie de lutte tous ensembles. RESIGNATION OU ACTION? TOUS ENSEMBLES, NOUS POUVONS FAIRE PLIER LA SNAV."

From informants' accounts, however, it was clear that the strike was failing. The original number in the occupation had been halved as men drifted back to work, although even they did not escape penalties. A CFDT leaflet of March 26 referred to the sacking of "un de nos camarades qui 'pris à la gorge' par des problèmes financiers importants reprenait le boulot après 4 semaines de grève." This leaflet nevertheless proclaims: "NOUS, TRAV-AILLEURS EN GREVE, OUVRIERS FRANCAIS ET IMMIGRES DU DEPARTE-

MENT CONTENEURS N'ACCEPTONS PAS L'INACCEPTABLE. NOUS
DONNONS L'EXEMPLE ET CONTINUONS LE COMBAT. NOUS APPELONS
TOUS LES TRAVAILLEURS DU REGION A LA SOLIDARITE POUR NOUS
AIDER A TENIR JUSQU'AU BOUT."

A last-minute postscript to this leaflet, however, indicated that other developments were taking place. Following the advice of the labor officer, the
CFDT in conjunction with the CGT proposed to the management to release
the two hundred containers (mentioned in the case before the tribunal) in
return for the lifting of the dismissals. Management replied that they required
the "liberation" of the container department, but would reduce the number
of dismissals to ten. Eighteen workers would, however, be suspended for
one to two days. No concessions were made to the workers' demands.

In fact, it is clear that by this stage discussions were about the conditions
for a return to work. Management kept up the pressure by laying off eighty
workers in another department. The principal objection to a return to work,
however, remained the dismissals. The CFDT organized a petition within
the factory on behalf of the sacked men, and made their case the central
theme of yet another leaflet issued on April 2. The leaflet is interesting in that
it reveals the speed of events at this time. On the front, dated April 1: "La
CFDT propose dès ce matin la suppression de toutes les sanctions pour faits
de grève . . . pour la reprise normale du travail." And under the heading
"Même une petite victoire sera aux Conteneurs la garantie d'autres victoires
prochaines pour ceux qui viendrons après," it notes that the labor officer
had promised to examine seriously the safety of employees in the container
workshop after a return to work. The back of the leaflet, however, contains a
last-minute revelation that following a meeting on Friday morning, there
would be a return to work on the following Monday with the number of
dismissals reduced from twelve to seven, the lifting of the threat of prosecu-
tion against six workers, and the lifting of the suspension of twenty-three
others. The CFDT promised to fight the remaining dismissals in the courts,
and, in fact, when later the cases came before the Conseil de Prudhomme,
the management was obliged to agree to pay compensation.

ANALYSIS

A full analysis of this material would take us in a number of
directions not germane to the theme of this chapter. I will therefore concentrate on what the dispute reveals about the relative
position of the two main unions. Let us begin with the issues.

There were, in fact, several issues at stake in the strike, some of
which changed as the conflict developed. There was, first, a background of disaffection and unease in the container department.
Some of the complaints made by the container men raised matters

of general concern in the industry (e.g., short-time working), others pertained to problems that were peculiar to them, especially conditions of work. A leaflet of March 26 states: "Les conditions du travail qui nous sont imposées sont terriblement contraignantes: soudure en atmosphère confine et polluente, peinture en tunnel à proximité des fours de séchage, espacements en chaîne de montage, bruit infernal de tôle torturée, coup d'arc, insultes des chefs, toilettes repoussantes etc." Initially, however, the workers met greater sympathy for their plight in the CFDT than in the CGT. And, as we shall see, the attitude of the CGT hardened as the dispute progressed. The reason for this may be found partly in the nature of the claims themselves.

In February and March 1976, the CFDT section formulated a lengthy package of claims based on the men's grievances. These included: a claim for workers in the department for a flat-rate wage increase of 250 francs per month; a set of demands for improvement in the physical conditions of work (noise, smell, lavatories); a set of demands for improvement in the social conditions of work (especially relations with supervisors); and a number of demands relating to conditions of service, in particular the recognition of foreign qualifications and improvements in the operation of the classification system. The way in which these claims were formulated and promulgated made them peculiar to the department concerned; they were not of general interest to the factory work force, still less the workers in the industry as a whole. As we have seen, the CGT's industrial strategy, which is formulated at a high level in the hierarchy, is to mobilize on a broad front, a mass front, as they would say.

At the time of the SNAV strike, the policy of the CGT-Métallurgie was to press for a wage demand expressed as an increase in the *valeur du point* to 14. 20 francs. (The slogan chanted on one of the March demonstrations: "Valeur du point, quatorze vingt!") This explains the CGT's attitude toward one aspect of the container men's claim. An increase in the *valeur du point* does not affect differentials (the coefficients). The distance between the pay of an OS2 and an OP1/OQ1 remains constant, for example, in a ratio of 140 : 160. A flat-rate increase, of course, reduces differentials. A CGT-Métallurgie (Rhône) leaflet of April 1976, addressed to the issues of the forthcoming national conference on immigration (see Event 2) remarked: "Quelquefois nous entendons dans certains ateliers: 'Nous demandons 300F pour tous.'

Ceci à première vue paraît normal, MAIS, AU FAIT, EST-CE
VRAIMENT JUSTE?" It explains why it is not and calls for a
collective defense of *la grille de la CGT*. The SNAV was not the
only factory in the region at this time where the CGT was opposing claims for a flat-rate increase of between 200 and 300 francs
supported by the CFDT.

A claim for 250 francs all around at the SNAV would be considered divisive by the CGT in that it altered differentials and therefore placed the skilled and unskilled workers at odds. In this
connection it is important to appreciate that although it recruits
widely among all workers, the center of gravity of the CGT's
support in this region is to be found in the established work force
of the main sectors of industrial employment, where it is especially strong among skilled workers. The large engineering factories of Vénissieux provide numerous examples of this. It is also
significant that Vénissieux is a PCF stronghold. The CFDT's support is much more varied, and at least in this region is stronger in
more marginal industries, and among unskilled workers, many of
whom are immigrants. For example, in one firm engaged in the
collection of refuse there was a clear division between the skilled
truck drivers who were French and in the CGT, and the loaders,
Algerian OS in the CFDT. Elsewhere the relative distribution is
not as obvious as that, but in general the (French) skilled worker is
the principal CGT constituent.

The other claims by the SNAV container men were also particularistic in that they related to the container department alone or
to the problems of one category of worker, the immigrants. Pursuit of such claims by strike action would in the CGT's view be
divisive because they bring out differences in the labor force,
pitting department against department, and worker against worker. Above all, the strike could be seen as a strike of immigrant
workers, with the danger that it would be confined to such workers.

In Chapter 3, I cited the views of one CGT official that the
CFDT contains elements who "believe that immigrant workers
are a revolutionary class," and subsequently cited another who
criticized the CFDT's advocacy of "action by agitating minorities."
Similar sentiments were expressed by the CGT branch at the
SNAV in a leaflet issued at the end of the strike:

> Les travailleurs se souviendront. Durant plus d'un mois, une équipe
> d'aventuristes a sciemment TROMPE, BAFOUE, réduit à la misere et à la

merci du Patron, quelques Travailleurs. RESULTAT DE L'OPERA-
TION? 7 LICENCIEMENTS. 7 licenciés victimes d'avoir courageuse-
ment agit au grand jour, alors que les manipulateurs se terraient lâche-
ment dans l'ombre. . . . Mais, qu'elles que soient les erreurs qui ont été
commises, nous devons considérer qu'elles font désormais partie du
passé. Car ce qui compte avant tout, c'est la satisfaction des revendications. SEULE L'UNITE DE TOUT LE PERSONNEL nous permettra
d'en obtenir satisfaction.

Strikes such as that in the container workshop at the SNAV are
in accord neither with the ideological position of the CGT nor
with its industrial and electoral strategies. At that time the CGT
firmly supported the "Common Program," which united the PCF
and the Parti Socialiste (PS) in an electoral pact. The election of
this coalition was seen as the first priority. The CGT characterized
the leftist propaganda at the SNAV as an "attack against the Common Program" (cf. Freeman 1979:245).

The situations in which such disputes are located do, however,
have greater ideological salience for the CFDT, or rather for
groups that associate themselves with the CFDT at the local level.
At the SNAV, the CFDT received full backing from the cell of a
groupuscule called the Parti Communiste Révolutionnaire – Marx-
iste Léniniste (PCR–ML), whose presence in this and other disputes I discuss elsewhere (Grillo 1979; cf. also Freeman
1979:237).

The journalist Bernard Lalanne, in a stimulating article on the
contemporary working class in France, asks the question: What or
who is that class? Having given "speakers" from the CGT and
CFDT their say, he provides this comment from a third party:
"Pour Marchais, c'est les métallos, la Régie Renault, les ouvriers
d'Hispano Suiza, les cheminots . . . davantage que les Lip. Pour les
gauchistes, ce qui est significatif, c'est cinquante types en grève
dans un patelin" (Lalanne 1975). This is highly apt. The CFDT
local militants are not infrequently found if not stimulating at
least fostering independent industrial militancy on the part of so-
called marginal groups such as immigrants. The oft cited "exem-
plary" strike at Penarroya symbolized such militancy for many
CFDT activists. Conversely, the CGT appears in a "demobilizing"
role, encouraging action only when it is in accord with its grand
strategy or involves its basic constituency.

The CFDT also often seeks to "popularize" a dispute, by drawing on support of people in the immediate locality and organizing

comités and *galas de Soutien* (see the Léon Grosse strike, Event 7, and the Caluire-Légumes strike, Event 9). This was not a factor in the SNAV dispute, where little attempt was made to encourage support even within the factory, let alone outside it. This may be a function partly of the nature of strikes in the larger factories (cf. the *caristes* dispute at Câbles de Lyon), partly of the residential location of workers. At both Léon Grosse and Caluire-Légumes a number of employees actually lived on the work site. My *impression*, however, from talking to CFDT militants at the SNAV, is that the isolation of the strike was in a sense willed, for ideological reasons. There was, I believe, a wish to see the strike succeed on its own terms, or fail, and be seen to fail, because of the ideological inadequacy of the CGT.

One other factor that influences CGT strategy in these disputes is the general background of racism. It is possible, as I suggested earlier, that racism is less manifest at work, within the factories, than outside work, on the housing estates. Nevertheless, as we have seen, racism does exist, is indeed a fact of life with which the CGT must contend. A dispute involving workers who are mainly, if not exclusively, immigrants (such as the container men) can too readily be dismissed in racist terms as one affecting only "those people, those Arabs." To that extent, such strikes "play into the hands of the boss" by allowing cleavages within the labor force to develop.

In 1975–6 the CGT and the PCF engaged in a campaign against these racist tendencies (see, for example, the special May Day number of the CGT's magazine, *La Vie Ouvrière*, No. 1652, April 28, 1976). As we have observed, the CGT *métallos* meeting (Event 2) and the PCF cell meeting at Vaulx Sud (Event 3) are better understood in part in the light of that campaign. It is clear, however, as I remarked in Chapter 5 à propos the dilemma of the communist local authorities, that subsequently both the PCF and the CGT resorted to a different kind of strategy, perhaps in an attempt to preserve their support among their basic constituents, the skilled French worker in the traditional large-scale industries. In the admittedly more difficult economic circumstances of 1981, the PCF adopted a much harder position on immigration and on the position of immigrant workers, as the speeches of their candidate in the 1981 presidential elections reveal.

At the conclusion of the SNAV dispute, the CFDT militant Marcel drew this lesson: "The strike showed that the workers are capable of governing themselves. It was the workers who took the decisions. The CGT has a hierarchical command structure. It is possible to change that structure. The working class must make its own decisions. In this strike the immigrants themselves conducted the strike." He may have been overly modest about his own contribution, but his remark provides a further illustration of what some see as a difference between the CFDT and CGT. It also illustrates another point. For if a picture emerges from the material presented in this chapter of organized labor and its activists as much concerned with the problems that immigrants pose for their *own* conceptual and organizational systems as with the problems of immigrants themselves, then it is an image that is not too misleading.

Immigrant workers in France form an integral part of the productive labor force, but they are located in certain sectors of production and at particular levels in those sectors. There are differences between immigrants of various nationalities, but by and large this is true historically of all groups of immigrants. In these sectors immigrants have a high concentration and high visibility – as they do in certain sectors of the housing market. In both housing and employment, immigrants are at the lower end of the French social system. They are, therefore, often distanced, socially and physically, from the French working class and their families. Immigrants may form an integral part of the productive labor force, but they are not thereby integrated with the working class, except at the level of grand theory.

This structural distancing in employment and housing has an interactive relationship with racism of both an institutional and a casual kind in that it is created in part by that distancing and is sustained by it. The trade unions are confronted with the implications of this day in and day out on the shop floor, and less hectically in the committee rooms where ideologies and strategies are elaborated. It is ironic that the ideological solutions of the problems created by one kind of division, that between French and immigrant workers, should be associated with bitter divisions of another kind, between the CFDT and the CGT. Who emerges the winner in these struggles I would not care to say.

10

"The strike is like a school"

This chapter continues the discussion of several of the themes explored in Chapter 9, which dealt with the problems of immigrant workers in employment. Its content also provides a bridge to Chapter 11, leading us directly into an examination of the position of certain groups and individuals who operate at the "interface" of the worlds of the French and immigrants. The chapter is ultimately about them and their roles as intermediaries and interpreters between two sets of cultures.

One of the issues central to this book is what I have termed the "problem of representation." The material presented in this chapter, which constitutes a single extended case study of a strike involving a small number of Tunisian workers, therefore illustrates what is a matter of more general concern, and is thus typical of much that occurs in Lyon. For various other reasons, however, the data are atypical. First, Lyon is an industrial city and migrant workers are concentrated in the sectors such as building and construction, mechanical engineering, and artificial textiles. The Tunisians in this case study, however, are agricultural workers, albeit in a sector that is highly industrial in character. They are employed by a market-gardening firm with premises on the outskirts of the *agglomération*. Second, the commune in which they are employed, and where they live, is a middle-class suburb (Caluire) to the north of the city, which contains relatively few foreigners (5.6 percent in the 1975 census). It is not therefore typical of the areas in which most immigrants reside – the inner-city tenements or the large working-class housing estates to the east and south. Nevertheless, the material is illustrative of a number of processes that characterize French-immigrant relations in Lyon.

Event 9A: The strike at Caluire-Légumes

The dispute to be described involved some nine Tunisians employed by a small market-gardening firm ("Caluire-Légumes") whose premises – farm, fields, and so on – are on the north side of the suburb of Caluire, on the edge of the built-up area. The firm is a Groupement Agricole d'Exploitation en Commun (GAEC) with about 30 hectares of salad and other vegetables that they supply to supermarkets. It is owned by two men, one of whom is the son of the deputy mayor of the commune. At the time of the dispute there were some 22 employees: 9 Tunisians, 5 Portuguese, 2 Spaniards, and 6 or 7 Turks. The Spaniards were classed as *chefs* (supervisors) and the Portuguese as *sous-chefs*. Some of the Turks, it was alleged, had no work permits and were therefore employed illegally. Most of the employees were housed by the *patrons* on the farm: the Tunisians and some others in *cabanes* or shacks in the fields, the rest in the farm buildings.

The strikes began in mid-May 1976 after a dispute between a Tunisian worker and one of the *chefs*. The Tunisians decided among themselves to raise the matter with the *patron,* but he simply supported the *chef* and stood by the work rules enforced in the enterprise (see full list of complaints given below). These rules were explained to me thus: "They were not allowed to talk at work, smoke, or even go for a piss." The Tunisians apparently concluded that these conditions of work were insupportable and decided to protest against them. As the idea took hold, they worked out what other grievances they had and began to draw up a list of claims. At this point – there was no trade union at the firm – they decided to seek help.

First, it appears, they went to the mayor of the commune. He suggested they return to work. Second, they went to the Bourse du Travail in central Lyon (the building where many unions have their headquarters) and approached the CGT, which explained that it did not have an organization dealing with agricultural workers in this area (but see the report on the meeting in Event 9B). They then went to the inspector for agricultural labor, again to no avail. Finally, at the Mutualité Agricole they met an employee (Claude) who was a CFDT militant. Through him they made formal contact with a trade union.

With Claude's help a complete list of grievances and claims were drawn up. These were spelled out in a leaflet produced immediately by the CFDT, and in a letter to the *patron*. This first leaflet went as follows:

> CFDT. Les travailleurs de "Caluire-Légumes" relevant la tête. "Cailuire-Légumes" : une entreprise de maraîchage, une vingtaine d'ouvriers, pour la plupart immigrés. NOS CONDITIONS DE TRAVAIL: Pour 17 ouvriers, 5 chefs + 2 patrons; Des horaires au bon gré du patron (différents selon les jours et les ouvriers); Toujours courbés a couper des salades. Pas de pause-casse-croûte. Pas le droit de se relever pour discuter avec le voisin. Si on va

au toilettes . . . remarques du chef. LA SEMAINE PASSEE UN COPAIN EST MORT SUITE A CES CONDITIONS DE TRAVAIL (position courbée – produits de traitements). On évite la fatigue, au tracteur (par mesure d'économie) mais pas aux ouvriers. Travail par tous les temps. L'accident n'est jamais reconnu – c'est toujours la maladie. Répression et brimade constante des chefs (réaction des travailleurs sanctionnés par engueulade des chefs et même diminution des salaires). NOS CONDITIONS DE LOGEMENT. Une chambre de 10m² pour 4. Pas d'eau chaude, pas de douche, pas de WC, pas de poubelle, en guise de séchoir à linge, les tondeuse et les tracteurs. Pas de verrou à la porte (les patrons et les chefs sont comme chez eux). L'environnement de la chambre: fumier, engrais, gas-oil. Tout le monde au lit à 10h. C'est un ordre! Pas le droit de recevoir quelqu'un dans notre chambre. ET TOUT CA POUR UN LOYER MENSUEL DE 100F. PAR PERSONNE ET SANS RECU. NOS CONDITIONS DE SALAIRE. 8.72F de l'heure. Una compte le 20 du mois à condition de l'avoir demandé 48h auparavant. La paye le 5. NOUS DEMANDONS. Un salaire horaire minimum de 10F. Un horaire fixe 7h30 12h – 13h30 17h. Un acompte le 15 de mois et la paye le 30. La suppression du travail le samedi. ½ heure de casse-croûte payée. La suppression du travail sous la pluie ou la neige. La liberté de discuter pendant le temps de travail. La suppression de toutes les brimades de la part des chefs. Tous les matins, l'affichage du travail à faire, pour chacun. Les réunions prise sur le temps du travail. Le logement gratuit avec toutes les mesures d'hygiène. L'amélioration de l'environnement des chambres. L'entière liberté de disposer et d'organiser notre temps hors du travail. Le droit de recevoir n'importe qui dans notre chambre. Des élections des délégués du personnel. Le paiement des heures de grève. L'assurance qu'aucune sanction ne sera prise suite de la grève. Notre lutte est la lutte de tous les travailleurs. DE VOTRE SOLIDARITE DEPENDERA LA REUSSITE DE NOTRE ACTION.

The tract, dated May 23, 1976, ended with a footnote: "Information de dernière heure. Hier matin un patron de l'entreprise a lancé sa voiture contre deux grévistes."

The list of demands remained much the same throughout the dispute, though at a late stage the wage claim was reduced to one for an hourly wage of 9.50 francs, and two additional claims were made: for a supplementary payment of 120 francs per month for those housed off the premises, and for the supplying of refrigerators in the shacks.

At first, the *patrons* refused any discussion, but on May 26 a first meeting was held and they "made a pretense of negotiating" (CFDT leaflet) in the presence of various employers' representatives, the *inspecteur des lois sociales en agriculture,* and the deputy mayor of Caluire (the father of one of the *patrons*). Nothing came of this meeting. During these *négotiations bidons,* as the CFDT described them, the only change in the *patrons'* position occurred at a meeting called by the mayor of Caluire, at which an offer of 50 centimes was made (i.e., to increase the hourly wage to 9.22 francs). The strikers reduced their own claim to 9.50 francs. The strike dragged on into June, when on June 24 more serious negotiations took place at the Chambre d'Agriculture du Rhône involving the Fédération des Syndicats Exploitants Agricoles (an employers' group). This is the meeting mentioned by Claude in the ACFAL meeting, Event 9B. Although nothing specific emerged from this meeting, it seemed to the union that there was disagreement among the ranks of the employers, some of whom appeared to oppose the way the Caluire-Légumes management treated its employees. A final round of negotiations was held at the Caluire town hall on July 6. It was presided over by the mayor and included the president of the *Fédération,* the two *patrons,* the *inspecteur,* two CFDT officials, and three of the strikers.

The outcome was as follows: Hourly salary was increased to 9.36 francs. Working hours were cut to forty per week with one quarter-hour paid break per day. The number of persons per shack was reduced to two, and the rent was reduced to 60 francs per person per month. Toilets and refrigerators were to be installed. In addition, twelve workers taken on during the strike (see below) would retain their jobs. This result received wide coverage in the press. *Le Progrès de Lyon* (July 7, 1976) described it as a "pyrrhic victory," weighing the fifty days spent on strike against the 64 centimes increase. In fact, as *Le Progrès de Lyon* also noted, the wage increase gained through the strike would have to be evaluated in relation to the whole range of claims that had been made, especially those concerning housing and conditions of work. Nevertheless, during the week in which the strikers won an increase of 64 centimes, the government announced an increase in the guaranteed minimum wage (SMIC) of 50 centimes. The result was that the strikers had in effect increased their pay by 14 centimes.

THE MANAGEMENT OF THE DISPUTE:
THE EMPLOYEES' SIDE

Let us go over this dispute and trace its development, first from the employees' side. A number of attempts were made to secure support for the strikers. The first was by the strikers themselves, who after a fruitless tour of various offices met Claude of the CFDT. This contact led to the involvement of a number of outside parties. First, its existence was brought to the attention of certain Tunisian organizations in two ways. Militants within the CFDT notified Jean-Paul, the worker priest and teacher of Arabic linked with ACFAL who appears in a number of Events discussed in this book. Jean-Paul invited a Tunisian postgraduate student (Amar), who taught Arabic classes at ACFAL (he was my own tutor) to accompany him on a visit to the strikers. They went and were, they said, very impressed by the strikers' determination. Through Amar, a Tunisian student organization and other Tunisian political groups became involved. As Amar put it: "A section of the Tunisian working class was in conflict." At the same time, the CFDT militants notified the student organization directly. According to one of these students (Milud), such information is regularly transmitted.

A second set of people was drawn in via the CFDT's own structure, in this case through the Union Interprofessionnelle de Base for Caluire and Rillieux. The UIB links the militants from different CFDT unions who happen to live in a particular locality. The CFDT also arranged for the strikers' participation at a conference (*rassemblement des luttes*) at the Bourse du Travail that was concerned with a number of disputes taking place in the Lyon area at that time. The Caluire-Légumes strike had a display with posters, photos, and leaflets. Some of the strikers and their student supporters were present to answer questions.

Through the UIB and other CFDT channels a third set of people entered the scene. These came from a variety of political groups, of which the most prominent was the local branch of the Parti Socialiste Unifié (PSU). From all these sources was drawn the membership of a Comité de Soutien which played a major part in the conduct of the strike. Claude (see Event 9B) said that the Comité de Soutien "was nothing very formal, not very structured," and that is a fair description. A number of organizations of the kind referred to above were represented at its meetings. For example, the one held on June 14 to discuss the *gala de soutien* scheduled for later that week was attended by some thirty people including five strikers, several Tunisian students, CFDT militants from the UIB, representatives from ACFAL and Accueil et Rencontre and from several *groupuscules* such as the PSU, "Homme Rouge," and other Maoist-leaning factions. The meeting spent thirty minutes discussing whether a full list of supporting organizations should be appended to the leaflets and posters advertising the gala. The list did appear on the gala poster, but not on others that were prepared in connection with the dispute. And all the "official" leaflets that I saw were issued in the name of the CFDT only.

Through the Comité de Soutien and the CFDT, publicity was given to the strike in a number of ways. In the early part of June, leaflets were widely circulated among trade unionists and leftist organizations. They were also distributed to customers at some of the supermarkets that bought Caluire-Légumes produce. Leaflets and posters also appeared on walls, telegraph posts, and so forth throughout the urban area. The design and printing of the publicity material was undertaken solely by the CFDT. The various supporting organizations also advertised the strike among their members. For example, ACFAL twice circulated cyclostyled notices, one of which advertised the June 25 demonstration described later. A number of brief notices were inserted in *Le Progrès de Lyon,* but until the dispute was concluded, when the industrial correspondent wrote two analytical pieces, only six short references to the strike appeared in the paper's news columns.

Money was collected, first through a general appeal, then through the sale of 5-franc *bons de soutien.* The *gala de soutien* also raised funds. This event was publicized by poster, by a notice in *Le Progrès de Lyon,* and by word of mouth. The previous week, for example, the forthcoming gala was announced at the *meshwi* that celebrated the successful conclusion of the Léon Grosse strike at Oullins (see Event 7). More than three hundred attended the gala, which was held in a cinema at the Croix Rousse in the Ist Arrondissment, and were entertained with music and singing.

Other measures in support of the strike included the maintenance of a picket outside the gates of the enterprise manned by strikers and their supporters, and an attempt (which was unsuccessful) to persuade workers at the supermarkets to refuse to handle Caluire-Légumes produce. Through the Comité de Soutien many local organizations in Caluire were asked for their support, including "liberal" groups such as the local Third World society. A certain amount of money came from such sources, but little else.

Three marches or demonstrations were organized. I attended the second of these on Friday, June 25, which had been advertised by leaflet, poster, and press notice to start at the Caluire post office at 6:30 P.M. I arrived at 6:00 to find a group of six young French people standing around. I sat and watched others arriving. Gradually the group of young people increased. "Voilà le gauchiste," they said to someone. I began to see people I knew, and soon it became apparent that several distinct groupings were involved who assembled, and later marched, together. The only group that actually publicized its identity, however, was the PSU, on whose part a leaflet was distributed, and the posters advertising the march had contained only the names "CFDT Agricole" and "Comité de Soutien."

At 6:30 the strikers themselves arrived, and then a loudspeaker van. Several banners were unfurled. These referred briefly to the basic facts of the strike, although one called for the "solidarity of workers and peasants." Trying to discuss the march with people I knew, I had great difficulty in ascertaining where we were heading or what was supposed to happen. The reason for this became apparent later. Finally, at about 7:00, we set out. There were about 150 marchers, among whom the great majority were young French women and men. There was, however, a fair sprinkling of older, well-dressed French people. "The revolution comes to Caluire," said one of these, rather self-consciously, I thought, to his friends. There were relatively few Arabs apart from the strikers themselves and some Tunisian students, though there was a small group of Moroccan workers whom I knew from elsewhere.

Someone told me that we were going to the town hall, but we passed that by with shouts and waving fists, and proceeded along Caluire's main street. Leaflets were distributed to the Friday evening shoppers and to motorists trapped in their vehicles by the passage of the march. There was little sign of emotion on their part. The police were notable for their absence – no one on traffic duty, for example. When by chance a police car was caught in the traffic jam, the procession was allowed to flow around it, and over it with the banners. Later someone pointed out an unmarked car that followed the procession to its end, halting some 50 meters from where the meeting was finally held.

The chanting of slogans was continuous: "Caluire-Légumes solidarité"; "Travailleurs français, immigrés, même combat, même patron, méme combat"; "Le patron va céder"; and so forth. There were others, too, about the *patron* and also about the police and fascism. Leaving the main street, we followed a route that took us through some plush suburbs toward the edge of the commune where the firm had its premises. Here I learned that the plan had been to hold a meeting at one of the large supermarkets that form a shopping center opposite the firm's farm. This had been forbidden by the police, so after winding our way through the shopping center's parking lots, we found ourselves outside the enterprise itself. No one seemed to know what to do. "Go into the yard [of the farm]," some shouted. The majority, however, decided to stay on the road, where a meeting now took place addressed briefly by one of the strikers, who simply stated the basic claims, and lengthily by a representative of the Jeunes Agricoles, who offered general support. The meeting ended with an invitation to those who wished to visit the shacks where the strikers lived.

The third demonstration was somewhat more dramatic than this. It took place on July 2 at a meeting of the Caluire council when some strikers and their supporters invaded the public gallery, unfurling banners and shouting slogans. The CFDT thought this demonstration played an important part in forcing a conclusion to the negotiations.

A fourth and, as it transpired, final rally was planned for July 6. This again was held outside the firm's premises. A socialist deputy was booked to speak, but at the last moment he had to return to Paris. The meeting in fact took place after the dispute had been resolved and became, in the words of *Le Progrès de Lyon* (July 7, 1976) a "victory rally." It was addressed at some length by representatives from the CFDT, the Parti Socialiste, and the PSU, and for two minutes by one of the strikers.

THE MANAGEMENT OF THE DISPUTE:
THE EMPLOYERS' SIDE

Some brief comments on the employers' actions in the dispute. First, there appears to have been considerable reluctance to negotiate. Only gradually were the management drawn to the table, and it seems that it was those who were otherwise on their side (the municipal authorities of Caluire, i.e., the mayor and the *Fédération*) who persuaded them to reach a settlement. According to Claude, as the dispute went on the *Fédération* split ranks with some of the employers expressing disagreement with Caluire-Légumes management's treatment of their employees. It was also suggested to me that other employers were worried about the effects on their own workers of a long strike in this sector, and the CFDT managed to obtain support from some farming groups, including the Jeunes Agricoles. In a final assessment of the dispute, *Le Progrès de Lyon* (July 10, 1976) commented:

> Ce que l'on peut déduire de cette grève par ailleurs, c'est qu'elle a ébranlé une profession "vorace en main-d'oeuvre" et en pleine mutation chez les maraîchers, car malgré la modernisation et la mécanisation actuellement en cours, ils ont besoin d'une main-d'oeuvre qualifiée et nombreuse surtout à certaines périodes de l'année. . . . Certains maraîchers, et notamment les dirigeants de "Caluire-Légumes," craignent qu'un développement de telles grèves à des périodes critiques mette en

péril non seulement les exploitations, mais aussi une part importante de l'alimentation de l'agglomération lyonnaise.

Just as an appeal to the *fédération* was in the end counterproductive for the Caluire-Légumes management, so too was their link with the municipal authorities. Although one of the directors was the son of the deputy mayor, the mayor himself seemed at an early stage anxious for a settlement to be reached. His anxiety apparently increased as the weeks passed. One informant thought that the mayor had been "dropped in the shit" by the dispute during a period leading up to municipal elections, then nine months away, in which at that time it was thought the left would do well (they did not). The CFDT certainly believed that the invasion of the municipal chamber, and the subsequent involvement of socialist councillors and deputies, was a crucial step in the strike. The suggestion that some of the firm's workers were employed illegally cannot have helped the management's standing with either the *fédération* or the municipality.

Four other developments during the strike may be noted briefly. First, there was direct action by management and police against the strike pickets. Twice the strikers and their supporters were "controlled" by the branch of the police known as the "Renseignements Généraux." Second, the management attempted to break the strike by engaging other workers. Initially they asked other market-gardeners in the area to help them out; later they recruited about a dozen workers on a temporary basis. These included some immigrants and also some students. Third, and of particular interest, was the recourse to the Tunisian consulate described in Event 9B (see especially the remarks by Milud).

This almost concludes the description of these events and their preliminary analysis. But before undertaking a further assessment of the dispute and drawing certain conclusions from it, I present an account of a meeting that took place at the conclusion of the strike. It covers some of the evidence already cited, but also includes important additional material.

Event 9B: The meeting to discuss "Les conflits – Caluire-Légumes," July 9, 1976

The setting: the ACFAL "Session d'Arabe," an evening meeting arranged as part of the program of *animation* that accompanied a three-week intensive

Arabic-language course organized by ACFAL. Several dozen persons were present including:

>Some half-dozen strikers from Caluire-Légumes, led by Bashir
>Belkacem – Algerian student, Arab teacher
>Claude – CFDT militant from the Agricultural Workers
>Françoise – primary-school teacher from Nanterre
>Amar – Tunisian economics postgraduate, Arab teacher
>Henri – adult-education teacher from Strasbourg
>Jean-Paul – worker priest, teacher of Arabic
>Charles – secondary-school teacher from Marseille
>Jo – worker and CFDT member from Nantes
>Milud – Tunisian student, Arab teacher

The meeting was scheduled for 5:30 P.M. In fact it was 6:30 by the time the strikers were fetched from their workplace in Caluire. They entered the meeting to general applause and took their seats at the front of the audience along with Amar, Milud, Belkacem, and another Algerian student. Jo, who intended to tape-record the meeting, also sat himself down at the front.

Amar opened the meeting by announcing that the ex-strikers would sing a song. This they did, and with Amar orchestrating, the audience joined in, clapping in rhythm and chanting the chorus. This lasted some five minutes. Amar then introduced Claude, who would say a few words.

Claude introduces himself as a "militant of the CFDT Agricole. I followed the strike on behalf of the CFDT." He then outlines briefly the background to the strike. "The enterprise [i.e. Caluire-Légumes] has twenty-two workers. Seventeen of these are *déclarés* [legally employed], and there are five Turks without papers. There are five Portuguese *chefs*. The role of the *chefs* was the motive for the strike. The enterprise is a GAEC and has two *patrons*. The strikers' demands were pay to be increased from eight francs seventy-two per hour to ten francs per hour; an end to insults from the chefs; better housing; better hours; a half-hour lunch break; an end to work in the snow; and one *chef* to be in charge so that they knew to whom to refer."

Jean-Paul: "Tell us about how the strike began."

Claude: "The strike began, more or less, on May nineteenth. The men were not in a union, so they went to the Bourse du Travail. Eventually they found me at the place where I work, the Mutualité Agricole. In the evening we put down the demands in black and white. A letter was sent to the patron and a leaflet was put out. The patron received the letter on the twentieth, after the leaflet had been put out. One of the problems was that the patron blocked the negotiations. He proposed Tuesdays and Fridays for the negotiations, but he didn't really want to discuss. In the final negotiations the participants were three of the workers, two people from the CFDT, the mayor of Caluire, the inspecteur de droit social, the president of the Fédération des Exploitants Agricoles. We had organized a strike picket in the mornings and two demonstrations. In my view, what brought about the negotiations was the presence of the strikers, with sympathizers, at the Caluire municipal council meeting, where we assembled with banners, chanting slogans like 'The patron is a fascist,' and so on. We asked to be allowed to speak. This was not permitted. But this is what pushed the mayor to negotiations.''

Belkacem now asks the strikers themselves to speak, in Arabic.

Milud and Amar turn to one of the strikers, the leader Bashir, and whisper to him.

Milud: "He prefers you to put questions."

Henri: "This is a flagrant example. Let them speak in Arabic and let someone translate." Loud applause from the youngest of the strikers.

Jo: "How long have they been at the *boîte*? How long have they been in France? Was this their first strike?"

Bashir begins to speak in French. There are several shouts of "Speak in Arabic!"

Bashir: "Was the question in French or Arabic?" Anyway, he begins again in Arabic.

Amar: "Slowly." At the end of Bashir's remarks Amar puts the reply into very simple Arabic for the benefit of beginners on the ACFAL course. He then translates into French.*

Amar: "He says that three of the men have been there for three years, two for one and a half years, the other for six to eight months. They have been in France since 1971–2." He turns to Bashir to prompt him on the third question.

Jean-Paul, from the floor, presses for an answer.

Amar: "Yes, one of them had participated in a strike at a factory." (It later transpires that this was Bashir himself.)

Q1: "Did many people support you?"

Q2: "What was the proportion of those who came out on strike and those who didn't?"

Amar again prompts a reply and tells them to speak slowly. "There was a lot of support: the Parti Socialiste, the CFDT, the PSU."

Milud: "The CFDT organized the strike from the start and support came from the Parti Socialiste and other organizations. [He lists them by initials.] And from the Syndicat des Etudiants Tunisiens."

Q3: "What about those without papers?"

---

*With certain exceptions that are marked in the text, I have not provided the verbatim record of the remarks by Bashir. I give here only the replies in French provided by Amar or Milud, that is, I give only their translations into French of the comments in Arabic made by the strikers, and their remarks based on the whispered conversations. The reasons for this will become apparent subsequently.

Amar consults with Bashir and announces, "There were four Turks working at the enterprise. Two of these were without papers. The patron sent
those two on holiday, and recruited others. The ones on holiday do not
know this yet."

Q4: "Where do they live?"

Bashir speaks, *Amar* translates: "Some live in cabins at the enterprise,
others live just outside the enterprise. One with his family lives in an HLM.
The Turks and the Portuguese are housed in the same building as the *patron*,
on the farm."

Belkacem (in Arabic, then in French): "What about the relationship between the Arabs and the others?"

Bashir (in Arabic): "There were seven Turks, four without papers. The
Turks said, 'We are not striking, but we are with you.' The Portuguese were
the *sous-chefs*, but otherwise the relationship with them was friendly."

Amar translates the first part of this as: "There were nine Turks, four
without papers. They didn't want to strike because of that. Out of solidarity
with their comrades they didn't strike . . . [etc.]"

Henri: How did they choose between the CFDT and the CGT?"

Amar (translates): "They didn't choose between them. They went first to
the Bourse du Travail, but the CGT didn't want them."

Milud: "No, no! The CGT said they didn't work in the agricultural
sector."

Amar: "They next went to the *inspecteur social*. Third, they met Claude,
who is in the CFDT."

Claude: "We held a meeting and produced a list of claims. The Fédération des Exploitants said they would support the patron, but we obtained
support from the Paysan-Travailleurs and the Young Farmers. That was the
first reaction on the part of the *fédération*. However, it's worth noting that
following this reaction, which was in a letter sent by the president and two
or three other people without consulting the grass roots, there was a reaction
among people who were favorable to the strikers. After that there was the
first round of negotiations within the Féderation des Exploitants. These were
in the presence of representatives of people who supported the strikers, the
president of the *fédération* and a certain number of others. Nothing came
out of it."

Charles: "I would like to know about the Comité de Soutien."

Claude: "It was nothing very formal, not very structured. It was formed
out of people who came to support the strike at meetings. The CFDT didn't
make an appeal to other organizations."

Françoise: "Was the one who had already participated in a strike already
in a union?"

Milud (answers directly): "When the Tunisians come to France, they are
not interested in unions. And then there is the Tunisian consulate, and
above all the Tunisian cops who follow them everywhere. Those who are

members of trade unions are known, and this poses problems when they return home."

Amar puts a question to Bashir, and there is a whispered conversation. "He was in a strike, but was not a member of a trade union. There is a repression exercised by the political leadership and the police in the Tunisian colony in Europe."

Q5: "What about the consulate?"

Milud: "The consulate intervened four times. The patron sent a letter to the consulate. Four times the consulate sent someone down to the cabins. Three times they didn't find anyone. On one occasion the man from the consulate took three of the workers back with him and said that if they left the CFDT hs would sort out the dispute, between the consulate and the patron."

Amar: "They refused this. They knew of another strike where this had happened. The strikers had left their union, and they had been sacked."

Belkacem (in Arabic, then in French): "What did the strike mean for you? What was the reaction of the French comrades?"

Amar prompts Bashir, "Answer, answer!"

Bashir (in Arabic): "The strike brought us various things that we hadn't seen and that we didn't know, and that we didn't imagine. And in this strike we also obtained some things, even if those things were not very great. Things were not very well done because we were not united, we workers, between ourselves, those who worked in the *boîte*. And because of that . . . *Inshallah,* we hope for another strike in which we will all be together, we workers, so that we can succeed at a very high level."

Amar (in simple Arabic at first – words in italics – and then in French): "*The strike – Now we know this word –* the strike, always the [la] – *The strike taught them what is the worker, one with others.* The strike is a good thing with *regard to the worker. Why? So that he might know his rights –* his rights – *and defend them –* and defend them. [Excitedly:] For them the strike is a school for the unity of the working class, and it explains how they can do something together. Separately they can do nothing. And in addition he says they hope, they are going to have other strikes so that really . . . [remarks drowned in laughter and applause] . . . to have other reunions of the working class. For them the strike is a manifestation of solidarity with the working class."

On this note the meeting is adjourned for supper. Later in the evening, after the meal, the discussion continues. Amar and Milud elaborate some of the points they have made.

Amar (in Arabic): "The strike is like a school. [In French]: The strike is *une école des luttes* and also an experience. For them, the way to better their standard of living is by means of struggle. For that reason it is a school. They distributed leaflets. . . . This was the first strike in the agricultural sector at Lyon launched by North Africans. Now they know what is solidarity with the French working class. The strike was something that brought them to-gether. They lived in the same village. [Now they know about getting] success for the claims, about struggling right to the end."

Milud: "Some French comrades who came never had discussions with the strikers. They discussed only with the militant French comrades."

Amar: "The *immigrés* form part of the French working class, but also part of the working class of Tunisia, Algeria, and Morocco. In this system they have their claims as part of the French working class, but also their specific claims. There are parallel struggles."

CONCLUSIONS

There are a number of issues raised by this case of interest to an urban and industrial anthropologist that must be left to one side (e.g., the structural implications of different types of industrial organization for social relations in an industry, the role of trade unions in industrial disputes in France, attitudes to jobs, pay and conditions of work, the reasons for the success or failure of a strike movement, and so on). I will instead concentrate on a few points that are of immediate importance to this study as a whole.

A significant feature of this dispute, compared with many oth-ers that occurred in Lyon during the course of fieldwork, is the total absence from it of the CGT, which is the predominant union in Lyon as it is in France generally. As other material shows, the CGT had in the mid-1970s elaborated a complete strategy for the handling of disputes in which immigrants were involved. This strike, however, fell into the hands of the CFDT, which has its own strategy.

To say "fell into the hands of" makes it sound as if sheer chance led the strikers to the CFDT. This is not so. As we have seen, the CGT in Lyon is best organized in, and concentrates its efforts on, the principal industrial groups in the public and private sectors. The small, and in some sense peripheral, sectors escape its net. The CFDT also organizes in the main sectors, but it is much more open to considering the problems of "marginal" industries and groups such as women, immigrants, and (in 1976) members of the armed forces. The CFDT is also more liable to promote what the CGT would see as sectional interests and claims within the work-ing class, and press for them with methods of action the CGT would call "divisive." These are some of the reasons why CGT officials describe CFDT militants as "leftist" and "adventurist."

This leads to a second point concerning the general structure of French-immigrant relations and the light that this case throws upon them. An affair that began as a local matter involving a handful of Tunisian immigrants and their employers was rapidly taken over by the CFDT and other groups on the left associated with it in this dispute. It was what I would term "incorporated" (some French writers might say *récupéré*) by what is essentially a French structure of organizations and relationships, and channeled into a particular framework of ideology and action by reference to which the events of the case were judged and evaluated, and toward which they were oriented. For the ideology provides both a code for the interpretation of events and a guide for their conduct.

This process of "incorporation" occurs across a wide spectrum of institutions in France. It is a very general process that characterizes the activities of both left and right, though the outcome in any specific situation varies considerably, depending, for example, on the issues, the organizations, the ideology, and the people involved. I am initially concerned here less with the reasons for the existence of this process than with its structural implications, but one factor may be mentioned that is of considerable importance when immigrants form the incorporated group.

French society consists, among much else, of a vast range of complex institutions and processes, not least those concerned with power. There is an equally complex array of formal and informal organizations that deal with those institutions and processes or "act on" the relationships they entail. When confronted by this system, one needs knowledge, often highly specialized knowledge, and if not power itself, at least an awareness of the ways in which power is exercised. One also needs knowledge of the "language" or "languages" used in the system, particularly by those with power within it. By this I do not mean knowledge of French as such (though that is important), but knowledge of the codes of French society. A small example might illustrate this. A Spanish crane driver, employed on a building site in Lyon, complained about the way in which the people working in the *office* bemused one with figures: "Suppose you get your pay slip and think you are 5 francs short. You go to the *office* and the man rolls up his sleeves and takes his pen and says: You have such and such and such and such, and we take away this and that and that. In fact you have received 50 francs too much!"

We may recall here the Algerians who sat through what was in effect a PCF recruitment meeting (Event 3) with the incomprehensible computer printouts detailing their water charges. Many immigrants, among others, usually lack the experience, knowledge, power, and perhaps confidence to handle these problems – or at least they are placed in that position by the French system, which then frequently characterizes them as possessing the *mentalité d'assisté*. The Tunisians at Caluire-Légumes knew that they wanted to do something about the utterly deplorable conditions in which they worked and lived, but were not sure what or how. So they hawked their problem round, as it were, until they could interest someone in it. They had to find a point in the system where they could "plug in" their problem. At that point the system takes over and articulates and manages their problem in its own terms.

The process of articulation was mentioned by a CFDT official in the building industry: "Generally the *chefs* do what they want and generally the immigrants don't react. But occasionally things build up, and then there is an explosion, a revolt over some matter that might be very small.* Our role was to go and ask people what the problem was, to find out what the claim was." The issues must be formulated in the "language" appropriate to industrial conflict in France and the dispute managed in an appropriate fashion. But it also means that the issues and their management will be given an ideological twist. The institutions that take them on will endow them with their own meaning.

Oversimplifying grossly for the moment, we may identify two sets of persons and institutions involved in this process: immigrant and French. Of particular interest is the position of those who operate at the "interface" between the two, who interpose themselves or who are interposed between French and immigrants. These are the people who effectively "represent," in both senses, the immigrant viewpoint to the French, who carry it to the French system, and vice versa. In Lyon the people in this position are generally French themselves. Independent articulation or action by immigrants themselves rarely occurs. There are some important exceptions to this (for example the Algerian Amicale, whose role is discussed in Chapter 11, or in a much earlier period

---

*Abuse by a supervisor is frequently cited as the trigger to industrial disputes involving immigrants, as was the case at Caluire-Légumes.

the FLN) and *non*-French persons do not entirely absent themselves from this process. In the Caluire-Legumes dispute, for example, the North African students obviously played an important part in articulating the men's grievances and interpreting them to the men themselves and to the French. An example of that occurred at the *"rassemblement des luttes"* mentioned earlier in this chapter. When I engaged in conversation with one striker, a Tunisian student physically interposed himself between us and took over the discussion.

By interpretation I do not mean simple translation, although the students do function as translators, preparing Arabic versions of leaflets and so on. The ACFAL meeting contains several examples that show that alongside translation between French and Arabic there was interpretation from one code to another. Amar's rendering of Bashir's assessment of the strike in Event 9B, is an excellent illustration of interpretation across language and across code. When I taxed Amar about his translation, he agreed that it was inaccurate but said that he was trying to convey what the strikers really meant. An interesting sequel to this may be found in the November 1976 issue of the ACFAL-CIMADE newsletter *Immigration*, which appeared after I had left the field. This issue includes discussion of the Caluire-Légumes dispute and has a piece entitled "Pour nous, comment nous avons vécu la grève," which is clearly intended to be a statement by one of the strikers but which internal evidence, the record of the ACFAL meeting (for example, the statement contains the phrase *la grève était comme une école*), and the written material produced during the strike by the CFDT suggest is a composite text compiled to convey a general sense of the strikers' views. This is accompanied by a *point de vue d'un militant qui a suivi la grève* that begins "Je reste persuadé cependant que l'acquis le plus important, c'est la prise de conscience politique nouvelle des ouvriers grévistes. . . ."

Some ten days before the ACFAL meeting I had discussed the organization of adult education with a left-wing social worker. Somewhat exasperated by the direction of the conversation, I complained that no immigrants appeared to be involved in the arguments about what should be done for them. She replied: "I think this is inevitable, given the system. They have no power of decision, and anyway, who could reply if one asked them? On the one side are knowledge and power, and it is on the other side that immigrants find themselves, except for a very small minority of militants. And who are the immigrants who speak when they speak? They are the bourgeoisie. The immigrants who speak represent the petite bourgeoisie which also exists among them. As for those who are spokesmen in the unions, he who speaks, when he speaks, it is what he has learned to speak. The *comités de quartier*, yes, but there also one is manipulated. Always there is a manipulation."

Some of her points are well taken. Many immigrants in France, especially those from North Africa, are placed in a subordinate social position. They also enter a society in which the possibilities for independent or autonomous organization in respect of the institutions of that society are severely circumscribed. But that system impinges on them in a multitude of ways, many of which have been described in this study. Struggling against this (or with the problem it poses) throws immigrants into sets of relations that often entail another kind of dependency and subordination. Thus it happens that even in contacts with radical groups who have the opposite intention, as another left-wing informant put it, "the relationship between French and immigrants is often willy-nilly that of *dominant-dominé*."

Some of the issues raised in these last pages are examined more fully in Chapter 11.

11

The representation of problems and the problem of representation

Early on, I stated that this book is about two central issues. We have so far been concerned mainly with the first of these: the ideological conceptualization of immigrant life, mainly by the French. We have seen how different elements in French society construe the nature of the population in question (whether they are to be thought of as "immigrants" or "foreigners") and of their problems as hostel residents, as residents in HLM and *cités de transit,* as husbands and wives and fathers and daughters, as schoolchildren, as adult learners of the French language, and as workers.

The focus now switches to the second issue: representation in a political sense, an aspect of which was discussed in passing in Chapter 4 (where we looked at the hostel committees) and in Chapter 9 (the trade unions). The present chapter is in six parts. The first three deal with the more formal side of representation on and through a variety of committees and associations. The first examines participation in the consultative bodies at department level, and the work of those bodies in the formation of official policy toward immigrants. The second deals with the formal representation of immigrants in certain French institutions. The third looks at the position of such autonomous immigrant organizations as exist in Lyon. Parts four and five are concerned with informal systems of representation, and also attempt to relate this aspect to the conceptual issue by examining the transmission and processing of information. The final section tackles the relationship of systems of representation to systems of control and incorporation.

Throughout the chapter the initial focus is on the flow of information about immigrants and their way of life. During fieldwork (see Grillo 1981) I conceived of this flow as a process through which "messages" were passed from one party to another. "Messages" implied "messengers" (see Figure 11.1), and that was a

	Source	"Messenger"	Audience
(a)	Immigrants ⟶	French ⟶	French
(b)	Immigrants ⟶	Immigrant ⟶	French

Figure 11.1 "Messengers."

term I used in early attempts to analyze the situation of those who are active in conveying information, by word of mouth or in writing, about immigrants and the phenomenon of immigration. However, no single word, such as "intermediaries" or "brokers," conveys the full range of activities in which these people engage, though they may, for example, take on a variety of roles for which terms such as "brokerage" are appropriate (cf. Dyck 1976).

Now, those who convey this information are often in fact French, and those who talk to each other about immigrants often do so without any immigrants participating in their discussions. Event 1 is almost, but not quite, an example of this. Thus, this chapter is once again focused on the French as the people who "represent" immigrants to the institutions of power and authority. Nevertheless, some immigrants are involved in this process: witness the parts played by Père Arderius in Event 1, by Yusuf in Event 2, and by Sherif in Event 4, to cite but three examples from the case material already presented. Their situation, and that of others like them who act inter alia as conduits for the passage of information between immigrants and the French, must be given as careful consideration as that of the French themselves who occupy similar intercalary roles.

Finally, I must state that there is here no discussion of the "immigrant vote," or of immigrant representation in parliament or on local councils, for the simple reason that foreign nationals resident in France do not have the vote. Their legal status is in this respect quite different from that of immigrants from the Commonwealth or the Republic of Ireland in Britain. Immigration may indeed become an issue in French elections (as in 1981, 1983, and 1984); but that is another matter, not considered here.

FORMAL REPRESENTATION AT THE DEPARTMENT LEVEL

Public organizations such as the DDASS, and private associations such as the SSFNA or the NDSA, are clearly in the front line of government social policy toward immigrants, though the views of their personnel do not always reflect that policy in its entirety – the SSFNA, for example, refused to continue with the role assigned to it by the prefecture in the processing of applications for HLM apartments. However, besides implementing policies, these organizations and associations have an important part to play at both national and local levels in the consultative process that accompanies the making of policy. An example of this was the participation of a number of bodies in the elaboration of policy concerning *animation:*

> Avec les encouragements des Pouvoirs Publics, les dirigeants des Associations d'aide aux migrants ont beaucoup réfléchi à l'échelon national ... sur le contenu de l'action socio-culturelle. ... Au cours de sessions d'étude, colloques, groupes de travail, réunions générales, organismes de concertation constitués à l'initiative du Ministère du Travail, ce qu'il fallait entendre par action socio-culturelle dans les foyers s'est précisé.
> [MTE Annual Report, June 1975:14]

At the local level, in the Rhône, there exists at the prefecture the Service de Liaison et Promotion des Migrants (SLPM), headed by a subprefect. Among other tasks, the SLFM coordinates the work of four *commissions consultatives* concerned with accommodations, reception, training and socio-educative action. This structure dates from 1973 and replaced an existing body, Comité de Liaison des Organisations du Rhône d'Aide aux Travailleurs Etrangers (CLORATE), which was dissolved as a result of political disagreement among its constituent members.

In theory each of the four *commissions* meets once a year, but "because there is a serious problem of housing in Lyon," the working party on accommodations met several times during 1975–6. As a result of its deliberations it was hoped to forward proposals to a national inquiry on housing. The composition of the *commissions* varies (see Lanier 1974:20) but included are representatives of the principal government departments (DDASS, Travail, ONI, Réglementation, Education), local government, trade unions and management ("naturally"), the HLM, SSAE, SSFNA, and a very large number of the other private associations (e.g., NDSA, MTE, ACFAL) engaged in working with immigrants.

These organizations are French, as are their representatives who attend the meetings. A senior official at the prefecture said this of foreign or immigrant representation: "It is a difficult matter. One cannot admit one group without the other. It is a delicate matter. There are forty nationalities concerned. One couldn't have meetings of that size. The representatives of the associations speak for the immigrants." For his own part, he said, "I meet ten to fifteen people each day in my office, who come to see me about housing. One gets to know their problems. That's how they are represented."

As other participants readily admitted, the immigrant viewpoint is represented only indirectly on these official bodies: "I feel myself on the consultative committee to be an intermediary between the immigrants and the committee" (SSFNA assistant). This form of indirect representation is one of the most striking features of French-immigrant consultative procedures. Let us take as an example a conference organized by the SLPM.

In 1969 the prefect of the region, working through the SLPM, convened a conference with the title "Groupe de Synthèse Régional de Promotion des Migrants: l'Alphabétisation des Etrangers dans la Region Rhône-Alpes," a cyclostyled report of whose procedings was subsequently published (SLPM 1970b). Of the 105 invitations to attend that were issued, 96 were taken up. A substantial number of participants were administrators attached to prefectures. Educational inspectors formed another large contingent. About 60 of the invitees, however, were representatives of various *comités* and *associations* operating in the region, together with two from Paris. Among others from Lyon came members of the MTE, ACFAL, Accueil et Rencontre, and the NDSA president, Gabriel Rosset. So far as I know, this was the largest gathering of its type ever organized in the region. There was only one immigrant present, a North African representative of the CFDT's Commission d'Immigrés, a body that was subsequently disbanded.

The conference began with a scene-setting of the *alpha* problem by Monsieur Cat, then of the Rhône prefecture. This was followed by a number of papers in which participants set out what they and their organizations saw to be nature of the problem, described their own activities, and gave their opinion on the measures that were required. The papers were usually followed by discussion.

An examination of the papers and of the discussion, extracts from which were included in the report, would show that the problem of *alpha* and the policies that might be adopted, were discussed for the benefit of French administrators with little or no direct contact with immigrants, by representatives of associations whose work brought them into closer contact with the target population, but who themselves were almost exclusively French. Their remarks included not only comments on the problems of their own organizations, but also (usually implicitly but sometimes explicitly) analyses of immigration and the situation of immigrants. They also offered their assessment of the subjective state of immigrants – their ideas, feelings, needs, and responses to life in France. The only immigrant to speak (and he did not speak because there was no time for his paper) was the man from the CFDT, whose contribution was a reiteration of the union's position.

This conference was part of a much wider process of consultation that culminated in the law of 1971 on "Formation Professionnelle pour Adultes," which in theory enacted certain benefits for migrants wishing to take *alpha* courses. It is, of course, difficult to assess the precise influence of such a meeting. Concrete proposals were made, and the administrators usually accepted them, adding that there were, however, all manner of difficulties, although in an ideal world, with adequate finance, and so on. Whatever the actual result, it is nevertheless clear that such conferences may channel information and ideas about the needs of immigrants to the administrators, and it is equally clear that the preferred medium for this passage is that provided by the French institutions and associations who are invited to attend.

Sometimes, as Event 1 shows, members of certain associations have direct access to senior political decision makers and clearly influence them. The MTE at Lyon, for example, conceived the idea for the reception center (CAIO) that the minister was in the city on that occasion to open. This raises the question of the connection between the associations and other bodies represented on the *commissions consultatives* and the institutions of power and authority. Of prime importance among those connections is the relationship with the state that, through the prefecture, coordinates their activities.

These connections are of four kinds. Some of the representative bodies are in fact branches of the state (e.g., DDASS, Education), others are *private* associations the state has created. This is the case, for example, with the AEE at the national level. Locally, there is the organization known as ALHTRAM, which runs four hostels in Lyon and which was created by the Direction Départementale du Travail. Third, a large number of the private associations receive financial help from the state in the form of grants that ususally come from the Fonds d'Action Sociale. ACFAL, for example, receives such funds for its work in *alpha*. Finally, the prefecture is often represented on the governing bodies of these private associations. One example of this is the MTE, an association that was in fact founded in the early 1950s at the instigation of the wife of the then prefect, Monsieur Massenet.

In addition to the connections with the state, many of these bodies are linked to other bastions of local power. The NDSA, for example, has very close connections with the Catholic Church and senior politicians in the city. The MTE has links with the politicians and with major businesses (see Chapter 4). The only bodies formally independent of these ties are the trade unions, though of course they have their own political links. There is, therefore, a complex network of connections between these associations and institutions and the local "power elite," at the center of which, in all senses, is the state, which has the key role of coordination.

The differential quality of these connections has an important bearing on another aspect of the associations involved in the SLPM's conference and in the work of the *commissions consultatives*. A wide range of organizations are involved, of several different types, engaged in many different social milieus: housing – hostels, *cités de transit*, HLM – education, *alpha*, social services, industry, and so on. They also range across the political spectrum and include conservative bodies such as the MTE as well as leftists such as ACFAL. The views expressed are inevitably different, sometimes radically different, refractions of the immigrant viewpoint. Representation via this method means that the immigrant voice is processed through the organizational structure of the different institutions and the ideological perspective of their personnel. But we should be clear that these alternative perspectives are not of equal power in terms of the attention they command.

REPRESENTATION WITHIN THE INSTITUTIONS

Few of the institutions represented on the *commissions consultatives* make formal provision for the representation of an immigrant viewpoint. The organs of the state apparatus (e.g., the DDASS) have none. Three systems of representation of a kind do, however, deserve attention: that to be found within the private associations, in the residents' committees of the hostels and *cités de transit* and in the trade unions.

Most of the private bodies discussed here are associations under the law of 1901. This law gives them quasi-charitable status (as *associations à but non-lucratif*). It also regulates their constitution by restricting foreign membership and the participation of foreigners on governing bodies (see discussion in Event 3).

Foreign members are not, of course, excluded, but with some exceptions most associations have very few. The exceptions are mainly the leftist associations such as ACFAL, and a handful of organizations under the auspices of the Catholic missions (see next section). Foreign members of both these types of associations come from a limited section of the community: that of ACFAL, for example, comes almost exclusively from students whose particular position is discussed later. Nevertheless, the annual business meeting of an association such as ACFAL does provide one forum within which immigrant participation in decisions about policy is formally possible. Event 4 took place within the context of such a forum, and one may see there how views may be formulated that subsequently inform the perspective of ACFAL's representatives on the *commissions consultatives*.

Another possible forum is that provided by the residents' committees in the hostels and *cités de transit*. In Chapter 4 we saw how, in 1974–6, all the hostels had been encouraged to form such committees as part of the program of *animation*. Where they exist, however, their personnel is often designated by the hostel director rather than elected, and their discussions are confined to the spending of the *budget d'animation* and to specific complaints about the hostel's fabric.

A leftist leaflet issued at the time of the hostel strike characterized these bodies as *comités de résidents bidons* and stated *la lutte s'est engager pour former des comités réellement représentatifs*. The evidence for that struggle was not obvious in Lyon, where even a leftist association that had a small hostel in the Vth Arrondissement (Accueil et Rencontre), and that was "struggling against paternalism," had difficulty in involving the residents in the particpatory process. "I regret the fact that when 'we' asked 'them,' the residents, whether they wanted a certain change, they had said yes. But it was us who had obliged them to say yes." Nevertheless, there were demands for the "democratization" of the hostels, especially the largest hostels run by the principal organizations (SONACOTRA, MTE, ALHTRAM), which the formation of the residents' committees was not designed to meet.

Be that as it may, the existing structure allows only an indirect form of representation or, to put it another way, provides an extremely tenuous channel along which "messages" may pass from immigrants to, say, a *commission consultative:* from hostel residents to committee representatives to the hostel director to the hostel organization directorate to their representative on a *commission.* Where the committee representatives or their equivalent are akin to the "customary chiefs," as one hostel director suggested, then there is indeed a similarity with the systems of "indirect rule" that operated in colonial Africa.

The only institutions in which there are attempts specifically to organize representation of immigrants and the immigrant viewpoint are the trade unions. Here I confine discussion to the CGT, whose interest in immigrants we have already illustrated: their bid for immigrant membership, their encouragement of immigrant candidates in union elections, their organization of *commission d'immigrés,* and their holding of a major national conference on the problems of immigration in April 1976, for which the meeting described in Event 2 was a preparation.

This was the second such conference to be held in the 1970s. The first, in 1972, had produced a Charte Revendicative that formed the basis of CGT policy on immigration. The results of the 1976 conference were not published while I was in the field, but provisional accounts were made available to the general public via the press, and to the membership via the CGT's own magazines and newspapers. Reports of representatives sent to the conference (see Event 2) were also discussed at local meetings.

The audience for such a conference is both national and international. Its message is directed toward overseas governments as much as it is toward French citizens and migrant workers in France. In fact, insofar as the conference paid particular attention to racism, it may be said to have been aimed as much at the CGT's French membership as at its immigrants. However, the latter did have a part to play in the production of the conference and its message.

The principal organizational vehicle used for this purpose was the *commissions d'immigrés,* which organize meetings in many of the larger factories. They are convened by a member of the section executive who is designated *responsable d'immigrés.* Such *responsables* have counterparts at higher levels in the union structure (e.g., the CGT-Métallurgie has one for the Rhône Department), and the *responsables* for a number of unions are grouped into a *commission* for the department, and so on to the national level. Most, but not all, these *responsables* are in fact French.

The *commissions* in the factories "prepared" for the 1976 conference by holding meetings, the results of which were passed on the next level. The meeting described in Event 2 formed part of this chain. For example, prior to that meeting, the factory *commissions* were asked to produce evidence on racism. For this purpose little notebooks were issued (see Event 2, Chapter 3). By chance, I happened to be with a *responsable* at one factory when Michel, the CGT militant, arrived with the notebooks and passed on the instruction that this task should be completed "by next week." At the meeting the notebooks were produced and some examples of racism discussed. Others were offered from the floor, and the discussion led to the formulation of a *revendication* to be forwarded to the Paris conference.

If this organizational structure (discussions within the factory *commissions* contributing to a central meeting of workers from factories in one industry and their deliberations to a meeting of *responsables* for the department, and thence to the Paris conference and dissemination to the membership and public at large) produces "messages," it also generates "messengers." At a factory like the Berliet plant at Vénissieux, for example, the meetings of language groups for what are called *débats casse-croûtes* are recruiting grounds for the *commissions,* and the latter provide a pool from which are drawn the potential candidates for union elections. From these in turn came, for example, the delegates who were sent to Paris for the big conference.

This procedure by which militants evolve (and which is similar to that through which *French* militants emerge) is in the control of those at the center of the union's organization who are largely, though not exclusively, themselves French (for example, Michel). In observing this process in the field, the image that occurred to me was of a football scout "spotting" some likely youngster and preparing him for the first team. Yusuf and the young Turk in Event 2 provide examples. Those who are brought on in this way tend to be youngish men who can express themselves well in French and who have a knowledge of their mother tongue, who have the respect of their compatriots, and who either show agreement with the basic ideological stance of the union or represent promising raw material who can be sent for suitable training on courses designed for this purpose.

Such militants have two audiences – the immigrants themselves and the French, though for the moment I am concerned only with the latter. An informant, cited at the end of the preceding chapter, said of such union militants, "He who speaks, when he speaks, it is what he has learned to speak." This is a harsh and somewhat cynical view, though one not without evidence in its support. It is certainly the case that in the CGT, immigrant opinion is firmly channeled through the existing union structure and subjected to a process of ideological transformation.

I have in this section concerned myself only with those institutions that participate in the work of the prefecture's *commissions consultatives*. There are many other bodies that immigrants might join and in which they can express an opinion, for example, the political parties, or the myriad committees and groups that exist in an urban or suburban quartier (e.g., APACS). However, apart from a certain number of Spanish and Italian residents, immigrant participation in such organizations is very small and generally confined to a handful of people whom the French would characterize as *evolués*.

It is often the case that the same kind of people who in the contexts discussed here emerge as formal representatives may in other contexts act as *informal* representatives of immigrant opinion. It is not unusual to find in hostels and *cités de transit,* or among parents of children in a school, or the residents of a tower building, individuals who establish a special relationship with a hostel director, a teacher, a social worker, or a housing administrator, and who through this relationship become in a sense "spokesmen" for their compatriots (see the section on "The immigrant-as-informant").

AUTONOMOUS IMMIGRANT REPRESENTATION

All too frequently, then, the immigrant voice is represented in the public arena by the French. On returning to Britain in the autumn of 1976, I was struck by the response of the British media to the violence that occurred that year at the Notting Hill Carnival. Interviewers and reporters immediately sought the opinion of a variety of spokesmen from the "communities" involved. Their response to the riots of 1981 in Brixton and Toxteth was similar. In the summer of 1976, in France, there was television coverage of a racist incident in which after a brief discussion with an inarticulate group of Algerians, the program switched to a lengthy interview with a French social worker, who presented the immigrants' viewpoint.

Immigrant voices are indeed sometimes heard in the media. A television debate on immigration in January 1975, for example, included the minister, an employer, the mayor of Grasse, and a social worker, together with the Algerian ambassador, the Portuguese consul-general, a Moroccan teacher of *alpha,* and a Yugoslav "immigrant." But in France generally, and in Lyon certainly, autonomous organizations that can claim in any sense to represent immigrant opinion are few and far between.

It is possible that in cities other than Lyon autonomous ethnic organization is much stronger. Recent research by Andrea Caspari (personal communication) shows that in Grenoble there is a wide range of Portuguese associations. Not all of these however, are autonomous (i.e., independent of the French), and in general there does not exist in France the array of ethnic organizations of the kind one finds in British cities (see Rex and Tomlinson, 1979: Chapter 8).

In Lyon, three types of association provide a relatively autonomous voice: organizations such as the Amicale des Algériens, which are in effect organs of the government of the sending society; those such as the Portuguese, Spanish, and Italian missions, which are under the auspices of the Catholic Church; and a variety of political groupings, mostly small and mostly leftist, such as the Mouvement des Travailleurs Arabes, and the Ben Bellist Comité des Travailleurs Arabes.

Although the Italian mission in Grenoble has taken an active part in encouraging Italian ethnic associational life in that city, its counterpart in Lyon does little more than exist. The Portuguese mission, has, however, through its head, Père Arderius, been heavily involved in organizing the Portuguese community and in representing the needs of Portuguese immigrants to both the French and the Portuguese governments. In 1964 was founded the Comité d'Accueil aux Portugais, an association that brought together a number of French citizens with a special interest in Portugal or Brazil, as well as Portuguese migrants linked with the mission. This *comité* coordinates a variety of work among the Portuguese, including (in the early 1970s) the reception of new families, help in finding accommodations, and help with the administrative system, especially in connection with the regularization of illegal entries. The mission itself also publishes, in conjunction with the Portuguese community at Clermont-Ferrand, a newspaper, *O Emigrante,* and has promoted a number of *tardes Portuguesas,* cultural evenings.

In 1974 the *comité* organized a *journée d'étude et rencontre* concerned especially with the *promotion* of Portuguese immigrants, their advancement in French society. In the cyclostyled "Compte-rendu" of the proceedings, the *comité's* president, Monsieur Jacques Vincent, is reported as saying: "Cette journée répond à un souci de notre Comité, association Franco-Portugaise dans laquelle les Francais, fondateurs en majorité, essaient de faire de plus en plus place aux Portugais. Nous sommes peut-être sur Lyon la seule association où les Portugais peuvent se fair entendre en tant que tels." The meeting in fact heard papers by three of the French activists, on employment training, on *alpha,* and on relationships with the law. There were also two papers by Arderius himself, one a general account of Portugese immigration, the other on *promotion,* and one by a Portuguese speaker on the problems of Portuguese youth.

A cyclostyled letter from Alfred Ancel of the church's Service des Migrants had in 1973 stressed the importance of allowing each ethnic group to conserve its own culture. The letter suggested that many Catholic migrants avoided the missions because some were concerned about links with the consulates of their countries of origin, while others *ne veulent pas être dirigés par des prêtres.* The solution proposed was the creation for each group of an association *composée principalement par des migrants et dirigée vraiment par eux.* The Portuguese *comité* was clearly influenced by this. In fact, throughout its existence the mission's leader had had a key role in the work of the *comité* and acted as its representative on CLORATE. He continued to act as a spokesman of the community (cf. Event 1) even in the changed circumstances of the Portuguese revolution. Certainly in 1975–6 he was the principal representative of Portuguese opinion to be heard by the French.

There was in 1975–6 no organized religious voice for Muslims in Lyon, indeed hardly any organized religious activity. There was no mosque, for example. There was an accredited leader of the Muslim community – a "nice old man. They bring him out for the fourteenth July" – but his work mainly concerned Harkis. There were, however, organizations sponsored by the North African governments, especially the Amicale des Algériens en Europe. In Chapter 8 we saw that this organization was concerned with the provision of Arabic-language classes and fostering other aspects of the culture of origin. No less significant is its political function. This has two sides to it. On the one hand, it mobilizes Algerian opinion in France on behalf of the Algerian government. In 1976, for example, it organized the diffusion of information about, and discussions of, the new "National Charter" proposed for Algeria. Through meetings held in public halls and elsewhere, Amicale officials claimed to have reached some 80,000 people in the region. On the other hand, the Amicale is concerned with various aspects of the life of Algerian immigrants in France.

The Amicale has offices in every part of France where there is a consulate. Attached to these are a number of full-time staff responsible for language courses and cultural activities. They are also responsible for liaising with Algerian residents about the problems of migration, though they are at pains to emphasize that this is all they do: "At meetings we talk about our problems, only our problems, those that touch on immigration." Closely involved with these discussions are a number of Algerian activists from the quartiers in which large numbers of North Africans reside. The structure of the Amicale's links outside the offices resembles the cell organization favored by the Front de Liberation Nationale (FLN) during the Algerian War. Some of those now prominent in Algerian affairs in Lyon were also active locally during that war, though many who had provided local leadership at that time returned to Algeria at the war's conclusion (see Institut d'Etudes Politiques de Lyon 1966). This network enables the Amicale, and thereby the consulate, to be informed about what is happening to Algerian citizens in the quartiers and the factories.

The Amicale has, over the years, organized a number of national conferences in France and in Algeria on immigration, and also publishes a journal (available in French), *L'Algérien en Europe*. There is also a National Day of Emigration (October 17), which in 1975 was celebrated in Lyon with a meeting and film show. Through the journal, the publication of conference proceedings (cf. Amicale des Algériens en Europe 1973), and such meetings, the Amicale projects a view of emigration and immigration. This is aimed at both its own citizens and members of the receiving society. Locally its officers are frequently invited to present their views to a wide range of French groups and organizations, especially in the education world. They were, for example, closely involved with the CEFISEM courses described in Chapter 7.

From the point of view of some, but by no means all, French people, the Amicale has a "legitimate" status as a "representative" body. After all, unlike its Tunisian and Moroccan counterparts, it can demonstrate widespread support among Algerians in France, and it certainly has deep roots within the community. This representative status is not, however, accepted by the extreme left, or by the extreme right (Amicale premises are often attacked by bombs), or indeed by the French government. The Algerian Amicale is a political body that in practice (e.g., in terms of personnel) is only with difficulty distinguishable from the consulates and the FLN – now Algeria's ruling party. It is the FLN's view that the Amicale voices, which is one of the reasons it is not favored by the leftists. In fact, in France the Amicale's closest political contacts are with the CGT, and indirectly with the PCF, via its own activists who are also militants in those organizations.

These three institutions often work in conjunction at both national (cf. PCF 1974) and local levels. In 1976 a number of joint public meetings were organized between the Amicale and the unions (including the CFDT) to celebrate the *solidarité des travailleurs français et algériens*. Occasionally the Amicale joins with the CGT or PCF in support of Algerian citizens in France. A propos the "segregation" of children in separate classes in the schools adjacent to the rue Olivier de Serres (see Chapter 7), one Algerian activist commented: "It took the combined efforts of the PCF, the Amicale, and the unions to approach the prefect and get him to abandon the idea."

In fact the Amicale believes itself to be extremely limited in what it can do: "We are not in our own country." If this then leads the Amicale to play down conflict between Algerian residents and French institutions, it also leads leftists to accuse the Amicale of playing a "demobilizing" role. "The Amicale is an extension of the regime [in Algeria]. The Amicale encourages a certain left tendency – the PCF, CGT – but discourages others. For example, at ———— the Amicale joined with the CGT and PCF to break the strike. The CGT and PCF are against strikes, which they label 'leftist'" (Algerian student). Such opponents of the regime often associate with one or another of the North African *groupuscules* that are accredited with representative status by those on the extreme left in France.

Although autonomous immigrant organizations of a kind exist that might be said to represent (in both senses) the immigrant voice, two points must be borne in mind in evaluating both what they say and how it is said. First, the principal organizations, such as the Portuguese Mission and the Amicale, are very much part of a nonmigrant established order: the Catholic Church on the one hand, the Algerian government on the other. Second, both the mission and the Amicale operate through important French links (the Comité d'Accueil, the CGT/PCF). These links are not just a "front." They are the means by which the associations are articulated with, and indeed incorporated by, French society.

THE MEDIATION OF INFORMATION

Earlier I wrote of the "processing" of the immigrant voice in public arenas such as the *commissions consultatives*. That is, that voice is encoded in a variety of ideological and institutional registers. A similar processing occurs when representations are made by the Portuguese Mission or the Amicale (though the actors may be different), or by immigrants who emerge as members of residents' committees in hostels, or as delegates of unions such as the CGT. Many of the Events described in this book provide various examples of this processing and the varied forms it may take (for it is not a single, undifferentiated phenomenon). It was during one meeting (Event 4, Chapter 8) where North African students and French teachers and social workers exchanged information and ideas about an absent third party – North African immigrant workers and their families – that I became fully aware of its implications.

The phenomenon is not, as I say, an undifferentiated one, and it operates in both directions, French to immigrant as well as immigrant to French, although for the moment I am concerned only with the latter. An example of one kind of processing is provided by organization of the Groupe Tiers Monde de caluire's exhibition on the problems of immigration, which I have described elsewhere (Grillo 1981). There, the passage of information about immigrants (ultimate source), via a variety of French informants ("messengers") to a French audience is particularly clearly demonstrated.

The French messengers in that case are similar to those we have encountered frequently in this book: social workers, hostel directors, teachers. Their professions bring them into constant and direct contact with immigrants as parents, mothers, wives, children, residents. In Chapter 1, I suggested that my own fieldwork among such people was relatively easy because "my role as investigator fitted exactly their role as informant." The significance of that remark may now be apparent. Such people are frequently involved in a variety of ways in the transmission of information, including acting as informants to "academic" investigators. A *permanent* in the building union complained: "One always had students coming in to find out about immigrants," and a social worker regretted that she had "given away a lot of her files to *stagiaires*" (i.e., trainees writing a *thèse* or *mémoire,* cf. ODTI 1974:7).

A smaller number of such informants are invited regularly to address meetings or conferences on immigration or provide professional advice to other institutions and associations. They may, for example, be asked to take the occasional seminars that form part of the training of social workers or teachers (see Chapters 6 and 7). And some, of course, sit on consultative committees.

There is, in fact, in Lyon a relatively small group of these specialists, some of whom have published work on immigration (Le Masne 1974; Pinot 1973), who are well known to each other. A number of them also form part of a loosely connected cross-service network of individuals who share a concern with the problems of immigration and a similar ideological viewpoint. They were described by one of their number as a *mafia gauchiste.* It was adherents of this grouping who, for example, at the time of the minister's visit to Lyon (Event 1, Chapter 3) produced a critique aimed at the minister under the label "A social workers' collective involving those working with immigrants." Many of these people are members of ACFAL (where in fact the critique was produced), and of the CFDT, and some were also involved in the Comités Français-Immigrés (see Chapter 9, discussion of Event 7).

Aside from the specialists who take on the task of informing French audiences about immigration, and groupings such as the *mafia gauchiste* who attempt to influence and organize opinion on immigration, ordinary social workers and teachers are, as we have noted, constantly providing information about that aspect of immigration with which they are familiar (and, indeed, about immigrants they know) to other parties, especially other branches of their service, or another service (e.g., social worker to teacher). They also provide links between migrants and those services. Social workers in particular frequently describe themselves as "intermediaries" ("between parents and teachers," "between the young and the Agence Nationale de l'Emploi"), in which role they often find themselves negotiating on the immigrants' behalf, for example, "unblocking a dossier" stuck in someone else's office.

In the 1974 annual report of the Société Lyonnaise pour l'Enfance et l'Adolescence, a group of *éducateurs* based in Villeurbanne comment:

> La troisième partie de notre travail dans le quartier est notre action par rapport aux structures. . . . Nous nous informons mutuellement de ce qui ce fait. D'autre part, nous prenons toujours le temps d'informer les pouvoirs publics (administrations, municipalités, préfecture). Les gens du quartier doivent être reconnus comme "interlocuteurs" valable, sans le besoin d'un intermédiaire. Notre information est la mise en contact direct des uns et des autres.
>
> [SLEA *Rapport Moral, Rapport d'Activite* 1974, p. 24]

This, it must be said, is a general reflection on the role of *éducateurs* and does not concern immigrants alone, though the gap between immigrants (as *gens du quartier*) and the *pouvoirs publics* is particularly marked. In many respects this gap is a general feature of French society.

THE IMMIGRANT-AS-INFORMANT

The information these and other "intermediaries" transmit derives in large part from their experiences at work. Some of this is garnered from casual contacts, for example, with those who file through their office (see the remark of the prefecture official cited above). Sometimes the source of information is even more haphazard, as when the director of a group of hostels admitted that his knowledge of the rent charged for *garnis* came from two men he had met on the street. However, I earlier pointed out that in certain contexts, social workers, teachers, hostel directors, and the like establish particularly strong relationships with individual migrants, who thus, in a sense, become spokesmen for their communities. In these cases the individual may be said to take on the role of "immigrant-as-informant."

One such was Chabanne, a skilled metalworker from Algeria, who had acted this role for a number of people including the director of the hostel where he lived; for Jean-Paul, the worker priest associated with ACFAL; and ultimately for the anthropologist. Directors of hostels and *cités de transit* often have such an informant on whom they draw for knowledge of the immigrants' way of life, and on whom they sometimes rely for detailed news of their residents' activities.

The immigrant-as-informant is often someone the French would describe as *évolué(e)*. Indeed, a social worker defined an *évolué* as "someone with whom you can discuss." There is a practical constraint in that few intermediaries speak the immigrants' language (though some certainly do, and others attempt to learn, for example, Arabic, see Chapter 8). The immigrant-as-informant is often, therefore, the immigrant-as-interpreter, in both a literal and metaphorical sense.

The immigrant-as-informant in the contexts discussed here (defined by the institutional framework within which the relationship occurs, and the particular roles involved – social worker/client, teacher/parent, director/resident) may sometimes emerge as a more formal "spokesman," for example when they are persuaded by a hostel director to become members of the residents' committees. Only rarely, however, do such individuals enter the wider *public* arena. Those who are found in that arena generally fall into one of four categories: officials from missions, consulates, and the Amicale; militants from trade unions and occasionally from political parties (especially the PCF); those, of whom there are very few, in professional occupations such as *éducateurs* (or in *alpha*, like the Moroccan who took part in the TV debate); and those in higher education, especially students. This last category deserves some consideration.

The majority of the students who associate with organizations such as ACFAL, Accueil et Rencontre, and CIMADE, are Algerian, with some Tunisians. Almost all were brought up in North Africa, where they received their schooling, but now follow university courses in France, mostly in the social sciences. They often have part-time jobs as instructors in Arabic. They are not immigrant workers in the strict sense, though they usually refer to themselves as *immigrés*. Ideologically they are usually firm supporters of the pan-Arab cause, but they would also place themselves on the far left and thus in opposition to their governments. All the ones that I met had contacts among North African immigrant workers in Lyon – relatives, family friends, and sometimes people from the *alpha* courses they also teach. They enter circles such as ACFAL via the language courses, or via *groupuscules*, or via a common cause, for example, a Franco-Palestinian medical-aid group. Linked with them is a small number of young immigrants born in France who associate with the student milieu.

Within associations such as ACFAL, the students act as inter-mediaries and interpreters, as their part in Events 3, 5, and 9 clearly demonstrates. In these contexts they are accorded a repre-sentative status they would not readily find elsewhere. My impres-sion is that they are viewed with suspicion bordering on resent-ment by the mass of ordinary immigrants ("these people are too proud to talk to us"), and their political position brings them into conflict with the Amicale. Their situation as young, left-wing in-tellectuals also makes them suspect in the eyes of many French people. It is precisely this, however, that makes them attractive to ACFAL. They are suited to their role as immigrant-as-informant in that context because they are highly articulate in French, and in other ways speak the same "language" as their audience, with whom they also share an educational and cultural experience. North African secondary schools still follow closely the French pattern, and of course these students are at a French university. They are interpreters who translate their information into an idiom (leftish, social scientific) with which ACFAL members are familiar and which they appreciate.

REPRESENTATION, INCORPORATION, AND CONTROL

This last point raises the question of the transmutation of infor-mation in its passage from immigrants to immigrant/French "messengers" to French. Such information is inevitably located within a conceptual and ideological framework, whether it con-cerns the selection and presentation of "facts," or whether it rep-resents an interpretative account of behavior. For some, this transmutation is implicit, indeed unacknowledged, but for others it is quite explicit. For those on the left, in particular, an in-terpretation that is *not* ideological (as I would use that term) is in fact suspect. Amar's translation of Bashir's assessment of the Ca-luire-Légumes strike (see Chapter 10) provides an especially clear example of an explicitly ideological interpretation.

Explicit or implicit interpretation of this kind occurs constantly and each Event contains several more or less obvious examples. Another occurs in accounts of the social and cultural organization of hostel residents furnished by the directors. Many of these, perhaps on the basis of their African experience, employ a "tribal" idiom: "They like to enclose themselves in tribal structures," "they share things and discipline each other," they have leaders who are the *sages de leur collectivité,* their fights are "a reckoning of accounts," "their" collective solidarity is opposed to "our" emphasis on the individual. And they "come from the same village." I once joined a discussion between Chabanne and the director of his hostel. Chabanne said the residents came from an area within 150 kilometers of Setif in Algeria. The director pressed him on this and insisted they came from a much smaller area. Afterward he commented: "Despite what Chabanne said, if you look at a map . . ."

This kind of transmutation is perhaps only important if it is taken into the public arena, and if it affects policy. When it does, that arena becomes the scene of a struggle between alternative versions of immigrant life. Now, entry to that arena is highly structured. Generally it involves French institutions with French representatives, or immigrant spokesmen incorporated within the French system on that system's terms: the consultative bodies, trade unions, political parties, residents' associations, and so on. The only serious alternative is provided by a limited number of institutions based on the sending society – in fact the church or state of the country of origin. It is extremely difficult to operate outside these two channels. The groups based on opposition elements within the sending societies (e.g., the Spanish Communist Party, or trade unions in Morocco or Tunisia) are only partial exceptions to this. Members of such groups in France are closely tied to their French counterparts (cf. the link between, say, the Comité des Travailleurs Arabes and the French *groupuscules*).

It is this structuring of representation (in both senses) that forms part of the process of the "incorporation" of immigrants in French society. In this process, information about immigrants, obtained only indirectly from immigrants themselves, is transmuted ideologically and carried by institutional spokesmen of unequal authority, influence, and power into those places where policies are discussed and formulated.

This, however, is only part of the story. We have, so far, been concerned with the transmission of messages *from* immigrants *to* the French. Let us reverse the arrows in Figure 11.1. If that is done, however, it ceases to be meaningful to confine discussion even in part to the flow of information and ideas. Certainly messages pass *from* the French *to* immigrants, and not infrequently the same conduits are employed, but the content and function of such messages is different. Some examples.

A hostel director: "A part of my job that is of primary importance is to be an intermediary between an employer and the residents. See this letter I received advertising a vacancy? I will show it around this evening to see if anyone is interested." An *éducateur:* "We are intermediaries between parents and the profs. The schools signal cases of absenteeism to us. The parents say they don't understand what's going on. Letters are sent, but the fathers can't read. The teachers at the CES ask us to make sure the parents read the *carnets scolaires,* or the children read them to their parents. We spoke to the children about it." A social assistant attached to a local technical college said of this person: "Do you know M———? He is very good, helping with their problems. He understands their language. The *éducateurs* are considered their friends. They can get what we can't."

Certainly social workers, teachers and the like, in their role as intermediaries, pass on information, though now it is about the *French* system, but even more important, they are a source of *instruction,* providing a means of socializing immigrants and aiding their incorporation within French society.

Those who operate at the interface between French society and immigrants, especially though not exclusively certain individuals who are themselves immigrants, also act as a medium of instruction in another sense, conveying ideas and ideological perspectives as well as information. Yusuf's speech on racism in Event 2 (Chapter 3) presented the immigrant audience with a summary of the CGT's position on that problem. "Comrade K" in Event 3 ("The best form of defense . . . ," Chapter 5) provided the *cité* residents with an ideological interpretation of the meaning of the PCF's organizational structure. It was also a statement intended to convert and recruit, just as Event 2 was in effect part of the CGT's drive for immigrant members.

For French institutions that wish to transmit a message to immigrants – whether that message is factual ("There is a job going at X"), or instructional ("You should follow your child's progress at school"), or ideological ("Racism is an idea that the bosses put into the workers' heads"), or exhortatory ("Join the PCF!") – a crucial problem, as we have seen on many occasions, is created by language. Those I have called "messengers" or "intermediaries," or "immigrants-as-informants," form links in a chain of communication that cuts through blockages of language. Some of these chains are quite long: teacher to school social assistant to *éducateur* to child to parent; others are brief; union to French-speaking immigrant to other immigrant workers. In either case, at some point or other there is an act of interpretation across language and across code.

This aspect of interpretation is perhaps, to an observer, most obvious in a political context, for example Amar's translation in Event 9B, or Comrade K——'s statement cited above. That statement was in fact made in French, and it was Comrade Ch—— who took the more active role in translating and interpreting between French and Arabic, across language and across code. As Ch——, a prominent figure in the CGT, PCF, and the Amicale, himself modestly put it: "I have a certain facility in the Arabic language."

Language/code translation, of course, operates both ways, as we saw, for example, in the industrial disputes in Chapters 9 and 10. Trade-union officials must "find out what the claim is." What are, or what seem to be, incoherent grievances must be converted into the code appropriate to industrial conflict and articulated as a set of "claims." The jargon must be right.

Throughout the passage from French to immigrant there is a strong element of control. This is especially apparent in institutions such as the hostels, where the director's immigrant-as-informant may also serve as a medium of instruction. Once when I was in conversation with a hostel director, the latter called into the discussion an aged resident. This was Ali, who had first come to France in 1923 and had stayed at the same hostel since 1956. Ali explained why he preferred the hostel to a lodging house. Commenting on the good atmosphere, he said, "I am a kind of intermediary between the director and the residents. They all respect me." The director added: "It is better to have someone of the same group tell them things." This usually means in matters affecting discipline. It really seems a form of indirect rule.

The French institutions and their personnel described in this and previous chapters, and the system of intermediaries, messengers, and immigrants-as-informants, provide a form of integration of migrants in French society, or what I would rather term "incorporation." By that I do not mean conjoined on more or less equal terms in a shared enterprise, which is Barth's usage (1966, cf. Paine 1976:64). I refer to an absorption of immigrants by the French, for the French, on French terms.

The intermediaries and the like have a crucial dual function in this process. On the one hand, they effect an indirect and controlled representation of immigrants, and on the other, some of them, at least, provide the channel for the issuing of instructions and exhortations. Many of them are, in effect, the instruments through which the policies of the French institutions of both right and left are enacted.

One of the reasons why some immigrants themselves serve this function so well is that they have a facility with language and codes. This, at any rate, is a necessary, though not sufficient, condition for entering the intermediary role. To describe them as "code masters" (Paine 1973) would, however, be misleading. They are jacks of many codes, but "masters," in the full sense, of none: "He who speaks, when he speaks, it is what he has learned to speak."

I have referred constantly to forms of "indirect," "processed," or "coded" representation, and this may be taken to imply that I believe that somewhere there exists a "pure" immigrant version of events that would tell things as they are in an uninflected voice, one unaffected by ideological transmutation. That is not so. Nor would I suggest that such speakers, were they to be found, would necessarily say anything radically different from some of those who take the word on their behalf. But at least an elementary justice might be seen to be done if the ordinary immigrant were enabled to speak directly and unaided in the public arena.

12

Conclusion: institutional and ideological structures

In this final chapter I shall attempt to place the material raised by this book in a wider perspective, taking up a number of points raised by the analysis of institutions and ideologies. I will also try to set the data in a comparative framework, drawing attention to similarities and differences between France and Britain.

METHODOLOGICAL PREMISES

When I have presented some of my findings to audiences of anthropologists, some participants have invariably sought to divert discussion from the French to the immigrants, as if *they* were considered the only appropriate field for anthropological inquiry. Indeed, on one occasion it was asked: "But what do the *real* people think?" I have suggested elsewhere (Grillo 1980a:4) that in the division of labor in the social sciences, anthropologists have allowed themselves to be accorded the role of expert in certain domains only, of which "immigrants" is one. To accept that role, however, is to ignore something that is both a methodological premise and an ethnographic fact: that the social and economic position of immigrants must be seen, in large part, in terms of their situation within the society to which they have migrated. Whether that situation may be described as "determined by," or a "reflection of," or a "response to," or "integration with," or even as "autonomous within" that society is a separate question.

This means that the systems of the receiving society, which of course affect not only immigrants, must be our starting point, and that an immigrant study is invariably concerned with that society. This is in no way to underestimate the importance of the sending society and its institutions, nor of the relationship *between* receiving and sending societies. Both at the macro-level of economic and political ties, and the micro level of individual migrants and their families, that relationship is of fundamental importance for our understanding of why migration occurs and the form it takes in particular cases.

There are, in fact, three focuses of analysis: the institutions of the sending society (and of the society of immigrants); those of the receiving society; and the relationship between the two. Ideally, a complete study of migration should take all three into account and give them appropriate weight. Many studies, however, stress one at the expense of another, and this book is no exception. This, of course, is the issue at stake in Watson's (1977a) criticism of Castles and Kosack (1973), and Dahya's (1974) argument with Rex and Moore (1967) about the precise relevance of the structure of the British housing market for analysis of the house-buying and residence patterns of Asian immigrants.

It is obvious that I come down on one side in this dispute by giving methodological priority to the institutions of the receiving society. However, I reiterate that this does not mean that the institutions of the sending society and its members (for instance their culture) are irrelevant. Far from it. But that relevance varies according to context and situation, and moreover depends in part at least on what leeway is allowed by the receiving society, or what kind of "autonomy" can be won (publicly or privately, openly or clandestinely) by immigrants for their culture.

I said at the outset that this study might have become a very different piece of research, by exploring the "view from within" the immigrant communities. Perhaps enough evidence has been cited in the text to suggest what shape such a study might have taken. It would have to be seen as one that complements the present analysis, documenting the other side of what is a *relationship*, not treating its material in isolation.

In practice it is very difficult for a single study, undertaken by a single fieldworker, to encompass all aspects of that relationship, and therefore choices must be made. This inevitably leaves gaps in the data. Take, for example, the growth of North African family migration to France, a phenomemon of central importance for the understanding of migration in Lyon in the mid-1970s. Clearly it is inadequate to discuss this solely in terms of the institutions of the receiving society, as I have tended to do in this book. Ideally, the student of this phenomenon should be working simultaneously on three fronts: with the institutions of the receiving society, among the immigrants themselves, and in the sending society.

To whatever we accord methodological priority, in an ideal world all migration studies should be at least "double-headed." The work of the Ballards on the Punjabis in Leeds (e.g., 1977), of Palmer on Italians in London (1981), and of Watson on the Chinese of London and Hong Kong (1977b) demonstrate the importance of this, albeit from the opposite point of view to that taken here, in that their priority is the sending society and its institutions.

INSTITUTIONAL STRUCTURES

Beginning, then, with the receiving society, I suggested in Chapter 1 that heuristically the French "system" may be treated as a series of institutional complexes entailing a variety of bureaucratically ordered organizations (firms, ministries, housing societies, supermarkets, etc.). The "system" is not just this – a housing or employment market consists of more than the organizations involved in it – but these organizations offer a point of departure for the anthropologist, just as they provide a point of contact for the ordinary citizen. They are the visible, indeed tangible, manifestations of the "system," and it is impossible to exist in the kind of society France has become without being constantly affected, directly and indirectly, by their existence. These institutional complexes organize two great classes of relationship – those of production and of consumption – and there is, analytically, a third set of institutions whose personnel "act on" those relationships.

Of the several features of this structure that make it seem typical of advanced or postindustrial societies, I would stress three. First, there is the fact of extensive organized institutional activity concerned with attending to relationships in production and consumption. There is the widespread belief that things need to be done, and can be done, about such relationships. Second, there is the equally widespread professionalization of, and training for, those who are to engage in this type of activity, which also frequently involves the extensive application of technical and socioscientific knowledge. Finally, much of the institutional activity concerned directly and indirectly with social relationships is state-organized or state-inspired (cf. Touraine 1977:216).

In this concluding chapter, I will deal with two of these points, beginning with the state: What is the role of the state in regard to the institutional activity described here? Why is the state concerned to "act on" the relationships in which people engage as producers and consumers? And why is there an especial concern with immigrants, in particular those from North Africa?

THE INSTITUTIONAL ROLE OF THE STATE

If we examine the range of institutions engaged with immigrants, we find a curious mixture of private and public organizations that is in fact wholly typical of France. The particular role of the *state*, however, needs underlining. "Today there is scarcely an activity in France which the State does not either totally control or markedly influence" (Suleiman 1975:24). Agreed. Consider the points at which the state intervenes directly or indirectly in the situation of immigrants. At the highest level are agreements between France and the sending societies that regulate the flow of immigrants in gross terms. The Office National d'Immigration controls the selection of groups of workers, and individual workers and their families, in the countries of origin, and supervises their conveyance to France. In France, in diverse ways, the DDASS, the prefecture, and the police monitor the location of immigrants and their movement. Their access to work is increasingly regulated, for example, by the linking of employment and residence permits. Until recently, the state regulated immigrant participation in trade unions. It directly controls their welfare benefits and the education of their children.

Many of the *private* associations described in this book are either creations of the state (like the AEE) or benefit extensively from state subventions such as those from the Fonds d'Action Sociale. The *offices* and *sociétés* HLM, the hostels, the *cités de transit*, private associations concerned with welfare (such as the SSFNA) or with *alpha* (such as ACFAL), are all extensively subsidized by a state that also regulates and monitors their constitution. The state also has a role, as we saw in Chapter 11, in the formation of policy and in the coordination of consultation about and implementation of that policy among both private and public-sector bodies.

Although the state may seem to play a particularly extensive role in regard to immigrants, intervention of the kind described is not peculiar to them, as Suleiman's remark testifies. France is, in a sense, a "state capitalist" system in which the state intervenes heavily to provide an infrastructure (or perhaps more accurately, a framework of infrastructural provision), and a flow of resources to create an environment within which the economic and social

order may function. Nevertheless, the very extent of state intervention regarding immigrants, and the nature of the matters in
which it intervenes, precludes any simple characterization of its
role so far as they are concerned.

It is clearly insufficient to argue that the state and its apparatus
provide the link between the other institutions of the society, in
particular the political apparatus and the realms of private finance and capital, though there are many instances where this
occurs in a straightforward way. The hostels provide one example
of this, as do the activities of the DDASS, albeit in a much less
obvious way. Nor can it be argued simply that the state is concerned with the "reproduction of labor power," or even, as my
account has suggested, the reproduction of "fit" producers and
consumers, though analysis of what are treated as "problems"
does reveal that immigrants are frequently conceived, inter alia,
to be poor consumers of housing, welfare, schools, consumer durables, and so on, just as they are sometimes seen to be poor
producers at work, or poor trade unionists.

Policies toward immigrants, however, encompass more than
this. *Insertion*, for example, as a policy certainly sets the institutions to work directly and indirectly on the immigrant's performance as producer and consumer – as we saw in Chapter 8, that is
what *insertion* is about. But it also defines how France might ac-
commodate *étrangeté*. That is to say, high on the agenda of the
state there is, and there has long been, a concern not just with the
reproduction of labor power, but with the definition and reproduction of a social order appropriate for the French nation.

To say that the French state seeks to regulate *étrangeté* might
suggest support for Banton (1967) and others who have presented a case for locating the structure of race relations (and interethnic relations generally) within a framework incorporating
notions of "strangeness," "distance," and "acceptance." I agree
with Rex's strictures on this perspective (1973:224). "Distance" is
not a natural phenomenon. The hierarchical ordering of cultures
in which *étrangeté*, construed as national, cultural, linguistic, religious, or racial difference becomes a salient way of differentiat-
ing humanity, itself requires sociological explanation.

Certainly the use of *étranger*, and the connotations of *étrangeté*
discussed in Chapter 3, and the concept of *évolué* (Chapters 5 and
6), show the importance for many French people of "distance"
from their culture, and the desire in some cases to reduce it.

Caillot (1969:113) and others whose surveys consistently demonstrate a scale of perceived ethnic distance from the French (usually in the order Italian, Spanish, Portuguese, Moroccan/Tunisian, Algerian) provide further evidence of this. But we have to examine closely by reference to what social and cultural features distance is measured, and by whom, to understand why it is salient in particular cases.

For the institutions, for reasons connected partly with their background(culture or origin), partly with their situation (economic and social status) in France, and partly with the organization and functioning of the French system itself, some immigrants do not "fit in." An obvious example of that is the way the housing stock corresponds to the needs of a certain size and type of family but not others. Families where the pattern is different are ipso facto "problem" families, unless they have the resources to find their own way through the housing market. This, of course, applies to certain French families as well (e.g., large families, gypsies), but the *décalage,* to use a favored term – or lack of synchronization between – immigrant families and the French system is generally much greater, and the likelihood of a "gap" between that system and North Africans is the greatest of all.

This suggests a somewhat different way of defining and interpreting "distance," by measuring it with respect to institutional norms and practices. The various policies implied by *insertion, intégration, assimilation,* and *évolution* thus represent different ways of thinking through the problem of "distance," and of closing, or eliminating, or accommodating the gap. As such, they also represent different conceptions of what the eventual social order of France might be, and it is in regulating that order that the state has a crucial role.

This does not, however, fully explain the special concern with North African immigrants, nor indeed the widespread, virulent hostility they frequently encounter.

INSTITUTIONS AND THE HISTORICAL CONTEXT OF INTERETHNIC RELATIONS

I suggested earlier that the sending and receiving societies and the relationship between them present three focuses for a "total" analysis of migration. At one point in time (e.g., 1976) any of these may be taken as given, thought of as part of the environing "structure." This must be acknowledged as the heuristic device it is. There is always a complex interaction between these elements, which only an examination of the historical record can document.

For example, some of the French institutions that deal with migration, and that affect at least contemporary patterns of North African immigration, were created in the early 1950s. The MTE, NDSA, SSFNA, ACFAL, all date from that time. Then they were a response to the prevailing pattern of migration (increasing numbers of single men). They were also, in contrasting ways, a response to the exigencies of the Algerian War.

By concentrating on the contemporary scene, I have perhaps paid insufficient attention to the interactive processes that analysis of a record of the past would reveal. I hope there may be an opportunity in the future to remedy this deficiency. There is, however, one area quite central to this book in which history, in the sense of the continuing presence of the past in the present, cannot simply be left to one side.

In a remark reminiscent of *Eighteenth Brumaire,* Hoffmann (1973:268) states that it was his intention "montrer au lecteur qu'une longue tradition pèse sur lui, que sa vision des Noirs ne diffère pas essentiellement de ces aieux." The point is this: Although the receiving society and its institutions must be accorded priority in the analysis of immigration, it should be acknowledged that they do not touch everyone in the same manner. Particular groups, of which immigrants are but one, are affected in distinct, often radically different ways. Nor are "immigrants" a homogeneous category, bearing in mind the differences of class, status, social and domestic situation, and cultural background found among them.

From the material presented it should be clear that the French institutional system weighs more heavily on immigrants from North Africa and in some contexts (for example, the schools) on the Portuguese, than it does on those from Spain or Italy. In my own experience and that of most observers, it is apparent that of all the national groups it is the Algerians who bear the brunt of the French institutional system, and indeed of French animosity toward immigrants.

The reasons are not far to seek. Of paramount importance are the continuing reverberations of the Algerian War. British readers who were in the 1950s and 1960s concerned with colonial freedom will recall all too well the landmarks of the era: Malaya, Cyprus,

Kenya. Their recollection of the Algerian War may be less vivid
because it had relatively little impact in Britain. In France the
events of that time are constantly in the background: "Al-gé-rie-
Fran-çaise," the barbed wire and the camps, half a million con-
scripts in Algeria, the grenades in cafés, the *plastiqueurs* of the OAS,
the *Barbouzes*, the generals' putsch, the *Paras* expected to land at
Orly, De Gaulle's "Françaises, Français, aidez-moi," Evian, and the
final rapid withdrawal of a million *pieds noirs* to the metropolitan
country. The scars of that period remain in the memories of both
sides as vividly as the cigarette burns on the legs of Comrade Ch.
To an extent I have taken that history, and its continuing significance, for granted in this book. Anyone who needs reminding had
best consult the historian Alistair Horne (1977), or perhaps
Ibrahim's horrific account of events in Paris in 1961 (Ibrahim
1981:91).

At this point it becomes relevant to cite the work of John Rex on
the genesis of racism elaborated by him in a series of publications
from the late 1960s onward (1970, 1973, 1979). The basic argument is that the racial(ist) nature of the relationship between
Third World immigrants and members of the "host" metropolitan societies must be understood in terms of the historical
relationship between metropolitan and colonized societies, and
the roles assigned to the various parties in that relationship. Thus:
"British people confronted with immigrants from what used to be
the Empire, cannot but be expected to react to them in terms of
the roles which the immigrants used to fill" (Rex and Tomlinson
1979:91).

Rex is not always clear about how this condition, which he in-
sists is not a "survival" from some imperial past, is sustained,
except in his occasional references to personal knowledge transmitted via networks of relatives and friends (1970:106), reinforced by the media (1970:154). Sometimes there is simply asser-
tion: "This is not a matter to be established by some naively
designed attitude test. It is a matter of history and of logic" (Rex
and Tomlinson 1979:91). This basic position is reiterated by others concerned with Britain (e.g., Benson 1981:42), and is shared
by Freeman (1979:30, 42) writing of both Britain and France.

The relevance of Rex's ideas to the understanding of the
French experience is not always made apparent. This is partly a
matter of the definition of racism. Although generally Rex adopts
a broad definition, he is sometimes led, perhaps influenced by his

South African and British experience, to equate racism with color prejudice, which he is prone to suggest is less important in France than in Britain (1970:110; 1979:12), and thus: "True, the colonial experience of Algerians and Moroccans may have more in common with that of British colonials, but here the geographical as well as the historical and cultural closeness of the countries surrounding the Mediterranean littoral may act as a countervailing factor" (Rex and Tomlinson 1979:13).

It is certainly true that the French frequently express the belief that color and other forms of discrimination are less common in France than in Britain. Many of my French informants made that very point. The works of Hoffmann (1973) and Cohen (1980), however, suggest that historically racism was as securely and elaborately founded in France as it was in Britain (see Curtin 1965, and Kiernan 1969).

Although this might be taken to reinforce Rex's position, Cohen in fact appears to think otherwise, at least insofar as racism as a rationalization for imperialism is concerned, since "until the 1880's, when empire building began in earnest, the racists were divided on whether Africans should be conquered" (1980:261). However, this has little to do with the point, that the racial structure of colonial society subsequently provided a model for contemporary relationships in metropolitan countries; and certainly Cohen, as we have seen, argues that ideas of an earlier period rationalize contemporary conflicts (1980:289). Thus, assuming that we can talk of the relationship between French and Algerians as racial (and not all would do so: it depends on how tightly one wishes to define "race"; see Cohen 1980:290, and Rex's argument with Banton in Rex 1973:xviii, 221), that relationship would appear, almost above any other, to be an example vindicating Rex's general argument.

Any account of the contemporary response to migration and migrants in France must, therefore, acknowledge the importance of a colonial past in defining and shaping interethnic relations – just as we must acknowledge that some of the arrangements for dealing with immigrants are in precise terms a colonial legacy. This cannot mean, however, that *that* past tells us all. Of comparable importance is the fact that since the French Revolution the problem of how to handle *étrangeté* – not just that of foreign immigrants, but also that of the constituent elements of the "hexagon" – has been a significant one in the development of a French

290 Ideologies and institutions in urban France

social order. So if colonialism provides one frame of reference, then the building of a *French* nation-state must provide another.

Both may be set alongside a third frame of reference, one provided by the type of society and economy that, along with others, I would characterize as "postindustrial." Each frame of reference provides insight into the ways in which countries like France and Britain perceive and handle the "others" in their midst. None may be properly overlooked if we are to understand why, in France, the "problems" of immigrants, especially those from North Africa, seems to cause such concern.

In various ways this leads us to questions of ideology, of ideological structure, and of the relationship between ideology and society. Before embarking on that discussion, however, I will conclude this section with some remarks on similarities and differences between France and Britain.

INSTITUTIONAL PRACTICES IN FRANCE AND BRITAIN

Originally my intention was to contribute to the comparative understanding of polyethnic urban and industrial systems. If that has been achieved, it has been by a different route from the one envisaged. As I have said, the study broadened to become an analysis of institutional arrangements and ideological structures in an advanced industrial society, with immigrants providing an illustration of how that society operates in a particular case.

Given the paucity of published work with a similar orientation, it is difficult to put my data in comparative perspective. It is even difficult to judge how far what I say about Lyon applied to other French cities. However, besides working extensively in Lyon, I have undertaken some research in Grenoble, Marseille, and the Paris region, and have supervised a number of students at Sussex who have also worked in France. Most of these have been "year abroad" French studies majors who have chosen to write dissertations on immigrants in places such as Aix, Marseille, and Toulouse. One, however, is a postgraduate student (Andrea Caspari) who spent fifteen months in Grenoble studying Portuguese immigrants. Their work, and extensive reading of the French migration literature, and observation of the French media, all suggests that two of the principal issues discussed in this book – the representation of problems and the problem of representation – reflect phenomena found generally throughout France.

This does not mean to say there is no variation, for example, in the way that the problem of representation is handled. There is, as Caspari's work will show. There are fair indications that the size and structure of the French community are significant factors in that variation, as are its social composition and political complexion. Lyon is a large industrial city with a strongly entrenched and powerful bourgeoisie. It is also a particularly violent city. In 1975, *Pravda* (reported in *Le Progrès de Lyon*) called it the "Chicago of France" on account of the extent of violent, casual and organized, crime in the area. It was in 1975, for example, that there occurred the famous assassination of a *juge d'instruction*. That episode later formed the basis of a film (*Un Juge Est Assassiné*), which was made in Saint-Etienne but which clearly refers to Lyon. Like *Z* and *Illustrious Corpses*, the film sought to unravel the social and political forces behind the murder of a prominent citizen. Its findings were, I believe, extremely accurate.

Thus, French-immigrant relations may be said to have a general structure of the kind outlined in this book, but that structure is given particular shape by the social environment in which those relations are located. In Lyon we almost certainly find, for example, a tighter control of the immigrant voice than occurs in other provincial cities. But nowhere is that control absent.

A second problem of generalization is this. I have stated that the situation of immigrants provides an example of how certain society-wide institutions operate. How far can we in fact generalize from an analysis of their handling of the particular problems of immigrants? Quite clearly some of what the institutions do with immigrants is limited to that category of the population, and only relevant to them. Nevertheless, the kinds of activities in which social workers, teachers, housing officials, or trade unionists engage when they deal with immigrants are similar to what they do in other cases too. There is a *pattern* of institutional and ideological activity about which we can generalize, and indeed which is generalized through the society. I would also argue with regard to the associations that are specifically concerned with immigrants (e.g., ACFAL or the MTE) that their very existence is a function of the general social order, and certainly their modes of institutional and ideological activity must be understood in relation to that order.

There is also the question of the comparison that may be made between France and other European countries. Certainly the basic position of postwar immigrants in many different European countries is very similar, as Castles and Kosack, for example, have shown only too well. A more detailed comparison of the situation of migrants in Germany (Rist 1978) or in a British city like Birmingham (Ratcliffe 1981, Rex 1973; Rex and Moore 1967; Rex and Tomlinson 1979), shows striking similarities in terms of the housing and employment markets, the school system, the language system, and the system of welfare distribution, with the position of migrants in Lyon.

With regard to the form of institutional activity described in this book and the issues of "representation," in both senses, with which I have been primarily concerned, the published literature offers relatively little help. There are studies that deal with policy (e.g., Jones 1977) but these, with few exceptions (e.g., Fred 1979), are mainly historical or deal with the national-political level. I would make the same point about the fascinating comparison of France and Britain made by Freeman, whose intentions are similar to my own, and with whose conclusions, so far as France is concerned, I largely concur.

There are, however, two general points that might be made about France and Britain. First, as Chapter 11 suggests, Britain allows more room for, and pays greater attention to, independent immigrant representation, just as it allows more room for cultural autonomy in certain defined areas. We are, of course, speaking relatively. Likewise, for a free society, France, or rather the French state, is engaged in a much closer monitoring and control of its citizens than we like to believe occurs in Britain. There is a contrast here between two traditions of nation and state that varies the way in which the advanced industrial order common to both countries is organized and operates, and that also tempers the way in which each country handles its constituent minorities.

Now, at a time of serious economic crisis, both countries are faced with a revolt of ethnic minorities (e.g., in Ulster and Corsica), though only in Britain has anything resembling a revolt occurred in the cities. Perhaps the tight control exerted over immigrants in France, directly and indirectly, accounts for this quiescence and acquiescence, and may also account for the glances, sometimes envious, sometimes horrified, directly toward the French riot police by their British counterparts, just as occasionally the French cast nervous glances toward Britain. Thus an article in the *Guardian* (September 19, 1981) referred to "Vennisieux" (*sic*) as France's nearest equivalent to Toxteth.

Paradoxically, the kind of violence experienced in Britain in 1981 has been relatively rare in recent British history, whereas the French, it seems, take to the streets at regular intervals (1870, 1936, 1968 . . .). It is to be hoped that no one will take the French institutional arrangements for handling immigrants as a model for imitation.

IDEOLOGICAL STRUCTURES AND INSTITUTIONAL PRACTICES

This book has been concerned both with institutional practices and the ideas that inform them. In particular it has focused on the views expressed by those engaged in acting on certain kinds of relations found in contemporary society. These persons have included both those who in various ways exercise power and authority within the dominant institutional system, and those formally outside that system (most obviously those on the left) who address themselves to it.

Although I use the term "ideology" to refer to ways of conceptualizing relations in production and consumption, this should not be taken to mean that ideology is defined by reference to those relations. That is, ideology, as I use the term, is not "about" such relations, and those alone. They happen to be the subject matter of the ideologies discussed in this book, not the subject matter of *all* ideology. This is one way in which the discussion of ideology here differs from that found in Althusser and in the anthropological literature influenced by his recension of Marx.

That recension presented a revision of the classical Marxist dictum that "the ideas of the ruling class are in every epoch the ruling ideas. . . . The class which has the means of material production at its disposal, has control at the same time over the means of mental production" (Marx and Engels 1965:60) by representing *all* the ideational and symbolic systems present in a society – indeed, the totality of culture (cf. McDonnell and Robins 1980: 166–7, and Poulantzas 1978:208) – as "ideological." Ideology is then identified with its function ("which defines it") of "'constituting' concrete individuals as subjects" (Althusser 1971: 171). This task it performs by representing "not the system of the real relations which govern the existence of individuals, but the imaginary relations of those individuals to the real relations in which they live" (ibid., p. 165; cf. Bloch 1977:287). Ideology not only produces "subjects," it "subjects" them. This is necessary "if the reproduction of relations of production is to be assured . . . every day, in the 'consciousness,' i.e. in the attitudes of individual-subjects occupying the posts which the socio-technical division of labour assigns to them" (p. 182). Thus the subjects "work by themselves" (p. 281).

This concept of ideology has been extremely influential in the study of discourse, for example, in the work of Michel Pêcheux in France (1969, 1978, 1982), and of the writers associated with the journal *Screen* in Britain. Its use in conjunction with approaches from semiotics and Lacanian psychoanalysis – what Pêcheux (1982:211) calls the "Triple Alliance," but which McDonnell and Robins (1980:179) term the "unholy Trinity" – has undoubtedly led to some important insights into the structure of political and literary texts. It is, however, beset with difficulties as recent criticism of its "functionalism," its anti-humanism, its dependence on Lacan's version of Freud, and its often implicit assumptions about its own "scientific" status make clear (cf. Thompson 1978, Clarke et al. 1980, among others).

Althusser's propositions may be reduced, crudely, to a functional chain of the following kind: mode of production to reproduction of labor power to ideology to "interpellation" of subject to subject in production. One major problem with this is its reductionism. Another is its simplification of the complex nature of discourse in contemporary society, and its relation to institutional practice.

For these reasons and others it is difficult to follow Althusser and identify all the institutions discussed in this book with "ideological state apparatuses," as he uses that term (1971:143). For a start, there is scarcely an institution that is not, for Althusser, a *state* apparatus. His view of capitalist society appears to be one in which all institutions (except perhaps the PCF) form a homogeneous entity serving the state, which in turn serves one purpose alone: "the reproduction of relations of production" (ibid., p. 148).

Undoubtedly some of the institutions I have discussed could be described in a commonsense way as "ideological state apparatuses." Directly or indirectly, many form part of the state system, and they and their personnel often seek to implement a point of view that at any moment might be called the "predominant," if not the "dominant," ideology. That is the prevailing orthodoxy, the viewpoint of those wielding power and authority in the public domain who advocate policies of *animation, participation,* socio-educative action, *insertion,* and so on. Undoubtedly, too, many of those policies are concerned with persons as producers (and, equally important, as consumers), but as I indicated earlier in this chapter, to assign such activity the sole function of the reproduction of relations of production is far too simple.

In a curious way, Althusser's concept of ideology is reminiscent of Malinowski's view of myth, but as Leach pointed out, myth (let us substitute ideology, discourse) "is a language of argument, not a chorus of harmony" (Leach 1954:278). Leaving aside the fact, which I would accept as a wholly secondary matter, that within state institutions in the ordinary sense teachers, social workers, and others attempt to put into practice views that are at variance with the prevailing orthodoxy, I would point to a range of organizations and groups, principally but not exclusively of the left, whose own ideology is avowedly in opposition to the dominant perspective.

If ideology/discourse is a site of struggle, however, those who find themselves ranged against each other cannot be assigned unambiguously to their structural position. Ideologies cannot be treated as if they were "political number-plates worn by social classes on their backs" (Poulantzas 1978:202, 205). There is no neat and obvious correlation between, say, ideology, political affiliation, socioeconomic situation, or, indeed, institutional location of any speaker or group of speakers. There may, of course, always be hints of this. Thus, the ideological position of the CGT, to which we may undoubtedly assign a political label, is relatable, at least in part, to the social composition of its main constituents – in Lyon, the skilled factory worker. A similar point might be made about, say, hostel directors. Nevertheless, there remains a relative degree of autonomy between these variables. A consideration of the structure of discourse will perhaps bear this out.

The analysis of discourse and ideology brings us back in a roundabout way to what had been my original aim: the study of ethnicity, class, and status among immigrant workers. For one of the principal features of the ideologies under discussion is the *language* (or rather *languages*) of ethnicity, class, and status (and also of culture and race) in which they are couched. When informants discussed immigrants, for example, with respect to their roles in production and consumption, they constantly used those languages to describe and analyze their situation. Which languages were deployed, and how they were employed, also provided the form of discourse on immigrants.

In a sense, class, culture, race and so forth constitute some of the "grammatical" components of discourse. Their usage reveals the underlying ideological structure. A simple example of this occurred in Chapter 3, where I suggested that statements might be ordered in such a way as to stress one component at the expense of another by referring to immigrants wholly in terms of their assumed class position or their ethnic origin. Similar examples occurred later in the discussion of the alternative perspectives revealed by such phrases as *ouverture culturelle* and *prise de conscience*, and in explanations of *retard scolaire*. Similarly, in Chapter 4 we observed opposing views of the problems of immigrant men in hostels where lack of "soul" was contrasted with too high rents, although there, and in the parallel debate about the hostel committees (*participation* versus *autogestion*), it is clear that key elements other than class and ethnicity are involved in ideological structuring.

Although these and other examples might suggest a fundamental contrast between two opposed ideological systems, which we can label right and left, in practice, as we have seen, there is a complex interweaving of ideological elements, especially at the level of individual utterance, although it may also appear in the ideological "system" espoused by a group of speakers. Such interweaving blurs any simple opposition between right and left. That, and the ideological differences within both right and left (see especially Chapter 3), often means that in practice it is difficult to identify a body of ideology that is undeniably and exclusively that of the "ruling class" (cf. Althusser 1971:146). An example is the weight given to the cultural dimension both by certain groups on the extreme left and by some of those on the Giscardian right (see Chapter 3.) This is not to say that the two groups make the same use of "culture" or articulate its relationship with some other element (e.g., class) in the same way.

There are other ways in which the contrast is blurred. First, although there may be a significant difference between what is *said* by two parties, there may be considerably less when we observe the import of what is *done*. Second, there may be greater differences between formal, official, publicly promulgated positions (the "line") taken by particular groups than between what their adherents say in casual, informal conversations. Finally, at another level entirely, those who might otherwise be said to be at different points on the political spectrum usually share a range of intellectual concerns of common origin. It is here, perhaps, that they reveal their Frenchness, their debt to a common *French* intellectual and cultural configuration. See, for example, the shared concern about the separateness of immigrants (both physical, as in a ghetto, and social), and the desire that they should "get out," or "open out," or perceive a common interest, although that perception may be variously described as a *prise de conscience* or an *ouverture culturelle,* terms to which we may attach a political tag.

This approach to discourse and ideology, which emphasizes the complexity of the domain, poses many problems. There is, for example, the question of the relationship between "ideological utterance" and "ideological system," and between an utterance and the discourse to which it pertains, which has a bearing on the status of the "subject" in this type of analysis. In that connection I cannot follow Foucault's search for a method "purged of all anthropologism" (1972:16). But this is a question that cannot be tackled here, although I hope to return to it on another occasion. One issue, however, demands immediate attention.

IDEOLOGY, INSTITUTIONAL ACTIVITY, AND THE SOCIAL SCIENCES

The discourses examined here, and the theories of social, cultural, and political relations they entail, are not just the property of informants encountered in the street, so to speak. They are part and parcel of French society and may be met anywhere. The views expressed outside the immediate place and time of fieldwork must, therefore, be considered pertinent to any inquiry of this kind, provided probable points of entry into that immediate locale can be identified.

One in particular suggests itself: the written word, which in this context knows no boundaries of time or space. Thus, as we saw, the ideas of Catani (1973) were made available to *alpha* teachers via a cyclostyled synopsis. Another, slightly different example is provided by the way in which the ideological views of adherents of certain groups (for instance, the PCF, the CGT, or the CFDT) are formed partly by texts put together "elsewhere," in the committees where the "line" is elaborated. When we then recall that

Althusser himself was a member of the Central Committee of the PCF, we can see that the boundary between what appears to be abstruse philosophical "literature" and the utterances of "informants" can become thin indeed.

In this way the writings of French social scientists and others about migration, for example, and many other matters, inevitably become part of the data of inquiry. There are other reasons, too, for so treating them. One of these is the way in which social scientists themselves participate in the system of institutions that "act on" relations of production and consumption, and within which the state has such an important role in defining and reproducing the social order. This, in fact, is the second major feature of postindustrial society to which I wish to draw attention.

Krishan Kumar notes that many writers, with widely differing theoretical perspectives, concur in asserting "the new structural importance of systematic and theoretical knowledge as a crucial 'resource' of present-day industrial society" (Kumar 1978:194). What is important, however, is the extent to which there is systematic *application* of such knowledge. The fact of the harnessing of science and technology to production is well known. Less well known, perhaps, is the application of social-scientific "knowledge" by institutions acting on relations in production and consumption.

I referred in Chapter 1 to the existence of a large body of social-scientific research (often local and ephemeral) concerned with immigrants in Lyon. Much of this is produced by or for institutions such as ministries, planning authorities and HLM. Many social scientists in French universities have, in fact, traditionally undertaken such research under contract, using the proceeds to finance their own "private" work.

This applied research is not about immigrants alone, of course. It is concerned principally with "problem" areas and groups, but by and large this inevitably means a great deal touches on immigrants, especially in the fields of housing and education. In quantitative terms it is probably in the domain of housing (*logement*) that applied social science makes its greatest impact. It should be no surprise to learn, therefore, that on the ZUP at Vaulx-en-Velin one of the earliest appointments made by the overall planning authority (SERL – Société d'Equipement pour la Région Lyonnaise – which is, in turn, part of SCET – Société Centrale pour l'Equipement du Territoire) was that of a sociologist, to work alongside the chief architect and the *paysagiste* designing the estate and monitoring its impact on the residents (and vice versa).

From the outset SERL sponsored a number of studies (e.g., SERL 1976), as they had begun to do, somewhat belatedly, at Vénissieux (see GSU 1974a, 1974b). The findings were discussed by a Groupe des Questions d'Aménagement de Cadre de Vie consisting of representatives from SERL, the commune authorities, the HLM, commercial interests, all the social service organizations, and later APACS.

At least a dozen meetings were held between 1971 and 1976. One that I attended heard a report on a recent study (SERL 1976) from the demographer concerned. This was followed by questions and discussion that ranged over such issues as traffic flows, the supply of telephone lines, the role of the new social center, and, something the mayor considered crucial, the number of children expected to take up school places at the following *rentrée*. An earlier study had, in fact, found that nearly 50 percent of primary-school children were foreigners. This, when reported to the prefecture and the HLM, had reinforced the view that there should be greater dispersal of foreigners, to prevent ghettoization.

In this way the activities of social scientists become part of institutional practice and, as such, part of a system of indirect representation. Those with whom I discussed the difficulties posed by such a role generally implied a pragmatic approach to policy questions: "The solutions I propose are practical. I bear in mind the financial constraints and the existing structure. There are certain problems created by the macro-structure that I cannot solve, for example, the general situation of immigrants." Sociologists with more radical views of their task certainly existed, although rarely were they as closely integrated with, for example, planning mechanisms as was the sociologist cited above.

Another reason for treating the social sciences as part of our data is the way in which social science forms a significant part of the training (*formation*) of those entering professions, such as teaching and social work, followed by many of the informants encountered in this book. In this way the social sciences provide a body of information and, indeed, a perspective on social relations, which may well inform day-to-day practice. Vocabulary is certainly influenced; witness the use of technical terms such as "psychodrama." This "trickling down" of the social sciences is apparent in much of what is said and done by such people as social assistants, teachers, and *alpha* instructors. It is also apparent in the way in which social-scientific ideas become part of "ordinary" discourses. The discussion of the so-called *seuil de tolérance* (see Chapter 5 and Event 1) provides a particularly clear-cut example of this.

But if French academics, for example, are to be treated as part of the data of inquiry and not accorded a privileged status as scientific observers of the French scene, then where do we stop? What can be said, for example, about a British anthropological study of French-immigrant relations? The issue here is not especially the extent to which such a study has become, or may become, part of the discourse of informants, it is the coincidence between the anthropologist's analytical language, that of his French counterparts, and that of informants in the field.

Anthropologists are always confronted by the problem of intersubjectivity, although this may be masked when they study societies where the language and concepts of informants differ widely from their own. When studying their own native society, the gap between the informants' language and what purports to be the analytical language of anthropology may be very narrow and, indeed, may cease to exist. A British anthropologist studying the French engages with a system of ideas and values that form part of a shared "European" tradition. This includes a shared vocabulary, in the broad sense. Thus, in both describing and analyzing French society I may use terms such as "race," "class," "ethnicity," and "culture," which are also everyday terms in both French and English.

In that the anthropologist specifies a technical meaning that differs from everyday usage, perhaps the only problem is one of confusion in presentation. In fact, in these examples, the technical and everyday usages may be closer than we think. But it is not just a question of vocabulary, for my informants not only use terms such as "class," and "culture" descriptively, they do so analytically, incorporating them in models of, and theories about, society and social relations much as I do. Add here the writings of French academic colleagues who use the same general vocabulary, and whose work may influence directly what my informants say, and we can identify three overlapping fields of discourse: that of "ordinary" French informants, that of French academics and intellectuals, and my own.

This is not to say that the linguistic usages or the analytical models of each of the three parties are precisely the same but is simply to remind us that there is a relationship here and that the difference needs to be defined. And in terms of their formal structure as analytical models of social relations, the difference between what each group offers may be hard to determine.

This leads to another difficulty. For if I am to treat "their" ideas as "ideological" (as organized and organizing bodies of ideas that are "constructed" and hence suitable for analytical attention), what can I say about the status of my own analytical constructs?

Now, I would not wish to argue that my analysis has a privileged, even "scientific," status that enables me to present a "true," still less a "correct," version of events, as some of my informants might wish to say about their own versions. I would aceept that my analysis is no more and no less ideological than theirs. I cannot offer "my" science in opposition to "their" ideology. To say "ideological," however, is not, as I have used the term, to say "false." Ideologies represent ways of reading the world and of illuminating it by placing elements in that world in a meaningful relationship with one another. That has been the purpose in writing this book.

The analysis here, and the research on which it was based, has moved some way from what anthropologists have usually considered their field, while remaining, I would claim, fundamentally anthropological. It may be hoped that it will thereby suggest new lines of inquiry for anthropologists and that, in particular, the discussion of the institutions of the "programmed society," to repeat Touraine's phrase, will have some value in indicating areas of contemporary society to which those concerned to demonstrate anthropology's intellectual and practical contribution might turn their attention.

Appendix: The French school system

Although 15 to 20 percent of French schoolchildren attend private schools, we are here concerned exclusively with the public-education system. In outline, the system does not differ markedly from that which operates in Britain, although some aspects are, on closer inspection, less familiar than they might seem. At the time of fieldwork the educational system was between two bouts of reform. The first, arising out of the events of the late 1960s, was still being assimilated. Its application was not everywhere uniform, and certainly the distinctive terminology of the old system was constantly employed alongside the jargon of the new. The second set of reforms was intended for implementation after fieldwork was completed (the Haby reforms).

The various types of school are as follows:

Elementary education: *maternelles* (nursery schools)
primary schools

Secondary education: Collèges d'Enseignement Général (CEG)
Collèges d'Enseignement Secondaire (CES)
Collèges d'Enseignement Technique (CET)
Lycées

There is also a variety of special schools and sections, e.g., Sections d'Education Specialisée, or SES, which are discussed below.

Nursery education is more highly developed in France than in Britain, and a very high proportion of children from the age of two and a half or three years onward attend part or full time an *école maternelle*, which in the cities is usually a separate school attached to a local primary school. The *maternelle* provides a basic introduction to school life (regular hours, discipline, contacts with teachers) for both pupils and parents, and allows children to make a start on basic skills such as writing.

At age six, when education becomes compulsory, the child normally enters a primary school, which caters to the six to eleven or twelve group. There are five classes, which are not streamed:

1. The *cours préparatoire* (CP)
2. The *cours élémentaire,* first year (CE1)
3. The *cours élémentaire,* second year (CE2)
4. The *cours moyen,* first year (CM1)
5. The *cours moyen,* second year (CM2)

The content of primary education in France is very similar to that of primary education in Britain – including, for example, the new mathematics. The style of education is, however, rather more formal, traditional even. For example, at the end of each term parents are sent a *livret scolaire*, a report book they must inspect and sign, which records their child's grades (from A for "very satisfactory" through to E for "very insufficient") in the subjects taught and in conduct. A poor result at the end of the year may mean that the child has to repeat that year. Toward the end of the CM2 year, a decision is made on the child's school for the following year, that is, whether the child will repeat the last year of primary education or proceed to secondary school.

The structure of secondary education requires some detailed discussion. There was "traditionally" a tripartite system with:

1. Lycée stream or school leading to the *baccalauréat* at age seventeen or eighteen and thence higher education
2. Secondary stream leading to a CET and a Brevet d'Etudes Professionnelles (BEP)
3. *Classes de transition / classes pratiques* leading either to a CET or to "active life"

These streams corresponded very closely to the grammar, technical, and secondary modern schools in Britain.

The reformed system, in theory, abolished streaming in the early years of secondary education. Secondary education, which is compulsory until age sixteen, is divided into a first cycle for pupils aged twelve to sixteen and a second cycle from sixteen onward up to higher education. In principle all pupils now enter a CES at age eleven to twelve and join the 6ème class (the French number their classes in the reverse order to us). In the 6ème and 5ème they follow a common course, and at the end of the 5ème their "orientation" for the following years is discussed. At that point, three possibilities are open: (1) Remain for a further two years, that is, to the end of the 3ème at the CES with a view to proceeding eventually to a Lycée and the *bac;* (2) Go immediately to a CET for a three year course to prepare for the CAP (Certificat d'Aptitude Professionnelle); (3) remain until school leaving age at the CES. Those in category (1) or (3) can transfer to a CET at the end of the 3ème. It is usually considered that categories (1) and (3) contain respectively the strongest and weakest pupils, while category (2) contains the average performers.

The system is a little more complicated than that preliminary account implies.

In the first instance let us take the 6ème and 5ème years at the CES.* In theory, all pupils admitted to the CES follow a similar course for these two years with classes in French, another language, mathematics (the *disciplines fondamentales,* which take up just over half the time), plus history, geography, civics,

---

*The CEG is a type of all-in school that was prevalent under the old system; it still exists in some rural areas but has been largely superseded in the towns.

biology, drawing, music, and manual work (*disciplines d'éveil*) and sport. In fact, in most schools in the Lyon area, from entry into the 6ème or at least shortly after, pupils are streamed into two groups: those following the course outlined above – the so-called traditional, or "normal," classes – and those following a *programme allégé*. The precise nature of these latter classes varies from school to school (they may involve reinforcement of work in French and math, phasing out of the foreign language, etc.). The essential point, however, is that entry to them involves a selection process. In the four principal communes of the *agglomération* (Lyon, Villeurbanne, Vénissieux, and Vaulx), pupils in the 6ème *allégé* represented 14 percent of the total in that age group, though there is considerable variation between communes and between schools (12 percent in Lyon, 24 percent in Vaulx).

A further selection occurs at the end of the 5ème. As one head teacher put it: "We at the CES retain the best and the worst." As we saw above, the middling pupils proceed, after selection, directly to a CET. This group includes some of the weaker pupils from the "normal" stream and the stronger ones from the *allégé* stream. The remainder of the normal stream proceed to the 4ème and 3ème and undertake the following: French, math, first foreign language, technology, history, natural science, drawing, music, and manual work and sport. They may also take, as options, Latin, Greek, a second foreign language, further work in first language. However, some of those in the 4ème or 3ème may take a less full program (referred to as the *classes aménagées*), which includes none of the options listed above but offers further work in the basic subjects. Those who follow this stream are likely to proceed to the CET rather than the lycée.

For reasons given in Chapter 7 it is those in the weakest group who interest us most. In the 4ème and 3ème, these pupils enter the Classes Préprofessionnelles de Niveau (CPPN) and Classes Préparatoires à l'Apprentissage (CPA). The latter are for older pupils, and the course involves consolidation of general education (reading, writing, and mathematics), 35 percent; art and so on, 11 percent; civics, 11 percent; sport, 20 percent; training for a trade, 23 percent. In addition, those taking the CPA may be attached part time (in a sort of sandwich course) to an employer. For the CPPN, pupils take general studies (reading, writing, math, some science and technology) and sport and practical work. At one CES, for example, the practical work is organized around five types of occupation, each of which is sampled by the pupils for a period of five weeks – for example: for boys, carpentry, electricity, plumbing, plastering, mechanics; for girls, cooking, sewing, laundering, training to be florists or shop assistants.

Some of those in the CPPN/CPA streams at the CES can go on to the CET, to take the lowest of the technical certificates, the Certificat d'Education Professionnelle (CEP), a one-year course. Other CET courses include: CAP ("Certificat d'Aptitude Professionnelle") – a three-year course taken by those leaving the CES at the end of the 5ème; BEP (Brevet d'Etudes Professionnelles) – a two-year course taken by those leaving the 3ème normal or *aménagée*. The cultural level of the BEP is higher than that of the CAP.

In addition there are a number of special schools and sections at both the primary and secondary levels. Special classes for foreign pupils (*classes d'initiation,* etc.) are discussed in the text. Here we are concerned with special sections for physically or mentally handicapped children. In fact, the latter category is of particular interest. Sections for children with moderate or mild mental handicaps exist at the primary level, but here I will mention those found attached to secondary schools: the Sections d'education specialisées, or SES. These are small annexes of the CESs, each taking some ninety pupils, who are recommended for admission at the time of the orientation at the end of the primary school. In principle they are intended for pupils who are "moderately mentally handicapped" with an IQ of between 65 and 80 (*Courier de l'Education* No. 28, April 12, 1976). Teaching in the SES anticipates to a certain extent the type of work followed in the CPPN and CPA classes: "The teaching in the SES . . . is characterized by . . . a constant reference to the concrete and to the interdependence between classwork and workshop."

Bibliography

Aboubacar, A. 1972. *L'immigration noire africaine dans l'agglomération lyonnaise.* Lyon: Institut d'Etudes Rhodaniens.

Aguilo, F. 1968. *Emigration et syndicalisme.* Paris: Les Editions Ouvrières.

Allal, T.; J. -P. Buffard; M. Marié; and T. Regazzola. 1977. *Situations migratoires, la fonction miroir.* Paris: Editions Galilée.

Althusser, L. 1971. *Lenin and philosophy and other essays.* New York: Monthly Review Press.

Althusser, L., and E. Balibar. 1979. *Reading capital.* London: Verso Editions.

Amicale des Algériens en Europe. 1973. *Conférence nationale sur l'émigration, Alger, Palais des Nations, 12–14 Jan. 1973* Algiers: Amicale des Algériens en Europe.

    1974a. "Situation sociale des travailleurs algériens." Document produced for VIIth Assemblée Générale, Paris, December 14–15, 1974. Cyclostyled.

    1974b. "La jeunesse algérienne en Europe." Document produced for VIIth Assemblée Générale, Paris, December 14–15, 1974. Cyclostyled.

    1974c. "Action éducative et culturelle de l'Amicale." Cyclostyled.

Anderson, M. 1974. *Conservative politics in France.* London: Allen & Unwin.

Anselme, D. 1972. "Penarroya" in G. Lorant et al. *4 grèves significatives.* Paris: EPI, pp. 143–73.

Armengaud, A. 1973. *La population française au XX siècle* (4th ed.). Paris: Presses Universitaires Françaises.

Asad, T. 1979. "Anthropology and the analysis of ideology." *Man* 14 (4): 607–27.

Augardes, J. 1970. *La migration algérienne.* Paris: Hommes et Migrations Etudes No. 116.

Autenrieth, Barbara. 1971. *Le groupe des Algériens dans l'agglomération lyonnaise.* Mémoire EPHE VIeme Section: Sociologie Musulmane.

Bailey, F. G. 1971. *Gifts and poison.* Oxford: Basil Blackwell.

    1973. *Debate and compromise.* Oxford: Basil Blackwell.

Ballard, R., and C. Ballard. 1977. "The Sikhs: the development of South Asian settlements in Britain," in J. Watson, ed., *Between two cultures.* Oxford: Basil Blackwell, pp. 21–56.

Banton, M. 1967. *Race relations.* London: Tavistock Publications.

Baroin, H. 1935. *La main d'oeuvre étrangère dans la région lyonnaise.* Lyon: Faculté de Droit. Unpublished diss.

Barth, F. 1966. *Models of social organisation.* Occasional Paper No. 23. London: Royal Anthropological Institute.

Belloula, Tayeb. 1965. *Les Algériens en France*. Algiers: Editions Nationales Algériennes.

Ben Sassi, T. 1968. *Les travailleurs tunisiens dans la région parisienne*. Paris: Hommes et Migrations Etudes No. 109.

Bendifallah, Smaïl. 1974. *L'immigration algérienne et le droit français*. Paris: Librairie Générale de Droit et de Jurisprudence.

Benson, S. 1981. *Ambiguous ethnicity: interracial families in London*. Cambridge: Cambridge University Press.

Biddiss, M. D. 1970. *Father of racist ideology: the social and political thought of Count Gobineau*. London: Weidenfeld & Nicolson.

Bienfait, J. 1970. "Le recensement de 1936 à Lyon, ou 120,000 lyonnais fictifs." *CNES* 1970: 487–502.

Bloch, M. 1974. "Symbol, song and dance and features of articulation." *European Journal of Sociology* 1:55–81.

   (ed.). 1975a. *Political language and oratory in traditional society*. London: Academic Press.

   (ed.). 1975b. *Marxist analyses and social anthropology*. ASA Studies No. 2. London: Malaby Press.

   1977. "The past and the present in the present". *Man* 12 (2): 278–92.

Böhning, W. R. 1972. *The migration of workers in the United Kingdom and the European Community*. London: Oxford University Press/Institute of Race Relations.

Bonnet, J. 1975. *Lyon et son agglomération*. Paris: Documentation Française.

Brettell, C. B. 1977. "Emigration and structuring of women's roles." *Urban Anthropology* 6 (2): 170–85.

Brunschwig, H. 1966. *French colonialism, 1871–1914: myths and realities*. London: Pall Mall Press.

Byrnes, R. F. 1950. *Antisemitism in modern France. Vol. 1: prologue to the Dreyfus affair*. New Brunswick, N. J.: Rutgers University Press.

Caillot, R. 1969. *L'insertion des étrangers dans l'aire métropolitaine Lyon-Saint-Etienne* Paris: Hommes et Migrations Etudes No. 113: 64–145.

Calame, P., and P. Calame. 1972. *Travailleurs étrangers en France*. Paris: Editions Ouvriéres. Collection Développement et Civilisations.

Calvet, L-J. 1976. *La production révolutionnaire: slogans, affiches, chansons*. Paris: Payot.

Castells, M. 1976a. "Is there an urban sociology?" in C. G. Pickvance, ed., *Urban sociology*. London: Tavistock Publications, pp. 33–59.

   1976b. "Theory and ideology in urban sociology," in C. G. Pickvance, ed., *Urban sociology*. London: Tavistock Publications, pp. 60–84.

   1976c. "Theoretical propositions for an experimental study of urban social movements," in C. G. Pickvance, ed., *Urban sociology*. London: Tavistock Publications, pp. 147–73.

Castles, S., and G. Kosack. 1973. *Immigrant workers and class structure in Western Europe*. London: Oxford University Press/Institute of Race Relations.

Catani, M. 1973. *L'alphabétisation des travailleurs étrangers: une relation dominant/dominé*. Paris: Tema-éditions.

   1981. "'Est-il possible de faire un enfant?' (des travailleurs étrangers, la sémantique et les valeurs)," in GRECO 13, *Recherches sur les migrations internationales: les travailleurs étrangers et la langue.* Special number, coordinated by Colette Noyau. Paris: Groupement de Recherches Coordonnées sur les Migrations Internationales, pp. 77–88.

Cavard, D.; A. Cordeiro; and R.-E. Verhaeren. 1973. *L'immigration et le système de prestations sociales.* Grenoble: Institut de Recherche Economique et de Planification.

CEDETIM. 1975. *Les immigrés.* Paris: Lutter/Stock 2.

CFDT. 1975. *Orientations et positions pour l'immigration.* Paris: CFDT. Cyclostyled.

CFDT Sections AEE. 1976. *A qui profite la formation des immigrés?* Paris: CFDT. Cyclostyled.

CGT. 1973a. *Charte revendicative pour une politique de l'immigration.* Paris: CGT.
   1973b. *IIIeme Conférence Nationale sur les Problèmes de l'Immigration.* Paris: CGT.

Chatelain, A. 1934. *Les étrangers dans l'agglomération lyonnaise en 1934.* Lyon: DES.

Chazalette, A. 1972. *Population de la ZUP de Minguettes à Vénissieux au mars 1969.* Lyon: GSU. Cyclostyled.

Chevalier, L. 1947. *Le problème démographique nord-africain.* Institut National d'Etudes Demographiques, Travaux et Documents, Cahier No. 6. Paris: Presses Universitaires de France.

Clarke, Simon, et al. 1980. *One dimensional marxism: Althusser and the politics of culture.* London: Allison & Busby.

Cohen, A. 1969. *Custom and politics in urban Africa.* London: Routledge & Kegan Paul.
   (ed.). 1974. *Urban ethnicity.* ASA Monographs No. 12. London: Tavistock Publications.

Cohen, W. B. 1980. *The French encounter with Africans: white response to blacks, 1530–1880.* Bloomington: Indiana University Press.

Colin, R. 1976. "Introduction à une analyse des migrations en relation avec les problèmes d'éducation interculturelle." Lyon: CEFISEM. Cyclostyled.

Comité de défense des travailleurs immigrés de Villeurbanne. 1972. *Histoire des immeubles Simon.* May 1972. Cyclostyled.

Cordeiro, A. 1970. *Eléments sur la condition des travailleurs immigrés algériens.* Grenoble: Institut de Recherche Economique et de Planification. Cyclostyled.

Courteuge, D. 1971. *Quelques aspects de la promotion sociale de la population étrangère dans le Département du Rhône.* Mémoire de Stage. Lyon: Association Lyonnaise pour le Développement de l'Enseignement du Service Social.

Crétaine, M. 1974. "Le logement de la population étrangère." *Regards sur la France:* 241–8.

Crozat, J. 1970. *Les travailleurs algériens dans le Rhône.* Lyon: Institut d'Etudes Rhodaniens.

Curtin, P. 1965. *The image of Africa: British ideas and action 1780–1850.* London: Macmillan.

Dahya, B. 1974. "The nature of Pakistani ethnicity in industrial cities in Britain," in A. Cohen, ed., *Urban ethnicity.* ASA Monographs No. 12. London: Tavistock Publications, pp. 77–118.

Daille, Roger. 1974. *Les étrangers dans l'agglomération lyonnaise.* Lyon: Université de Lyon II, Institut de Sociologie.

Davis, J. 1975. "Beyond the hyphen: some notes and documents on community-state relations," in J. Boissevain, and J. Friedl, eds., *Beyond the community: social process in Europe*. The Hague: Ministry of Education and Science, pp. 49–55.

———— 1977. *People of the Mediterranean*. London: Routledge & Kegan Paul.

de Mauroy, H. 1979. "Les étrangers et la nationalité française." *Points d'Appui* 5 (November): 9–22.

Dériol, C. 1971. *Lyon: ville mondiale*. Paris: Editions Stock.

Descayrac, C., and C. Dubois. 1981. "L'activité langagière des travailleurs migrants confrontés à une tâche de type technologique," in GRECO 13, *Recherches sur les migrations internationales: les travailleurs étrangers et la langue*. Special number coordinated by Colette Noyau. Paris: Groupement de Recherches Coordonnées sur les Migrations Internationales, pp. 107–20.

Deschamps, J. L. 1976. "Le parc de logements." *Points d'Appui* 5 (May). Special number.

Descloîtres, R. 1967. *The foreign worker: adaptation to industrial work and urban life*. Paris: OECD.

Dijoud, P. 1976. "La politique de l'immigration." *Droit Social* 5 (May): 3–5.

Dubreil, Dominique. 1975. "Les travailleurs immigrés." *Liaisons Rhône-Alpes* 23 (January-February). Special Number.

Dumont, L. 1977. *From Mandeville to Marx: the genesis and triumph of economic ideology*. Chicago: University of Chicago Press.

Duriez, G. 1976. "L'alphabétisation, où en est-on?" *ACFAL Info. No. Spécial "Alpha et formation."* (September): 13–16.

Dyck, N. 1976. *Advocacy, brokerage and leadership: an examination of interband political organisation among Saskatchewan Indians*. Manchester University: Unpublished Ph.D. diss.

Esprit. 1966. *Les étrangers en France*. Special No. (April 1966).

Faidutti-Rudolph, Anne-Marie. 1964. *L'immigration italienne dans le sud-est de la France*. Hautes-Alpes: Editions Ophrys-Gap.

Fleury, A. 1972. "Seuils de tolérance." *Bulletin de Gip* 5: 19–21.

FLN. 1966. *L'émigration algérienne: problèmes et perspectives*. Algiers: Front de Libération Nationale, National Seminar on Emigration.

Foucault, M. 1970. *The order of things: an archaeology of the human sciences*. London: Tavistock Publications.

———— 1971. *L'ordre du discours*. Paris: Gallimard.

———— 1972. *The archaeology of knowledge*. London: Tavistock Publications.

———— 1980. *Power/knowledge: selected interviews and other writings 1972–1977*. Brighton: Harvester Press.

Fred, M. 1977. "How Sweden works: a case from the bureaucracy," in S. Wallman, ed., *The social anthropology of work*. ASA Monographs No. 19. London: Academic Press, pp. 159–75.

Freeman, G. P. 1979. *Immigrant labor and racial conflict in industrial societies: The French and British experience, 1945–1975*. Princeton, N.J.: Princeton University Press.

Gani, Léon. 1972. *Syndicats et travailleurs immigrés*. Paris: Editions Sociales.

Gellner, E. 1978. "Notes towards a theory of ideology." *L'Homme* XVIII (3–4): 69–82.

Girard, Alain. 1971. "Attitudes des Français à l'égard de l'immigration étrangère. Enquête d'opinion publique." *Population* 26 (5): 827–76.

Girard, Alain, and Jean Stoetzel. 1953. *Français et immigrés: l'attitude française, l'adaptation des Italiens et des Polonais.* Institut National d'Etudes Démographiques, Travaux et Documents, Cahier No. 19. Paris: Presses Universitaires de France.

Gluckman, M. 1961. "Anthropological problems arising from the African industrial revolution," in A. W. Southall, ed., *Social change in modern Africa.* London: Oxford University Press/International African Institute.

Godefroy, F. 1884. *Dictionnarie de l'ancienne langue française.* New York: Kraus Reprint Corp. (1961).

Grandjeat, P. 1966. *Les migrations de travailleurs en Europe.* Paris: Cahier de l'Institut International des Etudes Sociales.

Grange, P., and P. Cherel. 1975. *Les enfants de partout et l'école française.* Paris: Hommes et Migrations Etudes No. 123.

Granotier, B. 1970. *Les travailleurs immigrés en France.* Paris: Maspero.

GRECO 13. 1981. *Recherches sur les migrations internationales: les travailleurs étrangers et la langue.* Special Number, coordinated by Colette Noyau. Paris: Groupement de Recherches Coordonnées sur les Migrations Internationales.

Griffin, C. C. M. 1973. *Italians into South-East France.* University of Sussex: Unpublished D. Phil. diss.

Grillo, R. D. 1978. *Report to the SSRC on Project No. 3410/2.* Ms. in British Library.
   1979. "Six ideologies in search of a movement." Paper presented to SSRC "European" Seminar, University of York. April 7–8, 1979. Cyclostyled.
   1980a. "Introduction," in R. D. Grillo, ed., *"Nation" and "State" in Europe: anthropological perspectives.* London: Academic Press.
   1980b. "Social workers and immigrants in Lyon, France," in R. D. Grillo, ed., *"Nation" and "State" in Europe: anthropological perspectives.* London: Academic Press, pp. 73–87.
   1980c. "The social context of anthropological research in Europe." Convenor's "Commentary" on Proceedings of Eighth Meeting of SSRC "European" Seminar. University of Sussex. January 1980. Cyclostyled.
   1981. "Coding the unknown: familiar and unfamiliar worlds in complex societies." Paper presented to seminar on "Complex Societies." Queen's University, Belfast.
   1982. "Alternative perceptions of language training in France: a case study from Lyon." *Journal of Multilingual and Multicultural Development* 3(3): 233–46.
   1983. "'An African railwayman is a railwayman . . .', or 'The subject of the subject of the Subject.' Paper presented to Social Anthropology Research in Progress Seminar, spring 1983. University of Sussex.

GSU. 1974a. *Etude de deux expériences de réhabilitation de cités HLM.* Lyon: GSU. Cyclostyled.
   1974b. *Etude démographique de la ZUP des Minguettes à Vénissieux.* Lyon: GSU. Cyclostyled.

Guiral, P. 1977. "Idée de race et pensée politique en France (gauche et droite) au XIXème siècle," in P. Guiral, and E. Témime, eds., *L'idée de race dans la pensée politique française contemporaine*. Paris: Editions du Centre National de la Recherche Scientifique, pp. 34–47.

Hainsworth, P. 1982. "Anti-semitism and neo-fascism on the contemporary Right," in P. G. Cerny, ed., *Social movements and protest in France*. London: Frances Pinter, pp. 146–71.

Hanley, D. L., A. P. Kerr; and N. H. Waites. 1979. *Contemporary France: politics and society since 1945*. London: Routledge & Kegan Paul.

Heidelberger Forschungsprojekt "Pidgin-Deutsch." 1978. "The acquisition of German syntax by foreign migrant workers," in D. Sankoff, ed., *Linguistic variation: models and methods*. London: Academic Press, pp. 1–22.

Hermet, Guy. 1967. *Les Espagnols en France*. Paris: Les Editions Ouvrières.

Hervo, M., and M. A. Charras. 1971. *Bidonvilles, l'enlisement*. Paris: Maspero.

Hessel, S. 1976. "Une politique culturelle avec les immigrés." *Droit Social* 5 (May): 178–80.

Hoffmann, L-F. 1973. *Le nègre romantique*. Paris: Payot.

Hommes et Migrations Etudes. 1967. *L'immigration portugaise*. Paris: Hommes et Migrations Etudes No. 105.

Horne, A. 1977. *A savage war of peace: Algeria 1954–1962*. London: Penguin Books.

Huguet, E. 1946. *Dictionnaire de la langue française du XVI*e* siècle*. Paris: Champion.

Ibrahim, Amr. 1981. "Syntaxe et culture: réflexion sur certaines formes de resistance à la langue étrangère," in GRECO 13, *Recherches sur les migrations internationales: les travailleurs étrangers et la langue*. Special number, coordinated by Colette Noyau. Paris: Groupement de Recherches Coordonnées sur les Migrations Internationales, pp. 89–102.

INED. 1954. *Français et immigrés: nouveaux documents sur l'adaptation: Algériens – Italiens – Polonais*. Institut National d'Etudes Démographiques, Travaux et Documents, Cahier No. 20. Paris: Presses Universitaires de France.

1955. *Les algériens en France*. Institut National d'Etudes Démographiques, Travaux et Documents, Cahier No. 24. Paris: Presses Universitaires de France.

1977. *Les immigrés du Maghreb*. Institut National d'Etudes Démographiques, Travaux et Documents, Cahier No. 79. Paris: Presses Universitaires de France.

Institut d'Etudes Politiques de Lyon. 1966. *Les travailleurs étrangers dans la Région Rhônes-Alpes*. Lyon: Chronique Sociale de France. Cyclostyled.

Institut National de la Statistique et des Etudes Economiques. 1975. "L'immigration étrangère dans la région Rhône-Alpes de 1970 à 1974." Etudes et Synthèses Rhône-Alpes. *Points d'Appui* 9 (October). Special Number.

1976. "La présence des étrangers dans la région Rhône-Alpes de 1967 à 1975." Etudes et Synthèses Rhône-Alpes. *Points d'Appui* 7 (July-August). Special Number.

Jones, C. 1977. *Immigration and social policy in Britain*. London: Tavistock Publications.

Kayser, B. 1971. *Manpower movements and labour markets*. Paris: OECD.

(ed.). 1972. *Cyclically determined homeward flows of migrant workers*. Paris: OECD.

Kiernan, V. G. 1969. *The lords of human kind: European attitudes towards the outside world in the imperial age.* London: Weidenfeld & Nicolson.

Kindleberger, C. P. 1967. *Europe's post-war growth: the role of labor supply.* Cambridge, Mass.: Harvard University Press.

Klaasen, L. H., and P. Drewe. 1973. *Migration policy in Europe: a comparative study.* Netherlands: Saxon House.

Klein, W., and N. Dittmar. 1979. *Developing grammars: the acquisition of German syntax by foreign workers.* Berlin: Springer-Verlag.

Kleinclausz, A.; et al. 1925. *Lyon: des origines à nos jours, la formation de la cité.* Lyon: Pierre Masson.

Kuhn, T. S. 1970. *The structure of scientific revolutions.* (2nd enlarged ed.) Chicago: University of Chicago Press.

Kumar, Krishan. 1978. *Prophecy and progress: the sociology of industrial and post-industrial society.* London: Penguin Books.

Lalanne, B. 1975. "Les ouvriers aujourd'hui." *L'Expansion* 91 (December): 76–87.

Lanier, Pierre (ed.). 1974. *Travailleurs étrangers et responsabilités collectives.* (3rd ed.). Lyon: Chronique Social de France.

Lapraz, Yves. 1972. *Etude sur l'évolution des familles en cité de transit.* Lyon: Bureau d'Etudes Sociales de NDSA. Cyclostyled.

Laroche, M. 1955. "La main d'oeuvre nord-africaine dans le Rhône." Compte rendu de la Commission Consultative Nationale pour l'étude des questions nord-africaines. April 1953. Ministère du Travail. Cyclostyled.

Latreille, A.; et al. 1975. *Histoire du Lyon et du Lyonnais.* Toulouse: Privat.

Le Masne, Henri. 1974. *Les émigrés Algériens et la perspective du retour.* University of Algiers: Mémoire pour le diplôme d'Etudes Supérieurs de Sciences Politiques.

Leach, E. R. 1954. *Political systems of Highland Burma.* London: Bell.

Leriche, J. 1959. *Les Algériens parmi nous.* Paris: Editions Sociales.

Lojkine, Jean. 1974. *La politique urbaine dans la région lyonnaise.* Paris: Mouton.
    1976. "Contribution to a Marxist theory of capitalist urbanization," in C. G. Pickvance, ed., *Urban sociology.* London: Tavistock Publications, pp. 119–46.

Lovecy, J. 1982. "Protest in Brittany from the Fourth to the Fifth Republics: from a regionalist to a regional social movement?" in P. G. Cerny, ed., *Social movements and protest in France.* London: Frances Pinter, pp. 172–201.

Maison du Travailleur Etranger. 1974, 1975. *Rapport moral et d'activité de l'année.* Lyon: Maison du Travailleur Etranger. Cyclostyled.

Mandel, E. 1978. *Late capitalism.* London: Verso Editions.

Marrus, M. R. 1971. *The politics of assimilation: a study of the Jewish community at the time of the Dreyfus affair.* Oxford: Clarendon Press.

Mars, G., and M. Nicod. 1984. *The world of waiters.* London: Allen & Unwin.

Marshall, A. 1973. *The import of labour: the case of the Netherlands.* Rotterdam: Rotterdam University Press.

Marx, K., and F. Engels. 1965. *The German ideology.* London: Lawrence & Wishart.

MATELT-SAEI. 1974. *Etude sur l'habitat insalubre, le logement des travailleurs immigrés.* Lyon: MATELT-SAEI. Cyclostyled.

Mathieu, J-L. 1961. *L'action sociale en faveur des musulmans dans l'agglomération lyonnaise.* Lyon: Mémoire de Stage de l'ENA.

Mazzoleni, M. 1970. *Les travailleurs maghrébins dans l'industrie lyonnaise.* Lyons: Mémoire, Faculté des Lettres et Sciences Humaines de Lyon.

McDonnell, K., and K. Robins. 1980. "Marxist cultural theory: the Althusserian smokescreen," in S. Clark, et al., *One dimensional marxism: Althusser and the politics of culture.* London: Allison & Busby, pp. 157–236.

Meury, A. 1975. "Enfants d'immigrés: des étrangers dans la classe." *Le Monde de l'Education* 3 (February): 7–10.

Michaud, Pierre. 1975. *Les travailleurs immigrés de la Région Rhône-Alpes et leurs conditions d'habitat.* Lyon: Université de Lyon II, Thèse de 3eme Cycle.

Michel, A. 1955. *Les travailleurs Algégiens en France.* Paris: CNRS.

Minces, Juliette. 1973. *Les travailleurs étrangers en France.* Paris: Editions du Seuil.

Miner, H. 1967. *The city in modern Africa.* New York: Praeger.

Ministère du Travail. 1975. "Résultats d'une enquête sur la main d'oeuvre étrangère, effectuée en Octobre 1973." *Bulletin mensuel des statistiques du travail* (Suppl. 31). Paris: Ministère du Travail.

    1977. *Les étrangers au recensement de 1975.* Paris: La Documentation Française.

Mohammed. 1973. *Journal de Mohammed.* Paris: Stock.

Montagne, R. 1953. "L'immigration nord-africaine en France: son caractère familial et villageois," in *Hommages à L. Febvre: eventail de l'histoire vivante.* Paris: Armand Colin, pp. 365–71.

    1954. *Rapport provisoire sur l'émigration des musulmans d'Algérie.* Paris: Ministère du Travail. Cyclostyled.

Muracciole, L. 1950. *L'émigration algérienne: aspects économiques, sociaux et juridiques.* Algiers: Feraris.

ODTI. 1974. *Office Dauphinoise des Travailleurs Immigrés: Rapport d'activité.* Grenoble: ODTI. Cyclostyled.

Olives, J. 1976. "The struggle against urban renewal in the 'Cité d'Aliarte' (Paris)," in C. G. Pickvance, ed., *Urban sociology.* London: Tavistock Publications, pp. 174–97.

Paine, R. 1973. "Transactions as communicative events." Paper presented to ASA Decennial Conference, July 1973, Oxford. Cyclostyled.

    1976. "Two modes of exchange and mediation," in B. Kapferer, ed., *Transaction and meaning.* ASA Essays in Social Anthropology 1. Philadelphia: Institute for the Study of Human Issues. pp. 63–86.

Palmer, R. 1981. *The Britalians: an anthropological investigation.* University of Sussex: Unpublished D. Phil. diss.

Papyle, H. 1973. *Les travailleurs étrangers en France: bibliographie.* Paris: Hommes et Migrations Etudes No. 120.

PCF. 1974. *Interviews et discours aux cadres du Parti FLN de Georges Marchais. Déclaration commune Parti du FLN-PCF.* Paris: PCF.

Pêcheux, M. 1969. *Analyse automatique du discours.* Paris: Dunod.

    1978. "Are the masses an inanimate object?" in D. Sankoff, ed., *Linguistic variation: models and methods.* London: Academic Press, pp. 251–66.

    1982. *Language, semantics and ideology.* London: Macmillan.

Perez, Mademoiselle. 1973. *Recrutement de la population Yougoslave et Marocaine.* Rapport de Stage, Berliet, Lyon. Mss.

Petitfils, J- Ch. 1973. *La droite en France de 1789 à nos jours*. Paris: Presses Universitaires de France.

Pétonnet, Colette. 1968. *Ces gens-là*. Paris: Maspero.

Philippe, J. 1973. "Notes de lecture sur 'L'alphabétisation des travailleurs étrangers: une relation dominant–dominé,' M. Catani." Lyon: CIMADE. Cyclostyled.

Pinot, F. 1973. *Travailleurs immigrés dans la lutte de classe*. Paris: Cerf.

    1976. "Quelques notions de législation applicables aux migrants étrangers et à leurs enfants." Lyon: CEFISEM. Cycostyled.

Piore, M. J. 1979. *Birds of passage: migrant labour and industrial societies*. Cambridge: Cambridge University Press.

Poliakov, L. 1977. "Racisme et antisémitisme: bilan provisoire de nos discussions et essai de description," in P. Guiral and E. Temime, eds., *L'idée de race dans la pensée politique française contemporaine*. Paris: Editions du Centre National de la Recherche, Scientifique, pp. 14–31.

Poulantzas, N. 1978. *Political power and social classes*. London: Verso Editions.

Power, J. 1979. *Migrant workers in Western Europe and the United States*. Oxford: Pergamon Press.

Pratt, J. 1973. *Friends, brothers and comrades: a study of social life in a Tuscan hilltown*. University of Sussex: Unpublished D. Phil. diss.

Rager, J. J. 1950. *Les musulmans algériens en France et dans les pays Islamiques*. Paris: Belles Lettres.

    1956. *L'émigration en France des musulmans d'Algérie*. Algiers: Rapport établi à la demande du Haut Comité Consultatif de la population et de la famille.

Ratcliffe, P. 1981. *Racism and reaction: a profile of Handsworth*. London: Routledge & Kegan Paul.

Rebérioux, M. 1975. *La République radicale? 1898–1914*. Paris: Editions du Seuil.

Rémond, R. 1963. *La droite en France de la première restauration à la Ve République*. Paris: Aubier.

    1971. *The right wing in France from 1815 to de Gaulle* (2nd ed.). Philadelphia: University of Pennsylvania Press.

Rew, A. 1975. "Without regard for persons: queuing for access to housing and employment in Port Moresby." *Development and Change* 6(2): 37–49.

Rex, J. 1970. *Race relations in sociological theory*. London: Weidenfeld & Nicolson.
    1973. *Race, colonialism and the city*. London: Routledge & Kegan Paul.

Rex, J., and R. Moore. 1967. *Race, community and conflict: a study of Sparkbrook*. London: Oxford University Press.

Rex, J., and S. Tomlinson. 1979. *Colonial immigrants in a British city: a class analysis*. London: Routledge & Kegan Paul.

Rist, R. C. 1978. *Guestworkers in Germany: the prospects for pluralism*. New York: Praeger.

Robert, P. 1960. *Dictionnaire alphabétique et analogique de la langue française*. Paris: Presses Universitaires Françaises.

Rose, A. M. 1969. *Migrants in Europe: problems of acceptance and adjustment*. Minneapolis: University of Minnesota Press.

Rosset, G. 1966. "Le relogement d'urgence à Lyon." *Esprit* (April): 671–78. Special number.

Sandillon, M. 1969. *Les étrangers dans l'agglomération roannaise.* Lyon: Institut d'Etudes Rhodaniens.

Schechtmann, J. B. 1962. *Postwar population transfers in Europe, 1945–55.* Philadelphia: University of Pennsylvania Press.

Seidel, G. 1975. "Ambiguity in political discourse," in M. Bloch, ed., *Political language and oratory in traditional society.* London: Academic Press, pp. 205–26.

  1979a. "On analysing political discourse." Paper presented to BSA/SSRC Methodology Conference, University of Lancaster, January 3–5, 1979. Cyclostyled.

  1979b. "Language, ideologies and the National Front." Paper presented to SSRC "European" Seminar, University of York, April 7–8, 1979. Cyclostyled.

  1983. "Political discourse analysis," in T. A. Van Dijk, ed., *Handbook of discourse analysis.* MS.

Seidel, G., and M. Billig. 1979. "Anti-christian pagan cults and the ultra-right: the function of Odinism as myth and ideology." Paper presented to the International Association for Semiotic Studies, Vienna, July 2–6, 1979. Cyclostyled.

SERL. 1976. *Vaulx La Grande Ile: études démographiques.* Lyon: SERL. Cyclostyled.

Shapiro, D. (ed.). 1962. *The Right in France, 1890–1919.* St. Antony's No. 13. London: Chatto & Windus.

Silber, A. 1973. "Racisme: l'allergie gallopante." *Le Point* 50:20–1.

SLPM. 1970a. "Note sur la situation de l'immigration dans la région Rhône-Alpes et le département du Rhône au 1er janvier 1970." Lyon: Préfecture du Rhône. Cyclostyled.

  1970b. *L'alphabétisation des étrangers dans la Région Rhône-Alpes.* Groupe de Synthèse Régional de Promotion des Migrants, Conference, April 17, 1969. Lyon: Préfecture du Rhône. Cyclostyled.

SONACOTRA. 1975a. *Compte rendu d'activité. Paris: SONACOTRA.*

  1975b. *Perception des foyers-hôtels SONACOTRA par la population environnante.* Paris: SONACOTRA, Direction des Etudes de Programmes, Services Etudes.

Soumille, M. 1977. "La notion de races chez les Français d'Algérie à la fin du XIXème siècle," in P. Guiral and E. Témime, eds., *L'idée de race dans la pensée politique française contemporaine.* Paris: Editions du Centre National de la Recherche Scientifique, pp. 242–45.

Sternhell, Z. 1977. "Le déterminisme physiologique et racial à la base du nationalisme de Maurice Barrès et de Jules Soury," in P. Guiral, and E. Témime, eds., *L'idée de race dans la pensée politique française contemporaine,* pp. 117–38.

Suleiman, E. M. 1975. *Politics, power and bureaucracy in France: the administrative elite.* Princeton, N.J.: Princeton University Press.

Tapinos, G. 1966. "Les immigrés." *Masses Ouvrières* 227.

  1969. *Les statistiques françaises d'immigration.* Paris: Hommes et Migrations Etudes No. 113: 4–45.

  1975. *L'immigration étrangère en France, 1946–1973.* Institut National d'Etudes Démographiques, Travaux et Documents, Cahier No. 71. Paris: Presses Universitaires de France.

Thompson, E. P. 1978. *The poverty of theory*. London: Merlin Press.

Touraine, A. 1974. *The post-industrial society*. London: Wildwood House.

   1977. *The self-production of society*. Chicago: University of Chicago Press.

Trébous, Madeleine. 1970. *Migration and development – the case of Algeria*. Paris: OECD.

Valabrègue, C. 1973. *L'homme déraciné: le livre noir des travailleurs étrangers*. Paris: Mercure de France.

Vallet, M. 1971. *L'immigration étrangère à Givors et son environnement*. Lyon: Institut d'Etudes Rhodaniens.

Véronique, D., and J. C. Tribollet. 1981. "Les comportements langagiers d'un groupe de travailleurs migrants maghrébins dans une tâche de production," in GRECO 13, *Recherches sur les migrations internationales: les travailleurs étrangers et la langue*. Special number, coordinated by Colette Noyau. Paris: Groupement de Recherches Coordonnées sur les Migrations Internationales, pp. 33–56.

Vieuguet, A. 1975. *Français et immigrés: le combat du PCF*. Paris: Editions Sociales.

Watson, J. (ed.). 1977a. *Between two cultures: migrants and minorities in Britain*. Oxford: Basil Blackwell.

   1977b. "The Chinese: Hong Kong villagers in the British catering trade," in J. Watson, ed., *Between Two Cultures*, pp. 181–213.

Weber, E. 1965. "France," in H. Rogger and E. Weber, eds., *The European Right: a historical profile*. London: Weidenfeld & Nicolson.

   1968. *The nationalist revival in France, 1905–1914*. Berkeley: University of California Press.

   1976. *Peasants into Frenchmen: the modernization of rural France, 1870–1914*. London: Chatto & Windus.

Whyte, W. F. 1943. *Street corner society*. Chicago: University of Chicago Press.

Wisniewski, J. 1973. *Les nationaux algériens en France*. Paris: Hommes et Migrations No. 848.

   1974. *Atlas de l'immigration en France*. Paris: Hommes et Migrations.

Zehraoui, Ahsène. 1971. *Les travailleurs algériens en France*. Paris: Maspero.

Map 1. Rhône-Alpes region: departments and principal towns.

N

0 1 2 3 4 5km

Genay
St. Germain-M.O.
Montanay
Neuville
Cury
Fleurieu
Albigny
Couzon
Caillioux
Poleymieux
Fontaines-St. M.
Rochetaillée
St. Romain
Sathonay-V.
Limonest
Fontaines-s/S.
St. Didier
Collonges
Sathonay-C.
Rillieux
St. Cyr
La Tour-
Salvagny
Dardilly
St. Rambert-l'I.B.
Crepieux-la Pape
Jonage
Champagne
Caluire-et-Cuire
Vaulx-en-Velin
Marcy-l'Étoile
Écully
Meyzieux
Charbonnières
Villeurbanne
Décines-Charpieu
St. Genis-
les Ollières
Tassin-la Demi-Lune
Lyon
Craponne
Chassieu
Francheville
Ste. Foy
Bron
La Mulatière
Oullins
Vénissieux
St. Priest
Pierre-Bénite
St. Genis-Laval
St. Fons
Irigny
Feyzin
Corbas
Mions
Charly
Solaise
Vernaison

Map 2. La Communauté Urbaine de Lyon (COURLY)

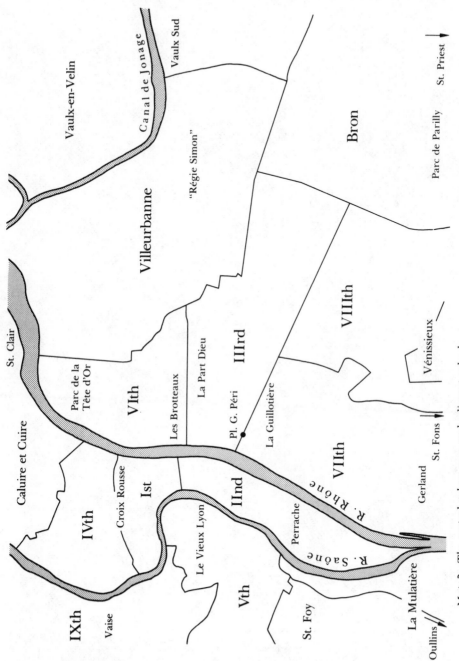

Map 3. The central urban area and adjacent suburbs

Index

322   *Index*

assistant scolaire, see education
assistant social, see social workers
associations, private, 27, 143, 191, 194, 262–3, 264, 284–5
  Law of 1901, 264
autogestion, see representation

baccalauréat, see education
"bachelors," 17, 32, 84, 99, 100–2, 128, 139
  housing market, 99
  see also hostels
Bailey, F. G., 11
Banton, Michael, 285, 289
Barrès, Maurice, 74
BEP, *see* education
Berliet, 39–41, 218, 219, 224, 227, 266
bidonvilles, see housing
bilingualism, *see* language
birth control, 149–52, 161
Bloch, Maurice, 8
blousons noirs, 185
Bourse du Travail, *see* trade unions
Britain, compared with France, 162, 186, 227, 259, 268, 289, 290–3
  immigration studies, 3
Bron, 91
BTP (building and construction), 42–4, 223, 227
  chantiers, 43–4, 227, 228, 229, 240
  see also Léon Grosse
bureaucracy, 5, 6, 283

Câbles de Lyon, 41–2, 57, 58, 59, 60, 61, 62, 224–5, 231
  caristes, 42, 218–21, 224, 238
cadres, see occupations
cafés, 17, 18, 19, 94, 230
Caillot, R., 286
CAIO, 52, 262
Caisse d'Allocations Familiales, 143, 175
Caluire, 19, 25, 91, 101, 115, 166, 240
  Groupe Tiers Monde, 245, 272
  Saint-Clair, 95, 115
Caluire-Légumes, 238, 240–57
CAP, *see* education
caristes, see Câbles de Lyon
Caspari, Andrea, 268, 290, 291
Castells, Manuel, 4, 5, 138
Castles, S., and Kosack, G., 12, 29, 282, 292
Catani, M., 3, 190, 216, 297
catégorie socio-professionnelle, see occupations
Catholic Church, 81, 150, 263, 272
  missions, 55, 193, 226–7, 264, 268
  Service des Migrants, 269
CEFISEM, 180–1, 187, 271
CEG, CES, CET, *see* secondary schools
CFDT, 66, 70, 207, 217, 219–21, 228, 229, 241, 249, 251, 253, 297

  analyses, 229
  comités de soutien, 244, 245, 251
  commission d'immigrés, 261
  and *étrangeté,* 76–7
  gala de soutien, 229, 238, 245
  and hostel strikes, 62, 110, 111
  and leftists, 224, 230, 231, 236, 244, 253, 273
  policies on immigration, 76–9, 81, 82, 221–3
  popularization of strikes, 229, 237
  rassemblement des luttes, 244, 256
  relationship with CGT, 76, 77–9, 221, 229, 231–9
  UIB, 231, 244
CFI, 230–1, 273
CGT, 169, 217, 219–21, 241, 251, 253, 295, 297
  AEFTI, 191, 206
  CGT-Métallurgie, 56–63, 235, 266
  commissions, 78, 120, 222, 265, 266
  conception of *immigré,* 66–70
  congresses on the problems of immigration, 57, 66, 221, 265–6
  débats casse-croûte, 78, 79, 266
  and demobilisation, 78, 237, 271
  policies on immigration, 66–70, 75, 78–9, 81, 82, 128, 193, 221–3, 265, 271
  racism, 60, 138, 222–3, 238
  recruitment of immigrants, 62, 223, 225, 278
  recruitment of militants, 266–7
  relationship with CFDT, 76, 77–9, 221, 231–9
  responsable d'immigrés, 78
  strategies, 67, 221, 225, 231, 235, 237, 239
  UDCGT, 57, 62, 63
chefs, 43, 228, 241, 251
  conflicts with, 77, 255
children, *see* North African immigrants; Portuguese immigrants
Chirac, Jacques, 49
CIMADE, 191, 275
Circulaire Marcellin-Fontanet, 230
cités de transit, 55, 95, 99, 112, 117–23, 125, 132–4, 138, 139, 153, 275, 284
  action socio-éducative, 132–40, 175
  definition, 132–3
  Fédération des Locataires, 119, 121
  PACT, 132, 134, 139
  residents, 130–2, 267
  see also NDSA
CLAP, *see* alpha
class, housing, 96–7, 99–100
  underclass, 50, 185, 186–7, 216
  see also immigré
classes de soutien, classes d'initiation, see education
classification, *see* occupations